UNACCOMPANIED BACH

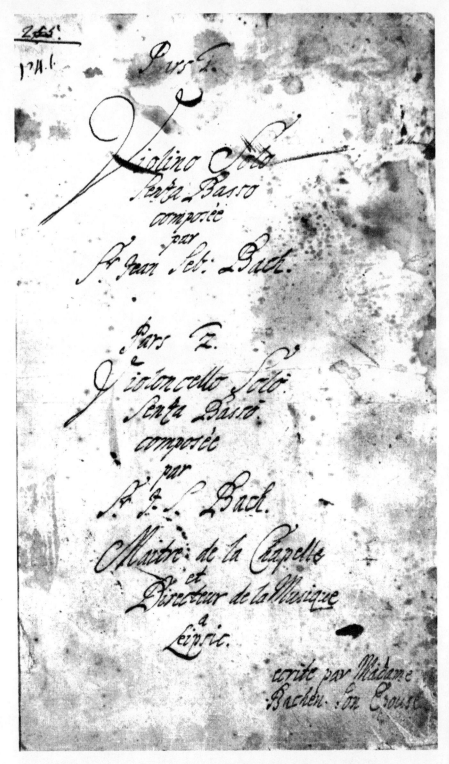

Title-page written by G.H.L. Schwanberg for Anna Magdalena Bach's copies of the violin *Sei Solo* and the cello *Suites* (Staatsbibliothek zu Berlin Preussischer Kulturbesitz, Musikabteilung mit Mendelssohn-Archiv, Mus.ms.Bach P 268)

Unaccompanied Bach

PERFORMING THE SOLO WORKS

David Ledbetter

YALE UNIVERSITY PRESS
NEW HAVEN AND LONDON

Published with the assistance of the Annie Burr Lewis Fund

Copyright © 2009 by David Ledbetter

All rights reserved. This book may not be reproduced in whole or in part, in any form (beyond that copying permitted by Sections 107 and 108 of the U.S. Copyright Law and except by reviewers for the public press), without written permission from the publishers.

For information about this and other Yale University Press publications please contact:

U.S. Office: sales.press@yale.edu   yalebooks.com
Europe Office: sales@yaleup.co.uk   www.yalebooks.co.uk

Set in Minion by J&L Composition, Scarborough, North Yorkshire

Library of Congress Control Number . . .

ISBN 978-0-300-14151-1

A catalogue record for this book is available from the British Library

Printed in the United States of America

10 9 8 7 6 5 4 3 2

Contents

Preface	viii
Abbreviations	x
Introduction	1
Chapter One: German Traditions of Solo Instrumental Music	12
1. Bach and the violin	12
2. German violin traditions	18
3. Violoncello and bass viol	35
4. The German lute tradition	46
5. Bach and the flute	57
Chapter Two: Concepts of Style and Structure	62
1. The German 'mixed style'	62
2. Dance and sonata styles	64
3. Fundamental and decorative note values	78
4. Division technique	80
5. Ritornello structures	81
6. The invention principle	85
7. Harmonic materials and structures	87
8. Aspects of fugue	91
Chapter Three: The *Sei Solo* for Violin BWV 1001–1006	95
Sonata Prima BWV 1001	95
Partia Prima BWV 1002	108
Sonata Seconda BWV 1003	118
Partia Seconda BWV 1004	129

Sonata Terza BWV 1005	145
Partia Terza BWV 1006	164
Chapter Four: The *6 Suites* for Cello BWV 1007–1012	**176**
Suite 1 in G major BWV 1007	176
Suite 2 in D minor BWV 1008	186
Suite 3 in C major BWV 1009	196
Suite 4 in E flat major BWV 1010	204
Suite 5 in C minor BWV 1011	213
Suite 6 in D major BWV 1012	227
Chapter Five: Works for Lute/Lautenwerk BWV 995–1000, 1006a	**238**
Suite in G minor BWV 995	238
Suite in E minor BWV 996	245
Suite in C minor BWV 997	252
Prelude, Fugue and Allegro in E flat major BWV 998	259
Prelude in C minor BWV 999	263
Fugue in G minor BWV 1000	265
Suite in E major BWV 1006a	267
Chapter Six: The *Solo* for Transverse Flute BWV 1013	**270**

Appendices
1. Heinrich Ignaz Franz von Biber, *Sonatae, Violino solo*, Sonata I, opening section — 281
2. Johann Jakob Walther, *Scherzi da Violino solo*, p. 30 — 285
3. Nicola Matteis, a) *Fantasia* for unaccompanied violin; b) *Alia Fantasia* — 286
4. Francesco Geminiani (?), *Sonata a Violino solo senza Basso* — 289
5. Johann Georg Pisendel, *Sonata a Violino solo senza Basso* — 292
6. François Couperin, Seventeenth harpsichord *Ordre*, [Allemande] 'La Superbe' — 297

Notes	299
Glossary	320
Bibliography	323
Select Discography	340
Index	341

Preface

Bach's unaccompanied Solos for violin, the cello Suites, the works for lute, and the flute Solo are part of the foundation repertory of their respective instruments. At the same time they are among the most complex and sophisticated manifestations of the union of French dance and Italian sonata styles that characterises the music of the early eighteenth century. This is what contemporaries of Bach call 'the mixed style' ('der vermischte Geschmack') and an understanding of it is vital for performers. Many movements headed with a dance title are not in fact dances at all, but sonata movements having little to do with the dance genre other than their time signature and binary structure. Modern performers with little experience of the surrounding repertory are puzzled by information about court dances and how to apply it to pieces where it is largely irrelevant. Bach was a connoisseur among connoisseurs of every nuance of style and genre. Conceptual aspects of style and structure are quite as important for interpreters of his music as where a slur begins or ends, or whether or not to use an open string. On another level, a performer emoting at large over the music in disregard of the composer's mind can only seem false to those who at least have an inkling of it. Not to share in the connoisseurship is to miss much of what interested Bach in composing the piece. It is also to miss the sensitivity to style necessary to interpret the notation. Fortunately, with the greatly increased knowledge of Baroque repertories and instruments now current the question of mixed style has come to the forefront and the full complexity and fascination of Bach's music can be savoured.

I have dealt with all the unaccompanied works BWV 995–1013 in a single book for two reasons. First, there are many links between works, particularly between lute and violin, and lute and cello. An appreciation of Bach's achievement is greatly enhanced by seeing this group of works as a whole. Second, as important, is that instrumentalists generally are too narrowly fixed on the repertory of their own instrument and need to broaden their horizons. For example, in order to reach a proper understanding of Bach's treatment of dance genres in the suite it is essential to be aware of his suite collections as a whole, whether for ensemble, keyboard, or solo instrument. Having all the instrumental solos under one roof, as it were, means that general concepts applicable to all of them can be explained in one place, and cross-references can be made freely between works.

An important part of the book is the figured-bass abstracts for some of the movements. These are essential for making points about harmonic structure in the text. They also show in easily visible form underlying harmonic movements, on larger as well as local levels, and the harmonic groundswell that is so important for performers to project. They are schematic, and designed to show the standard progressions of continuo harmony that underlie the music. A good knowledge of these is the first step to a real understanding of this music, which can be a puzzling expanse of surface detail on first acquaintance. They are also very useful aids to memorisation. The ability to read a figured bass is essential for playing Baroque music and the small amount of effort required is well worth making. To give a 'realisation' would add an extra layer of interpretation and would be too precise given the ambiguity of the originals. In the abstracts I have concentrated on broad outlines and strategic moments.

The commentaries are not intended to present finished analyses, still less to demonstrate any particular analytical method. They are intended to provide readers with materials and starting concepts on which they can build their own interpretation. Many players initially base their interpretations on favourite recordings. Although studying great performances is valuable in itself, it does not ultimately equip players to develop and deepen their own vision of the music. The commentaries are therefore based on concepts of Bach's time, which are known to have been fundamental to his system (figured bass, fugue, genre and style). My purpose is to deal specifically with these aspects; this is not intended as a general introduction in the manner of a handbook or guide. I do not deal with source study, editions, instrumental technique, reception history, social milieu, theories about expressive programmes and number symbolism, or modern performance/recording history and analysis, except inasmuch as these are relevant to the purpose of this book.

Readers will need scores of these works, and ideally also of very accessible works such as the Inventions and the French Suites for clavier. I would have liked to include more examples, particularly for Chapter One, had space permitted. Endnote references are used mainly for pointing to more detailed literature that readers may wish to explore about particular points. I have included some CD recordings of important works in the background to Bach, or to demonstrate particular points in the commentaries. The list is not intended to be comprehensive and I have kept it brief since reference to recordings is liable to be instantly out of date.

I wish particularly to thank the Arts and Humanities Research Council and the Research Committee of the Royal Northern College of Music for enabling me to have a research year for work on this book; also Karl Geck and the Sächsische Landesbibliothek–Staats- und Universitätsbibliothek Dresden, and Peter Wollny and the Bach-Archiv Leipzig for their assistance; and the Staatsbibliothek zu Berlin and the British Library for permission to reproduce illustrations. I also wish to thank Simon Rowland-Jones, whose work on his viola edition of the cello Suites gave me the initial concept for this book; Yo Tomita for much help of all sorts; Tim Crawford for advice about the lute; Pauline Nobes for lending me her dissertation; Jon Baxendale for setting the music examples; and Brigitte von Ungern-Sternberg for much support and hospitality in Berlin.

Abbreviations

A large number of sources for Bach's instrumental Solos are mentioned in this book. It is not possible to give full details for all of them: for further information the reader is referred to the NBA Critical Reports.

B-Bc	Brussels, Conservatoire Royal de Musique, Bibliothèque/ Koninklijk Conservatorium, Bibliotheek
B-Br	Brussels, Bibliothèque Royale Albert 1er
BG	*Joh. Seb. Bach's Kammermusik. Sechster Band. Solowerke für Violine. Solowerke für Violoncello.* Gesamtausgabe der Bach-Gesellschaft, Jahrgang XXVII/1, ed. A. Dörffel (Leipzig: Bach-Gesellschaft, 1879)
BR	*The Bach Reader* (ed. H.T. David and A. Mendel) (New York: Norton, 2/1966)
BWV	*Bach-Werke-Verzeichnis. Kleine Ausgabe*, ed. W. Schmieder; rev. A. Dürr, Y. Kobayashi, K. Beisswenger (Wiesbaden: Breitkopf & Härtel, 1998)
D-B	Staatsbibliothek zu Berlin Preussischer Kulturbesitz, Musikabteilung mit Mendelssohn-Archiv
D-Dl	Sächsische Landesbibliothek–Staats- und Universitätsbibliothek Dresden, Musikabteilung
DdT	*Denkmäler deutscher Tonkunst*
DEdM	*Das Erbe deutscher Musik*
D-Mbs	Munich, Bayerische Staatsbibliothek, Musikabteilung
Dok.I, II, III, V	*Bach-Dokumente*, ed. W. Neumann, H.-J. Schulze, A. Glöckner (Kassel: Bärenreiter, 1963–2007)
DTB	*Denkmäler der Tonkunst in Bayern*
DTÖ	*Denkmäler der Tonkunst in Österreich*

F-Pn	Bibliothèque nationale de France, Département de la Musique
GB-HAdolmetsch	Haslemere, Carl Dolmetsch Library
GB-Lbl	London, The British Library
H-SG	Szeged, Somogyi-Bibliothek
New Grove 2	*The New Grove Dictionary of Music and Musicians*, ed. S. Sadie and J. Tyrrell (London: Macmillan, 2/2001)
I-MOe	Modena, Biblioteca Estense
KB V/10	Eichberg, Hartmut and Thomas Kohlhase, *Johann Sebastian Bach. Neue Ausgabe sämtlicher Werke Serie V. Band 10: Einzeln überlieferte Klavierwerke II und Kompositionen für Lauteninstrumente. Kritischer Bericht* (Kassel: Bärenreiter, 1982)
KB VI/1	Hausswald, Günter and Rudolf Gerber, *Johann Sebastian Bach: Neue Ausgabe sämtlicher Werke Serie VI. Band 1: Werke für Violine. Kritischer Bericht* (Kassel: Bärenreiter, 1958)
KB VI/2	Eppstein, Hans, *Johann Sebastian Bach: Neue Ausgabe sämtlicher Werke Serie VI. Band 2: Sechs Suiten für Violoncello Solo BWV 1007–1012. Kritischer Bericht* (Kassel: Bärenreiter, 1990)
KB VI/5	Hofmann, Klaus, *Johann Sebastian Bach. Neue Ausgabe sämtlicher Werke Serie VI. Band 5: Verschiedene Kammermusikwerke. Kritischer Bericht.* (Kassel: Bärenreiter, 2006)
MGG1	*Die Musik in Geschichte und Gegenwart*, ed. F. Blume (Kassel: Bärenreiter, 1949–79)
MGG2	*Die Musik in Geschichte und Gegenwart*, ed. L. Finscher (Kassel: Bärenreiter, 2/1994–2007)
NBA V/10	*Johann Sebastian Bach. Neue Ausgabe sämtlicher Werke Serie V. Band 10: Einzeln überlieferte Klavierwerke II und Kompositionen für Lauteninstrumente*, ed. H. Eichberg and T. Kohlhase (Kassel: Bärenreiter, 1976)
NBA VI/1	*Johann Sebastian Bach. Neue Ausgabe sämtlicher Werke Serie VI. Band 1: Werke für Violine*, ed. G. Hausswald and R. Gerber (Kassel: Bärenreiter, 1958)
NBA VI/2	*Johann Sebastian Bach. Neue Ausgabe sämtlicher Werke Serie VI. Band 2: Sechs Suiten für Violoncello Solo*, ed. H. Eppstein (Kassel: Bärenreiter, 1988)
NBA VI/3	*Johann Sebastian Bach. Neue Ausgabe sämtlicher Werke*

	Serie VI. Band 3: *Werke für Flöte*, ed. H.-P. Schmitz (Kassel: Bärenreiter, 1963)
NBR	*The New Bach Reader*, ed. H.T. David and A. Mendel, revised C. Wolff (New York: Norton, 1998)
RISM	Répertoire international des sources musicales
rtl	Thaler
Schweitzer I, II	*J.S. Bach*, trans. E. Newman (London: A. & C. Black, 1923)
Spitta I, II, III	Spitta, Philipp, *Johann Sebastian Bach*, trans. C. Bell and J.A. Fuller-Maitland (London: Novello, 1883–5)
VBN	Beisswenger, Kirsten, *Johann Sebastian Bachs Notenbibliothek* (Kassel: Bärenreiter, 1992)

Particular pitches are referred to by means of the Helmholtz system, with middle C as c': GG C c c' c'' c'''

Generic pitches are written out in full: C sharp, B flat, etc.

Introduction

The aim of this book is to provide reasonably detailed guidance for those wishing to build an interpretation, or generally wishing to deepen their understanding of these works. It therefore centres on the four chapters of commentaries in Chapters Three to Six. Chapters One and Two deal with historical background and set up musical concepts in a general way, providing a point of reference for the discussions of individual pieces in the commentaries.

Chapter One gives a historical background for German instrumental traditions in the seventeenth century and in Bach's environment until around 1720, roughly the time when he completed the works for violin, cello, and flute (most of the 'lute' pieces are later and account is taken of that in their commentaries). The violin and lute developed virtuoso repertories in the earlier seventeenth century, establishing the genres of sonata and suite within which Bach was later to work. The initial stages of this development are necessarily described in a rather broad-brush way and will be familiar from general histories. Discussions become more specific as Bach's own time and place are approached. The cello was a relatively new instrument in Bach's time, and he was one of the first to write virtuoso unaccompanied music for it. The stringed bass instrument that already had a long tradition of solo virtuoso music in Germany was the bass viol, and some knowledge of that tradition is vital for understanding the cello Suites, both for style and playing technique. These traditions of violin, viol, and lute are not separate entities, but are all part of a unity. They are therefore dealt with as parallel strands in a single development. The discussions in this chapter aim to provide an overview from which those interested in further exploring particular aspects can branch out.

Chapter Two sets out basic concepts of style and structure that are worked out in detail in the commentaries. Part of the fascination of this music is that it comes after a century of stylistic development. The art of the suite and the sonata was to play on set forms in novel and inventive ways. The interesting thing is not how a particular piece conforms to a prototype, but the originality with which it uses the prototype, in terms of richness of invention of musical ideas, of ingenuity of developing them, or of playing against the expectations associated with the prototype in order to create strong expressive effects. A knowledge of standard genres, styles, and structures is essential for understanding the composer's intention, and for the delight of sharing in his act of creation. In this respect there is no more rewarding music than Bach's. Stylistic references in the music have crucial implications for performance. In a composite, mixed style such as Bach's the implications are subtle. Bach worked within certain structural principles and his manipulation of them is an aspect of his connoisseurship of musical materials. In cases where he plays against a structure it can be important to know what he is avoiding in order to understand what he is doing. Perhaps too much is sometimes made of the single-line nature of these pieces. The effect is strong and sonorous because the line is firmly grounded in the standard harmonic progressions of late Baroque music. A feeling for tensions and relaxations, for the movement of the harmonic groundswell, is essential for the large-scale projection of a piece.

In this chapter I have taken works of François Couperin and Corelli as examples. Couperin, whose works were known to, and admired by, Bach, is perhaps the best-known and best-documented example of mixing French and Italian styles in Bach's time. Couperin in Paris was quite specific about his admiration for Corelli, but in central Germany the situation with regard to Italian influences was more complex.[1] Corelli's works nonetheless provide classic examples of standard procedures. To illustrate the discussion I have tried to give as many music examples as possible, but in the case of longer Couperin pieces I have had to rely on the fact that the harpsichord works are easily accessible in facsimile and modern editions. For the explanation of basic concepts I have taken Corelli to represent Italian style, although in reality Italian style was not a single thing but developed in different ways in different centres, notably Venice, Rome and Naples.

Chapters Three to Six deal in detail with the violin Solos, the cello Suites, the pieces for lute/Lautenwerk, and the flute Solo. I have discussed each movement in varying amounts of detail, depending on its complexity. The discussions are designed to introduce the musical materials used in each piece in order to give players, and anybody wishing to study these pieces, basic information on which they can build their own interpretation.

1. *Terminology*

In the commentaries I have kept as closely as possible to Bach's own terminology since it is part of his artistic intentions. The violin works are commonly referred to nowadays by the unwieldy title Sonatas and Partitas for

Unaccompanied Violin.[2] This is to distinguish them from solo sonatas, which in late Baroque terminology normally means solo instrument with continuo bass accompaniment. But 'unaccompanied' is also awkward in that it implies that something is missing, as does Bach's own term *senza Basso*. Bach's title *Sei Solo* (Six Solos) is very neat and convenient, so for the purposes of this book I refer to them in English as the violin Solos, and correspondingly the cello Suites.

Some may find my use of the term Partia, rather than Partita, unfamiliar at first, but that is what Bach called them. The term Partia was standard in central Germany for suite-type works, and also in the south German and Austrian virtuoso violin tradition. An obvious model for Bach in suite formations and terminology was his predecessor as Thomascantor in Leipzig, Johann Kuhnau, who between 1689 and 1700 published two collections of *Partien* and two of *Suonaten* for keyboard, collections which were certainly known to Bach. There was a wide range of terminology available to Bach, as can be seen in the so-called Andreas Bach Buch and the Möller manuscript, collections of keyboard pieces made by Bach's eldest brother Johann Christoph, who took Bach into his home when their father died in 1695 and gave Bach his early keyboard training. Terms used are *Suitte*, *Partie*, *Symphonies* for arrangements of ensemble pieces, *Ouverture* for overture-suites, and *Pièces*, the normal term used for French solo instrumental suites. The Italian term *Partite diverse* is also used, though that can imply a variation-suite. Bach liked to provide examples of all available genres, and used almost all of these terms at various times. He used the term Partita for the six clavier Partitas BWV 825–830 published individually between 1726 and 1730, which were then all published together as a collection in 1731 with the overall title *Clavier Übung*, a title that again comes from Kuhnau.[3] Bach does not seem to have used the term Sonata in the *da camera* sense of dance movements.[4] In this the *Sei Solo* differ from Telemann's *Six Sonates* for violin (1715), which equally have three sonatas and three suites, though all are called Sonata.

One ought not to read too much significance into particular terms. One of Bach's agendas in seeking to be comprehensive was to use Italian terminology in the *Sei Solo* and French in the *6 Suites*. Generally he did keep to Italian terms in the violin Solos, other than in the dance movements of the E major Partia, but sometimes he slipped. The B minor Partia has a 'Sarabande', and the D minor Corrente is preceded by the instruction 'Segue la Courante'. We have no original title-page for the cello Suites. The *6 Suites* title-page was written by Georg Heinrich Ludwig Schwanberg, to whom Anna Magdalena Bach's copy was either given or sold; and Johann Peter Kellner's copy is entitled *Sechs Suonaten*. The movement titles are, however, French, including 'Prelude' (as opposed to 'Preludio' in the E major violin Partia), and each work is headed 'Suitte' in both of the early copies. This concern for contrast of language shows Bach's aim to be comprehensive, and is in itself an indication of 'mixed style'. Since the nineteenth century there has been a general move towards using Bach's own terminology. For example, where the old Bach Gesellschaft edition (BG, 1879) had 'Chaconne', the Neue Bach Ausgabe (NBA, 1958) has Bach's term 'Ciaccona' (common in suite-type works in German violin, viol, and lute repertories), but even NBA baulked at Bach's overall title for the violin Solos (*Sei Solo*, Six Solos) and at his 'Partia'. I see no reason not go the whole way now and call the pieces what Bach intended them to be called.

2. Sources

Sources of the works for lute/Lautenwerk and the flute *Solo* are dealt with in the individual commentaries. For the violin Solos there are four main sources.[5]

1. Bach's autograph fair copy, dated 1720 (*D-B* Mus.ms.Bach P 967), with the title-page: *Sei Solo. â Violino senza Baßo accompagnato. Libro Primo. da Joh. Seb. Bach aō 1720*. Individual works are entitled *Sonata 1ma* [*Partia 1ma* etc.] *â Violino Solo senza Baßo*. The repetition of *â Violino Solo senza Baßo* in each individual title implies that Bach was copying from separate fascicles. This is one of the finest of Bach's music autographs and has often been published in facsimile since it passed into public ownership in 1917.[6] It is the first evidence we have of Bach's policy of making a fair copy for personal reference of a group of works he considered to be an entity.[7] It is a model not only of calligraphic excellence, but also in practical matters such as avoidance of page turns within movements and, in spite of some anomalies, clarity of pitch notation and performance indications. The paper used is unique in Bach's works. It was made in Joachimstal in Bohemia, twenty kilometres from Carlsbad (Karlovy Vary), where Bach spent the early summer of 1720 in the suite of Prince Leopold of Anhalt-Cöthen.[8]

2. A copy by Anna Magdalena Bach, made between 1727 and 1731 (*D-B* Mus.ms.Bach P 268). This seems to have been made from the autograph, so is essential for the study of her writing characteristics and for assessing her copy of the cello Suites, for which no autograph survives. Illustrations 1 and 2 give Bach's autograph and Anna Magdalena Bach's copy of the first page of Sonata Prima for comparison.[9] P 268 was originally a pair with her copy of the cello Suites (P 269), as implied by their joint title-page (see frontispiece). The title-page was not written by Anna Magdalena Bach but by G.H.L. Schwanberg, mentioned above, a violinist and organist who studied with Bach in Leipzig in 1727–8.[10]

3. A copy by Johann Peter Kellner, dated 1726 (*D-B* Mus.ms.Bach P 804). The title-page simply lists the three Sonatas and the Partias in E major and D minor, in that order, and omits the B minor Partia. Individual work titles are as in the autograph P 967. Kellner's copy lacks all of the B minor Partia, the Allemanda and Corrente of the D minor, and the Loure, Menuett II, Bourrée and Gigue of the E major. In addition he has substantially shorter versions of the Ciaccona and of the fugues in the G minor and C major Sonatas. Günter Hausswald in the NBA Critical Report suggests that the cuts may not have been made by Kellner, but reflect an independent strand of transmission.[11] More recently Russell Stinson concludes that Kellner's versions of the fugues seem to reflect earlier versions than Bach's autograph, but that the evidence points to other pieces having cuts made by Kellner himself.[12] Details of Kellner's versions are given, where relevant, in the individual commentaries in Chapter Three.

4. A copy by two unknown copyists, made in two stages: BWV 1001–1005 copied 1721 or later, BWV 1006 copied in the late eighteenth century (*D-B* Mus.ms.Bach P 267). Once thought to be a Bach autograph, this is the manuscript that the music collector Georg Poelchau found in St Petersburg in 1814, in a stack of paper earmarked for wrapping up butter. The copy was made in close proximity to Bach and is of particular importance in that it seems to have been made from early versions. In particular it uses the flat sign to cancel a sharp, rather than the natural sign, a form of notation that Bach abandoned in the summer of 1714.[13] It has to be said, though, that the use of ♮ and ♭ is unsystematic (unlike Bach). Georg von Dadelsen points out that copies of other, definitely Cöthen, works have the same feature, and suggests that the copyist may simply have been conservative.[14] In fact, even Kellner's copy, dated 1726, occasionally uses the flat sign for a natural. P 267 does nonetheless raise the possibility that parts at least of the *Sei Solo* may go back to the time when Bach became concertmaster at Weimar.

The most important sources for the cello Suites are closely related to these. Since there is no surviving fair-copy autograph, the existing copies have been subjected to a great deal of scrutiny by editors and players. Neither Anna Magdalena Bach nor Johann Peter Kellner were evidently string players and their cursory, not to say careless, copying of bowings leaves much for players to decide. This is best done in the light of a close comparison of their copies of the violin Solos with Bach's autograph. Since facsimiles and commentaries for the cello Suites are readily available we need only briefly consider these sources.

1. A copy by Anna Magdalena Bach, made between 1727 and 1731 (*D-B* Mus.ms.Bach P 269). This was originally a pair with her copy of the violin Solos (P 268), and they shared a joint title-page (see frontispiece). Schwanberg

Illustration 1 First page of Sonata Prima for violin BWV 1001 in Bach's 1720 autograph (Staatsbibliothek zu Berlin Preussischer Kulturbesitz, Musikabteilung mit Mendelssohn-Archiv, Mus.ms.Bach P 967)

Illustration 2 First page of Sonata Prima for violin BWV 1001 in Anna Magdalena Bach's copy (Staatsbibliothek zu Berlin Preussischer Kulturbesitz, Musikabteilung mit Mendelssohn-Archiv, Mus.ms.Bach P 268)

later seems to have separated them, probably in order to dispose of them separately, and gave the cello Suites a separate title-page: *6 Suites a Violoncello Solo senza Basso composées par Sr J.S. Bach. Maitre de Chapelle*. This is a version of the cello element of the earlier joint title-page. Evidently the copies came without a general title-page since Schwanberg had to write his own, and judging by the formulation *Violino Solo senza Basso* he got his wording from individual work titles, not from Bach's general title-page for the *Sei Solo*. The formulation of the cello element of the joint title-page is modelled on the violin one. It used to be assumed that Anna Magdalena copied the cello Suites from a fair-copy autograph, now lost, equivalent to P 967. A more recent consensus is that, in view of the large number of mistakes, she may not have been copying from a fair copy but from a preliminary version, and there may in fact have been no final fair copy of the Suites.[15] In a preliminary version each Suite would have been in a separate fascicle, and there would probably not have been a general title-page for the set.[16]

2. A copy by Johann Peter Kellner, made in the same year as his copy of the violin Solos (1726) and in the same manuscript collection (*D-B* Mus.ms.Bach P 804). As we have seen above under Terminology, Bach did not otherwise use the term Sonata in the *da camera* sense, so it is unlikely that the title *Sechs Suonaten Pour le Viola de Baßo par Jean Sebastian Bach* stems from Bach. The term *Viola de Baßo* is rare. The lower strings of ensemble music were often marked 'Viola alto' and 'Basso', so 'Viola de Basso' may mean cello as distinct from viola (*basso* on its own could also mean *cembalo* or *organo*). Terms such as 'bassa viola' were used in late seventeenth-century Italy for the bass member of the violin family. On the other hand Bach is known to have favoured the viola, and Kellner's term was in use in Arnstadt for the largest type of viola (see Chapter One section 3). Or it may in some way reflect alternative possibilities. Perhaps we should not take this terminology too seriously since Kellner is unlikely to have made the copy for performance on a bowed stringed instrument. His copy lacks the Sarabande of the C minor Suite, and has only part of the Gigue. He wrote the C minor Suite at sounding pitch (working from a scordatura version, to judge by the mistakes), and he makes no mention of a fifth string in the D major Suite. In view of this, Russell Stinson suggests that Kellner may have made the copy for study purposes, or with a view to making keyboard arrangements of some of the Suites.[17]

The two other eighteenth-century manuscript copies are from late in the century and do not stem from Bach's direct circle.

3. A copy made by two anonymous copyists from the circle of C.P.E. Bach. The first is a Berlin copyist who also made copies in the circle of Johann Philipp Kirnberger, so this part of the manuscript probably dates from before C.P.E. Bach left Berlin in 1768. That copyist stopped during the Bourrée of the

C major Suite. The second copyist may have completed the work quite a lot later in Hamburg (*D-B* Mus.ms.Bach P 289).

4. A copy made by an anonymous copyist probably in northern Germany during the 1790s (*A-Wn* Musiksammlung, Mus.Hs. 5007). This manuscript was part of the stock of the Viennese music dealer, Johann Traeg.

The four eighteenth-century manuscript sources are readily available in facsimile in a supplement volume to the Critical Report (KB, Kritischer Bericht) for NBA VI/2. They are also in the Bärenreiter edition, edited by Bettina Schwemer and Douglas Woodfull-Harris, which includes facsimiles of all five sources listed below as well as a variorum edition of the notes that leaves players to make their own decisions about bowing and articulation. Since both the KB supplement and the Bärenreiter edition use the same alphabetical system for referring to the sources, I have followed it here, as follows:

A. Anna Magdalena Bach
B. Kellner
C. Copy No.3 above
D. Copy No.4 above
E. The first published edition (*Six Sonates ou Études pour le Violoncelle Solo*, Paris: Janet et Cotelle, *c*.1824). The edition was made by the French cellist Louis Norblin (1781–1854), who succeeded Levasseur at the Paris Conservatoire in 1824.

Sources C, D, and E appear to derive ultimately from the same lost *Vorlage*. NBA VI/2 gives two texts, one based on Sources A and B, and one on Sources C and D.

In addition to these facsimiles, two important recent editions, both published in the Bach year 2000, have taken different, and complementary, views of the sources. Kirsten Beisswenger (Breitkopf & Härtel) takes it that Anna Magdalena Bach copied from a companion fair-copy of the cello Suites to the 1720 autograph of the violin Solos. She therefore prioritises Anna Magdalena Bach's copy, and has a very revealing comparison (with facsimile examples) of traits of Anna Magdalena Bach's notation in bowings and articulations in the violin Solos, and those in the 1720 autograph.[18]

Ulrich Leisinger (Wiener Urtext), on the other hand, takes the view that Anna Magdalena, although a good singer and musician, was little acquainted with the specifics of string playing. If we did not have the autograph fair copy of the violin Solos it would be impossible to reconstruct the slurring from her copy alone. Since sources C, D, and E of the cello Suites seem to derive from a (now lost) common exemplar, which may have been a Bach autograph in the possession of C.P.E. Bach, Leisinger therefore prioritises the readings of these three later sources.[19] These two editions provide a most useful contribution to the materials available to anybody working on an interpretation of the Suites.

3. Genesis

Opinions differ as to whether the violin or the cello works were composed first. Hans Eppstein, NBA editor of the cello Suites, proposed the Suites as the first composed since Bach's trend is towards growing freedom in the treatment of form. A similar point is made by Günter Hausswald, NBA editor of the violin Solos.[20] The trouble with such stylistic assessments is that they can often be made to work both ways. It is unlikely that Bach, whose professional functioning as concertmaster in Weimar centred on the violin, would first have thought of writing a compendium of cello works. The title-page of the *Sei Solo* has them as *Libro Primo*; Schwanberg has the violin Solos as *Pars 1* and the cello Suites as *Pars 2*. It has been suggested that the flute *Solo* BWV 1013 may have been the beginning of a *Libro Terzo/Pars 3* for flute.[21] It has also been suggested that the Suites were not completed until Bach in Leipzig wrote a series of cantatas involving violoncello piccolo, in 1724–5 (see Chapter One section 3). All we can say for certain is that they were complete by early 1726 when Kellner made his copy.

The violin Solos are a more thoroughly speculative collection than the cello Suites. They have three large fugues, each in a different style (canzona, dance, and learned/mannered), each more elaborate than the one before and taking in more formal prototypes. Each of the Sonata third movements refers to a different scoring (solo sonata with continuo, trio sonata, concerto). Two of the Partias constitute a compendium of the variation, while the third presents an initial confrontation, and then gradual synthesis, of the opposite poles of Italian concertante and French dance styles, Bach's equivalent to François Couperin's reconciliation of French and Italian styles in *La Paix du Parnasse* (Paris 1725). In fact Bach covers in the *Sei Solo* virtually all the ground he was subsequently to cover in a whole series of instructive keyboard works, begun around 1720, including the Inventions and Sinfonias, the French Suites, and *The Well-tempered Clavier*. It says much for the importance of the instrument to him that his first great speculative compendium should be for the violin.

The cello Suites are also organized in increasing elaboration, including scordatura and a five-stringed instrument, although variety of possibilities is not so systematically exploited. In spite of their being suites, Bach manages to include a fugue in the guise of a French overture, but because they are all suites there is inevitably less variety of formal prototypes. There are nonetheless similarities with the French Suites for clavier in systematic working through different treatments of dance genres.

The order of composition of individual works within each set does not necessarily go with degree of elaboration, even though Bach in revising pieces virtually always enriched and elaborated rather than paring down. There is nonetheless a strong likelihood that the violin Sonatas were composed in the order that they appear in the autograph P 967. The Partias are less certain. Whatever the order of composition, Bach habitually arranged his collections in some coherent pattern of keys. In the autograph and Anna Magdalena's copy, Sonatas and Partias alternate in a key scheme: g–b–a–d–C–E. This has a neat palindromic shape in that the first three keynotes go up a 3rd and down a 2nd, and taking the second three as a mirror image (E–C–d) the keynotes go down a 3rd and up a 2nd. Taking the Sonatas and Partias separately (g–a–C : b–d–E), there is the same sequence of two minor keys and one major key, and another palindromic arrangement of keynote relations.[22] Kellner, however, presents a different organisation, with the three Sonatas together (in the same order), but then the Partias in E major and D minor (his copy lacks the Partia in B minor). Putting the B minor at the end, we get: g–a–C–E–d–[b], the first three having a rising 2nd and a rising 3rd, the second three a falling 2nd and a falling 3rd. Alternatively, with the B minor in its usual place the order is: g–[b]–a–C–E–d, two groups of a rising 3rd and falling 2nd. Whichever way one arranges them, these are the notes of the hard hexachord, starting on *g sol re ut*, the bottom note of the violin. The *Sei Solo* therefore provide the violin with an equivalent to *The Well-tempered Clavier*, which began as a series of finger-exercise preludes on each note of the natural hexachord (starting on *c sol fa ut*), though it ended up as a pair of preludes and fugues on every note of the keyboard octave. The cello Suites have not such a clear key pattern: G–d–C–E♭–c–D. Nonetheless, each group of three encloses a minor key between two major ones; while the outer major keys are a 4th apart, the inner major keys are a 3rd apart, and the two minor keys are a 2nd apart.

CHAPTER ONE

German Traditions of Solo Instrumental Music

1. *Bach and the violin*

Even though we have a far greater practical knowledge of seventeenth-century violin music now than at any time since Bach's violin Solos were first published in 1802, it is still being asserted that Bach's violin Solos are unique examples of unparalleled genius with very little to do with a pre-existing violin tradition.[1] This view of Bach's uniqueness goes back to those who promoted his reputation in the later eighteenth century. One of the prime movers to whom we owe the preservation of Bach's works is Johann Philipp Kirnberger (1721–1783), who had studied with Bach in Leipzig between 1739 and 1741 and later published a large composition tutor (*Die Kunst des reinen Satzes in der Musik*, Berlin 1771–9) purporting to be based on Bach's teaching method. Kirnberger grew out of sympathy with current musical trends in the 1760s and took refuge in adulation of Bach, to the extent of keeping a portrait of Bach behind a curtain in his teaching room as a kind of sacred icon.[2] Discussing the difficulty of writing satisfying harmony and melody in fewer than three parts, Kirnberger takes Bach's violin Solos and cello Suites as prime examples of single-part writing, so complete in themselves that no further melodic part could be added to them.[3] This thought was later repeated by Bach's first biographer, Johann Nikolaus Forkel (1802 p.31, NBR p.447). While it is certainly true that these works are complete in themselves, the notion that they are therefore uniquely perfect and immutable conflicts with what we are told elsewhere about, for example, Bach's continuo playing, in which he habitually added masses of harmony and extra melodic lines to compositions; and it is confuted by his own arrangement for lute of the C minor cello Suite (BWV 995) where he has in places added extra contrapuntal lines.[4] The only reference we have to Bach himself playing the violin Solos is on the clavichord, 'adding as much harmony as he considered necessary', something that may be reflected in the very elaborate keyboard arrangements of the A minor violin

Sonata (BWV 964) and the C major violin Adagio (BWV 968).[5] For one of the prime examples of single-part writing, the E major violin Preludio BWV 1006/1, Bach provided an entire orchestral accompaniment (Cantata 29/1). Too reverential an approach can blind us to the real nature of Bach's greatness.

Bach was far from the only composer of sophisticated music for violin *senza basso*. He was of course one of the very greatest masters who made extraordinarily more of his materials than did most of his contemporaries, but to ignore the tradition from which he sprang closes the door on understanding his artistic purposes and on reaching an informed appreciation of his achievements. During his lifetime, and for the rest of the eighteenth century, Bach was known as a keyboard virtuoso, partly because most of his pupils were organists, and partly because most of his published music was for keyboard. In that field he was proud to belong to a tradition of learned virtuosos going back in an almost unbroken teacher–pupil relationship to Frescobaldi, including Froberger, Kerll, Pachelbel and Bach's own eldest brother Johann Christoph Bach. The line of succession for the violin is less distinguished but no less important. Both Bach's father and grandfather were court and town musicians for whom the violin was central to their professional functioning, and we may assume that during the first decade of his life Bach received his first instruction from his father, Johann Ambrosius. Bach's command of the violin is highlighted by comparison with Handel, whose family background was of prosperous bourgeois rather than of town and court musicians. Handel never got further than playing 'die andere Violine' (i.e. ripieno violin) at the Hamburg opera when he first joined it in 1703. He only really came into his own when the harpsichordist was away and Handel was able to take over and show his quality as a keyboard player.[6] It has to be said, though, that Handel later, after his contacts with Corelli in Rome in 1707–8, came to command wonderfully aerated and sonorous string textures in his orchestral works, such as do not lie easily under a keyboard player's fingers.

Bach's first employment, for the first six months of 1703, was as 'lackey', i.e. rank-and-file violinist, in the private *Capelle* of Duke Johann Ernst of Sachsen-Weimar, following in the footsteps of his grandfather who had been a court musician at Weimar sixty years previously. Bach returned to Weimar as organist and court musician in 1708 when his functions would have primarily been as keyboard player. Nonetheless, it likely that he taught the violin to his pupils as part of an all-round music training, since one of them, Philipp David Kräuter, writes that he was receiving six hours instruction a day in composition and clavier, and also in other instruments.[7] It was when Bach was appointed concertmaster at Weimar in 1714 that the violin would have assumed a new importance. He was then within sight of eventually becoming capellmeister and it may have been at this stage that he wrote his first known piece for solo violin and continuo, the Fuga in G minor BWV 1026.[8] There is evidence to suggest that it was at this stage too that he started putting the violin Solos together. When he finally became capellmeister in 1717 it was at Cöthen, not Weimar, and that is where he gave them their final form in 1720.

The best-known testimonial to Bach as violinist is by Bach's second son, Carl Philipp Emanuel Bach (1714–1788) in a letter of 1774 to Forkel:

> As the greatest expert and judge of harmony, he liked best to play the viola, with appropriate loudness and softness. In his youth, and until the approach of old age, he played the violin cleanly and penetratingly, and thus kept the orchestra in better order than he could have done with the harpsichord. He understood to perfection the possibilities of all stringed instruments. This is evidenced by his Solos for the violin and for the violoncello *senza basso*. One of the greatest violinists told me once that he had seen nothing more perfect for learning to be a good violinist, and could suggest nothing better to anyone eager to learn, than the said violin Solos without bass.[9]

There is evidence of Bach's fondness for the viola in the sometimes unusually elaborate inner parts of his instrumental music, such as the Forlane of the C major Overture BWV 1066, or the Sarabande of the B minor Overture BWV 1067.

There are two main elements in C.P.E. Bach's account. One is the function of Bach's violin playing as his usual method of directing ensembles; the other is the 'learning' aspect. Bach's directing ensembles from the violin seems to have been something Emanuel was used to experiencing. Since Emanuel was born in 1714, Bach must at least occasionally have directed performances from the violin until the 1730s. There were other ways of directing: from the harpsichord, even from the organ, or with one or two rolls of paper.[10] It looks as if Bach's violin playing gradually went into abeyance after his move to Leipzig in 1723, compared with what it had been. In the one description of a particular concerted performance (1727) he is playing, and presumably leading from, the harpsichord.[11] By around 1738, with 'the approach of old age', when he was looking for concertos to play at the Leipzig Collegium Musicum concerts, it was in harpsichord arrangements that he presented a number of his earlier violin concertos. It was at about this time, too, that he is reported to have played the violin Solos, but on the clavichord.[12] In any case, the phrase 'cleanly and penetratingly' ('rein und durchdringend') suggests a good leader rather than a first-rate solo virtuoso.

The emphasis on 'learning' is perhaps important. One of the most quoted passages about the Solos is the following from Forkel:

There are few instruments for which Bach has not composed something. In his time, it was usual to play in the church, during the communion, a concerto or solo upon some instrument. He often wrote such pieces himself and always contrived them so that his performers could, by their means, improve upon their instruments. Most of these pieces, however, are lost. But, on the other hand, two principal works of another kind have been preserved which, in all probability, richly indemnify us for the loss of the others [here he mentions the violin Solos and cello Suites]. For a long series of years, the violin Solos were universally considered by the greatest performers on the violin as the best means to make an ambitious student a perfect master of his instrument. The solos for the violoncello are, in this respect, of equal value.[13]

It is always interesting to see what Forkel has done with his sources. In the case of Kirnberger's thought about the completeness of the Solos, referred to above, Forkel has clarified and improved on Kirnberger's formulation. Here, the comment about 'the greatest performers on the violin' looks like an intensification of C.P.E. Bach's 'one of the greatest violinists', though by 1800 there were certainly more admirers. Jean-Baptiste Cartier had published the C major Fuga BWV 1005/2 in his method and anthology *L'Art du violon* (Paris 1798); Johann Peter Salomon, who was introduced to the violin Solos by C.P.E. Bach, recommended them to his pupils and later played them in London.[14] It has often been suggested that the Solos were written for the Dresden virtuoso Johann Georg Pisendel (1687–1755), and he may indeed have been the violinist who praised them to C.P.E. Bach.[15] It might also have been Pisendel's pupil, Johann Gottlieb Graun (1702/3–1771), to whom Bach sent his eldest son Wilhelm Friedemann to learn how to compose for the violin in 1726–7. Yet there is no dedication of any sort on the title-pages of the surviving early sources. Bach liked to draw together groups of works into logical collections, partly no doubt for pupils to copy from, but also to make them more likely to survive the vagaries of time. Few works are dedicated to individuals, and of those only the Brandenburg Concertos (1721), the B minor *Missa* (1733), and the *Musical Offering* (1747) are substantial collections.[16] Most are dedicated to some combination of pupils, connoisseurs and amateurs, often with reference to 'Gemüths Ergötzung' (delight of spirit), a term in the Lutheran tradition implying that music can bring the spirit to a harmonious, and therefore God-like, state.

This therapeutic view of music was not only Martin Luther's, but was held generally during the Renaissance. One might pursue it further to ancient Greek symbolism, as represented very commonly in Renaissance and Baroque iconography, of the divine Apollo (representing the noble and god-like aspects of music), whose instrument was the lyre (its Baroque equivalent the violin), vanquishing and indeed flaying alive the goat-footed Marsyas, whose wind-blown Pan-pipes represented music's lewd and lascivious aspects. Fine and artistic violinists were very conscious of their superior social, as well as artistic, status. As Johann Jakob Prinner, a Viennese musician in the orbit of Schmelzer and Biber, put it:

> The violin is an artistic fiddle, on which virtuosity can be demonstrated *par excellence*, regardless of the fact that peasants and scullion-fiddlers take it upon themselves to scrape their cuts off it. This sort is definitely not artistic, laying the violin in their left fist and grabbing a note or chord with two flat fingers, more like bratwursts, gripping and wielding the bow with their right hand like a carter's whip.[17]

Unaccompanied violin music had various associations, from low-level dance fiddlers, to studying students, to great virtuosos.[18] There is no doubt that Bach was thinking of the noble aspect of the violin.

In 1720 Bach reached the age of thirty-five, half way through the biblical three-score and ten, and seems to have wanted to put together a summary of his achievements as composer and performer so far. For the capellmeister aspect there are the presentation manuscript score of the Brandenburg Concertos *Avec plusieurs Instruments* (1721) and the excellently calligraphic autograph of the *Sei Solo* for violin (1720). The cello Suites were at least intended to have an equivalent fair copy since the *Sei Solo* are billed as *Libro Primo* on their title-page, but it is not clear that such a copy was ever made.[19] These three collections represent the pinnacle of composition and performance. At the same time, in January 1720, Bach turned to educational concerns in the *Clavier-Büchlein* for Wilhelm Friedemann, who was approaching his tenth birthday. This contains elementary keyboard instruction and also early versions of the two-part Inventions and three-part Sinfonias (of which Bach later made a fair copy dated 1723), as well as some of the preludes of Book I of *The Well-tempered Clavier* (of which the fair copy is dated 1722). The earliest versions of the French Suites for clavier are in a *Clavier-Büchlein* for Anna Magdalena Bach, also dated 1722. The *Orgel-Büchlein*, demonstrating the techniques of elaborating chorales and playing the organ with pedals, was given a title-page around the same time. Taken as a whole, these collections from the early 1720s cover virtually the entire spectrum of instrumental music.

One might think that there was a decided gap between the elementary exercises and the virtuoso masterpieces. For Bach there was no gap, but a continuum. His pupils were virtually all aiming at a professional career in music, and the educational side of his functioning led seamlessly from the elementary instruction in clefs and ornaments at the beginning of Friedemann's *Clavier-Büchlein* to the great speculative collections of *The Well-tempered Clavier*, the *Clavier-Übungen*, and *The Art of Fugue*. Even an elementary finger exercise could be a rigorous 'research' of musical materials, as the Inventions show.[20] In view of this, the *senza basso* works for violin and cello, though peaks of their respective repertories, may still be regarded as works for 'learning', at the highest level. Bach's pupil J.F. Agricola says as much, comparing them to the Caprices (i.e. études) of the Berlin violinist Franz Benda, which had been recommended by J.F. Reichardt:

> Caprices are pieces designed for learning to master the most advanced possibilities of an instrument. They present all possible difficulties, so that the student has a firm grasp of how to compose for it. The harder they are, the better they achieve their aim. [Reichardt says that] such pieces should provide rules for composing a piece and, for the satisfaction and cultivation of good taste, should rightly be played only by those who have long since outgrown all such difficulties, and also derived the appropriate benefits. Why does [Reichardt] not rather instance the much more difficult 6 violin Solos without bass of Joh. Seb. Bach? They are certainly even harder and harmonically richer ['vollstimmiger'] than Mr. Benda's Capriccios. But they were made for a similar purpose.[21]

C.P.E. Bach tells us that his father had to devise ('auszudencken') a new keyboard technique, involving a more complete use of the fingers, in order to match the extraordinary changes in musical style ('Geschmack') during his lifetime. The height of this style-change was in the decade 1710–1720, and some of the exercises he devised may survive in Book I of *The Well-tempered Clavier*. One might see a similar intent in, for example, the Doubles of the B minor violin Partia. The *Sei Solo* may therefore be seen as encompassing in a single collection for the violin the elements of étude, prelude, fugue, sonata, and suite that are spread over a number of collections for the keyboard assembled at roughly the same time.

In view of the fact that there is no dedication of any sort on the title-page, Bach may have envisaged a variety of uses. They may have been played by Pisendel, or Joseph Spiess, virtuoso violinist and Bach's concertmaster at Cöthen. They would make excellent concert items for an audience of connoisseurs (Prince Leopold himself played the violin 'not badly'), sharing with the Brandenburg Concertos their exceptional scoring. Bach may have thought of the future training of his growing family, a concern evidenced in Wilhelm Friedemann's *Clavier-Büchlein*. And he assuredly played them himself. They are nowadays played by virtually every college student so it is difficult to believe that Bach, who was at least of the standard of a good orchestral leader, could not himself have played them.

2. German violin traditions

The new virtuoso school of violin playing that developed in Italy in the first decades of the seventeenth century spread very quickly to Germany. The 1620s saw the first great flowering of virtuoso violin style in Italy, and was also marked by a great burst of experimentation and invention, when virtuosos were intoxicated by new perceptions of the expressive possibilities of instruments. It was also the decade when new instrumental genres of canzona, sonata, capriccio became established, though there was no formal standardisation of these terms. The earliest publication to have specifically violinistic effects, at a time when most publications gave the option of violin or cornett, was the Op.1 *Affetti musicali* (Venice 1617) of the Brescian Biagio Marini (1594–1663), which features bow tremolo and also some double stops. Marini's Op.8 *Sonate* (Venice 1629) is generally considered the first real step into idiomatic virtuoso solo violin music, including multiple stopping and scordatura. Between 1623 and 1649 Marini was employed at the Wittelsbach court of Neuburg on the Danube (north of Munich, near Ingolstadt), and the dedication of Op.8 shows that it was composed at Neuburg.[22] It has been suggested that Marini learned these new techniques from German violinists there, but this is most unlikely since he was hired as one of the most advanced violinists of his day and a noted representative of the new Italian styles.[23] Scordaturas were part of the quest for new instrumental sonorities at the time and were, for example, a leading feature of lute music in the 1620s and 30s. The origin of violin multiple stopping is probably implied in Marini's *Capriccio per sonare il violino con tre corde a modo di lira* (1629). The 'lira' was the lira da braccio, an instrument much used from the late fifteenth century, designed to play four-part chords and accompany song, and as such is famously depicted by Raphael being played by Apollo.[24] A larger bass version, the lirone, with an ingenious re-entrant tuning designed to facilitate chord playing, was used for continuo in Marini's time.[25]

At the same time the Mantuan Carlo Farina (*c.*1604–1639) moved to Dresden where he was concertmaster from 1625–29, and would have been under the direction of Heinrich Schütz till Schütz left for Italy in August 1628. When Schütz returned in November 1629 he brought with him another Mantuan violinist, Francesco Castelli, who replaced Farina. During his time at Dresden Farina published all five of his surviving music collections. The best-known, and indeed notorious, piece is the *Capriccio stravagante* in the second book (*Ander Theil newer Paduanen* ..., Dresden 1627).[26] This is the most elaborate early example of the way in which representational music may encourage novel instrumental effects, a principle extending to Biber, Rebel, Berlioz and beyond. The *Capriccio stravagante* manages to include, in addition to multiple stops and bow vibrato, col legno, sul ponticello, glissando, pizzicato, as well as imitations of barking dogs, trumpets (*violino in tromba*, a very common effect in seventeenth-century Italian string music, also used by Biber), and a hurdy-gurdy, which is what at this stage higher positions on lower strings were thought to sound like. Apart from this, Farina's publications contain some of the most advanced violin music of the time, and he was a considerable influence on the development of virtuoso violin playing in Germany. In fact from his time onward the Dresden court was home to a virtuoso tradition that was to include figures directly in Bach's background, J.W. Furchheim, J.J. Walther, J.P. von Westhoff, N.A. Strungk, and J.G. Pisendel.

Other notable Italian violinists operating in the German area in the 1620s were Giovanni Battista Buonamente (c.1600–1642) and Antonio Bertali (1605–1669), musicians at the court in Vienna.[27] Later waves of Italians moving north of the Alps included Giovanni Antonio Pandolfi (*fl*.1660–1669) and Giovanni Bonaventura Viviani (1638–after 1692), both employed by the Habsburg court at Innsbruck; and Ignazio Albertini (c.1644–1685), chamber musician at the court in Vienna. Pandolfi's two collections of *Sonate ... per chiesa e camera* for violin and continuo Op.3 and Op.4 (Innsbruck 1660) seem to have had a dual influence: firstly on Johann Heinrich Schmelzer (c.1620/23–1680), whose *Sonatae unarum fidium* (Nuremberg 1664) were the first publication of Austrian virtuoso solo violin music; and secondly on Viviani's *Capricci armonici* Op.4 (Venice and Rome 1678), which in turn are a stepping-stone to Corelli's Op.5 violin Sonatas (Rome 1700). Schmelzer's *Sonatae* is the first of three publications representing the pinnacle of the Austrian violin school, the others being Biber's *Sonatae Violino Solo* (Nuremberg 1681) and Albertini's *Sonatinae XII Violino solo* (Vienna and Frankfurt 1692), all with continuo.

On the face of it, it is curious that the heights of virtuosity seem to have migrated north of the Alps after Marini, while Italians settled down to something more sedate. This impression is, however, more an accident of printing technology than a reflection of the true situation. Italian solo violin and ensemble music, when printed, was set in movable type, a relatively cheap process but one which at that time could not notate more than one note at a time on a stave, since each note and musical symbol required a separate piece of type. Multiple stops were problematical, as were high positions requiring many leger lines, and long bowing slurs.[28] In Marini's Op.8 the multiple-stopping passages are printed from specially carved wooden blocks, an expensive process. Engraving, also more expensive than movable type, was not used for solo violin sonatas in Italy until Corelli's Op.5 (1700). Some got around the problem by printing the violin part on two systems (Uccellini Op.7, 1668, G.M. Bononcini Op.4, 1671). Our image of Italian virtuoso violin music between Marini and Corelli is therefore incomplete. It is further clouded by the scarcity of manuscript sources, and such as there are tend to point up the limitations of the printing process. The twenty-five MS volumes of the Modenese Giuseppe Colombi (1635–1694) contain sonatas for one or two violins, some *senza basso*, with multiple stops and scordatura. Nonetheless, German MS sources greatly outnumber Italian ones, and are noticeably more technically demanding.[29]

Schmelzer's *Sonatae* of 1664, on the other hand, are engraved so could notate multiple stopping, though he hardly uses it in this publication.[30] Also engraved are the more technically advanced and elaborate 1681 *Sonatae* of Heinrich Ignaz Franz von Biber (1644–1704), the highpoint of published Austrian violin music, which uses both multiple stops and scordatura. As an example of the pinnacle of German virtuosity at this stage one might take the very brilliant first Sonata of Biber's 1681 collection.[31] In a manner that is traceable via Schmelzer to Uccellini in the 1640s, the sonata alternates sections in what one might call recitative style (*stylus phantasticus*) and sections in set rhythm, usually either on a dance model or on a ground bass. It has the following sections:

1) A complex and sophisticated blend of contrasting manners and effects, of the most powerful this seventeenth-century style has to offer (see Appendix 1). First, a highly dramatic free style over a pedal, featuring short statements separated by dramatic pauses, with technical effects such as a two-octave slurred-staccato scale, and various sorts of campanella in passages of racing 32nd notes. Then a contrasting Adagio (meaning recitative style, rather than particularly slow, in this repertory) that mixes steady movement with free style (bar 20). Generally speaking, when the bass has long notes the style is free, and when the bass moves in regular, shorter note values the movement is steady. Here the violin plays in two parts, as if it were two violins in a trio sonata (this two-in-one effect is brilliantly exploited in the eighth Sonata of the collection, which uses it throughout and manages to dialogue and combine voices in two different characters). This section concludes brilliantly (from bar 27), returning to the racing 32nds and covering a wide range of the instrument over a succession of pedal notes.

2) Presto in ¢-time in a regular dotted character, with two parts on the violin in ingenious imitations. This type of movement is common enough in ensemble music of Schmelzer and Biber, but has a particularly brilliant effect when the top parts are played by a single violin.[32]

3) A ground bass on a four-bar pattern, pairs of which support 8-bar variations. Several elements feature in these variation movements: character rhythms and textures, and moving into shorter note values on the division principle (see Chapter Two section 4). Generally, after a climax of movement there is a falling back to a quieter movement before the next, greater, wave of build-up. In this case the movement builds up to jagged patterns of sixteenth notes, then falls back to quieter leaping octaves and tenths, before the final build-up to long scales in 32nds.
4) The Finale returns to the movement of section 1, with brilliant 32nd-note patterns over a pedal.

Two of the sonatas require scordatura. One (Sonata VI) is in fact two pieces joined together, with the result that the violinist has to retune the E string down to d" during a linking passage for the continuo.[33] The continuo chords are neatly organised so that most of them can include the note d".

What J.J. Walther says about the reception of his *Scherzi* (1676) implies that many violinists did not publish, and indeed a large amount of German violin music survives in manuscript only.[34] Even so, there must originally have been a great deal more. In the 1660s and 1670s German courts wanted players who could play solos, with or without accompaniment, and violinists of the Viennese school were much in demand in south German courts. Schmelzer, who started out as a mere Stadtpfeiffer in Vienna, was well off and loaded with honours by the time he died. In 1670 he sent to Count Liechtenstein-Castelcorn a 'Ciaconna ohne ferneres accompagniomento' (i.e. unaccompanied; now lost) with a note that he had other 'bizarreries' of the sort. Ground-bass pieces were very suitable for displaying a full range of violinistic effects, from cantabile melody to coruscating *passaggi*. Like other virtuosos Schmelzer preferred to be booked in person, rather than distributing copies of his music. When the same patron asked him for a sonata featuring birdsong, Schmelzer said it was impossible to write it in notes, but he would come and play it himself.[35]

In 1636–7 Farina was in Danzig, where he is reported to have played violin solos even in the highly orthodox environment of the Lutheran church, though it is not clear whether the solos were with or without accompaniment.[36] This is one of a number of references to solo instrumental music in Lutheran services which may relate to Forkel's assertion that Bach instrumental works were on occasion played during the Communion.[37] Apart from solo instrumental pieces, concerted church music has some remarkable examples of expressive virtuoso violin writing, even though the composers were not primarily violinists.[38] Striking examples of this in Bach's direct background are the concerted church music of his uncle Johann Christoph Bach (1642–1703). This Johann Christoph was harpsichordist in the Eisenach court

Capelle under the violin virtuoso Daniel Eberlin (1647–1715), for whom these parts may have been written. Two sonata movements by Eberlin, with rapid runs and double stops, are in the Codex Rost (compiled *c.*1640–80), which also contains two anonymous unaccompanied movements.[39] Johann Pachelbel (1653–1706) is better known as part of Bach's keyboard background. In 1677 he was court organist at Eisenach and in 1678 organist in Erfurt where he taught Bach's eldest brother, also called Johann Christoph. Pachelbel's chamber music with violin includes a *Zwillingspartie à 2 Violini* in which the first violin has rapid passagework while the second accompanies with triple-stopped chords.[40] Clemens Fanselau suggests that the Adagio of Bach's G minor violin Sonata and the Grave of the A minor Sonata to an extent combine these on one violin, playing both chords and runs.[41] Pachelbel's violin works also include a *Partie* (six suite movements) for two scordatura violins and continuo, and an Aria and variations for scordatura violin and two bass viols. Through the Pachelbel circle Bach may have got to know of the Augsburg violinist Matthias Kelz (*c.*1635–1695) whose *Epidigma harmoniae novae* (Augsburg 1669), contains fifty dance movements for violin and bass viol in which the violin has bold leaps, goes up to ninth position, and has chains of double stops with contrapuntal parts. In fact it may have been via Pachelbel that Bach got to know works of the Italians Legrenzi, Albinoni, and Corelli from which he took subjects for early keyboard fugues.

In the choir library at Lüneburg Bach could have studied cantatas with elaborate violin parts by his uncle Johann Christoph Bach, Eberlin and Pachelbel, the north German violinists Nicolaus Bleyer (1591–1658) and Nathanael Schnittelbach (1633–1667), and the Dresden virtuosos Johann Wilhelm Furchheim (*c.*1635/40–1682) and Nicolaus Adam Strungk (1640–1700).[42] If we can believe J.G. Walther (1732), Strungk was able to amaze Corelli in Rome in 1685/86 with his skill and dexterity in scordatura and multiple stops, to such an extent that Corelli is said to have exclaimed, in effect, 'I am called Arcangelo, but you must be the Arcidiavolo!' Well-known figures tend to attract such archetypal stories.[43] Strungk is one of the composers C.P.E. Bach lists as those his father 'loved and studied' in his youth (Dok.III p.288).[44] He was one of the most brilliant virtuosos of his day on both keyboard and violin, so it is a pity that no copy survives of his *Musicalische Übung* (Dresden 1691), containing sonatas for violin and viola da gamba, and also several Ciaconas for two violins. During Bach's time at the Michaelisschule in Lüneburg (1700–1702) the well-travelled virtuoso Johann Fischer (1646–?1716/17) sought employment in Lüneburg in 1701 and donated several compositions to the school.[45] Fischer was a true pioneer of scordatura. His 'Das Eins-Drei und Drey Eins oder Der habile Violiste' (MS *c.*1686) requires the player to change between three different violins either between movements, or in mid-movement, and there are stretches of triple-stopping in three real parts.[46] Of north German violin virtuosos with Lübeck connections, Nicolaus Bruhns (1665–1697), with whose organ works Bach was certainly familiar, was a pupil of Schnittelbach for violin and viol. None of his chamber music survives, but some cantatas have brilliant polyphonic writing, showing the double- and multiple-stopping technique of the north German school. Like Strungk, he was a virtuoso on both keyboard and violin, and is said to have been able to play the violin while accompanying himself on the organ pedals.[47]

Strungk started by working in various northern courts, and moved to Dresden as vice-capellmeister in 1688. Dresden was by far the most prestigious musical centre in Bach's environment until the last decade of his life. Johann Jakob Walther (c.1650–1717) represents, with his contemporary Biber, the culmination of the German tradition of violin virtuosity in the seventeenth century: Biber in Austria, Walther in central Germany. Walther moved to the Saxon court in Dresden in 1674, but by 1681 had moved on to Mainz. Bach could have known his publications: *Scherzi da Violino Solo Con il Basso Continuo* (Leipzig and Frankfurt 1676, reprinted 1687), and *Hortulus Chelicus* (Mainz 1688, reprinted 1694 and 1705).[48] The number of reprints suggests a reasonable diffusion. The title-page of *Hortulus Chelicus* implies a partly instructive intention: 'a well-planted violinistic pleasure garden, in which all musicians and amateurs eager for art may find the way to perfection through curious pieces and pleasing variety, also through touching two, three, four strings on the violin in harmony. . .'.[49] In the preface Walther also says that he has included easier as well as more difficult pieces, so that weaker players can work to improve. The collection is a compendium of violin techniques and types of the 1680s and seems to have been repertory that aspiring virtuosos practised into the early years of the eighteenth century. Quantz tells us that in his apprenticeship days from 1708 he worked hard at the solos of Biber, Walther, and Albicastro, until he discovered those of Corelli and Telemann, at which he worked even harder.[50] This stylistic shift from German virtuosity to Corelli's smooth classicism was the general tendency in Bach's environment in the first decade of the eighteenth century.

Walther's works in particular show the stylistic distance covered in the forty years between 1680 and 1720, and at this stage it is well to reflect briefly on the nature of the seventeenth-century sonata. We tend to approach earlier repertories from more familiar later ones, with the attitude that they are 'precursors'. In the case of this style, the fact that it is based on short sections rather than long spans of music can give the impression of short-breathed bittiness (for the same reason some of Purcell's choral works were re-composed and extended in the eighteenth century when they were felt to lack the expansiveness of Handel). To appreciate the power and originality of Walther and Biber, they need to be approached from a starting point in the early seventeenth century. Then the aesthetic was not of unification, but of character and contrast. The 'second practice' of Monteverdi's generation had released the expressive power of dissonance, and instrumentalists explored in terms of their instruments the new emotional worlds opening up in solo vocal music, notably the opera. Strong character projection was the object, and character could be enhanced by putting several contrasting ones side by side. The effect is rather like the wall of a room in a palace, covered with paintings, each one presenting a different highly focused scene and character. Approaching Walther and Biber from the sonatas of Castello and Uccellini reveals them as supreme masters and the culmination of this seventeenth-century tradition, rather than as precursors of Bach. For the player they are extremely rewarding because of the range, depth, and subtlety of imagination required, and the freedom for expressive projection in music that is not driven forward in long spans by motor energy.

In an aesthetic where the aim is constantly to surprise and delight with novel and 'curious inventions' and 'pleasing variety', more depends on the originality of the composer/performer than in the post-Corellian type of sonata. Character can be in a manner (consort, recitative, aria etc.), an instrumental effect, an articulation, a time signature, a rhythmic figure, a dance type, and so on. One possibility for character that Walther firmly turned his back on was scordatura, telling the 'amateur of the violin' in *Hortulus Chelicus* to tune in 'good 5ths', not scordatura or tricks. Scordatura belonged to a period of individualism and experimentation, later ironed out in a classic phase. The era of scordatura tunings in French lute music was over by 1650; in German violin music it was largely finished by 1700 (neither Walther nor Westhoff used it). While it may seem part of the virtuoso style, it also has the advantage for less skilled players, clear in less demanding repertory such as the suites in the Klagenfurt MS, that certain chord shapes (therefore hand shapes) are basic to certain keys, and the music can be centred around them.[51] The variety of colours produced by different scordaturas is an aspect of the seventeenth-century quest for character and contrast, less urgently required when a smoother, more classic style supervened.

Generally, Walther tends to be less complex in his range of characters within a section than Biber, as one can see by comparing the first of Biber's 1681 Sonatas and the eighth of Walther's *Scherzi*, both very imposing works.[52] 1) Where Biber had a wide range of manners and textures in his opening section, with subtle juxtapositions as well as strong contrasts and an overall ternary shape, Walther's first section (all written in the same texture of three parts, with two in double stops on the violin) opens with a striking contrast of *forte* chords and *piano* bow tremolo. The tremolo is frequently used in concerted vocal music to represent 'fear and trembling', so this contrast is very suggestive of a dramatic situation. These two characters are then mixed with the dotted, imitative manner of Biber's second section.

2) Adagio, which generally means recitative style. This has the common contrast of vocal-style arioso opposed to brilliant, rapid passages featuring different note values and articulations.

3) A section in steady rhythm, in the manner of an imitative canzona, with two parts on the violin.

4) A section of bowing effects: first *ondeggiando* (i.e. slurred bariolage), then *arpeggiando con arcate sciolte* (rapid arpeggiation 'with loose bows') (see Appendix 2).

5) A section in gigue rhythm featuring constant *piano* and *forte* contrast.

6) A brief arioso leading to the usual, in this repertory, brilliant 32nd-note Finale.

Walther is unlikely not to have known works of Biber, since he had professional contacts with the court at Vienna, and around 1700 members of the Schönborn family, Walther's employers in Mainz, had violin lessons with Biber in Salzburg.[53] In addition, Biber's 1681 *Sonatae*, published in Nuremberg, were the chief monument of the German violin tradition since Schmelzer's of 1664, and judging by the number of surviving copies formed Biber's best-known and most widely circulated collection.[54] Bach may have known them for the same reason, and he may also have known Biber's extraordinary *Harmonia artificiosa-ariosa* for two scordatura violins and continuo, published in 1696 and reprinted in Nuremberg in 1712. Neither Walther nor Bach is likely to have known what is now Biber's best-known work, the so-called 'Mystery' or 'Rosary Sonatas' (the title-page is missing from the MS). These are the most thorough-going exploration of scordatura that survives from seventeenth-century Germany, with all except the first and last of sixteen sonatas in a different tuning. As far as we know they existed only in a presentation manuscript in Salzburg.[55] Bach therefore probably did not know the unaccompanied 'Pasagalia' that concludes the set. Nonetheless, some of the 'Mystery Sonatas' clearly date from some time before the compilation of the presentation manuscript, and there is the possibility that the Passacaglia dates from Biber's time with Bishop Liechtenstein-Castelcorn at Kroměříž in Moravia (1668–70). In the seventeenth century there was a chaconne by Biber in the Kroměříž archive, and the Passacaglia could have been copied further.[56] It hardly matters, though, since it is merely a single-violin version of a pattern that had been worked innumerable times in ensemble music in this tradition.

While some composers were content to have a succession of contrasting sections, there was a general move during the seventeenth century to bring some unity to sectional pieces. One way was to use a general manner, such as the free, recitative style, rather than a particular theme, as a refrain in which the manner returns but not exactly the same music. Another is to have thematic links between sections. A frequently cited example of this is the eighth Sonata of Uccellini's Op.5 (Modena 1649) where the pattern is: recitative style—steady canzona style in c-time—recitative style—steady canzona style reworked in triple time—recitative style.

By the end of the century patterns of this sort were being worked in a much more complex and sophisticated way in, for example, the free organ works of Pachelbel and, most sophisticated of all and in a way which has been compared to the nineteenth-century symphony, in the organ Praeludia of Buxtehude. There is little of this in Walther, but Biber could create substantial sections made from a subtle blend of manners, as we have seen in the first Sonata of 1681. Johann Paul von Westhoff (1656–1705) represents a slightly later phase. His *Sonate a violino solo con basso continuo* (Dresden 1694) generally have longer sections, with a single effect in each section.[57] The second Sonata, for example, has

1) Largo c: a very imaginative character texture of eighth notes and eighth rests, with the bass imitating the violin;
2) Presto c: *stile antico*-type imitations in double stops on the violin, with the bass in bustling triplets;
3) *Imitatione del liuto* presto $^6_4$: a rondo, obviously meant to be pizzicato; the lute imitation specially features the very characteristic lute effect of slurred pairs where only the first note is plucked by the right hand;
4) Aria grave c: this is moving towards a kind of Corellian style with walking eighth-note bass and small imitations occasionally (what Purcell calls 'reports') between violin and bass;
5) Finale c: very dashing double stops with repeated 32nds.

Here there is no return of manner or material, nor thematic linking, but a succession of highly characterised sections. At the same time there is a definite move towards the style of Corelli's Op.5 with slow (rather than recitative-style) first movements, second and fourth movements with polyphony in double and triple stops, much use of sequence, and moto perpetuo movements. What is missing is the logical, classic Corellian modulation structure, without which these longer sections can seem rambling. But given that character is the objective there is no doubt about the quality of the music, and by the same token one could sometimes wish that Corelli had more variety, not to say eccentricity, of character.

More important for us are Westhoff's six suites for unaccompanied violin (Dresden 1696), the only such collection to be published before Bach, though, as we have seen, there are a number of manuscript collections. Unfortunately both surviving copies lack the title-page and the last page of music, so we do not know what Westhoff called them.[58] Apart from being a virtuoso violinist, Westhoff was a highly educated and well-travelled courtier who had been in the Dresden court *Capelle* from 1674 to 1697, had played to Louis XIV in Paris in 1682, had also been in Florence, and for a brief period was professor of languages at Wittenberg University. From 1699 he was chamber secretary, chamber musician, and teacher of French and German at the court in Weimar, where he ended his days in 1705. He was therefore in Weimar when Bach had his first employment as a junior 'lackey' in the court band from around March until August 1703.

The six suites, as is also common in MS sources, are not headed Suite or Partia but each new key group begins with an Allemande, without any more general heading. In the dedication letter to the Electress Christiane Eberhardine of Saxony, written in impeccable French, he refers to them simply as 'pieces en Musique', a normal French way of referring to pieces that make up suites. One of the items he had played to Louis XIV was an unaccompanied suite (not one of these six suites) which was published in Paris as 'Suite pour le violon seul sans basse' (*Mercure galant*, January 1683).[59] Unusually in this violin repertory, all six suites have a uniform sequence of Allemande, Courante, Sarabande and Gigue, a situation more common in lute music (see section 4 below). In order to notate up to four parts on one stave, Westhoff and his engraver devised an ingenious eight-line stave, combining French violin (G1) and mezzo-soprano (C2) clefs. The bottom string (g) is therefore the space below the bottom line, and Westhoff's top note (c''') is one leger line above the top line. Suites of French dances tend not to use the upper range common in sonatas and, like Walther, Westhoff does not used scordatura. Suites for unaccompanied violin were a German, not a French, tradition, and in style the suites are in the German tradition of French dances, more directly melodic than, for example, the equivalent French lute repertory. They therefore lend themselves to polyphonic playing, and in some movements Westhoff develops textures of up to three parts. But he also varies the textural possibilities within this style by sometimes having a mainly single-line movement with occasional accentual chords, rather than a continuously two- or three-part texture. Sarabandes are generally in a very straightforward chordal texture that invites some decoration at least on repeats. In comparison with equivalent dance movements in Bach's violin Partias the chord-playing technique is similar, but stylistically Bach makes a blend of more sophisticated prototypes, the dances of François Couperin and the post-Corelli Italian sonata. The single line that implies more than one part, so common in Bach, is not usual here.[60]

How much contact 'lackey' Bach may have had with the senior and distinguished Westhoff is unclear. Bach was certainly avidly curious about traditions of music in his environment. On the other hand, Westhoff's employment was primarily as Chamber Secretary, and he may not still have been playing acrobatic violin music in the last couple of years of his life. Very noticeable in J.G. Walther's *Lexicon* entry (1732) is the full biographical information and the personal tone in which Walther, who was town organist at Weimar from 1707 and must at least have heard about Westhoff, writes about 'this very beloved and learned musician', listing the 1694 *Sonate* but not the 1696 unaccompanied suites, which he evidently did not know.

An Austrian counterpart to the suites of Westhoff is the *Artificiosus Concentus pro Camera* (1715) of the Salzburg violinist Johann Joseph Vilsmaÿr (1663–1722).[61] A pupil of Biber's, he carried on the Biber tradition in the Salzburg court *Capelle* after Biber's death in 1704. One of the Schönborn family (J.J. Walther's employers) had violin lessons with him in 1705 when previous members of the family had had them with Biber.[62] The collection consists of six Partias, four of which are in scordatura tunings. There is a slight dubiety about whether the pieces are actually unaccompanied because of the unusual formulation on the title-page: 'à Violino Solo Con Baβo bellè imitante'. There is no bass part with the unique copy in the British Library. Pauline Nobes has thoroughly examined the arguments for and against there being a missing bass part and concludes that this publication is almost certainly for unaccompanied violin.[63] The normal formulation for an accompaniment would be 'con basso continuo' (as in J.J. Walther's *Scherzi* and Westhoff's *Sonate*). The adverb 'bellè' is probably best translated as 'finely' or 'artfully', so the violin is 'artfully imitating a solo with bass', and the impression that these are unaccompanied is reinforced by the somewhat contrived compliment to Franz Anton, Archbishop of Salzburg, in the dedication letter: 'which express with one violin what is otherwise usually played on several instruments. They are an image of your great mind, who in one person holds together all the things that separately make for prosperous Princes'.[64] The title *Artificiosus Concentus* itself implies an 'ingenious consort' on one instrument, and there is nothing in the music to suggest that anything is missing.

The charm of these pieces is that, rather than being straight instrumental suites as Westhoff's, they combine aspects of Biber's style with more recent French dances of the orchestral type. Other than beginning with a Prelude, there is no standard sequence of movements, and seventeenth-century variety and contrast continue in preludes containing a complex mixture of manners and effects. Arias, variations, and ground-bass pieces are also in the Biber tradition, while menuets, gavottes, and a passepied represent more recent French fashion. This blend of traditional Austrian with Italian and French manners particularly recalls Georg Muffat, who had been organist and chamber musician at Salzburg from 1678 to 1687, two years before Vilsmaÿr joined the court *Capelle*.

Vilsmaÿr's Partias were available for sale at the Easter fair at Frankfurt in 1715, and J.G. Walther (1732) cites them from a catalogue of Lotter in Augsburg (including the phrase 'à Violino solo e Cont.', which is probably the result of a cursory reading of the title-page), so they were in circulation in Germany. Westhoff's suites are nonetheless the most likely such pieces for Bach to have known, in view of his proximity to the composer. Otherwise he may have known some of the pieces collected by the Dresden virtuoso Johann Georg Pisendel (1687–1755). Apart from being one of the outstanding violinists of his day, Pisendel was a keen connoisseur and collector of music, the greater part of whose collection is still preserved in the Saxon State Library, Dresden.[65] Bach seems first to have met Pisendel in 1709, when Pisendel stopped off at Weimar on the way to Leipzig.[66] It may have been he who introduced Bach to concertos by Giuseppe Torelli since Pisendel had trained with Torelli in Ansbach. There is also in Pisendel's collection a copy of parts for a Telemann two-violin concerto (TWV 52:G2) in Bach's handwriting and dating from around this time.[67] From 1712 Pisendel was first violin in the Dresden court *Capelle*, and from 1728 concertmaster. Bach may have met him again in 1717 when Bach was in Dresden for the competition with the French keyboard virtuoso Louis Marchand, one of the most repeated anecdotes about Bach.[68]

At that stage Pisendel had recently returned from a tour of Italy (March 1716–September 1717) where he had spent nine months in Venice in the suite of the Crown Prince of Saxony, followed by a study tour that included Naples; Rome, where he had lessons with Antonio Montanari; and Florence, where he got to know Martinello Bitti. Back in Venice he had lessons from Vivaldi, who remained a long-term friend.[69] Works by all three Italian composers are in the Dresden collection. Also in the collection, and probably acquired around this time, are (or were) unaccompanied violin works of Nicola Matteis the younger, Angelo Ragazzi, Francesco Geminiani, Pisendel himself, and Bach's Six Solos. The Bach, Ragazzi, and Geminiani pieces were in a convolute now lost.

Nicola Matteis (?late 1670s –1737), son of the Italian violinist whom John Evelyn described as 'stupendous' in London in 1674, moved from England to Vienna in 1700, where he was violinist and subsequently principal violinist in the court *Capelle*. Pisendel may have acquired his two Fantasias for unaccompanied violin on the way back from Italy in 1717, or during a trip to Vienna in the suite of the Crown Prince from August 1718 to March 1719. Music by Matteis was in any case known in Dresden since a violin concerto of his was performed there around 1710.[70]

Of the two Fantasias for unaccompanied violin in *D-Dl* Mus. 2045–R–1 (see Appendix 3) the first, in C minor, is in two movements, the second of which appears to be incomplete. The second Fantasia is in one movement. All three movements are of considerable interest stylistically. The first movement of the C minor has been compared to the Adagio and Grave first movements of Bach's G minor and A minor Solos.[71] It has in common with Bach's two movements the structure of chords and intervening flourishes, which some have related to the graces printed in the Amsterdam 1710 edition of Corelli's Op.5. Matteis's movement, however, differs in some important ways from Bach's, ways that throw into relief the nature of Bach's style. Most noticeable is that Bach's momentum is not interrupted; his movements proceed with a regular rhythmic tread, albeit with the freedom of florid ornamentation. Matteis's movement is marked 'Con discretione', meaning freely, in recitative style.[72] Matteis also makes dramatic use of silence, a feature in common with Telemann's violin Fantasias, but not part of Bach's style in the Solos. A more enlightening comparison is with the recitative section of the Chromatic Fantasia BWV 903/1 for keyboard: in fact the figuration in Matteis's bar 11 is virtually identical with that in bar 69 of the Chromatic Fantasia. This suggests a common style of improvisation rather than borrowing, and these three pieces by Matteis are in improvisatory genres. A strong characteristic in Matteis's movement is the dramatic use of chromatic harmony, which in the best tradition of such things is purposeful as well as colourful: the Neapolitan inflection in the opening upbeat bar also begins the second strain, and forms the climax of the sequence that runs from the end of bar 23 to bar 26. Here the Neapolitan D flat chord is juxtaposed to the dominant of C minor, giving the strong diminished 3rd leap d♭"–b♮', a progression favoured by Bach. Also in common with Bach is the structural use of tessitura, opening out to a very wide-spaced chord in bar 23 before narrowing down to the conclusion.

The following Molto adagio looks at first glance similar to Bach's G minor Fuga. In fact it belongs to a type of piece called variously Toccata, Tastada, or Arpeggiata in contemporary keyboard music.[73] As it is here, the piece meanders somewhat and may be incomplete. There is nonetheless skill in setting up expressive suspended dissonances, the objective of the keyboard equivalents by J.C.F. Fischer, F.X.A. Murschhauser and others. Bach's ultimate development of this genre is the B flat minor Prelude in Book I of *The Well-tempered Clavier*. Matteis's second Fantasia, in A minor (Appendix 3, 'Alia Fantasia'), has the appearance of another type of chord study, and has arpeggiated keyboard equivalents in the C major Prelude of Book I and the C sharp major Prelude of Book II of *The Well-tempered Clavier*, and a string equivalent in the Prelude of the G major cello Suite. Again, the objective seems to be to demonstrate variety in the layout of chords, with a structural contraction to very close intervals (bariolage, bars 43, 50 etc.), opening out to a variety of wide-spaced possibilities, and there is a skilful use of dissonance. If the C minor first movement seems to be a more finished composition, with its binary structure, the second movement and the A minor Fantasia seem demonstration studies for chord technique and improvisation.

The *Fantasia a Violino solo senza Basso* of Angelo Ragazzi (?1680–1750) is no longer extant and all we know of it is a description by Bruno Studeny and a brief quotation given by Andreas Moser (Ex.1.1).[74] According to Moser, Ragazzi's Fantasia was in no way inferior to those of Matteis, with wilful harmonic progressions, sequences up to seventh position, and demanding multiple stops. Studeny adds that it was in three sections: a free 'phantastic' Adagio, excellent both musically and violin-technically (apparently similar to the first movement of Matteis's C minor Fantasia); a weaker Allegro; and a final section in ⅜-time. Ragazzi was a court musician in Vienna from 1713–1722 and Pisendel may have acquired this Fantasia at the same time as the Matteis ones.

Ex.1.1   Angelo Ragazzi, from *Fantasia a Violino solo senza Basso*

Also lost is the *Sonata a Violino solo senza Basso* in B flat major attributed to Francesco Geminiani (1687–1762), but in this case there is an edition in a series of 'Masterpieces for Violin Solo', published in 1911 and (rather heavily) edited by Karl Gerhartz.[75] Later editions are based on this (see Appendix 4; I have given a version without the interpretative markings in the Gerhartz edition). Given the circumstances of Pisendel's collecting, it is likely that this sonata dates from before Geminiani's move to England in 1714. In style it is post-Corellian, though with some Corellian features, and with movement types and a stylistic eccentricity more in common with Vivaldi. There may also be an element of the style of the eccentric Milanese virtuoso Carlo Ambrogio Lonati (*c.*1645–*c.*1710/15), with whom Geminiani may have studied.[76] Lonati's Sonatas of 1701 include multiple stopping and scordatura, and reveal a pre-Corellian Italian tradition parallel to the Austro-German one (Biber was Lonati's exact contemporary), that Corelli only partially represents. Lonati's Sonatas were dedicated to the Emperor Leopold I. Pisendel somehow got hold of the dedication copy in Vienna and took it back to Dresden, where it is possible that Bach may have seen it.[77]

In Geminiani's Sonata there are also decided similarities to the sonatas of Bach's Solos. The first two movements (Adagio and Vivace) form a prelude and fugue pair, as in Corelli's *da chiesa* sonatas. The Adagio is noteworthy for notating arpeggiando with a wavy line. In his edition Gerhartz includes his own realisation of the Adagio, and whatever one thinks it (the opening arpeggiated section is rather too like the first-movement cadenza of Mendelssohn's Violin Concerto) he is surely right to say that it is not necessarily all arpeggiated, but is the basis for improvisation. From bar 15 he realises it in the style of Matteis's C minor Fantasia first movement. Working on an elaboration of this movement would be an excellent preparation for gaining freedom in the first movements of Bach's solo Sonatas. What Matteis and Geminiani have, and Bach has not, are dramatic pauses. These give surface articulation to an artful harmonic argument that starts ambiguously and quickly cadences in G minor (which misled the publisher into putting that key in the title of the Sonata). Moves in the direction of B flat major are constantly sidetracked, and when an obvious B flat major chord comes (at the beginning of bar 12) it is as the submediant of D minor and sounds remote from the key of B flat. Only the descending bass scale from bar 18 takes us ultimately home to the tonic. Considering that an identical harmonic strategy is thought supremely original in the first-movement introduction of Beethoven's Fourth Symphony one can only admire the previous originality of Geminiani. The ambiguity of key prefigures the key scheme of the entire Sonata since the second and fourth movements are in B flat, and the third in G minor.

The following Vivace fugue has a two-voice exposition such as is usual in the second movements of Corelli's Op.5 sonatas, yet manages to suggest four subject entries, with the subject at a soprano pitch in bar 3 and, at least the beginning of it, at a 'bass' pitch, in bar 5 (a similar effect of a four-voice exposition, expressed as a single line, is in the ¾ section of the Prelude of Bach's C minor cello Suite). There are remarkable similarities to the Fuga of Bach's G minor violin Sonata: in the subject itself (imagine Geminiani's subject beginning with three eighth-note f's); in the use of concertante-style, single-line episodes, where the arpeggiation suggests several parts and also elements from the subject; and in the use of subject entries to mark the main structural key centres: B flat—D minor (bars 14–15)—B flat (bars 18–20). On the other hand, a comparison with Bach's fugue is instructive in contrasting Italian lucidity with German rigour. It is extraordinary how much Geminiani manages to suggest with no more than one or two parts, including such contrapuntal ingenuities as the augmentation that marks the return to B flat from bar 18, and the hint of counterpoint at the 10th from bar 26. Bach uses predominantly three- and four-note chords: his ingenuity is in what he can suggest in an aerated texture.

Of the other two movements of this Sonata, the third (Affettuoso) shows a mastery of expressive chromatic harmony, more like Vivaldi than Corelli, featuring leaps of the diminished 3rd in the second strain. Good dramatic use of melodic dissonance is the essence of single-line writing. The concluding Giga again features characteristic dissonance and is so similar to the Gigue of Pisendel's A minor solo Sonata that one may assume Geminiani's was the model for it. Less sophisticated is the *Giga senza basso* in the D minor Sonata of Antonio Montanari (1676–1737). This is the only unaccompanied movement in a group of three sonatas that Pisendel presumably acquired from Montanari when he had lessons from him in Rome in 1717.[78] Like Geminiani, Montanari uses an obsessive figure (useful for unaccompanied pieces), but without Geminiani's highly characteristic use of melodic dissonance, or sense of economy.

Pisendel's A minor *Sonata à Violino Solo Senza Baßo* (*D-Dl* Mus. 2421–R–2) has traditionally been seen as a prime piece in the background to Bach's Solos (see Appendix 5).[79] Pisendel's headings for these works are identical to Bach's in the *Sei Solo*. There is no doubt that Bach, when he visited Dresden in September–October 1717, would have wished to see Pisendel, just returned from Italy, a friend of Vivaldi's and *au fait* with the latest in Italian music. It is by no means so likely that Pisendel had already composed his Sonata and played it to Bach.[80] The one firm date is provided by Telemann, who published the Giga as 'Gigue sans basse' (without its Double) in *Der getreue Musikmeister* (Hamburg 1728–29).[81] Pisendel's handwriting did not undergo the kind of development that assists in the dating of Bach's autographs.[82] One has therefore to make an assessment on grounds of style, and it has to be said that the date 1716 given by some seems too early both for musical style and for the way of writing for the violin. Here Geminiani's Sonata, which almost certainly dates from before 1714, is a useful point of comparison. Where Geminiani's first movement leaves much to be improvised by the player, Pisendel has written out all he wants and there is no question of adding further florid ornaments. The tendency to write out florid ornaments, with a rhythmic sophistication expressed in a great variety of note values, became general in the 1720s. Where Geminiani's first two movements, and those of Bach's Sonatas, form a prelude and fugue pair, Pisendel's first movement is in the style of a caprice, or cadenza, while the second is an Italian-style homophonic Allegro.[83]

In the first movement (without title, but plainly an Adagio) we can believe Quantz when he says that Pisendel was noted for his 'exceptionally touching way' of playing Adagios.[84] The violin style shows the sophisticated bowing technique of the 1720s and later, in Leclair, in Vivaldi's later works, or in the style Geminiani described in *The Art of Playing on the Violin* (London 1751). The dramatic, dotted, repeated chords are similar to those in the Praeludio of Bach's E minor Suite 'aufs Lauten Werck' BWV 996 (oldest copy 1714/17), but otherwise the comparison again throws into relief the impression that Pisendel's style is later. Here they have the effect of orchestral interjections in an accompanied recitative that demands fire and fantasy as well as much expressive nuance. The dramatic use of melodic dissonance, observed in the solos of Matteis and Geminiani, is much enhanced. This movement, and indeed the whole Sonata, takes the art of Ragazzi, Matteis, Montanari and Geminiani as represented in their solos and puts it to more powerful expressive use.

The Allegro seems also to belong in the 1720s, with elements of the 'Lombardic' style (dotted pairs with the short note first, as in bar 2 etc.), the arrival of which Quantz dates around 1722.[85] The rhythm in itself is not uncommon, but Pisendel makes a feature of it here, and it is a characteristic feature of the oncoming galant style as is rhythmic variety generally, so different from a Corellian Allegro or even from Vivaldi's violin Sonatas (1712, 1716). Less like the galant style, at least in its most straightforward form which normally has a predominance of four-bar dance phrases, is Pisendel's very artful irregular phraseology, and the organic way in which he develops later in the movement the motifs exposed in the first twelve bars. The variety of ways of using the solo violin is also masterly, ranging from three parts in one (bars 31–6 etc.), to straight arpeggios, to scale patterns, and often with highly expressive melodic dissonance (bars 52–4 etc.). Strongly purposeful and dramatic, in comparison with Montanari and Geminiani, is his use of an obsessive figure to build a climax in bars 81–90. In spite of being a less overt demonstration of skill than a fugue would be, this is music by a considerable connoisseur of styles and techniques. Allowing that stylistic datings are susceptible to being proved wrong by harder evidence, it would seem reasonable to date this Sonata around the mid-1720s.

The most notable collection of sonatas and suites for violin published in Germany in the years before 1720 is Telemann's *Six Sonates*, published in Frankfurt in 1715, and dedicated to Prince Johann Ernst of Sachsen-Weimar. Various things here overlap with Bach's plan for the violin Solos. Telemann's sonatas have three of each sonata type (i.e. 3 church and 3 chamber; Telemann, who studied the works of Corelli from an early age, uses the Corellian terminology of Sonata for both types; Bach uses German terminology of Sonata and Partia). More significant is that Telemann works systematically through different versions of genres. Of the three Correnti, for example, one (in A minor) is a straight moto perpetuo of eighth notes, another (in A major) has a witty, chasing effect in an interlocking pattern, and the third (in D major) features a mixture of note values (eighths, triplets, sixteenths).[86] Telemann also uses a structure more typical of Vivaldi than Corelli. While Corelli sets up a phrase structure in the first strain and then plays with expansions of it in the second, Telemann sets up a series of thematic motifs in the first strain, moving from the tonic to the dominant, which he then reruns in the second strain, with extensions and developments, back to the tonic. This plan is also Bach's standard practice from around 1720 for pieces in a binary structure (see Chapter Two section 5).

3. Violoncello and bass viol

Compared with the violin, the violoncello was a relatively new instrument in the first decade or so of the eighteenth century and there was nothing like the repertory tradition of the violin. The instrument itself dates back no further than the 1660s in Bologna, when the new technology of silver-wound strings allowed a relatively small member of the violone group to have a good bass as well as agility in the tenor register. With regard to the nature of the instrument, there was nothing then like the standardisation of instrument types we are used to nowadays. Around 1700 there were basically two types of violoncello: one played on the shoulder (*da spalla*, not to be confused with *da braccio*, i.e. on the arm), with violin technique; and one played between the knees (*da gamba*). The second of these was usually played with the viol, underhand bow-hold, and indeed the virtuoso instrument with which it was sometimes compared was the bass viol.[87] The question of the instruments that Bach may have used will be discussed later. Out of the great variety of bass stringed instruments in the seventeenth century, the emergence of the violoncello is associated with the shift to new Italian styles, particularly associated with Corelli but by no means limited to him, from the 1690s. By the 1710s there were a number of outstanding Italian virtuosos, notably Giovanni Bononcini who spent several years at the court of Sophie Charlotte in Berlin from 1702. Also in the Berlin *Capelle* at that stage was Christian Bernhard Linike, an excellent cellist who joined Prince Leopold's *Capelle* at Cöthen in 1716 and is the most likely person for Bach to have written the cello Suites for, if indeed he wrote them for a particular person. At the same time instrument-making had reached its classic phase, never to be surpassed. The fact that Bach could write some of the defining repertory of the instrument around 1720 shows not only his genius, but also the responsiveness of German courts to current fashion. In the same way Bach wrote superbly imaginative horn parts in the First Brandenburg Concerto, probably originally composed in 1712/13, shortly after the Waldhorn came into Germany.

Details of the early Italian repertory for cello are readily available.[88] Of the two early examples thought to be for unaccompanied cello, the twelve *Ricercate sopra il violoncello o clavicembalo* Op.1 (Bologna 1687) of Giovanni Battista degli Antoni must be discounted since a violin part has been found in the Estense Library in Modena.[89] The other, a manuscript collection of Ricercari by Domenico Gabrielli (1689), also in the Estense Library, is worth considering briefly since it makes a number of important points about unaccompanied pieces. The main one is that this is instructional material. No.1 (Ex.1.2a) looks like a teaching bass that sets up situations for the teacher to comment on (and improvise a melodic part to?) such as the expressive e♭ in bar 3 which, in the custom of unfigured bass realisation of the time, would take a major 7th, resolving to 6, suspension, and so on. No.2 can only be an exercise for clef-reading, since it jumps randomly between five different ones, using standard figurations together with rhythmic points such as syncopation, and ends in a new time-signature ($^{12}_{8}$). No.3 (Ex.1.2b) is a catalogue of D major effects, with trumpet-call outlines, *basse de trompette* leaps of an octave etc., repeated sixteenth notes as in the first movement of the Fifth Brandenburg Concerto, and similarities to the subject of the D major organ fugue BWV 532/2, showing how traditional were the materials that Bach dealt with. No 4 is in a more difficult key (E flat major). No.5 in C major is a study in leaps, then scales that move into sharp keys. All these pieces look like practice for basso continuo parts rather than independent solo repertory. Also probably instructional is the (well-written) canon for two cellos. Such *bicinia* were traditional for teaching, the pupil could imitate the teacher, and they also demonstrate composition technique. One Sonata for two cellos has different characters, time-signatures and so on, in which the pupil could first accompany the teacher, then take the solo role. Imitation of a master was standard practice for learning at the time, and certainly tallies with what we know of Bach's teaching methods. An important point is that two Ricercari (Nos. 6 and 7) have multiple stopping, and a second Sonata for two cellos even has hints of inner parts for the accompanying cello, evidence for chordal cello accompaniment in some of the earliest repertory. The instructional intention, so evident here, links with Forkel's comment that Bach 'always contrived his [instrumental pieces] so that his performers could, by their means, improve upon their instruments'. When the cello Suites were first published (by Janet et Cotelle in Paris c.1824) it was as *Sonates ou Études*.

Ex.1.2   a) Domenico Gabrielli, *Ricercar Primo*, bars 1–6;

b) *Ricercar Terzo*, concluding bars

The fashion for the violoncello passed rapidly into Germany. The first concerto composer to elevate the cello to the status of the violin was Vivaldi, with twenty-nine solo concertos and one for two cellos. Some of the earliest cello concertos, and probably some of the very first concertos he wrote, were sent to, and perhaps written for, the enthusiast Count Rudolf Franz Erwein von Schönborn, at Wiesentheid (near Würzburg) in 1709.[90] If they are relatively undemanding and written as for a large violin, Vivaldi later made up for this in exploiting the expressive potential of different registers of the cello's wide compass. Bach used the cello as soloist in cantatas from 1708 onwards. BWV 71, published in that year and Bach's only cantata to be published in his lifetime, again shows the cello treated as a large violin. With a range of G–e♭" (in the autograph part) and figurations that imply obvious diatonic violin fingerings, it implies the *da spalla* option in which the same player could play all members of the violin family (soprano violin, alto and tenor viola, bass cello).[91] At Weimar Bach could call on the cellist Gregor Christoph Eylenstein, 'Cammer-Musicus', though instrumentalists there were expected to be versatile, rather than specialists as at Dresden. In BWV 199 (1713) the cello part implies that the player took up the oboe for an obbligato in one movement, and the viola in another.[92] There are some notable violoncello obbligatos in the Weimar cantatas: in BWV 172/5 (1714) and BWV 132/3 (1715), and in particular the remarkable aria for Bass, two obbligato cellos and continuo in BWV 163/3 (1715).

If the cello was a relative newcomer, stemming from the violin family, the bass viol (commonly called viola da gamba) had a German virtuoso tradition in the seventeenth century second only to the violin's, based on multiple stops and polyphonic playing. Bach's gamba Sonatas, in their almost exclusively single-part writing, are not in that tradition and, other than perhaps the D major BWV 1028, are unlikely to have been originally for viol. Nearer is the obbligato in the aria 'Komm süßes Kreuz' in the St Matthew Passion, though that also exists in a lute version. If one strand feeding into the cello Suites is the German tradition of suites for unaccompanied violin, the other is the German virtuoso viol tradition.

The question of viol influence is not a merely theoretical one, but radically affects performance style. In the seventeenth century the two main centres of viol playing were England and France, with quite different playing styles. Towards the end of the century there came in addition the strong influence of Italian violin music. Some seventeenth-century German viol players went to England to improve. There they encountered the English lyra viol (smaller, chord-playing viol) with its full range of double stops, chords, pizzicato, *col legno*, bow tremolo, echo dynamics and other dynamic effects.[93] As we have noted above (in section 1) the Lübeck violinist Thomas Baltzar, who worked in England from 1655 to 1663, seems to have been more influenced by this in his unaccompanied violin pieces than by the German violin tradition. The French, meanwhile, evolved a very distinct manner of viol playing. The difference is well explained by Jean Rousseau in his *Traité de la viole* (Paris 1687), who naturally regarded the French style as perfection. Where the English concentrate on chords and diminutions (improvised division technique) and are 'more admirable for their skill than good taste', the French excel in 'their sensitivity in imitating the voice', that is, the very subtle and subtly ornamented type of melody associated with the *air de cour*.[94] Chord-playing was nonetheless an important part of the French tradition, which was closely allied to that of the lute and theorbo. The earliest French publication of suites for unaccompanied bass viol is the *Pieces de violle* (Paris 1685) of Demachy (his first name is not known).[95] In the preface (*Avertissement*) Demachy lists four manners of playing: 1) chord playing; 2) accompanying oneself singing; 3) playing a part in an ensemble; and 4) plucking. Pizzicato was an important viol effect, and Demachy regretted that he was unable to include 'Pieces à pincer' in his book. Marin Marais, in his third Book of viol pieces (Paris 1711), has a Gavotte 'dans le goût du théorbe que l'on peut pincer si l'on veut'.[96] To these four ways, Jean Rousseau (1687) adds developing a subject extempore. This ultimate skill, called by Christopher Simpson 'driving a point [of imitation]', is related to Bach's 'invention' principle (see Chapter Two section 6). Generally, though, the two main elements of the French tradition may be summed up as chord playing ('jeu d'harmonie') and melodic playing ('jeu de mélodie').

Of the two main representatives of the French viol school in Bach's day, Marin Marais (1656–1728) and Antoine Forqueray (1672–1745), Marais represents the classic phase of the French style and the highly distinctive French manner of playing. We are very well informed about it by the prefaces to his five Books of viol pieces, and by the large amount of performance detail Marais includes in his notation. His influence was great and his published works were known throughout Europe, as J.G Walther tells us (1732). The defining aspect was the characteristic French bow-stroke which, as it were, plucks the string in a manner often compared to the lute or harpsichord.[97] The bow is prepared at rest, and the pluck is done by tensioning the hair with the middle finger so that it scratches the string. The pluck is caused by releasing the tension on the bow hair. Given that some German cellists used the viol, palm-up, bow-hold into the late eighteenth century, it is possible that this may to some extent have affected German cello playing in French-style music, particularly in the early decades of the century.[98] The essence of the French style of bowing was variety of bowstrokes, and Marais is reported to have used six distinct types of bowstroke.[99] This contrasted strongly with the Italian style of bowing, which was imitating a radically different style of singing from the French, one that emphasised continuous cantilena rather than subtle, detailed nuance. The difference is vividly described by a French lawyer and viol enthusiast, Hubert le Blanc, in an informative defence of the 'noble' viol against the Italian violin and violoncello that were threatening to drive it out of use (1740). Le Blanc compares the way of playing an Italian sonata, drawing a continuous sound as the voice does, to a potter modelling clay on a revolving wheel, whereas he describes the way of playing French *Pièces* (suites) as:

> *tic-tac*, with lifted bow-strokes, all in the air, which take so much from the pluck of the lute and the guitar, on which model Marin Marais composed his *Pièces*, and which, although he varied them with six different bow-strokes, one might criticise as having something of the lack of expression of the harpsichord in that they suffer from the central defect of being *simple* (i.e. striking the string of the viol as the jack does that of the harpsichord), and not *complex*, as in the Italian manner where, by the use of smooth and well-connected up-bows and down-bows whose changes are imperceptible, there is produced an endless chain of notes that appear as a continuous flow, such as those emanating from the throats of [the famous Italian sopranos Cuzzoni] and Faustina'.[100]

For Le Blanc the ideal is represented by Forqueray, who united French resonant harmony with Italian vocal melody, 'where one draws a sparkling sound from a marbled style' ('où l'on tire un Son petillant d'un goût persillé', a typically French gastronomic comparison to champagne and meat, marbled with fat so combining two things).[101]

The gradual mingling of French and Italian styles, the leading movement in French music from the 1690s epitomised by François Couperin's quest for a fusion of styles (*Les goûts réunis*), had a corresponding movement in Germany. There these styles, initially at any rate, were combined also with German traditions of virtuoso string playing. Out of the rich German viol culture, only some leading strands need be mentioned here.[102] The *Primitiae Chelicae* (Nuremberg 1695) of Konrad Höffler (1647–in or before 1705) show an initial phase of this.[103] It consists of twelve suites in different major and minor keys, several of which have highly virtuosic preludes in a variety of contrasting manners, very much on the lines of Vilsmaÿr's for violin. In the first suite this is combined with a Fuga, much of which consists of standard sequences in chords, with a run of sixteenth notes towards the end, and with the main structural points marked by an entry of the brief subject. The dances are quite French in character, recognisably in the same world as Marais, and would presumably have been performed in the French style. Höffler was gambist at the court at Weissenfels till his death around 1705, a court with which Bach was to have many contacts from at least 1712.

A more complex blend is in the *Sonate ô Partite* (Kassel 1698) of August Kühnel (1645–c.1700).[104] Kühnel certainly knew his styles at first hand, since he seems to have studied in Paris in 1665, and in 1682 he was in England 'because that is where the viola da gamba comes from'.[105] From 1695 he was capellmeister at the Italophile court at Kassel, where the Landgrave Carl of Hessen-Kassel was a keen and good gambist. The title and dedicatory letter of the *Sonate* are all in Italian. The Landgrave was one of a number of princely devotees of the viol until well into the eighteenth century, another being Bach's employer, Prince Leopold of Anhalt-Cöthen.[106]

Of the fourteen sonatas and partitas, Kühnel says in his Preface that the first three (for two viols) and the last four (for one viol) are written so as to be playable without continuo. This means that the last four are effectively for unaccompanied bass viol since the basso continuo part does little more than double notes that are already in the solo part. In view of the prevalence of chord-playing, and 'monodic polyphony', in viol music generally, much repertory could in fact be played without accompaniment if the player were to add the occasionally necessary harmony notes. Marais did not publish the *basse continue* part of his first Book (1686) until three years after the solo part, and then recommended the theorbo as the accompanying instrument. This avoids the heavy effect of two viols doubling bass notes much of the time. The theorbo was also at that stage the preferred instrument for accompanying the voice, for which the viol was considered in France to be the closest instrumental equivalent.[107] Various writers have commented on the redundancy of the basso continuo in much eighteenth-century viol repertory and the growing tendency to dispense with it.

Performance style in the partitas of Kühnel is not so clear-cut as with Höffler. There is a rhythmic regularity, common in German versions of dances, that is untypical of central French style. Yet he always has the character of the dance clearly in focus, and there is not yet the admixture of Italian sonata features that was ultimately to transform binary dance genres into binary sonata movements. Some dances, particularly allemandes, could be played either with or without *notes inégales*. On the other hand there is a perceptible and growing tendency in the early eighteenth century for composers in the mixed style to notate the rhythm they want. All in all, the partitas of Kühnel demonstrate the central performance issue of these repertories: much is left to the connoisseurship of players, who may choose a more or less French manner of performance according to their taste.

Kühnel's *Sonate* were published at the very end of his career. In the same year Johann Schenck (1660–after 1710) published his *Scherzi musicali* Op.6 (Amsterdam 1698). Schenck's publications, in luxurious editions widely distributed, and also in manuscript copies, were an influential model of the mixed style in the first decade of the eighteenth century. From 1696 Schenck was employed at the Düsseldorf court of the Elector Palatine, himself an amateur viol player. The *Scherzi* continue to have first movements (called variously preludium, fantasia, or capriccio) in 'fantastic' style with contrast of movement and character, but now, as we have observed with Westhoff, the sections are longer and there are changes of time signature. Where Kühnel keeps to the traditional solo instrumental dances (allemande, courante, sarabande, gigue) Schenck also has the Lullian lighter dances (rondeau, gavotte, bourrée, menuet) in their plain form, as yet without sonata-type phrases. Also Lullian are the overture, in a style similar to Dieupart's keyboard versions, and chaconne. On the other hand Schenck has the Corellian type of fugue, starting with two entries of the subject on the viol in double stopping, followed by the bass (this is in the fourth Sonata, marked 'con Basso obligato': in the other sonatas the accompaniment is optional).

The fusion of styles is further pursued in *Le nymphe di Rheno* Op.8 (Amsterdam [1702]) and *L'Echo du Danube* Op.9 (Amsterdam [1704]). In spite of the latter's French title, the echo could as easily be of the Tiber, since this is Schenck's most Italianate collection.[108] In Op.8 there is evidence for the importation of sonata features into the more stately dances, particularly the correnti and sarabandes, which can have two types of movement: one in the rhythmic character of the dance, the other in continuous eighth notes. One Corrente (in Sonata I) is written with dotted eighth notes. This is probably not a notation of *notes inégales* but a character rhythm, since other correnti are written straight, but it implies that the application of strong inequality would be inappropriate where dots are not notated. The lighter dances are in straightforward dance style. Of the ten Sonatas, four have an initial slow movement followed by the traditional solo-suite dances; three are Italian-type sonatas; two have the lighter Lullian dances (Sonata IV begins with a Ciacona), and one (Sonata X) has a mixture of both suite types.

Of the six Sonatas of Schenck's Op.9, the first two have basso continuo, and are in very Corellian violin-sonata style, mostly with a single line and little chording; the second two have optional accompaniment and have French dances with a good deal of chording; and the last two are unaccompanied. There is a decided move to the Italian sonata style over Op.8, with a noticeable increase in the importation of sonata features into the dances, including both of Corelli's manners of doing this: turning a dance into a moto perpetuo of a single note value, or alternating phrases in a dance rhythm with ones in a single note value, usually with the antecedent in the characteristic dance rhythm and the consequent in continuous eighth notes (see Chapter Two section 2). The *pièce de résistance* is Sonata VI for unaccompanied viol.[109] In A minor, it has a passionate opening movement in the German tradition of several highly contrasted sections. This acts as a prelude to a *stile antico* fugue, not very contrapuntal but nonetheless ingenious in adapting the common progressions of this type of fugue to the viol. The remainder of the Sonata consists of short, highly contrasted sections ranging from florid recitative to moto perpetuo, and ending with a Giga. Two further unaccompanied sonatas, from a manuscript source, are edited in DEdM 6. *L'Echo du Danube* must have had numerous admirers since it was reprinted c.1742 in Paris.

Most distinguished of all German viol virtuosos was Ernst Christian Hesse (1676–1762), who became known as an excellent viol player in his youth at Eisenach. He was subsequently employed by the Landgrave Ernst Ludwig of Hessen-Darmstadt, who had been in Paris during Lully's last years and who was, musically at any rate, Francophile. The Landgrave sponsored Hesse to study in Paris with Marais and Forqueray from 1698–1701. Very few of Hesse's works survive, though they must have been numerous since E.L. Gerber mentions many suites and sonatas, some for unaccompanied bass viol and some with accompanying bass, in the mixed style but leaning towards the French.[110] Hesse's pupil Johann Christian Hertel (1697–1754) had thought of studying in Paris but decided to study French style and technique with Hesse instead. From 1718 he was a viol player in the court *Capelle* at Eisenach, and met Bach in Leipzig in 1726.[111] According to J.A. Hiller (1784), Hertel visited the court at Cöthen in 1718.[112]

How much of French viol technique may have affected the cello Suites as they might have been played at Cöthen can only be guessed. Bach's version of the mixed style in them leans decidedly towards the Italian. Nonetheless some types of movement, particularly sarabandes, and the lighter dances, preserve their French character. The Sonatas of the Italian cello virtuoso Antonio Maria Bononcini (1693, younger brother of Giovanni Bononcini) are overtly virtuosic, but with nothing of the intellectual weight of Bach's Suites.[113] The intellectual tradition lay with the French viol. Some aspects of viol technique, such as the *enflé* (swelling on a note), *coupé* (sound cut off), *soutenu* (sound evenly sustained through the note) were common currency on both instruments.[114] The French viol repertory was certainly part of Bach's environment, and it would be well worth cellists' effort now to familiarise themselves with Marais's performance instructions and at least some of his viol works in good performances.

As far as the instrument itself is concerned, opinions are almost as varied as for the lute. In the seventeenth century a large number of stringed bass instruments were in use and standardisation was only beginning in the first two decades of the eighteenth century. Nearest to Bach is the definition of his cousin J.G. Walther, organist of the town church in Weimar, who wrote in 1708: 'Violoncello, is an Italian bass instrument, not unlike a viola da gamba, which is treated almost like a violin, i.e. it is partly held by the left hand, that also forms the hand-shapes, but partly it is hung on the coat button on account of its weight, and bowed with the right hand. It is tuned like a viola'.[115] Walther is presumably comparing it to the gamba for size, while describing the *da spalla* way of holding the instrument. A clearer description is given by Mattheson in 1713, who lists three smaller basses: the *violoncello*, the *bassa viola*, and the *viola da spalla*.[116] These may have up to five or six strings, and since they are relatively small one can play all sorts of quick things, divisions and ornaments on them. Mattheson particularly recommends the viola da spalla ('shoulder-viola') for accompaniment on account of its penetrating tone, making the bass line distinct and clear. It is secured on the chest by a belt which is thrown over the right shoulder, and there is nothing to impede its resonance (i.e. resting an instrument on the leg, *da gamba*, damps the sound). Mattheson's list is by no means the whole story, but it does give the general range of instrument types in use in Germany at the time: a violoncello of various sizes, a bass viola (not a viola da gamba since Mattheson discusses that separately), and a shoulder-viola.

Bach evidently used the term violoncello for the *6 Suites*, though the 'Viola de Baβo' on the title-page of J.P. Kellner's copy is interesting in the light of Mattheson's 'bassa viola'. There are, however, two other instruments in question: in 1724–5 Bach wrote a series of cantatas involving what he calls *Violoncello piccolo*; and later in the eighteenth century he was credited with the invention of an instrument called the *Viola pomposa*. With regard to the violoncello piccolo, the question is whether it was played on the leg or on the shoulder, or indeed if it is a single instrument. Two of the cantatas have the violoncello piccolo movements in the Violin I part, and a further two have the C3 clef changed to G2, the point being that an instrument tuned C G d a e' would be perfectly playable by a violinist, sounding a octave lower than the violin (Anna Magdalena Bach put a bracket around the notes G d a e' in the tuning instruction for the D major cello Suite, though that does not use the G2 clef). The question of whether the violoncello piccolo was played *da gamba* or *da spalla*, or whether it was a single instrument, can be argued both ways. A further question is whether or not it is it in fact the same as the viola pomposa. Was the 'Bassettgen' listed among Bach's stringed instruments at his death an instrument of this sort?[117]

The first mention of the viola pomposa was in 1766 by the Leipzig musician and writer on music J.A. Hiller.[118] He attributes its invention to Bach, and describes it as follows: 'It is tuned like a violoncello but with an extra top string, is somewhat larger than a viola, and is secured by a belt so that it can be held on the arm in front of the chest'. This description is in a footnote to an anecdote about the Dresden violinist Pisendel playing the viola pomposa to accompany Franz Benda on the violin. In a later edition Hiller adds that the Leipzig luthier J.C. Hoffmann had made several to Bach's specifications. Around 1777 another Leipzig writer, J.F. Köhler, repeats the fact that it is used to accompany violin solos, and adds that it is half way between a violin and a cello.[119] In 1782 J.N. Forkel, who knew both Wilhelm Friedemann and C.P.E. Bach, repeats Hiller's description word for word and expands on Köhler's comment about its usefulness for accompanying the violin.[120] So far everything seems to derive from Hiller's initial footnote and the anecdote about Pisendel accompanying Benda. The invention of the viola pomposa entered the Bach hagiography as an example of his all-round musicianship (it is mentioned again as such in a music journal article in 1789).[121] The instrument is nowhere specified in Bach's works, but does figure in a Duo for transverse flute and viola pomposa or violin by Telemann (Hamburg 1728) and in a concerto with the same specification by J.G. Graun.

A different, and more plausible, strand of tradition is represented in a description by E.L. Gerber in 1790.[122] E.L. Gerber was the son of H.N. Gerber, who was a pupil of Bach's in Leipzig probably between the end of 1724 and the beginning of 1726, just when Bach was writing the cantatas with violoncello piccolo. E.L. Gerber's account harks back to Mattheson rather than Hiller: 'The stiff manner with which the violoncellos were handled at that time made it necessary for [Bach] to invent what he called the viola pomposa for the lively bass parts in his works. It added an extra 5th, e', to the low-pitched four strings of the violoncello, and it was played on the arm. This convenient instrument allowed the player to perform more easily the said high and quick passages.' In a listing of instruments and their inventors, Gerber identifies Bach as the inventor of the viola pomposa 'around the year 1724'.[123] The conjunction of H.N. Gerber's presence in Leipzig at that date and Bach's cantatas with violoncello piccolo has prompted most recent writers to identify the violoncello piccolo with the viola pomposa.[124] Not all are convinced, however. Winfried Schrammek (1977), in an expert survey of literary sources and surviving instruments, points out that the viola pomposa was a large viola, not a small cello, and proposes a violoncello piccolo played 'in shoulder position' for the four cantatas where it seems to have been played by a violinist. Schrammek's attitude may have been coloured by the acerbic pre-war arguments about these instruments, and the sometimes dubious activities of instrument dealers and curators. Georg Kinsky, for example, curator of the Heyer Collection of musical instruments in Cologne in the 1920s, had a four-string violoncello piccolo quietly converted to five strings and put in his catalogue as 'viola pomposa'.[125] Schrammek lists a number of surviving instruments that correspond to the descriptions of the viola pomposa.

Ulrich Drüner (1987) proposes that Bach's contribution was not to invent a new instrument, but to add the proportions of a small cello to the viola da spalla in order to get a better sound quality. He then proposes a special 'Bach' violoncello piccolo for the cantatas, again applying cello dimensions to the viola da spalla, though smaller than the violoncello piccolo proper, and not identical with the viola pomposa. This would be for use on Sundays when Bach did not have a sufficiently skilled cellist available for tenor-register obbligatos, and could be played by a violinist or violist. One is always suspicious of special 'Bach' instruments, whether violin, lute, or cello, but Drüner is right to emphasise that versions of the violoncello were played on the shoulder. In fact, in the 1680s in Italy, when the very first solo cello literature was being produced, the very word 'violoncello' probably meant a *da spalla* instrument, the version played on the leg being termed 'violone' (as in all Corelli's sonata publications).[126] In 1762 a Breitkopf catalogue listed 41 works for 'Violoncello piccolo, ô violoncello da braccia'.[127]

The relevance of all this to the D major cello Suite has been explored by Mark M. Smith (1998) in a very wide-ranging survey of tenor- and bass-register stringed instruments in the first half of the eighteenth century. Pointing to the elaborate nature of the Suite from the points of view of both instrumental technique and composition, Smith concludes that this Suite is unlikely to have been a one-off experiment in Cöthen and was probably written around the time of the violoncello piccolo cantatas (1724–5). This is reasonable in view of the fact that the earliest copy of the cello Suites (by J.P. Kellner) dates from 1726–7, and that Bach's suite and other collections were generally not written in one go but assembled over a period of time. With regard to an instrument, the fact that the range extends to a 10th above the top string (whereas the other suites never exceed an octave), together with the first chord in bar 6 of the Sarabande, imply a small instrument. Smith cites a great deal of interesting supporting evidence, including that Kellner's term 'Viola de Basso' was used in the Arnstadt court *Capelle* in the 1690s for the largest size of viola.¹²⁸ All this points to an instrument with cello characteristics of viola size, which Smith equates with the viola pomposa as designed by Bach and J.C. Hoffmann. It is tempting to think of the very enjoyable obbligato in the aria 'Mein gläubiges Herz' from Cantata 68 being played by Bach himself on the instrument that he and Hoffmann cooked up.

More recently the argument has been moved forward in a practical way by Dmitry Badiarov (2007), who makes and plays a small size of violoncello da spalla with doubly-wound bass strings. This instrument has been used for the Bach Suites with persuasive advocacy by Sigiswald Kuijken. It does seem, though, that in the surviving iconographic evidence the violoncello da spalla looks rather larger than this. In a wide-ranging survey of iconographic evidence it was found that cellos played *da spalla* were common in northern Italy but not in Germany, where only *da gamba* playing is depicted, often with underhand (viol-style) bow hold. Badiarov's instruments with double-wound lower strings are in any case rather smaller than the iconographic evidence suggests.¹²⁹

While the wealth of information provided in these discussions is fascinating, and there is much enjoyment to be had from a well-constructed argument, it has to be said that ultimately we are dealing with no more than likelihoods. The notion that one instrument is more 'correct' than another is alien to Bach's environment, and Bach himself would assuredly be amazed and delighted to hear a brilliant performance of the D major Suite on a four-string modern cello.

4. The German lute tradition

If the violin was the centre of experimentation and new genres in Italy in the 1620s, the lute was in France, and there are many parallels between the two developments. Italian violinists explored new expressive possibilities of instrumental sonority in terms of new techniques of hand and bow, some pictorial, many in imitation of the new expressive powers of virtuoso singers in the second practice. French lutenists explored new sonorities in terms of scordaturas. From the 1620s the old Renaissance *vieil ton* tuning (the six fingered courses tuned to g' d' a f c G, or the same intervals down from a') was abandoned in favour of a plethora of new tunings containing more 3rds.¹³⁰ This meant that the lower courses were raised in pitch and gave a better response, encouraging the use of *sans chanterelle* textures (i.e. not using the top string). From this experimentation there emerged what was to be the standard tuning of French lute music from around 1650, known as D minor tuning (f' d' a f d A; first known use 1638). With this tuning, the normal lute of the classic phase of French lute music (from around 1650) had, in addition to these six courses, an extra five bass courses going down diatonically from G to C, giving a total of eleven courses.

Just as Italian violinists moved to Germany, so French musicians moved around German courts. But whereas Italian instrumentalists brought either virtuoso solo or ensemble music, the French brought dance music, whether as dancing masters, as ordinary string players in court bands, or, on the most prestigious level, as virtuoso lutenists playing highly stylised and abstracted versions of dance genres. In this respect there is a remarkable similarity between Italian and French styles in the 1620s. In sonatas by, for example, Castello there is a contrast between relatively short phrases of dance type (like verse lines), and much longer, open-ended phrases, usually building up to a climax (like prose sentences). The spinning out of long phrases of no set length was to be a feature of the sonata style throughout the century and is one of its leading characteristics in the time of Bach (see Chapter Two section 2). Correspondingly, the leading French lutenist in the new style in the 1620s, René Mesangeau (d. 1638; he may actually have been of Italian origin), was writing courantes which elided the clear phrases of dance music so that an entire strain may have a single unbroken phrase that does not touch the ground harmonically until the double bar.[131] It was also in the 1620s that the main genre of French solo instrumental music, the suite, began to emerge, consisting of unmeasured or semi-measured prelude, allemande, courante, and sarabande, with (after around 1650) the addition of the gigue. Sometimes, mostly in groups in rarer keys where there are fewer pieces, the movements seem to belong together as an entity, but in many sources there are multiple movements of each type within a key group, particularly courantes, from which the player would presumably make a selection. Lutenists collected individual pieces as they found them, and arranging them in key groups in a manuscript was a way of keeping together pieces in the same tuning. Germans tended to integrate things more, with mostly only one of each dance and sometimes thematic links between dances. Nonetheless, Bach's A major English Suite for keyboard BWV 806, with its two Courantes and their Doubles, is a relic of this looser type of suite, possibly influenced by François Couperin's first book of harpsichord pieces (Paris 1713), in which the first group of pieces also has two Courantes, one with a Double.

Of the leading instruments in seventeenth-century Germany the lute was the one virtually exclusively associated with France, as testified by the enormous amount of French lute music surviving in 'retrospective' German (including Austrian and Bohemian) manuscript sources. Numerous French lutenists circulated in the German lands, and French style was associated with them to such an extent that, until well into the second half of the century, when German keyboard players wished to play French music they usually made arrangements of lute pieces rather than looking for original French harpsichord pieces. In this situation, the German lutenist who most influentially took on the French style was the younger Esaias Reusner (1636–1679). He was born and spent most of his early life in or near what was then the German city of Breslau (now Wrocław), cradle of some of the finest German lutenists. He studied with his father, also a noted lute virtuoso, and with an unidentified French lutenist, and in 1667 published in Breslau his first main collection, *Delitiae testudinis*. The prestige of this landmark publication is evident from the fact that it was reprinted in the following year and again in Leipzig in 1697, long after Reusner's death (the 1697 edition was renamed *Erfreuliche Lauten-Lust*). In 1672 Reusner moved to Leipzig, where he taught lute at the university and played the theorbo in concerted music at the Thomaskirche under Sebastian Knüpfer, one of Bach's predecessors as Thomascantor. In 1674 he moved to Berlin as chamber lutenist to the Elector of Brandenburg, and there in 1676 he published his second collection, *Neue Lauten-Früchte*.

Reusner's thoroughgoing adoption of French style is evident from his introductory remarks in both publications. Apart from giving basic information about technique and notation, he stresses the importance of French *notes inégales* for bringing out the correct rhythmic character 'according to the present manner'.[132] Both books are for 11-course lute, mainly in D minor tuning though there are a couple of scordaturas. While the French aspect of Reusner's style is clear, it is far from being a straight copy of the style of Denis Gaultier and others, and differs in ways that are typical of German musicians taking over foreign styles. There is a more consistent organisation, with each key group centring on a regular sequence of one each of allemande, courante, sarabande, and gigue, sometimes with thematic links between movements in the manner of Froberger's keyboard suites.[133] A gavotte frequently figures before or after the gigue. Reusner uses the word 'Suite' in his instructions, but key groups have no other heading than an initial type of movement such as prelude, pavane or allemande. Two groups from of the 1676 book end with a Ciacona and a Passagalia respectively, not an uncommon arrangement and one behind the organisation of Bach's D minor violin Partia.

A second difference from the classic French lute style is Reusner's greater continuity of line and solidity of texture. Pavanes particularly are fully chorded and with contrapuntal lines more in the manner of the first generation of French *style brisé* lutenists represented by Dufaut, whose published works appeared in the 1630s. Sarabandes also can be very fully chorded, and sometimes have a rhythmic regularity quite alien to French style. This quest for coherence and unification is a German trait, evident as much in Schütz's treatment of principles taken from Monteverdi, as in Bach's treatment of elements taken from Venetian concertos. Reusner's preludes are either measured (with bar-lines and rhythm signs) or semi-measured (with complete rhythm signs but not bar-lines), rather than unmeasured (with only partially notated rhythm signs) in the manner of Denis Gaultier. They nonetheless make an elegant play on positions and sonorities idiomatic to the instrument, entirely in accord with the great French lutenists. Courantes are, as one might expect, closest to the French style, and one Gigue (from the C minor group of 1676) is in a continuously *brisé* texture throughout, with hardly any notes sounded simultaneously. This texture of what one might call total *campanella* is characteristic of French *style brisé* lute music from its earliest manifestations around 1600. It is also in some of Reusner's sarabandes, as it is in some German keyboard sarabandes of this time such as the suites of Johann Adam Reincken, and the effect may be one of the elements behind the single line, with rich harmonic implications, in the Sarabande of Bach's C minor cello Suite.

A comparison of the D major Passagalia that ends the 1676 book with a C major Chaconne on the same bass by one of the founders of the French *style brisé*, Ennemond Gaultier, uncle of Denis Gaultier, highlights what is French and what is un-French in Reusner's style.[134] The Gaultier piece is a sort of free rondeau, typical of French lute music before Lully's orchestral dance music became a predominant influence. It is entirely *sans chanterelle*, with mostly spare, *brisé* texture. Form, harmony, melody, all are suggested rather than plainly stated; the refrain returns at irregular intervals, and there is no clear division between one couplet and the next. As is common in sarabandes, chaconnes, and *passacailles* there are some strummed chords (a device known in French as *tirer et rabattre*), a reminiscence of the guitar origin of these dances. Reusner's Passagalia is more a logical set of variations over a ground bass, each variation having a different character, with more continuous lines. In fact it is closer to an Italian treatment of this bass than to Gaultier's, though Reusner also has some strummed chords and *brisé* moments. Reusner is in fact writing in a mixed style here, that has something French, something Italian, in a characteristically German blend. This macaronic musical style is reflected in the macaronic movement titles, whether Latinate (Praeludium, Paduana, Couranta), Italianate (Allemanda, Sarabanda), or French (Gavotte, Gigue), a mixture continued by Bach in his first two violin Partias. German court musicians constantly worked with French and Italians, as well as having their own fine tradition of learned counterpoint, and the mixture of technical languages corresponds to the blend of styles in Reusner's music. In the learned tradition, Reusner has a liking for the sort of *obligo* (a self-imposed technical constraint) used in keyboard works by Frescobaldi, a tradition also continued by Bach.[135] In the 1667 book there is a 'Couranta â 3. literis' that uses only fret letters a, f and h; and a 'Couranta sine quintâ, quartâ et tertiâ' that avoids the top three courses.[136] This sort of overtly learned effect is quite alien to contemporary French lute music.

Of numerous German lutenists in German-speaking parts of Europe, two may be considered as in some degree in the background to Bach. The first is a well-travelled aristocrat, Philipp Franz Lesage de Richée, who was a lutenist in Breslau in the 1690s where he taught the father of Johann Kropfgans (the Kropfgans who, together with Silvius Leopold Weiss, visited Bach in Leipzig in 1739). Most of what we know about Lesage is contained in the letter to the reader of his *Cabinet der Lauten* (Breslau 1695). In it he puts himself firmly in the French tradition as a pupil of Charles Mouton, one of the last generation of great French lutenists. His pieces are, he says, 'arranged according to the principles of the most famous masters Dufaut, Gaultier, and Mouton'.[137] Since Mouton's two lute books were published (at the end of his life) in the 1690s and he was preceded by two generations of Gaultiers, this makes Lesage the recipient of the accumulated experience of all three generations of the golden age of French lute music, a claim that says much for the prestige of French lute music in Germany at the time.

Lesage has much in common with Mouton in his handling of the lute, but combines this with the harmonic richness of Reusner in a very attractive mixed style. Preludes are semi-measured (unbarred but with rhythm signs), a type favoured also by Weiss, and together with the dances show a sensitivity to harmony and texture typical of French lute style. Lesage does not use the word suite (few do), but the title-page describes the key groups as *Partien*, the term Partia being the commonest equivalent for suite in this environment. It implies that the movements are intended to belong together, something not necessarily implied by the French word *Pièces*. Regularity of organization is also a feature with Lesage. The usual prelude, allemande, courante, sarabande and gigue are typically followed by gavotte, minuet, and bourrée. Various types may come at the end, in one case a Chiacone, in another a Pasagallia (to be played very slowly and 'mit discretion').

The main stylistic shift in French music between the generation of Denis Gaultier and that of Mouton was brought about by the arrival of Lully and by the influence that the vocal and instrumental styles of Lully's stage works had on French music generally, and by extension on French-influenced music elsewhere. The enthusiastic reception of Lully's music in the German area (including Austria and Bohemia) is reflected in arrangements for lute, for viol, and for keyboard of pieces from his stage works. The rhythmic and melodic clarity of Lully's dance music is reflected in the clearer and more dance-like melodic profile in many of Mouton's pieces, together with a simpler treble-and-bass texture and generally higher tessitura than was usual in the preceding generation. This newer manner co-exists with more traditional low, sometimes *sans chanterelle*, writing and sensitive *brisé* textures. Lesage tends to stay with the older, more complex style in the core dances and in the chaconne and *passacaille*, which are closer to the traditional lute chaconne and passacaille than to Lully's manner. The lighter dances, on the other hand, are more straightforward, and the G minor group has a Lullian *Ouverture*.

Much of what one might say about Lesage could equally be said of the most important lutenist in this area in the generation before Bach, Jan Antonín Losy von Losinthal (*c*.1650–1721). Of minor Bohemian nobility, Losy (also spelt Logy) was also well travelled, having spent time in Italy and probably also France. Losy's celebrity is evident from the number of tributes paid to him. Lesage describes him as 'the Prince of all artists' on the lute and prints a 'Courante extraordinaire' of Losy's in homage ('extraordinaire' because it is the only piece in the book not by Lesage; it is another piece that is almost entirely *brisé* throughout, as noted above in some of Reusner's gigues). Otherwise Losy's works, in common with those of most lutenists, circulated only in manuscript among connoisseurs. Johann Kuhnau, Bach's predecessor as Thomascantor, is equally complimentary in the dedication to Losy of his *Frische Clavier Früchte* (keyboard pieces entitled 'Suonata'; Leipzig 1696), as rich a mixture of things German, Italian and French as one will find around 1700. Ernst Gottlieb Baron, in his very informative treatise on the lute (Nuremberg 1727), presents Losy as being a pioneer of just this blend of styles. Losy, says Baron, had already (in the 1690s) combined the new Italian and French method of playing the lute so happily that he could be pleasing and cantabile (as the Italians) and at the same time artful (as the French) and firmly grounded (as the Germans).[138] Baron is another lutenist whom Bach may have known since Baron visited various courts, including Cöthen, in the years before 1720.[139] Baron's word for artful ('künstlich') is interesting here since it can mean learned in counterpoint (not a particularly French characteristic in this repertory), but was also used to describe Bach's manner of playing French harpsichord suites, 'very lightly and artfully' ('sehr flüchtig und künstlich'), presumably with all the subtleties of rhythm and ornamentation that one would expect.[140] Yet in spite of all the praise for mastery of many styles, what we have of Losy is nothing like as German or Italian as Kuhnau's *Suonaten* of 1696, and certainly not as Italianate as the earlier works of Weiss. They appear in manuscript collections alongside works of the classic French lutenists Ennemond and Denis Gaultier, Pinel, Dubut, Gallot and so on.[141] There is, of course, no knowing what Losy improvised, although Gottfried Heinrich Stölzel, who heard him play in Prague around 1716, mentions only full-voiced textures and *brisé* French style.[142] The most telling tribute to him is by the greatest of German lutenists, known and admired by Bach, Silvius

Leopold Weiss (1687–1750) in his highly expressive and learned *Tombeau sur la Mort de M. Comte de Logy*.

Weiss was yet another Breslau lutenist, and from a family of lutenists.[143] He was the supreme lutenist of his time, who set a new technical standard, to such an extent that, according to Baron, 'it makes no difference whether one hears an ingenious organist performing his fantasias and fugues on a harpsichord or hears Monsieur Weiss playing'. He was equally exceptional in all other respects: 'In arpeggios he has an extraordinary full-voiced texture, in expression of emotions he is incomparable, he has a stupendous technique and an unheard-of delicacy and *cantabile* charm. He is a great improviser, for he can play extemporaneously the most beautiful themes, or even violin concerti directly from their notation, and he plays thorough-bass extraordinarily well on either lute or theorbo'.[144] Weiss's earliest works are in the thoroughly mixed style of the first decade of the century. Crucial for his development was his stay in Rome from 1710–1714 in the suite of the Polish Prince Alexander Sobiesky, whose mother, Queen Maria Casimira, employed both Alessandro and Domenico Scarlatti there. He may conceivably have heard Corelli, though Corelli was at the very end of his life by the time Weiss arrived in Rome, had retired from public view in 1708 and died in January 1713. Weiss would nonetheless have been thoroughly familiar with the Roman violin tradition. He was at the Saxon court in Dresden in 1717, and took up a formal appointment there in 1718 at the high salary of 1000 rtl a year. There is no direct evidence for Bach meeting him other than when Wilhelm Friedemann Bach brought Weiss and Johann Kropfgans to Leipzig from Dresden in August 1739, when 'something extra fine in the way of music happened'.[145] But they may well have met during Bach's documented visits to Dresden in the 1720s and 30s, and during Weiss's visits to Leipzig where his pupils included Luise Gottsched. Much later J.F. Reichardt (who also played the lute) tells us that Weiss and Bach competed in improvising and in playing fugues (which ties in with what Baron says about the 'ingenious organist'), something one can readily believe given their prowess as improvisers and Bach's evident love of competitions.[146] It was from around 1739 that the 'lute' works BWV 997, 998 and 1006a originated, and that Bach made the arrangement of a Weiss lute Sonata in BWV 1025.

We are lucky in having two main manuscript sources of Weiss's works (one in London and one in Dresden) from which it is possible to get a good impression of his development both as composer and lutenist.[147] The London source, which is partly autograph, is particularly relevant here since it contains works from the earlier part of Weiss's career, up to the early 1720s, and so is important evidence of the development of the German mixed style at the time when Bach was putting together his first suite collections. It has Weiss's earliest surviving Sonata (No.7 in C minor, dated 1706) and the *Tombeau* for Losy, which presumably dates from the year of Losy's death in 1721.[148] In addition to dated sonatas, it is possible to date pieces by the fact that Weiss began to change from the 11-course to the 13-course lute around 1717 (with two extra bass courses going down to AA, apparently Weiss's own invention) and changed completely to the 13-course instrument after 1719.[149]

Weiss used the terms 'Suonata' or 'Parthia' for his key groups. In outward appearance these are suites, based on the usual prelude, allemande, courante, sarabande, and gigue, with a tendency to have a bourrée or other light dance before as well as after the sarabande. While this is the general pattern, Weiss is by no means systematic in detail. There are many other lighter types, as well as overtures, a chaconne and a passacaglia, and occasional character pieces: virtually every Sonata has a different configuration. Within this framework, the leading characteristic is the thoroughgoing influence of the Italian sonata style, in a way that is hardly evident with Lesage or Losy. Weiss was often compared to Bach in the eighteenth century, notably by Forkel (1782), who compared Weiss's 'genuine and gritty style' to that of Bach's clavier works.[150] By this Forkel presumably means the full, sonorous textures and strong harmony that Weiss certainly shares with Bach, and that had come to seem old-fashioned in comparison with the lighter galant style of the generation of Johann Kropfgans and Adam Falckenhagen.

There are certainly striking similarities in materials between works of Weiss and Bach. The Courante of Sonata 22 starts with an anacrusis and descending scale very similar to the Allemande of Bach's C major cello Suite; the Bourrée of Sonata 2 has little runs of four sixteenth notes, as has Bourrée I of Bach's E flat major cello Suite; the Ouverture of Sonata 4 has similarities with that of Bach's C minor cello Suite, and it ends with chords articulated by a repeated ♪♩ rhythm reminiscent of the Adagio of Bach's C major violin Sonata; very suggestive is an unpublished Caprice (Ex.1.3), which cannot be dated and is not certainly by Weiss but is intriguing in view of Bach's arrangement of the E major violin Preludio in BWV 1006a.[151] As well as similarity of materials, Weiss's style resembles Bach's in strong character projection and rich, sonorous harmony.

Yet when one pursues these surface similarities further one is brought up against some fundamental differences between Weiss and Bach. By far the most significant is that Weiss lacks Bach's fascination with profound 'research' into the possibilities of a single idea and his obsessive integration of materials. Weiss has an Italianate flow of ideas, and there is quite as much to remind one of Handel as of Bach. Weiss's version of the mixed style at times recalls keyboard works of Johann Caspar Ferdinand Fischer (an influence on Bach) rather than Bach himself. The key to Weiss's style is in Baron's praise for him

Ex.1.3 Silvius Leopold Weiss (?), Caprice for lute, bars 1–19

as a great improviser ('ein großer Extemporaneus'), which is what his fame depended on apart from his brilliant and novel technical innovations ('stupende Fertigkeit'). Weiss's preludes are a good case in point. Far from exhausting the possibilities of a single idea, as do many of Bach's, the more elaborate of them are more in line with what C.P.E. Bach describes as 'fantasiren', of continually surprising and delighting the listener with new ideas and turns of phrase. In this they form a link in a genre development from the semi-measured lute preludes of Mesangeau in the 1630s and the subsequent French lute tradition of the Gaultiers and Mouton, via such pieces as the keyboard *tombeaux* of Froberger, to C.P.E. Bach and ultimately to the classical Development sections of Haydn. The obvious example by J.S. Bach in this manner is the Chromatic Fantasia BWV 903/1. This has been compared to Weiss's chromatic Prelude in E flat major (pp.145–8 in Weiss-Smith 1990), which also leads to a fugue with a subject in moderate, even notes, though not chromatic like Bach's. Weiss's Prelude is certainly remarkable, with some surprising and indeed bizarre turns, but Bach's Fantasia is a rigorous exploration of the diminished 7th and its enharmonic possibilities. Although the diminished 7th is central also to Weiss's 'Fantasiren', his use is essentially dramatic and lacks that speculative edge. Another telling comparison is between the Prelude of the G major cello Suite and that of Weiss's Sonata No.5, also in G major. Both begin with a similar decoration of the first chord, but Weiss gradually expands this into a melodic line which he spins out, whereas Bach sticks doggedly to his opening pattern as his *inventio* throughout the piece. To say that he lacks Bach's obsessive concentration is in no way to denigrate Weiss. Few would dispute the greatness of Handel because he did not share Bach's obsession. The fact that Bach's attitude appealed so strongly to composers of the Classical period and after has distorted our view of Bach's contemporaries.

Allemandes generally are of a march type common in the French lute tradition, which Weiss interprets in an air-like way. They move in eighth notes, lacking the subtle *brisé* web of sixteenths that is the other main type of lute allemande. Weiss's allemandes are therefore of a different type from Bach's. Their stylistic distance from the French tradition is emphasized by the inclusion in a manuscript of Weiss's doubles (*c.*1720) of a French *style brisé, sans chanterelle* allemande 'L'amant malheureux' by Jacques Gallot (?–before 1699).[152] This piece also underlines the fact that the sort of French performance conventions that are appropriate for Lesage or Losy would be largely out of place with Weiss. Weiss's courantes are Italianate, generally with a moto perpetuo of eighth notes, a type much used by Bach. Weiss also has a type in sixteenths. Courantes by Bach of this type are in sonata style (G major and E major French Suites, D minor cello Suite), whereas Weiss tends to a more spacious type with violin-concerto figurations (Sonatas 2 and 5). In classic French lute music there are two types of sarabande: a grave, chordal type with emphasis on the sarabande metre; and a lighter, more air-like type generally in a higher tessitura. While Bach favours the grave type, Weiss favours the lighter one with a tendency to use common features of Italian arias in this metre. A particularly noticeable one is to leave the third beat of the second bar empty:

3 ♩♩♩ | ♩♩ 𝄾 | ♩♩♩ | ♩♩ 𝄾 |

a type of sarabande/aria also favoured by Handel. Gigues, with courantes, are as a whole most similar to Bach's. Gigues featuring campanella/bariolage are endemic at this time in repertory for lute, bass viol, and violin.[153] Once again, Bach has taken this manner and developed it far beyond what one would normally expect in the Prelude of the D major cello Suite.

Some formal aspects are part of the common currency of the time. The pattern in lighter dances of having an antecedent phrase in dance metre and a consequent in continuous eighths, and of increasing the eighth-note, sonata-style component as the piece proceeds, is common in Corelli and related repertories. Also common is the formula in the core suite dances of having a characteristic phrase (usually of self-contained type) at the opening, followed by an open-ended sequence that modulates to the dominant cadence at the double bar. This pattern lies behind many Bach movements. A classic example of it by Weiss is the Allemande of Sonata No.25, one of the few to move mainly in sixteenth notes (see Ex.2.9b). Each strain begins with the same two-bar head motif, followed by sequences that develop shapes from the motif. While Weiss is endlessly fertile in highly characterised and attractive ideas, and has a good practical control of form, one cannot help feeling sometimes that the sequences are too drawn out; they are certainly not as tightly controlled as Bach's. A courante of 184 bars, as in Sonata No. 51, would be unthinkable from Bach. Here again, it is Handel's suites that come to mind rather than Bach's and assuredly for the same reason: both Handel and Weiss used the dance genres as vehicles for improvisation, in which the traditional dance characters and formal schemes both suggested ideas and allowed extempore development. And, as with Handel, behind this lay the last of Weiss's skills in Baron's list, his expertise in continuo playing. The harmonic basis for the sequential extension and development of ideas was at his fingertips and needed only to be adjusted to the requirements of the moment. Bach was no less of an 'Extemporaneus', but his written music is more rigorously worked, concentrated and controlled, a trait summed up in the word 'arbeitsam' (worked-at) that C.P.E. Bach used of his father's style (see Chapter Two section 6).

It is clear from Bach's 'lute' works that he himself did not play the lute, even though he possessed a good lute at the time of his death, as well as two Lautenwerke (probably made by the organ-builder Zacharias Hildebrandt).[154] If the violin Solos contain difficulties, even sometimes impossibilities, there is also a natural, practical feel for the instrument not evident in the lute works. This practical feel is so important on the lute that lutenists rarely wrote other than in tablature, which notates the action of the hands on the instrument rather than the sound as such. Nonetheless, the works do show Bach imagining lute effects, even technical possibilities. The consensus among players now is that Bach made his staff-notation versions for lutenists to adapt to their instrument. This adds a dimension of creative recreation for the lutenist not available to keyboard players and others, who are expected to play what Bach wrote. There is no need to imagine, as some have done, that Bach had a special instrument in mind along the lines of the Vega 'Bach' violin bow.[155]

If the lute had largely gone out of fashion in France by 1700, in the German area it was cultivated until late in the eighteenth century, and there were lutenists in Bach's environment throughout his career.[156] Baron tells us of Johann Michael Kühnel, skilled lutenist and gambist and perhaps son of the gambist August Kühnel, who was at the Prussian court with the cellist Linike, and subsequently moved to the Weimar court, presumably when the Berlin *Capelle* was disbanded in 1713.[157] At Cöthen there was a mysterious 'lutenist from Düsseldorf' who visited the court in August 1719 and may have been a member of the Weiss family.[158] In Leipzig Bach was not only a friend of one of the most prestigious lute-makers in Germany, Johann Christian Hoffmann, but he also had a number of lute players in his circle. He used the lute in several earlier Leipzig works, the first version of the Saint John Passion (1724), the *Trauer Ode* BWV 198 (1727), and the early version of the Saint Matthew Passion (probably also 1727). He seems to have been particularly friendly with Johann Christian Weyrauch who made the intabulations of three movements from BWV 997 and also of the G minor Fuga BWV 1000.[159] The lutenist Adam Falckenhagen, a close contemporary of Weyrauch's who grew up in the same village near Leipzig, may have made the intabulation of BWV 995 (see the discussion in Chapter Five). Several of Bach's pupils played and composed for the lute, notably Johann Ludwig Krebs and Rudolf Straube, though there is no evidence of their having studied the instrument with Bach.

In spite of Bach's having more or less constant contact with lutenists throughout his career, there will always be the suspicion that what we know as the lute works were in fact conceived for a favourite keyboard instrument of his, the Lautenwerk or gut-strung lute-harpsichord. It is particularly striking that the earliest sources of most of these works are from times when Bach is known to have been involved with the Lautenwerk: BWV 996 from around 1715 when Duke Ernst August in Weimar acquired one from Bach's cousin Johann Nicolaus Bach in nearby Jena; BWV 997, 998, and 1006a from the later 1730s when Bach is known to have had contact with Silvius Leopold Weiss and Johann Kropfgans, and when he made the arrangement of a Weiss lute Sonata in BWV 1025. It was also around 1740 that Johann Friedrich Agricola saw a Lautenwerk in Bach's house, designed by Bach and built by Zacharias Hildebrandt. These were sophisticated instruments. J.N. Bach's had three manuals, each controlling a separate set of jacks which plucked at different points along the string, partly for dynamic variation, but also allowing the colour change of the lutenist's hand moving nearer or farther from the bridge. Hildebrandt's had only one manual, but had a complex system of stops, including a buff stop to give a 'fingered' effect since otherwise all notes would sound as open strings. The possibility of imitating the nuanced sound of lute or theorbo (often said to be the ideal instrument for accompaniment since it supports unassertively), yet without the technical difficulties, must have been very appealing and these works are certainly at home on such an instrument.[160]

5. Bach and the flute

Both the horn and the transverse flute were relatively new instruments in the form in which Bach used them. He was quicker to write for the horn, starting in 1713, than for the flute. There is no evidence of his writing for the transverse flute before 1717, nor did he have flute players at Mühlhausen or Weimar. The transverse flute, though initially a quintessentially French instrument, rapidly became a prime vehicle for the mixed style. The first tutor (by

J.-P. Freillon-Poncein) was published in Paris in 1700, and the first music for solo flute and *basse-continue* (by Michel de la Barre) in 1702. La Barre, a leading virtuoso in the French royal music, claims in his *Avertissement* that he has developed a completely new character for the flute, and that his aim is to do for the flute what his colleague Marin Marais had done for the bass viol. In other words, he aimed to equal on the flute the subtlety and sensitivity of expression for which Marais was noted. This being so, La Barre would almost certainly have used a full battery of ornaments analogous to those of the viol, including the *flattement* (finger vibrato) and *enflé* (swelling on a note), though his notation has nothing like the wealth of performance indications that Marais managed to include in his five Books of viol pieces. The music is relatively straightforward and is an excellent introduction to playing in a pure French style.

Until around 1720 the French style predominated in Parisian flute publications, although they were no means immune to the vogue for Corelli's violin sonatas in Paris at this time. Jacques Hotteterre, who spent 1698–1700 in Rome and was nicknamed 'le Romain', moved to a decidedly more varied and sophisticated range of expressions.[161] His *Pieces pour la flute traversiere ... Livre premier* (1708) on one hand emphasises French aspects of sensitive low tessitura and subtlety of articulation and ornaments (of which he provides an explanatory table), and on the other adopts to a certain extent Corelli's admixture of sonata elements. The pieces in G major include an Allemande 'L'Atalante', an Italian allegro in running sixteenth notes with imitations, similar to the piece of the same title in François Couperin's second Book of harpsichord pieces (1717), and a Sarabande with a bass of continuous eighth notes, a sonata feature used influentially by Corelli in his violin Sonata Op.5 No.8.[162] Italianate gigues, of the type popularised in Corelli's Op.5, are ubiquitous. The collection ends with a substantial piece ('Echos') for unaccompanied flute. Hotteterre's *Deuxiéme livre de Pieces pour la flûte-traversiere* (1715) adds some typically mixed genres of this time. The second Suite has a two-section Prelude loosely based on the French overture pattern, having a 2-time first section with the usual French dotted rhythms and tiratas, but a *vivement* second section in ¢-time in the style of an Italian canzona allegro, with invertible counterpoint. The third Suite has an Italian adagio-style Prelude with constant eighth-note movement in the bass and a melodic line that includes French ornaments and almost certainly also French rhythmic inequality in the sixteenth notes.[163] It also has a sonata-style Courante in ($\frac{3}{4}$-time with violinistic arpeggio outlines in almost constant eighth notes. All of these types are paralleled in François Couperin's chamber music of 1690–1715, and elsewhere, and their derivation from Italian models, mainly Corelli, will be discussed in Chapter Two section 2. After around 1720 what one might call the international mixed style of the late Baroque emerged, typically represented in the *Sonates* Op.2 (1732) of Michel Blavet, with French lighter dances and character pieces, and French ornamentation, mixed with Italianate floridly decorated Adagios, and sonata-style Allemandas and Allegros.[164]

The situation in central Germany to a certain extent ran parallel with this, though with a much stronger violin influence from the Venetian concerto composers. Telemann was using the transverse flute as a solo instrument in concertos from around 1712. Even in relatively undemanding chamber music such as his *Six Trio* (Frankfurt 1718) the writing for flute in Trio 3 is noticeably more violinistic than that for the recorder in Trio 2. The relative paucity of woodwind publications in the first two decades of the century meant that flute players adapted violin or oboe pieces.[165] Some collections, such as Johann Mattheson's *Der brauchbare Virtuoso* (Hamburg 1720), were for either violin or flute.[166] In this situation woodwind players had to develop a technique equal to the passagework of Italian violin concertos, just as Bach had to extend his keyboard technique for the same purpose. The outstanding virtuoso for this was, according to Quantz, Pierre-Gabriel Buffardin, who joined the Dresden court *Capelle* in 1715 at the large annual salary of 500 rtl. Quantz tells us that during his brief period of study with Buffardin they played only quick pieces since that was where Buffardin's strength lay, as is evident in his surviving works.[167] Buffardin was clearly exceptional, but equally clearly there were by 1720 very competent woodwind players at many German courts. Some of these were the virtuosos at Dresden, Berlin, and Darmstadt to whom Telemann dedicated his *Kleine Cammer-Music* (Frankfurt 1716). Telemann was always keen to write within the nature of a given instrument, and here he says he has avoided violinistic extremes of range, wide leaps, and covered (i.e. elaborately fork-fingered) and other inconvenient notes.[168] A similar reaction against virtuoso violin style is in the *Sechzig Arien* (Freiberg, n.d.) for violin, oboe, or traverso by the Dresden woodwind player Johann Martin Blochwitz. As with other instruments, Bach seems to have ranged over the whole spectrum of possibilities, from the relatively undemanding flute parts in cantatas written at Cöthen, to the flute Solo BWV 1013 which is virtually a catalogue of all the things that Telemann claims to have avoided.

The unique source of the flute Solo (not autograph) dates from after 1725 (see the discussion in Chapter Six). There is no need to imagine that it must have been written for Buffardin himself, and attempts to engineer a meeting between Bach and the great flautist in Dresden in 1717, 1718, or in Leipzig after 1723, are purely speculative. Bach evidently did meet Buffardin in Leipzig at some stage, but it is not known when.[169] He had very competent flute players at Cöthen in Johann Heinrich Freytag (d.1720) and Johann

Gottlieb Würdig (who disappears form the accounts in 1722). At 94 rtl and 84 rtl *per annum* respectively they were nothing like on the same plane as Buffardin, but still paid twice as much as an ordinary tutti player.[170] Bach's Cöthen flute parts do not necessarily give a fair picture of the capabilities of Freytag and Würdig since the Fifth Brandenburg Concerto puts the harpsichord firmly in the foreground, and in cantatas BWV 173a and 184a two flutes play as a pair. None of these pieces gives any real impression of what a full-blooded flute solo might have been. A Sonata that may be by this Freytag is in a manuscript of German woodwind sonatas of around this time (*B-Bc* 15.115), a source that gives a very favourable impression of woodwind repertory in Bach's environment at this stage.[171] It is also highlights what is characteristic of the surrounding tradition and what is individual in Bach's writing for solo flute.

Leipzig was at this time the main Saxon centre of woodwind-instrument making, and flutes of the most recent design were to be had there.[172] Right from the beginning Bach had at least two good flute players in Friedrich Gottlieb Wild and Christoph Gottlob Wecker. Wild entered Leipzig University as a student in April 1723, one month before Bach moved to Leipzig, and Wecker entered the University the following December. Bach depended heavily on university students for more experienced singers and instrumentalists. A university training, particularly in law, by no means precluded a career in music and was considered an advantage for a musician aiming at a senior appointment as cantor or capellmeister: C.P.E. Bach studied law at the University of Frankfurt an der Oder, and both Wild and Wecker were later professional musicians. Both were pupils of Bach, who later wrote in particularly warm terms about Wild, specifically mentioning his ability as a flute player. Bach also wrote favourably about Wecker's musical abilities, though without specifying the flute.[173] In 1724 Bach produced a spate of twelve cantatas involving the transverse flute, one most weeks from July to November. These are virtuoso solo parts, decidedly more advanced than the Cöthen flute parts, and it has been assumed that they were written for a virtuoso flautist who was visiting Leipzig at the time. While that is possible, it may alternatively have been that Bach, with some keen players to hand, went through a period of 'research' of the transverse flute in 1724, involving also BWV 1013 and perhaps the E minor Sonata BWV 1034 (whose earliest and principal source, a copy belonging to J.P. Kellner, dates from *c.*1726–7). Bach made further use of the transverse flute in 1725 (ten cantatas) and 1726 (six cantatas), making these years a rich source of flute repertory.[174]

Summary

Looking at Bach's instrumental solos as a whole, it is striking that, although the violin and lute had long virtuoso traditions in Germany, the cello and traverso were relative newcomers. Particularly in the case of the cello, Bach's Suites are a remarkable compendium, summing up the virtuoso attainments of the time, and exploring to the full the possibilities of the instrument in a way that matches and surpasses the bass viol. Nowadays, Bach's cello Suites are regarded as the foundation repertory of the instrument. Then, they were at the cutting edge of developments, forward-looking and innovative in technique, style, and scope.

CHAPTER TWO

Concepts of Style and Structure

1. *The German 'mixed style'*

It was natural that a mixed style should develop in Germany during the seventeenth century since the courts that were the centres of musical activity employed both French and Italian musicians. Their German colleagues would have to be familiar with French and Italian styles, as well as contributing their own German traditions. We have seen details of this in Chapter One, particularly with regard to the violin, the bass viol, and the lute and only a broad summary of the general situation is needed here. At a highly sophisticated level French music was represented primarily by lutenists, cultivating the dance genres of the solo instrumental suite, and at a more ordinary level by players of violin-family instruments, who formed the court dance bands. This violin repertory was technically undemanding, but required a good knowledge of the characters of many dance types and the conventions for playing them. Italian music was represented mainly by singers and violinists, in the brilliant solo concertato and sonata styles deriving from Giovanni Gabrieli, Monteverdi and their contemporaries. Germans themselves developed these traditions and brought them further, particularly the virtuoso violin tradition, adding their own predilection for full harmony and contrapuntal logic. The main development towards the end of the seventeenth century was the overwhelming influence of Lully for French dance music, and by extension of French composers of the following generation such as André Campra and Marin Marais.

The corresponding Italian influence towards the end of the century is normally considered to be Corelli, partly because both he and Lully were pioneers of orchestral discipline and partly because their works were printed and distributed all over Europe. While Corelli was certainly the predominant influence in France and England he was not on quite such a pedestal in Germany since many Italian musicians were employed at German courts, and southern Germany had close contacts with northern Italian centres, particularly Venice. Corelli was nonetheless an important figure on account of his publications. His works provide classic examples of some of the leading features of the mixed style and so are a useful point of reference. Telemann, whose solo and ensemble instrumental works were models of the German mixed style in the first two decades of the eighteenth century, tells us that in his youth (around 1700) he took the works of Corelli, among others, as his model for the Italian style, and Lully and Campra 'and other good masters' for the French style.[1] Quantz, who started out as a violinist, says that he correspondingly (around 1710) began with works in the German tradition (Biber, J.J. Walther, Albicastro), until he discovered the Solos of Corelli and Telemann.[2] But there were other Italian influences in Germany, notably Giuseppe Torelli who worked at the court at Ansbach in the 1690s where he taught Pisendel, and Agostino Steffani, who in the same decade provided an influential model of mixed styles in opera at Hanover.[3] More important than Corelli for the German mixed style were Venetian composers such as Albinoni and especially Vivaldi, whose works were sought avidly by German connoisseurs from around 1710.

There are many examples one might take of collections of ensemble music by German capellmeisters showing the mixture of styles from the 1690s on. Some have suggestive titles, such as the *Duplex genius sive Gallo-Italus instrumentorum concentus* of Johann Christoph Pez (Augsburg 1696; Bach at Weimar copied out part of a Mass setting by Pez, and probably knew the ensemble suite copied by his eldest brother Johann Christoph Bach into the so-called Möller manuscript).[4] Pez had worked in Rome from 1689–92 and was familiar with Corelli's music. The twelfth Sonata of the *Duplex genius* has a Fuga in E minor on a subject identical to that of the C sharp minor Fugue of Book I of Bach's *Well-tempered Clavier* (1722), a commonplace of the time also used in Corelli's Concerto Op.6 No 3. Later in the piece Pez combines this with a second subject in running sixteenth notes.[5] The following Dolce, on the other hand, is in French style, similar to the Rondeau by François Couperin that Bach may have arranged for organ as BWV 587.[6] In this instance the styles keep their integrity in separate movements.

A sophisticated blend of styles was cultivated by the Austrian Georg Muffat, the prime example of German mixed style around 1700, who was not only an exceptionally fine composer but also, uniquely, left substantial and invaluable performance instructions for both styles. Muffat worked with Lully in Paris in the 1660s and had contacts with Corelli in Rome in the 1680s. The prefaces to his *Florilegium primum* (Augsburg 1695) and particularly *Florilegium secundum* (Passau 1698) are by far the most detailed information we have about the performing style of Lully's orchestra. The preface to his *Auserlesene*

Instrumental-music (Passau 1701, an expanded version of *Armonico tributo*, a 'harmonic tribute' to Corelli published in Salzburg in 1682), gives information relevant to the performance of Corelli's concertos.[7] Here Muffat describes his own concertos as a mixture of serious and light, of lively ballet airs in the Lullian mould and the profound and rare expressions of the Italian manner, with various witty and artful inventions. He tells us that he learnt this mixture in Rome from Bernardo Pasquini on the keyboard, and from the concertos of Corelli. Muffat's most important point for us is that this mixed style is not suitable for the church because of the ballets and arias, nor for dancing because of the changes of mood. It is for the delight of the ear at gatherings of connoisseurs and virtuosos.[8] It is therefore not practical dance music, but a witty play of styles for the delight of the knowledgeable.

In the first decades of the eighteenth century the mixture of styles was the norm in German music, taking different forms in different places. In Bach's environment the main centre was Dresden, which at that stage had the most prestigious musical establishment in Germany. The Dresden orchestra was brought to a peak of perfection in the French style from 1709 by the Flemish violinist and dancing master Jean Baptiste Volumier (Woulmyer), who had trained at the French court and who introduced the Lullian discipline in Dresden. Bach was well acquainted with Dresden musicians: it is said to have been Volumier who arranged the competition between Bach and the French keyboard virtuoso Louis Marchand in Dresden in 1717.[9] The mixed style, though with a heavy Italian bias, was cultivated by the violin virtuoso Johann Georg Pisendel, whose style and career have been discussed in Chapter One section 2. Pisendel was a supreme connoisseur and collector of music and a fine composer. It was the well-paid Dresden musicians whom Bach cited in his letter to the Leipzig town council in 1730 as capable of playing all sorts of music, whether Italian, French, English or Polish, a capability he had difficulty matching with his ill-paid students in Leipzig, but one that was essential for the performance of his music.[10]

2. Dance and sonata styles

We have seen in Chapter One that the abstraction of practical dance music into the genres of solo virtuoso instrumental music can be traced back to the initial rise of virtuoso instrumental music in the first decades of the seventeenth century, in Italian violin sonatas of Dario Castello and French lute courantes of René Mesangeau, both dating from the 1620s. Towards the end of the century the distinction between dance and sonata styles is given classic expression in Corelli's chamber sonatas. The Corrente of Op.2 No.1 (Ex.2.1a) is a typical French dance, with clear dance phrases and a melody moving mainly by step in a narrow pitch range. The commonest note value is the quarter note, and the characteristic swaying rhythm is given by the accent of a dotted quarter (or half note in the bass) switching from the first to the second beat of the bar and back. There is a two-bar chord at the end of each strain, as in practical dance music. Dances of this sort are generic in Lully's stage works, and in cognate repertory such as Marin Marais's *Pièces en trio* (Paris 1692). In which case Corelli's dance seems bare, to say the least, without the usual French essential ornaments and *notes inégales*.[11]

The opposite pole, a piece with a dance title that is effectively a binary sonata movement, is the Corrente of Op.4 No.3 (Ex.2.1b). Here melody is dissolved into a moto perpetuo of eighth notes, making the piece a solo for the first violin. Phrases are of no set length, and are based on harmonic sequences patterned out with instrumental figurations consisting largely of broken chords. The traditional way of defining these two types as French courante and Italian corrente is really not adequate to explain the fundamental difference between them. The terms *da ballo* and *da camera*, used in Corelli's environment, more accurately reflect it.[12] The point of the second type is that it is not in the set phrases of a dance. Its charm is that it goes beyond them in an intoxicating expansiveness, building up climaxes beyond the reach of the dance, with an effect of liberation similar to the final extended phrase of a Handel aria. In Ex.2.1b, after a pattern of two 12-bar phrases in the first strain, the second strain begins with an irregular phrase of seven bars, followed by an enormous phrase that does not touch the ground for eighteen bars. Other correnti in Op.2 and Op.4 can be located stylistically at various points

Ex.2.1 a) Arcangelo Corelli, Corrente from *Sonate da camera a tre* Op.2 No.1, first strain

b) Corrente from Op.4 No.3

between these two poles. The infection of the dance by the sonata is largely the story of the instrumental suite between 1680 and 1720.

The question posed by Ex.2.1b is whether it is a dance that has been expanded into a binary sonata movement, or a binary sonata movement based on dance characteristics. It can be looked at in both ways. The second violin

b) Continued

and bass have the fundamental corrente note values of half note and quarter note, with the swaying rhythm, in which case the first violin has a sort of division descant. It demonstrates that one origin of this sonata style is in division (diminution, double) variation technique, in which note values are regularly divided into smaller values (see section 4 below). On the other hand, in the second strain even the lower parts are drawn into the long harmonic sequence that builds up the climax. An example of a dance expanded into a sonata movement is the second Allegro of Corelli's Concerto Op.6 No.4 (Ex.2.2b). This appears to be a rewriting in concertante style of the Gavotta of the trio Sonata Op.2 No.1 (Ex.2.2a; I use the term concertante simply because Ex.2.2b is in a concerto rather than a sonata; for present purposes the principles of concertante and sonata style are the same). The first four-bar phrase has the rhythmic characteristics of the dance, but the consequent is spun out into an extended phrase of eight bars in which the division values of triplet and eighth note predominate. This represents one very common way of combining dance and sonata styles, particularly in the lighter dances of minuet, gavotte, bourrée, rigaudon and so on: to have an antecedent in dance rhythm and a consequent in a division note value, in sonata/concertante style. Often the sonata/concertante element gradually takes over. Later in this Allegro the sequential element becomes more prominent, there are echo effects, plays of light and shade between soloists (*concertino*) and tutti (*concerto grosso*), in fact just the witty play of ideas ('scherzige Einfäll der Kunst') that Muffat describes as the essence of Corelli's concerto style.

Another common way of infusing a sonata/division element into a dance is to have a moto perpetuo of a division note value in one part. This is particularly characteristic of sarabandes in Corellian style, with running eighth-notes in the bass (Ex.2.3). Jacques Hotteterre (see Chapter One section 5) tells French performers of these pieces to play the eighth notes in the bass equally.[13] One assumes that they played the melody with the usual *notes inégales* (i.e. unequal eighths, with the lilting rhythm of dotted quarter followed by eighth note), as one certainly would in a sarabande with this feature by François Couperin.[14] In this instance the effect is at a slowish tempo (Largo), but Corelli uses it just as often at a quick one: two other Sarabandas with this feature (in the Concertos Op.6 No. 4 and No.12) are marked Vivace. Bach uses this effect in the Forlane of the C major Overture-suite BWV 1066, in itself an excellent example of the combination of dance and sonata/concertante styles (Ex.2.4b). The forlane (a gigue-like Venetian dance) was one of the dances popularised by André Campra in the ballet *L'Europe galante* (Paris 1696; Ex.2.4a). Campra's Forlana has short, clearly defined phrases, each with the characteristic ending of a repeated note (every 2 bars). Bach has added a concertante element in the moto perpetuo eighths in second violin and viola throughout, but the difference goes deeper than that. Bach has reserved the phrase-ending gesture until the end of the strain (elsewhere it is elided into a continuation of the phrase) with the result that the entire first strain is a single spun-out phrase that does not touch the ground before the double bar. Here the question whether this is a sonata version of a dance, or a surface of dance characteristics applied to a sonata structure, becomes more difficult to disen-

Ex.2.2 a) Corelli, Gavotta from Op.2 No.1, first strain

b) Allegro from *Concerti grossi* Op.6 No.4, bars 1–12

tangle. One performance detail in Bach's version is his slurring of the division eighth notes into pairs. He does this again in the division sixteenth notes in the Allemanda Double of the B minor violin Partia and it may imply a slight inequality, perhaps in the Forlane to align the off-beat eighth notes to the lilting dotted rhythm of the dance.[15]

Moving on to the more substantial dances of the solo instrumental suite, the allemande and courante, the balance swings decidedly in favour of the sonata. When one comes to a mind as subtle and inventive as François Couperin's the play of styles provides a rich field for the composer's imagination. In the chamber music of the 1690s Couperin tended to keep styles separate, but in the harpsichord works and the later chamber music he found many ways of combining them in a single composite style. As in most works in mixed style, the blend is different in virtually every piece. Closest to a classic model of French allemande, at least in its sophisticated solo instrumental form, is *Les Graces incomparables* from the Third Book of harpsichord pieces (Paris 1722; Ex.2.5a). Like most allemandes of this type it has a two-bar opening phrase with a caesura at the beginning of the second bar, similar to the twelve-syllable alexandrine line with a caesura after the sixth syllable. The remainder of the strain plays with this shape in various expressive ways such as internal sequence and *enjambement*.

In contrast to *Les Graces incomparables* is *La Laborieuse* from the First Book (Paris 1713; Ex.2.5b). Here Couperin seems to be demonstrating the advantages of infusing the French genre with Italian techniques. The 'laborious' aspect is the systematic motivic working—'travaillé' as the French called it, 'où le dessus et la basse travaillent toujours', as Couperin says of the little Italian-style demonstration Allemande in *L'Art de toucher le clavecin*, in other words the treble and bass are continually 'working' figurations rather than the bass just accompanying the treble. In the first strain Couperin has the usual two-bar opening phrase, but with the left hand in the second bar imitating the right hand in the first, invention-wise. After a French-style bar 3 the rest of the strain does not touch the ground harmonically until the double bar, systematically working motifs over sequences. The blend of styles is matched by the performance instruction 'Sans lenteur, et les doubles croches un tant-soit-peu pointées'. In other words this is quicker than a French allemande with the usual level of rhythmic inequality, and getting towards an Italian sonata allegro, with notionally equal sixteenths. The inequality should therefore be

Ex.2. 3   a) Corelli, Sarabanda from *Sonate a Violino solo* Op.5 No.8, first strain

b) Vivace from Op.6 No.4, first strain

less than French but more than Italian, perhaps more in the French phrases than in the Italian ones. There are many levels on the way and clearly the connoisseurship of the performer must match that of the composer. The most brilliant example of a *sans lenteur* allemande is *La Superbe* from the Third Book (Appendix 6). Here Couperin exploits the typical allemande two-bar phrase with a caesura in the middle by having in the first strain a series of two-bar phrases that are French in one half and Italian in the other. Then in the second strain he spins out long, sonata-style phrases from the Italian elements, showing how these can be used to build up grand climaxes beyond the reach of French dance phrases of set length.[16]

Bach comes closest to this Couperin-type mixed style in the Allemanda of the B minor violin Partia (see the commentary in Chapter Three). Characteristically, though, he treats the unequal rhythm as not just an incidental feature of performance style but notates it in full, thereby making it one of two fundamental rhythmic elements from which he constructs the piece, the other being triplets. The Allemanda has the usual two-bar opening phrase with a caesura, but the rest is in longer, sonata-style phrases. Here we are very close to a sonata movement woven from an economical selection of dance features.

The allemande and the courante were traditionally a pair of dances of similar structure, one in duple and one in triple time. In the manner of the variation-suite (the original meaning of the Italian term *partita*, i.e. divisions on a theme) there are often similarities at least in the openings of the two dances, an obvious example in Bach's case being the Allemanda and Corrente of the D minor violin Partia. In 1720, at the time when Bach made the fair copy of the violin Solos, he began a series of educational works for keyboard that were not just exercises and examples of composition techniques for the benefit of his eldest son Wilhelm Friedemann, but sum up his philosophy of

Ex.2.4 a) André Campra, La Forlana from *L'Europe galante*, refrain

b) J.S. Bach, Forlane from Overture-suite in C major BWV 1066, first strain

composition as it had evolved in his time at Weimar and his first years at Cöthen. Works include the two-part Inventions and three-part Sinfonias (autograph fair copy 1723), the first Book of *The Well-tempered Clavier* (1722), and the so-called French Suites (if Bach made a final fair copy it has not survived, but there is an initial autograph copy in Anna Magdalena Bach's first *Clavier-Büchlein*, of 1722). This was foundation repertory that Bach then used in his general teaching practice: for example, they are the works he gave to H.N. Gerber to copy when Gerber was studying with Bach around 1725. These collections work fairly systematically through different materials and possibilities for their treatment. Of primary interest in this context are the French Suites, which demonstrate different treatments of dance genres. This is particularly clear in the case of the courante, since the examples in these Suites cover a spectrum from fairly close to French dance style to a purely sonata/concertante style.

Ex.2.5 a) François Couperin, [Allemande] 'Les Graces incomparables' from the Sixteenth harpsichord *Ordre*, first strain

b) Allemande 'La Laborieuse' from the Second *Ordre*, first strain

As a model of the purest French style one might take the Courante of Couperin's *Troisième Concert* (1722; Ex.2.6a). The tempo is moderate and, if the usual performance conventions are observed, should suggest itself. The conventions are: unequal eighth notes (probably in something like a triplet rhythm), and quarter notes played separately (for details see the commentary on the Courante of the C minor cello Suite in Chapter Four). Like an allemande, Couperin's Courante begins with a two-bar phrase with a caesura after the first note of bar 2 (I have added punctuation in the example). Typically, Couperin then plays on this shape in subtle ways for the rest of the strain. In bar 3 the first phrase ends in the first half of the bar with a *coulé de tierce* in $\frac{6}{4}$-time, whereas the second phrase begins in the second half of the bar with an upbeat in $\frac{3}{2}$-time. The final phrase (beginning on the second $\frac{3}{2}$ beat of bar 8) has the effect of being an extension of the phrase before. Most importantly, the texture is of treble melody and bass accompaniment, there is no 'laborious' motivic working. In all Bach's works the closest he comes to this pure French style is the Courante of the C major Overture-suite BWV 1066 (another variation-suite, earliest surviving source 1724; Ex.2.6b). Bach's Courante differs from the French model in having a first phrase of three bars rather than two (perhaps because this is a variation on a pre-existing theme), and he has a little eighth-note link in bar 4 that neatly elides the first phrase into the second, but otherwise it is a straightforward melody-and-bass piece. As with the Corrente from Corelli's Op.2 No.1 it would seem reasonable to play this piece in the French style, with unequal eighths, separated quarters, and quite a lot of extra ornaments.

An important feature to note here in working out the phraseology of a piece is the use of the *coulé de tierce* (in the first half of bar 3 of the Couperin Courante Ex.2.6a, and at the beginning of bar 8). This is a conventional intermediate phrase-ending formula, equivalent to a comma or caesura in French poetry, normally used in French music to set feminine words ending in mute 'e' (e.g. 'belle': the second 'e' is pronounced, but very lightly), so the accent is on the first note and the rest is phrased off, with a slight pause afterwards. It outlines a falling 3rd and ends on a weak beat, whereas final phrases normally end on a downbeat (bar 10). In the subtle balance of asymmetrical phrases the varied weightings of phrase endings play an important part. The two *coulé de tierce* phrase endings here have different weights in that the one in bar 3 is obviously the ending of the first phrase, whereas in bar 8 there is an *enjambement* (i.e. in verse when the meaning of one line runs on into the next): the *coulé de tierce* in the first beat ends the phrase that began on the second beat of bar 6, but it is also the first element of a strong, three half-note rhythm in bar 8 that has the effect of a hemiola. On the other hand, the downbeat ending

Ex.2.6 a) Couperin, Courante from the Third *Concert Royal* for melody instrument and bass, first strain

b) Bach, Courante from the Overture-suite in C major BWV 1066, first strain, Violin I and Bass only

on the first beat of bar 6 is not final in that it ends on the 3rd of the chord, is an imperfect cadence, and the upbeat eighth notes that begin the next phrase follow hot on its heels. The alternation of off-beat phrase endings (bars 3 and 8) and on-beat phrase endings (bars 6 and 10) therefore has the effect of a verse setting with alternating feminine and masculine rhymes. This Courante is an excellent example of French classicism of the *grand siècle*, where the object was to say strong and subtle things using only commonly understood materials, without overt learning, 'labour', or extremes of pitch or dissonance.

In the music of François Couperin the grace-note *coulé* would normally be played during the time of the first note, though slurred to the second (in the rhythm ♩. 𝅘𝅥𝅮 ♩).[17] Bach, however, when he wrote this figure out in full notes, normally put the *coulé* in the time of the second note (Ex.2.7c), and that is the interpretation also in French tables of ornaments that Bach knew.[18] Ex.2.7a gives the *coulé de tierce* in its most usual form, with a trill on the upper note, and a small grace note (*coulé*) to the lower note; Ex.2.7b gives a minor-key version with the upper note approached from below, so the trill is, as it were, inverted to a *port de voix pincé* (i.e. an appoggiatura from below on the beat, plus a mordent, then the *coulé* before the second beat). Ex.2.7c is in the form often written out by Bach, and Ex.2.7d has a written-out appoggiatura to the upper note (Bach does not always write in the slurs). In continuous runs of notes of the same value it is important to be sensitive to the fact that this figure may imply an intermediate phrase ending. In Ex.2.6b, for example, Bach has it at the beginning of bar 4, but then runs it on (*enjambement*) into the beginning of the next phrase, which is why he has put a slur over all eight notes. These examples are in eighth notes, the commonest decorative note value. Some genres have different decorative values: in **c**-time allemandes it is sixteenths; in $\frac{3}{2}$-time sarabandes it is quarter notes. Ex.2.7e gives the *coulé de tierce* figure as it often appears in $\frac{3}{4}$-time sarabandes, with two common decorations in Exx.2.7f and g. Many references to different types of *coulé de tierce* will be found in the commentaries in the following chapters.

Taking the C major Courante of BWV 1066 as the dance-style end of the spectrum, we can then arrange the courantes of the French Suites in a sequence that gradually shades over to the sonata style:
1. Overture-suite in C major BWV 1066: $\frac{3}{2}$, as near as Bach ever got to a genuine French courante, which could be played in all respects as one would a courante from Couperin's *Concerts*.
2. French Suite in D minor BWV 812: $\frac{3}{2}$, the same time signature and general metre, but sonata concerns are evident in the moto perpetuo of eighths and the Invention handling of motifs (note the exposition structure of the first two bars, with the right hand in bar 1 imitated by the left hand in bar 2); more

Ex.2.7 a–g) Examples of *coulé de tierce* formations

than a slight inequality would impede the projection of larger eighth-note shapes.

3. French Suite in B minor BWV 814: $^6_4$, the time signature and general movement imply a fleeter tempo; much systematic motivic working, such as would normally be more common in a gigue; with these long runs of eighth notes we are approaching Corelli's correnti *da camera* and only a slight inequality of stress, as recommended by Quantz, with flexible shaping of groups, seems in order.

4. French Suite in C minor BWV 813: $^3_4$, a sonata allegro; note the complete rising scale from bars 9–14, such a systematic shape is quite un-French. In this piece Bach uses a favourite sonata structure for a minor key of a square four-bar opening phrase, then a sequential modulation that passes through the relative major (bars 5–16) to the dominant at the double bar (see section 7 below); basically even performance, though with shaping of the very varied sub-phrases.

5. French Suite in E flat major BWV 815: $^3_4$, as type 4 but with triplets and a dotted rhythm that aligns with the triplets. Types 4–7 progress systematically through the basic division note values of eighth notes, triplets, and sixteenth notes.

6. French Suite in G major BWV 816: $^3_4$, a sonata allegro with mixed eighth notes and sixteenth notes; even sixteenths.

7. French Suite in E major BWV 817: $^3_4$, another sonata allegro, this time with continuous concertante sixteenths; this Courante uses Bach's favoured sonata structure for a major key of a square opening phrase (bars 1–4), a sequential modulation to the dominant (bars 5–13), and a closing theme featuring a pedal (bars 13–16; see section 5 below); even sixteenths with phrase shaping.

In the instrumental Solos these types are represented as follows:

1. E minor 'Lautenwerk' Suite.
2. C minor cello/G minor lute suite.
3. not represented.
4. B minor violin Partia, C major cello Suite.
5. D minor violin Partia.
6. Cello Suites in G major, D major, E flat major (also has triplets); Flute Solo.
7. B minor violin Corrente Double, D minor cello Suite (though not so allegro).

3. *Fundamental and decorative note values*

There is plenty of evidence for Bach's knowledge of French performing style in general, and for his admiration for the works of François Couperin in particular.[19] Kirnberger, a pupil of Bach's, evidently worked on Couperin's harpsichord pieces with his own pupils, in imitation of Bach's teaching practice.[20] Couperin's works are the best introduction to the language of ornamentation, variety of time signatures and metres, and most importantly are invaluable for the study of the subtleties of mixed style since Couperin had devoted his life to a union of French and Italian styles (*réunion des goûts*) as represented by Lully and Corelli. Not only Kirnberger, but modern writers since the 1920s have recommended study of the works of Couperin as the best possible preparation for Bach's.[21]

Apart from ornamentation, the most noticeable aspect of French performance is the practice of rhythmic inequality (*notes inégales*).[22] In the ordinary form of a French dance there are normally three main note values, of which two are fundamental and played as written, and one is decorative and played unequally. In the decorative value it is usual to lengthen the notes on the beat and shorten the notes off the beat, though the opposite (Lombardic) rhythm with the short note on the beat is also a possibility. This division of function in note values was a fundamental aspect of music from at least the Renaissance period, related to the three note values (whole notes, half notes, and quarter notes) of the old species counterpoint, best known in its formulation by Johann Joseph Fux (1725). In the case of French dance music, the commonest note values are the half note and quarter note as fundamental, and the eighth note as decorative (a good example is Corelli's Corrente in Ex.2.1a). An exception is the allemande, where the fundamental values are quarter notes and eighth notes, and the decorative value is the sixteenth note. In a straightforward version of a French dance, triplet inequality would be normal, but of course the essence is flexibility and expressive rhythmic projection, so the degree of inequality can always be adjusted to the expressive moment. The more sophisticated the music, the more subtle and varied the inequality. The important thing is that the decorative note value should be flexible: if it is treated as fundamental (with equal weight on each note) the piece loses its rhythmic shape and character, and therefore its expressive nature. In a very sophisticated piece such as the Sarabande of Bach's D minor cello Suite it would be absurd to treat the eighth notes as if this was a straightforward French dance, yet it is essential that they preserve some flexibility and feeling of on-beats and off-beats. To treat the eighth notes, and even more the sixteenths, as fundamental is to lose the rhythmic shape.

In principle Italian music is played with equal notes, yet even there contemporary Italian tutors talk of on-beats and off-beats as 'good' notes (*note buone*) and 'bad' notes (*note cattive*). The type of bow and the articulation syllables of wind instruments ensure this difference. When we come to sophisticated mixed styles from around 1700, and particularly from the 1720s onwards, there are infinite possibilities of rhythmic moulding and articulation.[23] As the

French violinist Mondonville says (1748), the player must be sensitive at every moment to the style of each phrase.[24] The most useful accounts of variable inequality are in Quantz's *Versuch* (1752) and in his manuscript *Solfeggi*, which gives a large number of examples from contemporary repertory.[25] Quantz's formative years were in the 1710s and 20s in Dresden where he learnt from Zelenka, Buffardin, and particularly from the mixed style of Pisendel. He was personally acquainted with Bach, and is in fact the only person to have left an eye-witness account of Bach's harpsichord technique.

4. Division technique

Closely connected to the relative weight of note values is the technique of division variations. If the art of division as presented in Renaissance tutors is rhythmically complex, and in Christopher Simpson's *Division Violist* (London 1659) embraces melody and counterpoint as well as dividing metrical units into ever smaller note values, the ordinary technique of division (diminution, double) was a standard way of learning freedom in improvisation. At its simplest the technique is to take a melody and vary it successively in constant eighth notes, constant triplets, and constant sixteenths. Alternatively one could take a ground bass pattern and improvise over it first a slow melody, then decorate it successively in the same manner. This technique, which is fundamentally an improvised one, is the best way to learn how to improvise florid decorations, and is the basis for many sets of variations into the Classical period and beyond. Instructive tutors from Ganassi (1535) to Quantz (1752) generally organize their material around intervals: how to decorate a unison, a rising 2nd, a rising 3rd, a rising 4th and so on.[26] The art is to string these shapes into elegantly balanced patterns (Ex.2.8).

The Corrente in Ex.2.1b shows, if it needed to be shown, that the origin of the Corellian sonata style lies in the technique of division ornamentation. One could not wish for better evidence of this than Bach's B minor violin Partia, in which each movement has a division variation (Double): the Tempo di Borea in eighth notes, the Sarabande in triplets, the Allemanda and Corrente in sixteenths. The list of courante types given above (section 3) for Bach's French Suites shows how fundamental is the concept of division note values to variety of dance treatments. Related to this is the concept of the variation-suite, in which a melody, a ground bass, or a chord progression is varied successively in the style of an allemande, a courante, a sarabande and so on. Some of the earliest examples of this principle are in keyboard *partite* of Frescobaldi (Rome 1615 etc.), and the type became common in seventeenth-century Germany. A relic of it is in the thematic connections between movements in many seventeenth-century German suite groupings, and in some Bach suites

Ex.2.8 a and d) Johann Christoph Pepusch, minuet with sixteenth-note division;
b and c) eighth-note and triplet divisions (author)

such as the D minor violin Partia, where the same initial chord progression is worked in different dance genres in each successive movement from the Allemanda through to the Ciaccona.

There is a difference here between an ordinary division on a dance (*da ballo*) and a true sonata movement (*da camera*). The division is based on dance phrases; the sonata is not.

5. Ritornello structures

Apart from taking a pre-existing theme, a common way of improvising in dance genres was to use a standard structure. A common structure in seventeenth-century Italy for the *soggetto* of an instrumental movement or aria was to have three elements: 1) a characteristic head motif, then 2) a sequence and 3) a cadence.[27] Bach used this shape in longer fugue subjects, as in Ex.2.9a, though in his mature fugues he tended, as here, to avoid having a definite cadence at the end of the subject since it impedes the construction of longer continuous sections. As a formula for improvising a dance movement

Ex.2.9 a) Bach, simple ritornello shape in the subject of BWV 543/2

b) Silvius Leopold Weiss, Allemande from Sonata 25 in G minor, first strain

this structure has the advantage that one can improvise a phrase or two in the character of the dance, and then have one or more of the harmonic sequences that were standard in continuo playing and so were in the fingers of virtually all musicians, decorating them with motifs from the character opening. In a binary movement the sequential passage would normally modulate to the dominant, and have a cadence in that key at the double bar. The second strain could then start with the same opening character motif in the dominant and use further sequences to return to the tonic, again with a cadence at the final double bar. Improvements and variants could be introduced in the repeats. An example of this formula in an allemande by the lutenist Silvius Leopold Weiss is in Ex.2.9b. Weiss was noted for his skill in improvisation, as was Handel, and their suite movements preserve a feeling of *ex tempore* freedom. After gaining fluency in division technique, practising this sort of improvisation is highly recommended for instrumentalists wishing to develop their feeling for the Baroque suite.[28]

The great advantage of this structure is its flexibility. It can be used simply in a fugue subject or in the instrumental ritornello at the beginning of an aria, or it can be the basis of something much more elaborate. The ritornellos of Vivaldi's concerto movements vary enormously in their degree of elaboration. Among the concertos that Bach arranged for keyboard, the first-movement ritornello of Vivaldi's Op.3 No.8 is the most elaborate (arranged for organ as BWV 593; Ex.2.10). It is an expansion of the *soggetto* just described, and forms a section structure that Bach was to use many times. The elements are: 1) character opening; 2) sequential continuation; 3) a closing motif, often with a pedal or chromatic tinge; and 4) a cadence. The rich variety of material provided in Ex.2.10 clearly appealed to Bach on account of its possibilities for development, and this is in fact one of Vivaldi's more systematic movements. This was Bach's favoured structure for large-scale fugal movements. The Fuga of the G minor violin Sonata, for example, opens with a section (bars 1–14) that corresponds to Vivaldi's ritornello. The character opening corresponds to the exposition with its four subject entries (bars 1–5); the sequential continuation corresponds to the passage in concertante style in sixteenth notes (bars 6–10); which builds up to a climactic re-entry of the subject with added chromatic tinge, corresponding to the closing motif with its cadence (bars 11–14). The opening sections of the two other violin Fuga movements are essentially expansions of this shape (see the commentaries in Chapter Three).

Since these examples are concerto-style opening ritornellos they stay in the tonic. By making the sequential continuation modulate to the dominant the structure can be used for the first strain of a sonata movement. In dance movements, or movements in dance metre, Bach tends to use a pair of balancing antecedent and consequent phrases for the character opening. This provides the additional neat contrast of a closed shape for element 1, and an open-ended shape for element 2. This structure is endemic in the instrumental solos and Bach was infinitely resourceful in varying it. Part of the connoisseurship and pleasure of these works is in seeing what ingenious and novel use he makes of it in each instance (see for example the commentary on the Courante of the G major cello Suite in Chapter Four). It is essentially a sonata/concertante (*da camera*) structure; a true dance structure (*da ballo*) has relatively short, balancing phrases, without open-ended phrases of indefinite length.

The attraction of this ritornello shape is its flexibility; it can be worked in dance, sonata, or fugal styles. Joel Lester has shown how Bach then constructs pieces in a series of sections, each parallel to the first, with a successively heightened level of development.[29]

Ex.2.10 Antonio Vivaldi, *L'Estro Armonico*, opening Allegro ritornello of Op.3 No.8, arranged by Bach for organ as BWV 593

6. The invention principle

The term 'invention' can refer to something quite straightforward, or have a more subtle implication.[30] Bach used it for a type of piece in the two-part Inventions, but explains in his title-page that the term '*inventiones*' applies to initial ideas, and that there is also the aspect of working them out ('sondern auch selbige wohl durchzuführen').[31] For roughly half of them the meaning is straightforward in that the piece develops from a brief motif treated imitatively at the beginning; the rest have various other sorts of basic material. We have seen the principle in operation in Couperin's Allemande 'La Laborieuse' (see section 2 above). The equivalent word for 'laborieux' in German ('arbeitsam') was used by C.P.E. Bach to describe his father's style, and the invention principle, which builds a piece by 'working' an idea rather than just spinning out a melody, was fundamental to Bach's musical thought at this time.[32] Johann Adolph Scheibe (*c*.1730), who was later to criticise Bach publicly for this, also criticised German composers generally for having too much artifice and working ('gar offt zu viel Kunst und Arbeit') in their compositions.[33] The principle is related to the idea of fugue in that all develops from an initial idea or group of ideas (*inventiones*). But the material does not necessarily have to be imitative, or even contrapuntal, though in the particular case of the two-part Inventions themselves invertible counterpoint is part of the demonstration. Virtually any musical element can constitute an *inventio*, and this possibility is an important component in the technique of treating dance genres in a sonata manner.

Take the case of the French overture. There is a great difference between the tune-and-bass dance overtures of Lully in the 1670s and 80s and the late-Baroque overtures of Telemann, Bach and Handel in the 1710s and 20s. Lully's overtures are virtually without any real counterpoint. He is said to have composed only the melody and bass and left the three inner parts of his five-part string band (the so-called *parties de remplissage*) to be filled in by assistants. The overture is in two sections in which the contrast is not so much slow—quick as duple time—(usually) triple time. The duple time sometimes returns at the end. The overture is therefore similar to a duple-triple dance pair such as the allemande and courante. The character of the first section is given by dotted rhythms and *traits* (or tiratas, short rapid scale segments). The second section opens with lively imitations of a short theme, the entries always starting with the top part and coming in in successively lower parts down to the bass (in the sequence violin, viola 1, viola 2, viola 3, bass). After the bass has entered imitation stops and the texture reverts to being tune-and-bass with harmonic-filler inner parts. This was Lully's formula, but other composers treated it in their own manner. Purcell, for example, in the 1680s and 90s often took the hint of imitations in the second section to write an elaborate Italianate canzona-style fugue, full of contrapuntal artifice. Bach and Handel often wrote an extended concerto-style fugue for the second section (all Bach's Overture-suites BWV 1066–1069 provide examples).

The first section was not normally susceptible to fugal treatment as such, but Scheibe's 'Kunst und Arbeit' can still be brought in here. A selection of pieces by contemporary composers who Bach thought suitable for his eldest son Wilhelm Friedemann to learn from is included in the *Clavier-Büchlein* that Bach started to put together for him in 1720, the year in which Friedemann reached his tenth birthday. One is a Partia by Gottfried Heinrich Stölzel, copied out by Friedemann in 1722–3 (Ex.2.11; Stölzel was capellmeister at Gotha, and is best known for his setting of 'Bist du bei mir' in Anna Magdalena Bach's 1725 *Clavier-Büchlein*). Stölzel's *Ouverture* could not be more remote from Lully's tune-and-bass dance overtures. He makes an *inventio* of the dotted rhythm and tirata, gives it a miniature exposition in the first two bars, then treats it systematically to contrapuntal techniques of inversion and extension exactly in the manner of a Bach Invention. Stölzel's skill in treating French decorative ingredients in this way is presumably why Bach gave the piece to Friedemann to study.[34] A comparable use of ingredients in Bach's Solos is the Allemande of the C minor cello Suite (see the commentary

Ex.2.11   Gottfried Heinrich Stölzel, *Ouverteur* [sic] from Partia in G minor, first strain

in Chapter Four). Here Bach has taken the dotted rhythm and the tirata, included his own favoured figure of extended runs in even sixteenths, and applied these to a sonata structure. In the D major fugue of *The Well-tempered Clavier* of 1722 he did the same in the genre of fugue. People have criticised Stravinsky for taking in his Violin Concerto the gestures of the slow movement of a Bach concerto and applying them in circumstances foreign to the harmonic world from which they originally grew. One could equally criticise Bach and his contemporaries for taking decorative features from a melodic, dance style and treating them as contrapuntal elements in their own right in a different context, without the melodic lines that were their original justification.

The workings of the invention principle are many and varied. Perhaps the most subtle in all these pieces is the Allemanda of the B minor violin Partia (see the commentary in Chapter Three). In this piece Bach has taken two rhythmic characters, the dotted effect of *notes inégales* in a French allemande and the triplets of the newer galant style, and concentrated on them exclusively throughout the piece. Further, he uses the 6/5 chord on a leading note, which first appears in the middle of bar 1, as a fundamental building block. This collection of elements is far less obvious as an *inventio* than the motif at the beginning of the C major two-part Invention, yet the principle is the same: to develop them ('selbige wohl durchzuführen'). Other composers were working along the same lines, but the degree of Bach's concentration and integration of materials is exceptional, a degree of technical control that is matched by the exceptional force and concentration of expression in these works.

7. Harmonic materials and structures

When Bach described his two-part Inventions as demonstrations of good initial ideas (*inventiones*) and how to develop them (*distributio*, in the terminology of traditional rhetoric) he was not just thinking of the opening motifs and the usual contrapuntal techniques of melodic and contrapuntal inversion, sequential extension and so on, but of the whole structure of the piece. For this the aria-ritornello structure outlined above is the fundamental shape. The character head corresponds to the invention, and the sequential tail to the development. Normally Bach runs this shape three or more times during the course of the piece, with cadences in the important key centres. The purpose of working such pieces out on paper was partly to demonstrate contrapuntal techniques with a density not normally possible in improvisation, but it was also to improve and refine improvisation itself. In audition tests for prestigious organ posts, for which Bach prepared his pupils, the test items consisted entirely of various sorts of improvisations; playing printed repertory did not come into it.[35] When Dr Burney toured Germany and the Low Countries in 1772 he judged organists entirely by their skill and ingenuity in improvisation; he considered players of written pieces to be amateur.[36] At the same time the structures of written music (*gesetzt*) seem to have been little different from those of music that was improvised (*praeludirt, fantasirt*).

In the Inventions, Bach is demonstrating not only a motivic surface, but also the use of standard harmonic materials. As usual in his educational/speculative works, such as *The Well-tempered Clavier* and the French Suites, he works through the available materials in a fairly systematic way. These consist of opening gambits (for the *inventio*) and harmonic sequences (for the *distributio*). These are standard elements and as such were fundamental to both improvisation and composition in Bach's time. An understanding of them is vital for understanding the instrumental solos. The harmonic strength of the single-line writing depends on them, and observing Bach's manipulation of them yields a substantial part of our pleasure in the music.

The *Clavier-Büchlein* for Wilhelm Friedemann Bach contains two sets of pieces that between them demonstrate the main harmonic opening gambits: the two-part Inventions (which he calls *Praeambulum* in the *Clavier-Büchlein*) and eleven of the first twelve Preludes of *The Well-tempered Clavier* of 1722 (which he calls *Praeludium*). The opening gambits are as follows, with the relevant piece in brackets:

1) A prolonged tonic chord: I ⎯⎯ (F major Invention)
2) An alternation of tonic and dominant: I V I (G major Invention); this may be repeated several times: I V I V I (A minor Invention)
3) A tonic pedal with changing harmonies: I— 5/3 6/4 7/4/2 5/3 (B flat major Invention)
4) A similar effect: $I^{5/3}$ $II^{6/4/2}$ $V^{6/5}$ $I^{5/3}$ (C major Prelude)
5) A version of this with root-position 7th chords: I I^6 II^7 V^7 I (D major Prelude)
6) A progression involving the subdominant: I IV V I (F minor Invention).
7) Not in these pieces, but an important building-block for Bach since it is one of the three themes in the cryptic canon he holds in his right hand in the famous Haussmann portrait (BWV 1076), and is the first eight notes of the bass of the theme of the Goldberg Variations. It goes round the following notes of the scale: 8 7 6 5 3 4 5 1. This is one of the commonest Baroque progressions, related to the Italian ciacona bass, with versions from Monteverdi's 'Chiome d'oro'/'Beatus vir' to Bach's 'Sheep may safely graze', Handel's 'The Arrival of the Queen of Sheba', and Arne's 'Rule Britannia'. If Bach chose it as the ultimate representative of a harmonic phrase he could not have chosen better.

Examples of these progressions from the instrumental Solos are:
1) Preludio of E major violin Partia (Ex.3.25).
2) Presto of G minor violin Sonata; a very common version that balances two inversions of the dominant 7th (I $V^{6/5}$ $V^{4/3}$ I); the opening of the Prelude of the D minor cello Suite balances two inversions of the leading-note 7th (Ex.4.4).
3) Prelude of G major cello Suite (Ex.4.1); a slightly more elaborate version: I— 5/3 7♭ 6/4 7♮/4/2 5/3 is in the Prelude of the E flat major cello Suite (Ex.4.14); the minor-key version of this is very commonly used as a final pedal: I— 5/3♮ 7♮/3♯ 6♭/4 7♯/6♭/4/2 5/3♯ (for example at the end of the first strain of the Allemanda of the D minor violin Partia, Ex.3.13).
4) This is the gambit behind the opening of the Adagio of the C major violin Sonata (Ex.3.18), but consider the sense of spaciousness and complexity that results when the bass goes on down to b♭ in bar 4 rather than back up to c', an effect comparable to that at the opening of Handel's anthem 'Zadok the priest' (1727).
5) Allemande of the G major cello Suite (Ex.4.2a).
6) Courante of G major cello Suite (Ex.4.3).
7) Largo of C major violin Sonata (*cf* Ex.3.23).

These gambits are used for the closed shape at the beginning of a piece. The sequential continuations are based on the standard progressions in Ex.2.12. Ex.2.12a–c are scale sequences: 2.12a harmonises a descending scale starting on c" or e"; 2.12c is a standard decoration of 2.12b.

Ex.2.12 Standard Baroque progressions:
a–c) scale sequences

Ex.2.12d–f are three versions of the circle of falling 5ths progression, using different inversions of the 7th chords.

d–f) circle of 5ths

Ex.2.12g–j are other standard progressions: 2.12g is a pattern of falling 3rds, as in the A major Invention (it may also be stepped out with passing notes, as at the opening of the first chorus of 'Wachet auf' BWV 140); 2.12h is a rising pattern, alternating a rising 4th and a falling 3rd; 2.12i is a version of this that gains a chromatic scale by using first inversions and secondary dominants; 2.12j is a pattern of rising 5ths.

g–j) other common progressions

These materials are rarely used in their crude primary form, but selected, varied and moulded together to form a naturally flowing movement. Within the aria-ritornello structure there are various ways in which they can be handled to make a complete piece. In a prelude, or other type of piece not in a set form, the ritornello shape may be run several times in the course of the piece, modulating to, and cadencing in, important related keys. The most straightforward way of dealing with it in a binary dance/sonata movement is to re-run the events of the first strain, which ended in the dominant, back from the dominant to the tonic in the second strain, with extensions and developments of individual elements. For this there are two standard tonal schemes used by Bach, one for major-mode and one for minor-mode pieces. The scheme for the major mode is:
Tonic—Dominant :|: Dominant—relative—Subdominant—Tonic :|
The peak of harmonic density and dissonance tends to be at the relative-minor phase. The scheme for the minor mode is:
tonic—Relative—dominant :|: dominant—subdominant—tonic :|
Minor-mode pieces therefore tend to have more complex first strains since they visit an extra key centre before the double bar. The commentaries on individual pieces in the following chapters provide numerous examples of the subtlety and variety, as well as skill and ingenuity ('Kunst und Arbeit'), in Bach's treatment of these straightforward, common materials.

8. *Aspects of fugue*

Friedrich Wilhelm Marpurg, who knew Bach and discussed fugue with him, and was the first to publish a treatise on fugue based on Bach's works (1753–4), divides fugues broadly into two types: strict fugue (*fuga obligata*) in which the subject is ever-present in that all is derived from it and its countersubject; and free fugue (*fuga libera*) which has subsidiary material of similar character to the subject, but not directly derived from it. Marpurg gives Bach as the great practitioner of strict fugue, and Handel of free fugue.[37] All the fugues in these works, even the free-seeming 'lute' Fuga in BWV 998, are highly concentrated examples of strict fugue, worked by Bach on the Invention principle. Marpurg is not quite accurate, though, since to derive all from the subject and countersubject alone is too narrow a definition: it could be from an initial block of material, all of which constitutes the *soggetto* (see, for example, the commentary on the C minor 'lute' Fuga BWV 997/2 in Chapter Five). Marpurg's distinction between strict and free is nonetheless a useful one.

Fugue is not a form in itself, but a technique and, in a way, a formula since, however the details may vary, a fugue must have an exposition.[38] Otherwise it can embrace all the topics discussed above: dance, sonata, concerto, and division technique. Most important is the Invention aspect since fugue, at least as it developed in the seventeenth century, provides the model of a piece developing from a *soggetto* in the manner of a speech or debate. Within this, an important further aspect is the form taken by the answer to the subject, since that is the first variation on the subject and often suggests further development.

In Bach's time, the one defining characteristic of fugue proper, as opposed to mere imitation, was that the answer to the subject in the exposition should enter at a perfect interval (i.e. a unison, 4th, 5th, or octave). In the seventeenth century this had been related to the modal system where, if the subject was in the authentic version of the mode, the answer would normally be in the plagal version.[39] In tonal terms, to put it at its simplest, the subject is in the tonic key, and the answer in the dominant. But there are problems. One arises if you want to bring in the answer immediately after the subject has finished. The answer will then have to start in the tonic key before it moves to the dominant. But if the subject has the fifth degree of the tonic scale in its first few notes, the fifth degree of the dominant scale, being the second degree of the tonic scale, will not harmonise with the tonic triad. The usual way of dealing with this is to replace the fifth degree of the dominant scale (= the second degree of the tonic scale) with the fourth degree of the dominant scale (= the tonic note itself). The details of working this out give wide scope for pedantry and dogma, but for Bach this warp in the universe was a spur to invention, and the surprising and felicitous ideas it often prompts are part of the intellectual delight in his music. Understanding the principle is essential for joining in his connoisseurship. The form of the answer is not just a local problem for the early bars of the piece. One can see in Bach's handling of it that long-term strategies are present in his formulating the solution.

In these Solos there are three fugues for violin, one for cello, and three for lute, plus two for lute that are arrangements. In all of these, even in the relatively early BWV 996, an understanding of what Bach has done with the answer is essential for understanding what he has done in the fugue as a whole. Most straightforward is the C minor cello Prelude, which just changes the 5th of the tonic C minor to the 4th of the dominant G minor (Ex.2.13a; the examples omit decoration). A similar case is in the C major violin Fuga. Ex.2.13b gives the answer in its expected form, but in the Fuga itself Bach sharpened the third c" because he wished to have the chromatic tetrachord as the countersubject, leading to further agendas at all levels of compositional thought. An analogous case is in the A minor violin Fuga, where the initial

Ex.2.13 Bach, subjects and answers:
a) from the Prelude of BWV 1011;

b) from the Fuga of BWV 1005;

c) from the Fuga of BWV 1003;

d) from the *Prelude pour la luth* BWV 998

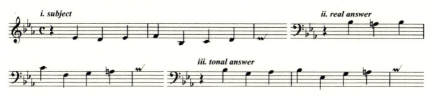

e) from the Fuga of BWV 1001

adjustment is made in the usual way (Ex.2.13.c), but continuation of the answer has been adjusted so as to lead into the chromatic tetrachord, a strategy that equally has large-scale implications for this fugue. Interesting here is the d♯" at the beginning of the subject: why did Bach make the auxiliary chromatic? (Mattheson gives this subject without the sharp, see the commentary on BWV 1003 in Chapter Three.) It is probably because the answer, since it begins on the tonic note of A minor, would sound odd without the sharpened leading note (g♯'). Bach therefore retrospectively sharpened the d" to match.

A very beautiful example is in the E flat major lute Fuga (Ex.2.13 d[i]). Since the subject does not have the fifth degree of the tonic scale until its fifth note, the answer could perfectly well be a simple transposition, known as a 'real answer' (Ex.2.13d[ii]). The drawback of is that it makes for a crude and banal switch to the dominant immediately after the end of the subject, which firmly cadences on the tonic. Bach has therefore adjusted the beginning of the subject to stay in the tonic, giving what is known as a 'tonal answer' (Ex.2.13d^{iii}). The answer therefore moves to the dominant only for its last three notes, and the intervallic relations of the first six notes are changed. The use Bach makes of this deformation of the subject is one of the most delightful *jeux d'esprit* in all these fugues (see the commentary on BWV 998 in Chapter Five).

In formulating a tonal answer, what covered the interval of a 5th in the tonic now has to be compressed into a 4th in the dominant. This creates problems in a subject that outlines notes 5 4 3 of the tonic scale. In the dominant scale it would have to be adjusted to notes 4 4 3. A tonal answer for the subject of the G minor Fuga would therefore be as in Ex.2.13e. This is not only banal, it also denatures the subject by removing its sense of direction. Bach has therefore used a real answer instead. The fact that this makes the answer end in C minor, rather than the usual D minor, has implications not only for this fugue, but links with the emphasis on C minor in the preceding Grave, which functions as a prelude to this fugue.[40]

CHAPTER THREE

The *Sei Solo* for Violin BWV 1001–1006

Sonata Prima BWV 1001

1. *Adagio*

This has been compared to a number of pieces by Bach and others, and such comparisons are undoubtedly useful in focusing its stylistic identity. The texture of chords separated by flourishes seems to have particularly interested Bach in the years before 1720. An early example is the opening Sinfonia of the cantata 'Weinen, Klagen, Sorgen, Zagen' BWV 12 (1714) which, in F minor, shares the mood of high tragedy with this Adagio, though it has to be said that Bach later worked similar motifs with totally different effect in the first movement of the E major Sonata for obbligato harpsichord and violin BWV 1016. Other pieces are difficult to date, but include the organ arrangement of Vivaldi's 'Grosso Mogul' Concerto (RV 208, BWV 594) from his Op.7 concertos (published in Amsterdam in 1716–17 but Bach used a different, manuscript version so the print is no indication of dating); the G minor Fantasia for organ BWV 542/1; the Chromatic Fantasia for clavier BWV 903/1; and the second movement of the First Brandenburg Concerto (autograph fair copy dated 1721, though part may date back to 1712/13).[1]

Both the second movement of BWV 594 and the recitative section of the Chromatic Fantasia are marked 'Recitativ', and in the case of BWV 594 also Adagio, a useful reminder that Adagio can mean a free, rhetorical style, not necessarily dead slow. There is a crucial difference, though, between these two movements and this Adagio in that this has regular chords every half bar throughout the piece, so proceeds with a steady tread. The essence is the combination of a rapidly moving surface over a grave and measured framework. Freedom in the ornamentation is essential, but clearly must be on the basis of the written note values. Closer to this is the G minor organ Fantasia (Ex. 3.1), whose opening bars share the regularity of the violin Adagio, though it later goes into quite different textures and, in common with the Chromatic

Fantasia, has a freedom of chromatic harmony that must have seemed experimental, or very 'learned', at the time. This is not shared by the violin Adagio except at one dramatic moment. In fact the G minor Fantasia is a very good foil to the violin Adagio in showing the difference between a large-scale, public style as opposed to more intimate chamber music. Large scale is in the sheer volume of sound produced by the organ, and by the long, insistent pedal effect throughout the first seven bars, making dramatic use of a large building. The old style of violin playing that attempted to reproduce organ effects is mercifully now far less general than it used to be.[2] Telemann says that in his youth he learnt to compose properly for instruments, not like the unskilled composer who writes for the violin in the style of the organ, or the flute and oboe in the style of the trumpet.[3] Nobody could accuse Bach of being unskilled in writing for instruments. The only description we have of him playing the violin Solos himself is on the clavichord, not the organ, and although the Fuga of BWV 1001 exists in a version for organ, it also exists in a version for lute (neither version by Bach).[4]

Ex.3.1 Bach, organ Fantasia in G minor BWV 542/1, bars 1–4

There are in any case plenty of string antecedents for this manner. The one most often mentioned is the Amsterdam printing of Corelli's Op.5 violin Sonatas (1710) which has ornaments in the slow movements attributed to Corelli.[5] These are in quite a different style from later ornamentations for Corelli's Sonatas by Geminiani and others in that they tend to have very light filigree ornaments at the end of the note, rather than a steady level of rhythmic ornamentation (Ex.3.2).[6] If they are indeed Corelli's ornaments, he was not alone in this style. The manner is to be found in Marin Marais's viol Preludes (1686 etc.), and nearer to Bach in several of Johann Schenck's unaccompanied bass viol Sonatas.[7] It is also in the third movement of Albicastro's

Op.5 No.1 (Amsterdam 1703), from a very Corellian set of violin Sonatas. Arnold Schering has extracted a plain, unornamented line for the G minor Adagio, such as Corelli might have written.[8] When Bach adopted the manner is uncertain. If the keyboard adaptation of the A minor trio Sonata from Johann Adam Reincken's *Hortus Musicus* (Hamburg 1687; Ex.3.3a and b) stems from the early stages of Bach's career, then it would be a prime early example, but it could just as well date from his later Weimar days.[9] Certainly what distinguishes Bach's use of this manner in the G minor Adagio is the fact that the ornaments are compositionally significant and part of an expressive scheme that could not be left to chance.

Ex.3.2   Corelli, violin Sonata Op.5 No.5 with 'Corelli's Graces', bars 1–5

Joel Lester has written very perceptively and in detail about this Sonata.[10] The most important aspect from the point of view of style and structure is the expressive and structural use of the ornamentation. As is commonly the case, the opening four-chord unit outlines the tonic key (see the figured-bass digest Ex.3.4). A Schenkerian view would see the neighbour-note concept ($\hat{3}\overset{N}{4}\hat{3}$) as significant here for structural outlines in successive movements (i.e. the 'alto' notes b♭'-c"- b♭' in the first four chords).[11] It is certainly true that the fourth degree is structurally important in this movement since the opening section, modulating up a 5th to the dominant (bars 1–9), is reprised beginning in the subdominant C minor (fourth degree) and modulating up a 5th to the tonic (bars 14–22). The principle of the subdominant reprise was commonly used by Bach at this time.[12] Within this general scheme there is a remarkable unity of surface and structure, characteristic of Bach, which is also the expressive argument. The first note outside the tonic and dominant chords in bars 1–2 is the e♭" at the end of bar 2, emphasised by the decorative tirata that leads up to

Ex.3.3   a) Johann Adam Reincken, *Hortus Musicus*, Sonata 3, bars 1–6

b) Bach's keyboard arrangement BWV 965

it. This note provides the grit from which the Adagio develops. It is resolved onto d" in the appoggiaturas in the first beat of bar 3, but immediately is strongly emphasised again in the bass on the third beat (though Bach forgot the flat in the autograph), with the resolution d" now itself converted into a strongly dissonant major 7th.[13] The dramatic tension of this is expressed in the shower of ornamentation of the Phrygian cadence from here to the beginning of the next bar. So far we are in G minor. The c♯' at the beginning of bar 5 swings the harmony round to D minor, where the e♭" in the second half of the bar is now the expressive Neapolitan note in that key, resolving in Bach's favoured way onto a last-inversion dominant 7th chord at the beginning of bar 6, with the strong melodic dissonance of the diminished 3rd. The very directional 6/4/2 chord, with the 7th in the bass, gives solidity to the modulation to D. The Phrygian cadence in the second half of bar 7 to bar 8 is therefore not dramatically important in itself, so although the 7th now resolves onto the richer 6/4/3 (*quarta italica*, end of bar 7 in Ex.3.4), it is not decorated so extravagantly as the equivalent in bar 3.

Ex.3.4 Adagio of BWV 1001, figured-bass abstract

The middle section (beginning in bar 9) has, as one would expect, some intensification of materials, particularly in the more dissonant version of the sixteenth-note appoggiaturas in the first half of bar 11 (compare the beginning of bar 3). C minor here seems to be just a stepping stone to a main cadence in E flat major, strongly prepared in bar 12. The expected close in the major key is contradicted in the most dramatic moment of the piece, where the e♭" at the beginning of bar 13, far from bringing major-key relaxation, is part of a tense diminished 7th on a♮. This diminished 7th is wrenched bodily up a tone to one on b♮, the leading note of C minor, and when e♭' next appears, on the third beat of bar 13, it is part of that dark key. The darkness is reinforced in bar 14 by having the reprise begin at the bottom of the instrument. The emphasised note at the end of bar 15 is now a♭" and this takes the place previously held by the e♭" at the end of bar 2: part of the Neapolitan 6th in G minor in the second half of bar 18, complete with diminished 3rd; the Neapolitan 6th to dominant 6/4/2 progression is repeated from the second half of bar 20 to the first beat of bar 21; and there is a final flicker in the prefix to the cadential trill at the end of bar 21.

Comparison with the Chromatic Fantasia shows how different this is from recitative style. As C.P.E. Bach says, strange and distant modulations are unsuitable for pieces with a regular beat.[14] The one chromatic lurch in the

Adagio is powerful because it is unique and the surprise is thoroughly prepared. The expression is concentrated by the economy of material, and also by the technical concentration inherent in an instrument of four strings.

In the autograph Bach's policy for stem directions is to keep the notes as much as possible within the stave, and he is very ingenious in avoiding collision with notes from adjacent staves. Dörffel (BG) has put most of the stems up, which has the advantage of legibility, and also shows the continuity of the decorated line in bar 1, and how a prefix and trill are part of the same shape (as in bar 2). Hausswald (NBA) has preserved Bach's directions. On the other hand he has divided short note values in flourishes into groups of four, in accordance with modern convention, which suggests a rhythmic rigidity not present with Dörffel and certainly not in Bach's very suggestive graphic flourishes. Hausswald also has an unnecessary triplet mark on the second beat of bar 21: the compulsion to make the notation 'add up' can very often undermine an intention of rhythmic freedom. Hausswald's slurs are much closer to Bach's than Dörffel's. Joel Lester has listed ambiguities, to which one might add the third beat of bar 17.[15] The small extra slur in the autograph looks like an extension of the preceding one, so the intention may be to have a single slur begin on b♭' and end on g".

2. Fuga

The combination of Adagio first movement and fugal second, common in sonatas in the Corelli tradition, forms a prelude and fugue pair, and there are many links here between the Adagio and the Fuga. On a local level, the e♭'' in bar 2 of the fugue corresponds to the e♭'' at the end of bar 2 in the Adagio, and the harmonic progression in the fugue from bar 2 to half way through bar 3 corresponds in the Adagio to the progression from the end of bar 2 to the beginning of bar 4, including the major 7th on e♭'.[16] As Joel Lester points out, this means that the instrumental hand-shapes are virtually the same.[17] As in the Adagio, the key of C minor is also emphasized here: the answer in bar 2 necessarily uses the notes of C minor since, if it had to be crammed into the 4th g'–d', it would lose its melodic and harmonic character (see Ex.2.13c).[18] The subdominant key of C minor is also as strongly emphasized on the larger scale in the Fuga as in the Adagio, with the longest episode building up to the subject entry in C minor at bar 52. The lute version (BWV 1000) dramatises this moment with a fermata on the chord in the first beat of the bar. This C minor section is also emphasised by having the largest and most sonorous chords.

Canzona-type subjects with repeated notes are common in the Corelli tradition: the second movement of Corelli's Op.5 No.6 has material similar to this Fuga, as has the second movement of the B flat unaccompanied violin sonata attributed to Geminiani, discussed in Chapter One section 2. Denser workings of these materials are in Albicastro's sonatas: the last movement of Op.5 No.1 has a repeated-note subject in $^6_8$ time, with double stops virtually throughout the movement. Such subjects have an obvious practical convenience for polyphony on stringed instruments, and are used also in the virtuoso viol tradition of Kühnel and Schenck. Subjects commonly begin on a rhythmically propulsive weak beat and need a countersubject that will be not only invertible but also playable.[19]

Bach's subject here begins after the downbeat in ¢ time, making the entire subject an upbeat to the second bar. The fact that the middle of the bar is not a downbeat as it would be in c time gives the necessary feeling of fluency, with the subject as a single, highly directional unit, and emphasizes its fundamental shape of three descending notes of a scale (5 4 3). Descending scales are then the principal shape around which Bach constructs the large paragraphs necessary in such a substantial piece, even though based on such a brief subject. The first one, a scale of G minor (g'–g) in the lowest sounding part from bar 2 to half way through bar 4, unites the events of the exposition. One can then follow a slowly moving scale down through the first episode from b♭" at the beginning of bar 6 to b♭' in the middle of bar 10, repeated more quickly from the b♭" on the second beat of bar 11 down to g', in a sentence that clinches this section in the tonic.

The exposition is very neat in that it in begins with what must be the 'tenor', then has the answer twice, an octave apart, on either side of it ('bass' and 'cantus'), returning in bar 4 to an 'alto' entry of the subject at the same pitch as bar 1. Bach used this pattern of subject-answer-answer-subject in fugues where he wished to have a particularly compact exposition.[20] Both the lute and the organ arrangements of this fugue make their main changes in the exposition, since repeating the subject at the same pitch, necessary on the violin, was evidently felt to be a weakness. Bach knows how to turn a limitation of this sort to good dramatic use: he saves the 'missing' entry on the bottom string for the final entry of the fugue in bar 82, where it provides a delayed fulfilment of the expectation of an entry at that pitch in the exposition. In any case, the effect of the fourth entry in the exposition is inevitably quite different from the first, given the intervening events and the fact that it is accompanied by chords.

The exposition is not a self-contained entity. Already in the second half of bar 5 Bach begins a sequential extension of the subject, taken up again and developed from bar 11. The exposition corresponds to the character head of Bach's favoured ritornello shape of character head—sequential tail—closing motif—cadence (see Chapter Two section 5). This all constitutes section 1 of the fugue (bars 1 to the beginning of 14). The sequential tail is the sixteenth-note episode beginning at bar 7; the closing motif begins on the second beat of bar 11 (it often has a chromatic tinge, as here in the Neapolitan A flats at the beginnings of bars 12 and 13); and a cadence figure in bar 13 to the beginning of bar 14. This material is then rerun with extensions and developments ('rotated' in various ways, some might say) a number of times during the piece.[21] Section 2 runs from bar 14 to the D minor cadence in bar 24; section 3 to the C minor cadence into bar 55; and section 4 to the G minor cadence into bar 87, followed by what one might call a coda, including a cadenza in bar 93.

On the Invention principle, Bach 'researches' elements of the subject as he builds up the first section. Apart from its descending-scale outline, the subject consists of repeated notes, a lower auxiliary, and a falling 3rd. It is not difficult to see the elements of scale segments and 3rds embedded in the sixteenths from bars 7 to 10. They are yet more apparent in the equivalent episode from bar 42, where Schumann brings out the subject outline in his piano accompaniment, not a good idea since this passage is clearly intended to be a prolonged respite from the subject before its dramatic return at bar 52. The circle-of-5ths sequence on which the sixteenths are based is in the countersubject in bar 2. The closing motif from bar 11 turns the three elements of the subject into a descending scale sequence, with falling 3rds in the bass of bars 11–12. As well as the Invention principle, there is a large element of the Italian solo concerto in this fugue. As is common in, particularly Venetian, concertos in the first two decades of the century, the solo episodes are distinguished from the tutti by having a different, quicker note value. The violin chords at subject entries are not really polyphonic, but correspond to the full sonority of the concerto tutti in a way similar to the violino piccolo part in the third movement of the First Brandenburg Concerto. Paradoxically, the solo episodes in this Fuga are a relaxation from the effortful sound of violin chords, the opposite of the usual effect of quicker note values in the solo passages of a concerto.

Section 2 takes up the descending scale sequence that ends section 1, starting at a new high pitch, and treats it to a substantial development. The series of overlapping entries that ends the section (alto and cantus in bars 22–3) was evidently felt to be a weakness by the organ arranger, who dissolved it into *brisé* figurations (BWV 539/2 bars 23–4), presumably because these adumbrations of the subject weaken the effect of the entry at the beginning of section 3. In the violin version they have the logic of taking up and developing the imitation already noted at the end of the exposition (from the middle of bar 4 to the middle of bar 5).

Ex.3.5 Fuga of BWV 1001, J.P. Kellner's abbreviated version of bars 34–42

Sections 3 and 4 correspond in various ways. They both start low in pitch and use a new, rising countersubject (outlining notes 5 6 7 8 of the scale). If one could say that the countersubject in bar 2 pushes the subject downwards, one could say that here the subject pushes the countersubject upwards. The correspondence between these two sections is more obvious in Kellner's copy, which omits bars 35–41, and has bar 34 leading into bar 42 as in Ex.3.5.[22] Both sections would then be expansions of the shape of section 1, with exposition, sixteenth-note episode, extension of the subject down a descending scale, and cadence. The practical Bach managed to get this fugue onto a single opening in the autograph, in which case it is noticeable that the extra stave he drew at the bottom of the page has roughly the same number of bars as those lacking in Kellner's copy. It may therefore be that Kellner was given an earlier version of the Fuga to copy.[23] The function, and performance, of bars 35–41 are matters for debate. From the structural point of view it is not obvious why there should be such a prolonged dominant pedal of G minor at this stage when that really belongs at bars 69ff. More obvious is the change of note value and texture. Up to this point there has been an aerated texture with chords when the subject is present, alternating with a texture of continuous sixteenths. At bar 30 a new articulation is introduced, of slurred pairs, which may be intended to give a calming effect, subsequently developed in the calm 3rds and 6ths in eighth notes from bar 38. Most players arpeggiate from the second half of bar 35 to the end of bar 41, and various ways are suggested by Joachim, Boyden, Champeil and others.[24] Some have suggested using the pattern in the C major Fuga in BWV 1005, bars 186ff and 273ff.[25] If it has any bearing, Kellner cut most of these sections too (bars 188–200 and 277–86). Yet, as Russell Stinson says, Bach did not specify arpeggiation in his very carefully prepared holograph, nor is it indicated in any other source, in contrast to the D minor Ciaccona where he did notate it.[26] Bach also wrote out the pattern he wanted in the C major Fuga. The organ and lute versions treat this as a moment of calm, with smooth 3rds and 6ths over a pedal.[27] On the other hand, in his organ arrangement of Vivaldi's 'Grosso Mogul' concerto BWV 594, Bach interprets Vivaldi's chords as in Ex.3.6.[28] Pedal points can be static and calm (as in a pastorale), or tension-building (as in bars 69ff of the G

Ex.3.6 a) Vivaldi, 'Great Mogul' concerto RV 208, first movement Allegro, solo violin bars 26–32

b) Bach's organ arrangement BWV 594

minor Fuga). Another possible factor to consider is that bar 40 runs up to the highest pitch in the fugue (f'''). Whatever the player decides will have to be part of an overall strategy for the piece.

The organ version BWV 539/2 (in D minor) is worth comparing in order to gain a perspective on the violin original. Far from being student work it is in fact a skilful arrangement.[29] Two extra bars are added (between bars 5–6 and 28–9 of the violin version) in order to accommodate extra subject entries, the latter deftly enhancing the effect of accumulating entries in bars 24ff of the violin version. There are numerous differences of detail, but specially pleasing are the left-hand parts added in bars 44–7 and 70–5 (of BWV 594) in the manner of the flute and violin parts in the first movement of the Fifth Brandenburg Concerto (bars 81ff), and the complementary left-hand accompaniment in bars 93–4. The fermata at the beginning of bar 95 of the organ version is implied, though not notated, in bar 93 of the violin Fuga.

3. *Siciliana*

Joel Lester has written so persuasively about this piece that I need only add a few points.[30] Each of the Sonatas has a third movement in a contrasting key, and each refers to a different scoring. This is in the manner of a trio, the Andante of Sonata II of the slow movement of a Venetian concerto, and the Largo of Sonata III is in the manner of a violin sonata.

It is customary with reference to this movement to cite Quantz's advice for playing sicilianos, and rightly so since his description of the dance corresponds exactly to Bach's ingredients. It is a light dance, in $\frac{12}{8}$ time with dotted notes, to be played not too slowly and with few graces other than some slurred sixteenth notes and appoggiaturas.[31] Elsewhere Quantz advises that dotted eighth notes should be leant on, and the sixteenth note after the dot be played briefly.[32] The sixteenth note certainly needs to be light, and perhaps with some feeling of background triplet inequality to give the characteristic lilt of the dance. As with a number of Bach pieces in this metre, the art is to reconcile this lilting dotted rhythm with groups of even sixteenths.[33] Though the two rhythms do not occur simultaneously in this particular piece, the feel of the sixteenths here is no different from the same rhythmic effect in pieces where they do. The effect is best achieved by following Leopold Mozart's advice to lean slightly on the first note under a slur.[34]

The time signature $^{12}_{8}$ is light since there is only one strong downbeat in every four dotted quarter notes, the third beat of the bar being a lighter downbeat. The triplet division of the beat then makes the eighth and sixteenth notes very unemphatic. Quantz gives an approximate pulse-based tempo for a siciliano of ♩. = 53, which is on the quick side since the violin has not only to play the two upper parts (as in those sonatas by Biber and J.J. Walther where the violin has to play the two upper parts of a 'trio' sonata in double stopping throughout), but the bass as well.[35] The rhythmic character of the siciliano can still be preserved at a slower tempo. An indication of the distance travelled in performance since the late nineteenth century is in Spitta's description of 'this charmingly conceived *Siciliano* in B flat major, with marvellous polyphonic working out, but the tenderness of this dance-form is injured by the strength and harshness of tone necessarily resulting from the employment of several parts'.[36] Mercifully these genre characters are well understood nowadays.

The structure of sections is similar to that in the Fuga, though here there are only two main sections. In this case the opening sentence is a four-bar antecedent-consequent phrase, with a half close at the end of bar 2 answered by a full close half way through bar 4. The remainder of the section modulates to a new key at bar 9, as it would in a binary dance or sonata movement, except that the new key here is not the expected dominant (F major) but the relative (G minor). Since the Adagio and Fuga have hardly used B flat major, concentrating instead on D minor and C minor as alternatives to the tonic, the return to G minor in this major-key movement is particularly affecting. The second section returns to B flat in a way that transforms the significance of the C minor triad (see below).

The unity of materials in this seemingly light piece is extraordinary: it is perhaps the most concentrated example of the application of the invention and sonata principles to a dance genre. The descending sixteenth notes in the second beat of bar 1 can be read as an inversion and division of the rising triad in the first beat. The sighing eighth-note appoggiaturas in the second half of the bar are then an augmentation of the descending 4th motif, a relationship reinforced by the sixteenths in bar 2, which further unite the appoggiaturas to the sixteenth-note scale figure in bar 1. Bach, as was common practice at this period, wrote in the articulation he wanted in the first bar, but notated it only patchily thereafter, usually to show a different articulation from the initial one (as in the slurred pairs in the first beat of bar 4).

The concentration of materials is matched by the concentration of expression. In spite of its lighter feel and major mode, this movement has strong links with the Adagio. There is already an accent on C minor half way through bar 3, and the following bars dramatize the note E flat as the Adagio did. In the fourth beat of bar 5 it prepares a dominant pedal of G minor, and the whole of bar 6 involves moving up from a dominant 7th c" to e♭", the very plangent dominant minor 9th that unleashes a shower of ornamentation outlining the diminished 7th from the e♭" on the last beat of bar 6 to the f'♯ at the beginning of bar 7. The expected G minor is replaced by C minor for the second half of bar 7, and again the cadence in the second beat of bar 8 is thwarted by resolving onto a first inversion on the third beat, followed by another shower of decoration, whose rising shape balances the falling flourish at the end of bar 6 and whose e♭" is at last brought down to g' at the beginning of bar 9.

The goal of G minor brings the main motif down to the bottom note of the violin. One therefore expects the return to the major to be accompanied by a brightening of pitch levels, and this is indeed what happens. The motivic sixteenth notes move up the instrument till the highest note of the piece (c''') is reached in bar 13. This peak dramatises the fact that the expected B flat chord at the beginning of bar 13 is replaced by one of C minor, with the significant e♭" melodically emphasised. But the effect of C minor is now very different from what it was in the first section, being the supertonic in B flat major rather than the subdominant in G minor. As such it now contributes much to the warmth of this final section. After bar 13, pitch subsides to a half close in B flat into bar 15, and a full close into bar 19. The final two bars have the effect of a miniature tonic reprise, returning to the chord layout of the opening.

The 6/4 chord that resolves directly onto the B flat chord on the third beat of bar 4 has puzzled some, who have played c" instead of d" at the end of the second beat; alternatively, some decorate it so that it forms the usual dominant.[37] In fact this type of 6/4 is common enough in lighter genres at this time. It is in the main cadence in the Forlane from the fourth of François Couperin's *Concerts royaux* (Paris 1722) and in a number of Handel arias. There is a curious similarity here to the equivalent cadence into bar 19, where the tonic B flat chord could equally be preceded by a 6/4 on e♭'.

Bach's use of the fermata is significant in the grouping of movements.[38] The Adagio has a fermata over the final chord and the instruction 'VS.Volti', implying a pause on the final chord, then going straight into the Fuga. The Fuga has a fermata over the final barline, implying a pause before the next movement. The Siciliana has no fermata, though it has got rests, which must mean that the Presto begins like a dramatic bolt from the blue.[39]

4. Presto

The time signature and barring are important indicators of the metrical feel of this movement. Why write it in $\frac{3}{8}$-time with half bar-lines, rather than in $\frac{6}{8}$? One could say that $\frac{3}{8}$ is in a sense the opposite of the $\frac{12}{8}$ of the Siciliana in that in $\frac{3}{8}$ time individual eighth notes have more weight (as in the $\frac{3}{8}$ Gigues of the D minor and E flat major cello Suites, or in Bach's numerous passepieds). The half bar-lines and the marking Presto suggest greater fluency of sixteenth notes than in these, but with a certain weight to allow the kaleidoscopic rhythmic groupings to tell, one of the main points of this moto perpetuo. The beat after the half bar-line is a lighter downbeat, not an upbeat as in $\frac{6}{8}$ time, and the pairing of bars into stronger and weaker makes possible all sorts of rhythmic counterpoints.

A firm grasp of harmonic structure and of the strategy of pitch levels is essential for the projection of this movement. The essence of a moto perpetuo of this sort, at least in Bach's case, is that surface figurations and rhythms relate to fundamental harmonic function and structure. The normal pattern is to have static harmonic rhythm at the main centres, and more rapid change in the transitions. Within that, Bach's normal harmonic structure for the first strain of a binary piece in a minor key is to visit the relative major (as a secondary key centre) on the way to the dominant (at the double bar; see Chapter Two section 7). The first chord of the Presto is already an irregular (sesquialtera) shape of three bars. Bars 4–9 have an accent each bar, but the ping-pong effect of low notes and high notes gives the effect of two-bar units. This is more relaxed than the single-bar units in bars 9–11, which imply harmonic change at the rate of two chords a bar in the rhythm ♪♩, made more active in effect by the bowing, in bars 12–17.[40] A slower sequence of two-bar units (bars 17–24) climbs to the goal of b♭", where there is an upper pedal lasting four bars. The accelerando of harmonic change in the first bars of the movement had the function of taking the leading pitch line up from g" (bar 1) via a" (bar 7) to b♭" (bar 9), the highest note in the strain. In fact bars 1–8 could be regarded as a large upbeat to bar 9. The b♭" pedal in bars 25–8 revisits that pitch, and ultimately takes it down to the dominant d" at the double bar. The move from B flat to D minor is marked by the brief pedal a in bars 33–5, and the swirling cross rhythms over it. This dominant pedal is taken up again more emphatically again in bars 47–51.

The second strain expands and develops elements of the first, working through the same materials as it moves from the dominant back to the tonic.[41] The inversion of the opening arpeggio takes the pitch level up to d''', the highest note in the piece. The harmonic plan is to return to the tonic via the subdominant, so there is a cadence in C minor into bar 66. The e♭" in bar 67 is an important goal pitch, corresponding to the b♭" in bar 9, so is built up to in the same way, and has the same quicker descent afterwards. We leave C minor in bar 83, to return to G minor via B flat major. As is common with Bach, the tonal move is quickly achieved: there is a main cadence in G minor in bars 87–90. The rest of the piece is a highly resourceful variation of motifs from the first strain, broadly with the same main events. The emphasised pitch corresponding to the pedal a at bar 33 is now b♭, as the 3rd of G minor, at bar 110. Literal repetition of events is avoided. There is no final dominant pedal, but the climbing effect in bars 49–52 is extended from bar 129–34, opening out the pitch range to the final chord. This chord was outlined by the opening arpeggio, and has been, as it were, the source and origin of the whole Sonata.

This is a classic example of single-part polyphony. Figurations tend to move between a high note and a low note, outlining two parts, and there are some standard part movements, such as the parallel 6s in bars 43–6, or the two-part formula inherent in bars 12–17 etc. (Ex.3.7).

Ex.3.7 Presto of BWV 1001, outline of bars 12–17

Partia Prima BWV 1002

In his suite collections Bach liked to work systematically through types of piece, as we have seen in the range of courante types in the French Suites for clavier (see Chapter Two section 2). In the discussion of the G minor Sonata we have noted different types of fugue subject in the second movements of the violin Sonatas, and reference to different ensemble groupings in the third movements. The three Partias correspondingly represent three different types. The first two are of the solo instrumental suite type (allemande, courante, sarabande, and gigue), though the B minor Partia substitutes a Borea (bourrée) for the Gigue. This is probably because the Double of the Sarabande was already in 9/8 time, rather than because, as Spitta suggests, that a gigue was hardly suitable for variations.[42] There is a variation (Double) of the Gigue in BWV 997, and also in Pisendel's A minor violin Sonata *senza basso* (Appendix 5). The third Partia is of the overture-suite type as far as its dances are concerned, though the Preludio is Italianate in style. Within that broad plan, dances normally associated with the overture-suite (bourrée, chaconne) occur also in the solo type of suite, as they commonly do since these are not hermetic categories but general types. The first two Partias are themselves of different types within the solo instrumental suite format, in that they explore different possible relationships of the suite to the variation: the B minor has variation Doubles, while the D minor recalls the variation-suite with its strong variation element between the movements. The Ciaccona is in itself the dance genre in which the variation principle is fundamental. There is also the consideration that the Doubles of the B minor, with their repeats, make the first Partia as substantial as the D minor with its Ciaccona, which would otherwise unbalance the collection.

For variation technique Bach uses the traditional note values of basic division technique (discussed in Chapter Two section 4). Divisions can decorate either a melody, or a harmonic progression (as with Renaissance dance basses, or English 'divisions on a ground'). Handel demonstrates the standard pattern in the G minor Passacaille of his harpsichord *Suites* (London 1720), where successive variations regularly divide the note values into eighth notes, triplets, sixteenth notes. Bach is less obvious in the B minor Partia, with eighth notes in the Tempo di Borea, triplets in the Sarabande, and sixteenths in the Allemanda and Corrente.

This Partia is the one that plays most subtly with styles and genres. It could be described as a research into the ideas of dance and sonata, and their blending in the 'mixed style'.[43] The first movement has the Italian term Allemanda for a French-style dance, and the French term Double for its reworking as an Italianate moto perpetuo (rather than Pisendel's term 'Variatione'). Within his general policy of having Italian titles in the violin Solos Bach occasionally slips back into what seems to have been for him familiar terminology.

1. *Allemanda and Double*

As the first suite movements of this collection, the Allemanda and Double of the B minor Partia have the appearance of a stylistic pair, the Allemanda representing the French dance style and the Double the Italian sonata style (the moto perpetuo of sixteenths in the Double is in the spirit of similar movements in Corelli's Op.5). Neat as this distinction would be, the reality is more subtle and more interesting. The Allemanda looks like a dance genre but has a fundamentally sonata structure. The Double looks like a sixteenth-note division on a dance, but cannot be that since the Allemanda has a sonata, not a dance, phrase structure, so it is in fact a reworking of a sonata structure in another manner. In addition, the stylistic reference in the dotted notes and triplets in the Allemanda is vital to understand for performing it.

Surface complexity of rhythm, expressed in variety of note values, was a common feature of what is usually called the galant style in the 1720s, but it is difficult to find examples from before then. It is therefore striking that Bach appears to have been one of the first to have this style fully developed, in both of the Allemandas of the *Sei Solo*, which must date from 1720 or before, and also in the Allemande of the F major English Suite for clavier, which may also date from around that time. If it is true that the violin Solos were written, at least in part, in Weimar, and perhaps also the English Suites, then Bach was indeed in the vanguard, unless other composers simply did not notate as much as he did, which is also quite likely. Triplets are rare in allemandes before 1720. They do not feature in French harpsichord suites of the first two decades of the century. Very occasionally they occur in allemandes of Johann Mattheson (1714), Christoph Graupner (1718), and Silvius Leopold Weiss (1719), but only as a momentary effect, not subjected to the thoroughgoing use that Bach made of them.[44]

The other feature of the B minor Allemanda apart from triplets is the dotted rhythm. A pair of sixteenth notes, whether notated dotted or plain, has numerous possible interpretations, some of which overlap, and the stylistic reference is all-important for their interpretation. One possible source of dotted rhythms is the Italian adagio, in Quantz's generic sense of a slow movement, usually the first movement of a sonata. Within the general species there is a dotted genus of adagio, with examples in Albinoni's *Trattenimenti* violin sonatas Op.6 (Amsterdam *c.*1711), a collection known to Bach.[45] Nearer to 1720, the Preludio of Vivaldi's Op.5 No.6 (RV 72; Amsterdam 1716), is binary and features dotted sixteenths, 32nds, and sixteenth triplets. In this type of adagio the dotted rhythm gives a pleasing, stately poise to the movement if quite sharply dotted. A comparison of the first movements of both church and chamber sonatas in Telemann's 1715 violin *Sonates* shows how much the allemanda was infected by the sonata adagio, just as the corrente was by the sonata allegro, and one explanation for the genre of allemande with many note values is just this infection.

Another possibility for the dotted rhythm is the French *entrée*, or first section of an overture. This has been suggested for the B minor Allemanda, but the note values are wrong.[46] As can be seen from the Prelude of the C minor cello Suite BWV 1011, the dotted values in the overture are ♩. ♪ and ♫. Sixteenths themselves are not dotted. An Allemande that uses the dotted eighths, tiratas, and runs of sixteenths of the Bach-style overture is that of the same C minor cello Suite (see the discussion in Chapter Four). Yet another type of dotted piece is represented by the aria 'Komm süßes Kreuz' in the Saint Matthew Passion. Superficially this might look as if it is related to the B minor Allemanda, with its dotted sixteenths and chords on lute or viol, but in fact it relates to a type of Italian aria where dotted rhythms have particular expressive associations.[47]

If not related to the dotted type of adagio, the dotted rhythms of the B minor Allemanda may alternatively be Bach notating the rhythmic inequality usual in a French allemande. In this case the dotting would be gentler, something like that suitable for Couperin's *Les Graces incomparables* (see Chapter Two section 2). Of course we cannot know quite how Couperin played, but we can at least come to an informed estimate based on contemporary instructive literature, original notation, and large experience of the relevant repertories. As far as notation is concerned, an extensive look at music in the German mixed style in the first decades of the eighteenth century gives the impression that composers frequently notated inequality when they wanted it. This is certainly true of Graupner's clavier *Partien* of 1718, but also of Telemann's overture-suites, and of similar mixed-style ensemble music by Dall'Abaco, or Johann Christoph Pez. Even in French music there are lute sources that notate rhythmic inequality by means of dotted notes throughout.[48]

The phrase structure of Bach's Allemanda is similar to that of a Couperin allemande, but in Couperin's Italianate vein. There is a two-bar opening phrase with a caesura at the beginning of bar 2. Bach uses a strong major 7th here, just as Couperin uses a highly coloured, and typically French, augmented 5th at the equivalent point in *La Superbe* from his seventeenth harpsichord *Ordre* (1722; Appendix 6). Bach's 7th gives him the opportunity for a sonorous chord based on the two lowest open strings. The first phrase has an on-beat ending (beginning of bar 3); the second (beginning of bar 5) has the typical French *coulé de tierce* off-beat phrase ending, notated in the reverse inequality that Couperin indicates in his first Book of harpsichord pieces (1713) by means of a slur and a dot.[49] Phrases for the rest of the strain are irregular, sonata-style, with only one intermediate cadence into bar 8. To say that the dotting is less than written is not to say that it must be regularly so throughout the piece. Moulding the level of inequality to the expressive moment is a prime resource in this style.

If there could be any doubt about the French background of this Allemanda, a look at the use of identical ingredients in the Allemanda of the third of Veracini's *Sonate a Violino solo, e Basso* (Dresden 1721) should convince as to how different an Italian-based style is from a French-based one (Ex.3.8). Although published in 1721 these sonatas probably date from the years before, since part of the twelfth Sonata had already appeared in the first of the manuscript 'Sonate a Violino, o Flauto solo, e Basso' presented by

Veracini to the Crown Prince of Saxony in 1716.[50] Veracini's Allemanda already shows the mixture of manners and variety of rhythmic surface that were to be standard in adagio movements from the 1720s. There are about half a dozen different types of sixteenth-note articulation, of which the dotted arpeggios at the beginning very definitely come from the Italian adagio, not from the French allemande. Triplets here are part of this surface variety and there is no question of assimilating anything else to them. Their function is decorative, sometimes to intensify a progression in a rising line, or they may have a relaxing effect in a falling one.

Ex.3.8   Francesco Maria Veracini, Allemanda of violin Sonata Op.1 No.3, first strain

As one might expect, Bach's use of triplets in his B minor Allemanda is more subtle and more purposeful. Deeply wedded to the 'invention' principle (of developing everything from a limited amount of material presented in the first bar or so), rather than variety and diffusion, his essential building block in this piece is the 6/5 chord on a leading note, which first appears half way through bar 1 (see the figured-bass outline in Ex.3.9). Of the other versions of this chord in the first strain, that on e♯' in bar 9 is the crucial one structurally since it achieves the modulation to the dominant. Bach therefore introduces the new rhythmic value of triplets in bar 8, and works them up first to an augmented 2nd outline, and then in bar 9 to outline the dissonant 7♯/6♮/4/2 chord, an effect very different from Veracini's smooth divisions. The increase of tension associated with the dominant key at this point is further expressed by the jagged wide leaps in bars 10 and 11. The triplets in bar 12, in contrast, are of the falling, relaxing type, having reached the dominant goal. These opposite uses of triplets underline this difference in function. The extended phrase from bar 8 to bar 12 has the character of a large upbeat from F sharp major, as the dominant of B minor (bar 8), to F sharp minor (with *tierce de Picardie*) as a tonic at the double bar.

Ex.3.9   Allemanda of BWV 1002, figured-bass abstract

Another aspect of Bach's use triplets in this piece is the distinction between stepwise melodic elaboration and outlining chords, as an alternative to simultaneously notated chords. The second strain uses triplet chord outlines for the lovely colour change from E minor to C major in bars 17–18, and the diminished 7th on d♯' in bar 22.

The moto perpetuo nature of the Double implies that it is an allegro, and the time signature ¢ implies that quarters are, notionally at any rate, twice as fast as in the c-time Allemanda.[51] A notable performance feature is that almost the entire Double is to be bowed in pairs, as are the concertante eighths in the Forlane of BWV 1066. If we can believe Tartini, Corelli's movements of this sort were to be bowed out in separate bows for each note, and in fact were used as basic bowing exercises throughout the 18th century.[52] A similar movement with paired bowings is the Allegro third section of Telemann's Sonata IV (1715). Both reflect the increased sophistication of bowing technique developed by Dresden violinists such as Pisendel and Veracini. The pairs may also imply a slight ('un tant-soit-peu') swinging of the sixteenths.[53]

In accordance with the editorial policy of making notation add up, Bach's ♩. 𝅘𝅥𝅰𝅘𝅥𝅰𝅘𝅥𝅰 has been replaced by ♩.𝅘𝅥𝅰𝅘𝅥𝅰𝅘𝅥𝅰 in NBA, an exact rhythmic value not necessarily implied by Bach's freer notation.[54]

2. Corrente and Double

As in the Presto of the G minor Sonata, Bach has used half bar-lines (mostly looking more like quarter bar-lines), presumably for the same reason of avoiding having too many strong downbeats. It is useful to compare the

Courante of the B minor French Suite for clavier, in $^6_4$ time where eighth notes are light and flexible being a relatively small value in that time signature, with that of the C minor French Suite, in $^3_4$ time where they have more weight and equality. The violin Corrente lies between these two, with a lighter downbeat on the even-numbered bars, rather than an upbeat as it would have in $^6_4$. The Corrente is also an Italianate sonata moto perpetuo with few of the shifts between $^6_4$ and $^3_2$ of the French courante, and a true hemiola only in bars 50–1. It preserves the classic French shape of having three phrases in the first strain (with phrase ends at bars 10, 18 and the double bar), but the phrases are much extended, sonata-fashion, beyond the length of Couperin's. Also un-French is the fact that the first reprise has only one instance (bar 9) of the half-note accent shifting to the second beat of the bar. As the figured-bass digest shows (Ex.3.10) this detail is not wasted, but taken up in the second reprise (bars 34–40) in a climbing sequence that leads to the subdominant E minor. The Corrente has Bach's usual harmonic structure for a binary sonata/dance movement, with a visit to the relative major in the first strain at bar 18; and to the subdominant at bar 48 in the second strain.

Ex.3.10   Corrente of BWV 1002, figured-bass abstract

As with all these moto perpetuo movements, the surface of a single note value overlies great rhythmic vitality in the kaleidoscopic changes of shape in the figurations. One feature of rhythmic variety is the shifting of the slurred three-note arpeggio from half-bars to whole bars. John Butt, in a final virtuoso demonstration at the end of his book on Bach's articulation signs, has given a detailed analysis of this Corrente relating the rhythmic play of slurs to the harmonic structure.[55] Also useful for contemplating the infinite variety of this piece is Günter Kehr's notation of it as a single line over three staves, with realised *tenues* in the manner of the lute to show implied part movements.[56]

While the Allemanda Double turns the melodic Allemanda into arpeggio figurations, the fleeter Corrente Double turns the arpeggiated Corrente into stepwise scale figurations. If the Corrente blends aspects of the B minor and C minor Courantes from the French Suites, the Double is in the toccata manner of the Courante of the E major French Suite. Unlike the E major Courante, however, it is not in the usual ritornello structure. A distinguishing feature of these violin suites in comparison with the French Suites is the Solos' extraordinarily long harmonic phrases, something Bach seems to be exploring in this collection. It is also one of the major differences between these Solos and Telemann's unaccompanied violin Fantasias (1735). This Double is far more than just a division on the Corrente. Though the harmonic goal notes of the figurations (b–a♯–b) are the same, the first bars of each strain invert the direction of the equivalent bars in the Corrente, and the Double deals independently with its own motivic network, which entails paraphrase of the original harmonic structure in places.

The word Double here seems to mean that the predominant note value doubles the surface movement from eighths to sixteenths, rather than the 2:1 time-signature ratio of the Allemanda and Double. The direction Presto implies there should be no relaxation of tempo. Each movement and its Double has a pause over the final barline, meaning a slight pause between the movement and its Double, no doubt welcome to both player and listener in view of the relentless nature of this Partia. The direction 'VS volti' at the end of this Double, as before the second reprise of the Corrente and elsewhere in the autograph, means no more than that the Partia continues overleaf, until the word Fine at the end.

3. *Sarabande and Double*

Bach's use of French terminology uniquely for this movement is probably just a slip of the pen; far from being typically French, this is a mixed-style working.[57] Of dance genres, Bach's sarabandes tend to stay closest to the typical phrase structure of the dance, in this case of four-bar phrases. The shape of the first reprise, of eight bars in the pattern 2+2+4, is a common one. There is also play on typical French features, such as the *coulé de tierce* intermediate phrase endings that lie behind the eighth notes in bars 2 and 4, a figure used again for the different purpose of leading back in the first-time bar.

Initially the most notable thing about this Sarabande is its very full texture, a feature shared with the Sarabande of the D minor French Suite for clavier, and comparison with that is useful in defining the type and performance feel. The D minor Sarabande is fundamentally a sonata type, with eighth-note movement virtually throughout, and passages where the melodic line is in the bass. The similarity to the final chorus of the Saint Matthew Passion is striking. The B minor violin Sarabande is inevitably lighter in texture, but shares the fact that Bach in these pieces has reduced the normal rhythmic variety of the genre to two rhythms only: the steady tread of three quarters to a bar (with various decorations), and the rhythm ♩ ♪♩ , which gives a downbeat feel to the even-numbered bars and enhances the processional tread of the pieces. The limitation of ingredients concentrates the sombre mood. Given the sonata orientation, a marked French inequality for eighths, as proposed by Arnold Dolmetsch for the D minor French Suite Sarabande, would be quite inappropriate.[58] Nonetheless, in order for this highly expressive processional metre to tell, quarter notes should not be too heavy, the downbeat feel of the even-numbered bars is needed, and Quantz's distinction of on-beat and off-beat eighth notes is appropriate.

There are several types of eighth note, each of which may suggest a slightly different style of performance. The linking figure in bar 2 etc. has been mentioned. The leaps in bar 13 would normally be considered a *style brisé* compound melody, but might also be thought of as an expressive Italianate vocal line. The figures in bars 10, 26 and 28 are identical to sonata figurations in the Corrente. On the other hand, there are many eighths that seem to be in pairs. Bar 15 in particular recalls the Sarabande of the D major cello Suite, which has fully notated paired bowings throughout. The only slurred pairs are in bars 21 and 23, presumably because Bach wanted a new effect in this sequence. There are a few cases where he omitted slurs in this autograph, but in general he was exceptionally careful to indicate what he wanted. The difference between down-bows and up-bows gives natural pairing, and the bowings work out unproblematically with unslurred eighths and an occasional retake over a barline, as recommended by Georg Muffat (1698).

The Double can hardly be intended to fill the place of a Gigue, but is a triplet division on the Sarabande. According to Kirnberger, in a treatise that he claimed to represent Bach's teaching method, the signature $\frac{9}{8}$ is derived from $\frac{3}{4}$ and shares the same tempo, though the eighth notes are lighter in $\frac{9}{8}$ (for reasons already explained in the commentaries on the Siciliana and Presto of Sonata I).[59] In Cantata 147, the well-known chorale setting 'Wohl mir, dass ich

Jesum habe' (better known in English as 'Jesu, joy of man's desiring') has all the parts in ¾-time with the exception of the first violins which are in 9/8, being a triplet division on the chorale melody. These Doubles are far removed from ordinary études in that, within the stream of notes of a single value, there is great variety in the relative weighting of notes.[60] In the first strain here, for example, the archetypal rhythm of the first strain of a Sarabande is very perceptible behind the triplets, with the figurations and sensitive harmony notes suggesting the following accents:

$$\frac{3}{4}\ \flat\flat\flat\ |\ \flat.\ |\ \flat\flat\flat\ |\ \flat.\ |\ \flat\flat\flat\ |\ \flat\flat\flat\ |\ \flat.\ |$$

Pieces of this sort that rely on a single note value throughout, such as the G sharp minor Fugue from Book II of *The Well-tempered Clavier*, require great maturity on the part of the player to mould the phrases with subtlety and sensitivity to the harmony and figurations. Bach himself wrote not a single slur in this Double, in spite of there being several pairs that would seem to benefit from them (such as in the second and third beats of bars 25 and 27, compare bar 43 of the Borea Double). The slurs in the autograph at strain ends are *chapeaux*, i.e. indications of first- and second-time bars. Part of the maturity must be to achieve the necessary variety and subtlety with the Double bowed out all through.

4. *Tempo di Borea and Double*

Corelli used the term 'tempo di' for pieces in a dance metre which are in fact sonata movements. In these lighter dances Bach often uses Corelli's pattern of having a dance-rhythm antecedent and a sonata-style consequent (as for example in Bourrée I of the C major cello Suite). In the B minor Borea, however, he has kept the dance metre clear until well into the second strain, no doubt to avoid anticipating the effect of the eighth-note variation in the Double. This has the same time signature and is plainly meant to go at the same speed. One of the many patterns of this Partia is the gradual convergence of speed between dance and Double, more interesting and purposeful than the usual regular division into eighths, triplets, sixteenths. Bach has reserved the move into eighth-notes to bar 44 of the Borea, where they can provide a foretaste of the Double. Typically, he converts what could be a failing into a virtue by picking up the figurations again at bar 61 of the Double, making the final sense of reprise all the stronger.

The feeling of two beats in the bar, with the middle of the bar as an upbeat, is important for the lightness of this dance metre. Having said that, the very strong second beat of bar 1, matched by a very light second beat in bar 2, is almost a parody of the bourrée metre. The effect is of joviality, not grimness, in the spirit of the German 'Kehraus', or final dance of an evening. This very emphatic bourrée metre pays off in the Double, where it is very strongly felt behind the eighth-note figurations in bars 1 to 4:

¢ ♩ | ♩♩ | ♩. ♩ | ♩♩♩♩ | ♩.

The first strain, after the initial four-bar phrase, has a second phrase in the common 2+2+4 pattern (bars 5–12), but the 4 does not come to an end in bar 12. It is thrown forward in a sequence that makes a single extended phrase in D major (this is the only movement to cadence at the double bar in the relative major). This extended phrase, avoiding the regular phrase endings of a dance, is the sonata element implied by 'tempo di'.

The little phrase-ending figure in bar 4 of the Borea is slurred in pairs in bar 4 of the Double. The slurs in the second half of bar 48 of the Double are not repeated in bar 50, perhaps an intentional variation, also the first three notes of bar 52. Perhaps some intensification is intended, or maybe they were considered obvious in a sequence.

Sonata Seconda BWV 1003

The main general issue concerning this Sonata is the status of the clavier arrangement BWV 964 since it is a good quality arrangement that clarifies the harmony and structure, having a bass part throughout that is not adjusted to the necessities of the violin. For instance, the clavier version shows that the bass in bar 1 moves in steady quarter notes from a down to d at the beginning of bar 2. The violin version breaks back an octave to f' on the third beat of bar 1, which obscures this and encouraged Dörffel in BG to make the second note g♯. The arrangement also has suggestive details for violin interpretation.

The only account we have of Bach playing these pieces is by Johann Friedrich Agricola, who was a pupil between 1738 and 1741. Agricola tells us that he heard Bach playing them 'often' on the clavichord, 'adding as much harmony as he thought necessary. He recognised the necessity of sonorous harmony, which he had not been able to achieve in those compositions.'[61] This was late in Bach's life when, 'with approaching age', he had ceased to play the violin (see Chapter One section 1). Jakob Adlung, another who knew Bach, put the '6 Sonaten und Partien ohne Baβ' in a list of Bach's keyboard works, with a note to say that, although they were actually violin solos *senza basso*, 'they lend themselves very well to being played on the clavier' (by 1758 when this was published clavier often meant clavichord).[62] Of all keyboard instruments, the clavichord is the most suitable for playing the pieces as they stand (perhaps an octave down) since what in keyboard terms is a thin texture suits the clavichord's capacity for the most sensitive dynamic moulding, and vibrato. It has the nearest approach to the player actually making the note on the string, as the violinist's finger does, though of course it can never really be a substitute for the violin since the music is fundamentally conceived in terms of the strategy of four strings and the language of the bow. The clavichord does not absolutely require much addition to the texture. On the other hand, what we know of Bach's improvisation is that he liked 'masses of harmony', so the rather full textures of BWV 964 and the arrangement of the Adagio of the C major Sonata (BWV 968) may represent something like what Bach played.[63]

Both arrangements are in a single source (*D-B* Mus.ms.Bach P 218) copied by Johann Christoph Altnickol, who was a pupil of Bach's between 1744 and 1748, and in 1749 became his son-in-law. The title of BWV 964 in the manuscript is 'Sonata per il Cembalo Solo del Signore J.S. Bach', but that is no indication of who the arranger was. Spitta was convinced that it was Bach, since his primary view of Bach was as cantor and organist and these 'proved' that Bach thought originally in keyboard terms.[64] Rudolf Steglich (1935) and Hermann Keller (1950) were also convinced that the arrangements were by Bach, but more recently the style of the arrangements has been thought to belong more to the generation of Bach's sons than to Bach himself.[65] The most reasonable consensus is that they are probably the work of a skilled arranger, perhaps Wilhelm Friedemann Bach or Altnickol himself, perhaps under Bach's supervision. One of the features that is taken to indicate a later style is the chromatic scale passage in the second last bar of the Adagio (as the first movement is headed in the arrangement): a suggestive representation of the curious wavy lines and trill sign (of which more below) at the equivalent place in the violin original.

1. Grave

This has much in common with the Adagio of Sonata I. In terms of the initial slow movements of sonatas the words adagio and grave often seem synonymous, and the fact that Bach uses different terms may simply reflect his liking in collections of this sort to run systematically through terminology, rather than meaning anything more fundamental.[66] The heading Adagio in the arrangement presumably reflects the heading in the arranger's *Vorlage*. It has been suggested, on the basis of cantata movements in French-overture style where the two sections are labelled successively grave and vivace, that the Grave of this Sonata corresponds to the first section of a French overture, and the Fuga to the second.[67] There are a few dotted rhythms in the Grave, and some tiratas, so there may be a slight element of this, but it is hardly an accurate assessment of the genre for reasons given in the discussion of the B minor Allemanda. The A minor Grave and Fuga are not a French-overture type pairing. Their combination of rhetorical section followed by imitative section is a sonata pairing, that goes back virtually to the origins of the sonata in the first decades of the seventeenth century in Italy. The A minor Grave is another example of the floridly decorated sonata adagio (in the general sense), with perhaps a touch more of the speaking style of recitative than in the G minor Adagio, bringing it nearer to the first movement of Pisendel's A minor violin Sonata *senza basso*.

The rhetorical aspect of this movement is in its florid ornamentation, wherein lies much of its expressive force. For this reason it is the best demonstration of how necessary it was for Bach to write out all the ornamentation he wanted. Structurally it is one of Bach's most flexible and organic uses of his binary sonata plan. It has the usual visit to the relative major at bar 7, and the dominant cadence into bar 12 (where the double bar would be if there was one). After that there is only a brief link before a subdominant reprise at bar 14, but these two bars (12–13) set up the reprise in a uniquely expressive and dramatic way.

The usual regular shape at the opening is on a harmonic formula that leads to a half close in the middle of bar 2. If half bars were full bars, this would be a four-bar phrase. As in the G minor Adagio, Bach sets up accents in the first phrase that are important subsequently. Here too the minor sixth degree, the most expressive degree of the minor scale, is emphasised: as a harmony note f' on the third beat of bar 1 (making a virtue of the change of octave), and as the most expressive melodic note f", emphasized by the tirata into bar 2. The expressive implications of falling and rising scales here are powerfully realised later. The move towards the relative major is prepared by the brightening arpeggio at the beginning of bar 3, taking the line up to a higher pitch. Bar 4 has a more structural accent on f' (preceded by its dominant) as part of the move to C major. New rhythms are introduced in bar 5 for the first climax: first triplets, then a magnificent triple tirata, this time up to an emphatic f♯" at the beginning of bar 6, part of the dominant of the dominant of C major, with the highest notes so far. The tiratas are the first development of the scale motif, and powerfully dramatize the move to C major. These events are intensified in the following move to the dominant minor (E minor), with a darkening plunge in pitch in bar 7, and a yet more emphatic dominant of the dominant of E (a♯' at the beginning of bar 11). The tightly spaced diminished 7th in the clavier version here is perhaps more effective than the mere two notes on the violin.

The balance of falling and rising scales is now given its most powerfully dramatic development. The falling scales in bar 12 seem to be relaxing from the dominant back into the tonic A minor, when suddenly in bar 13 a rushing upward scale climaxes on b♭", expressive minor sixth degree of D minor and agonising dominant minor 9th over a chord of A major. This crisis induces a new figure of sobbing paired sixteenths down to the reprise at bar 14. So affecting was the crisis in bar 13 that the reprise is barely recognisable beneath the shower of florid decoration and kaleidoscopic chord changes that have been unleashed in a cathartic flow of emotion. The clavier version shows more clearly the original bass progression at this point, though the mere diminished 7th on the keyboard is no match for the violin's wide-spaced dominant minor 9th in bar 13. The reprise is shortened by four and a half bars (there is no visit to F major) and largely recomposed. It ends in the middle of bar 21, which is clearly an important point of repose. The remainder of the movement is a link to a Phrygian cadence, with yet more florid decoration of the 7–6 suspension in bar 22, as observed in the G minor Adagio.

Two points in the notation are important for performance. The first relates to the triple tirata in bar 5. As so often with modern editions, the NBA policy of making the rhythm add up destroys the quite clear performance implications of Bach's notation. A tirata is an ornament and as such is not necessarily played in an exact rhythm, but rapidly.[68] Bach's values are ♩. ♫. ♫.♫. The dot signifies an accent and slight pause, rather than an exact value, so there is a four-note tirata, then a six-note tirata, then a more regular final ornament. Dörffel in BG follows Bach for the first group, but in the second he omits the dot on e", so depriving the six-note tirata of its little accent and pause. Since the intended effect is a development of the tirata that led up to the crucial f" at the beginning of bar 2, it is vital that Bach's intention be respected for the expressive development of the piece. Bach's notation shows that it is sometimes more exact to be inexact.

The other point of notation is the pair of wavy lines leading to a trill sign at the end of the second last bar. Since this seems to have something to do with going up a semitone, one obvious possible interpretation is the vibrato (*flattement*) followed by glissando up a fret (*coulé du doigt*) common in French viol repertory.[69] The *flattement* can be either a finger vibrato (striking lightly, repeatedly, and as closely as possible to the fixed finger with the finger adjacent to it), or can be a wrist vibrato. Marais and others use a horizontal wavy line for this. This may be what is meant by the wavy lines for mysterious *pianissimo* rising semitones in the solo flute and violin parts in the first movement of the Fifth Brandenburg Concerto (bar 95), though equivalent places in the Organ Sonatas BWV 526/1 and 530/2 would have to be trills.[70] In the Brandenburg Concerto the solo parts are accompanied in the ripieno by a sort of bow vibrato (repeated notes under a slur), and that also is a possible interpretation of the wavy lines.[71] J.J. Walther (1676) uses repeated notes with a wavy line to indicate this. For arpeggiando Bach uses a vertical wavy line, as in the second movement of the A major Sonata for obbligato harpsichord and violin BWV 1015, so this is unlikely. But ondeggiando is a definite possibility, again indicated by a wavy line in J.J. Walther 1676 (Appendix 2), and this is perhaps also the meaning of the wavy lines in the first movement of the B flat major violin Sonata *senza basso* attributed to Geminiani (see Appendix 4). It has been well described as 'A shimmering effect ... obtained in a kind of bow vibrato which crosses two strings, breaking the double stop and alternating the two notes in a slurred bow'.[72] There is no certain answer and it is worth experimenting with the options. The clavier version gives a rising chromatic scale implying a crescendo, so a crescendo into the trill is likely.

At the end Bach has a Phrygian cadence, no fermata, and adds the time-signature of the Fuga as a kind of direct at the end of the final stave, implying that the player is to go straight into the Fuga without a break (he does the same at the end of the Adagio of the C major Sonata). It was customary for the prelude to end on the dominant when the fugue subject begins on the dominant note, as happens here, the last note of the prelude putting the note into the mouth, as it were, of the first voice to enter in the fugue.

2. *Fuga*

If the G minor Fuga represents the canzona type, with ¢ time signature, repeated-note subject and four-voice exposition, the A minor represents the type of fugue in a light dance metre, so much cultivated by Bach, so has a light French time signature and a three-voice exposition. A light three-voice texture is suitable for a subject with an octave leap. The time signature is important since it means that the first main accent is the a' at the beginning of bar 2; in ¢-time the first main accent would be the c" at the beginning of bar 3. This subject has been compared to various other A minor subjects of Bach's. Of them, the closest is that of the Prelude of the A minor English Suite BWV 807, which comes close to being its inversion. The combination of fugue and concerto plans is also common to both pieces. A further example that may have been written about the same time is the A minor Fugue in Book I of *The Well-tempered Clavier*. Its subject has the same rhythmic character, and the fugue works systematically through a programme of contrapuntal devices including inversion, as the violin Fuga does.[73] But the clavier fugue has next to no episodes, just a succession of expositions, each concentrating on a particular contrapuntal device, whereas the violin Fuga has substantial, developmental, concerto-style episodes.

Johann Mattheson (1737), in a discussion of fugue subjects, complimented Bach on being able to develop such a substantial fugue out of such a short subject:

> One often finds the most excellent workings-out upon the fewest notes, or shortest fugue subjects, almost as the best sermons can be made on three or four words of text. Who would believe that these eight short notes [Mattheson omits the c" at the end of the subject] would be so fruitful as to bring forth a counterpoint of more than a whole folio of paper, without extraneous extension and quite naturally? And yet the skilled, and in this genre particularly felicitous, Bach in Leipzig has set the following before the world; indeed, he has in addition introduced the subject here and there in inversion.[74]

Mattheson then quotes the first eight notes of the subject, though without the sharp on d". It is not clear what Mattheson saw since he does not mention the most remarkable thing about this fugue, its scoring for solo violin. Since the subject is quoted inaccurately he may have worked from hearsay.[75]

Length does seem to have been an objective here. Mattheson is right about the Fuga spreading over more than a folio ('Bogen'). Where the G minor fugue fits on a single opening in the autograph, the A minor extends over two (with the hard-pressed violinist having to 'V:S: volti presto' in the middle). This is significant, given Bach's careful use of paper and the fact that he can be seen in some other works to be gearing the length of a piece to a single opening. Bach relished setting himself challenges and triumphantly meeting them. It is certainly a challenge to write a piece of this length that is varied, makes structural use of pitch levels, yet is based on a tightly economical motivic network, for an instrument with four strings and a three-octave range. But large expansion of forms was perhaps the single most important new move in music during Bach's lifetime, as the many-sectioned sonata of the seventeenth century gave way to the sonata with three or four substantial movements of the eighteenth. There is a clear progression in the fugues of the Six Solos from the G minor, to the longer A minor, to the C major which is longest of all, perhaps showing that the order of composition was that of their ordering in the autograph.

Apart from this progression towards larger dimensions, there are other strong motivic connections between the three fugues. The leap of a 3rd in the subject of the G minor is used again here, particularly obvious when the A minor subject is inverted (compare bar 25 of the G minor with bar 126 of the A minor). Both subjects also outline three notes of a scale, falling in the g minor, rising in the A minor (outlining a' b' c" in bars 2–3). Mattheson is not correct in saying that the fugue is entirely based on the first eight notes of the subject. The little invertible block from the end of bar 4 to the beginning of bar 7 is just as important, and one might say that the *inventio* of this fugue, from which all is derived, includes all of bars 1–7, rather than just bars 1–2.

Two broad formal principles are in operation here: the concerto ritornello plan, as in the English Suite Preludes, and the binary sonata plan, which we have observed in most pieces. The sonata shape is best to start with for getting a grip on the overall form. Taking the main tonic cadence at bar 280 (before the coda) as effectively the end of the piece, the dominant cadence at bar 137 (just under half-way through) is at the equivalent of the double bar in a binary sonata or dance movement, and gives the harmonic proportion 2:1 as the dividing point, common with Bach in minor-key movements.[76] The usual visit to the relative major is from bar 87, with a main cadence in C major into bar 103. In the second 'strain', the visit to the subdominant comes with the move to the flat side from bar 197 and a main cadence into bar 232. D minor also provides some dramatic moments in the final stages, one of a number of connections between the Fuga and the Grave.

In the combination of fugue and concerto schemes, Bach generally likes to have a substantial 'tutti' paragraph in the tonic to begin with. In the Prelude of the A minor English Suite this is 55 bars long; here it is 45 bars. Within that, he can set up on a smaller scale what can later be developed on a larger scale. The move from less to more is also evident even within this section. The exposition begins with the middle voice of the three, with a tonal answer in the bass at bar 3. The little block of invertible counterpoint in bars 5–7, based on the descending chromatic tetrachord, provides a codetta leading to the cantus entry with the answer in bar 7. As in the G minor fugue, Bach plays on expectations here. Since the exposition ends with the answer we expect the subject proper to enter at any moment, rounding it off. This does not happen until the bass entry at bar 39, which provides the climax of the section and binds it all together in an arch of expectation and fulfilment.

This opening section could in itself be a normal-size binary sonata movement, so prefigures the shape of the whole Fuga. It has a visit to the relative major at bar 13, emphasized by a chord and a new run of sixteenths; a Phrygian cadence into bar 18, where the double bar would be; and subdominant emphasis in bars 35–7. Within that there is a clear strategy of motivic working. The subject introduces a lower auxiliary, and leaps of an octave, 4th and 3rd; the actual countersubject in bar 4 is no more than a four-note cadence figure; the invertible block in bars 5–6 introduces the descending chromatic tetrachord, a new element, and it is clear that this will eventually be combined with other things. All the main ingredients introduced so far are susceptible to both contrapuntal and melodic inversion. Bars 10–12 introduce an upbeat chordal pattern; bar 13 extends the auxiliary sixteenths (inverted in the first three notes of the bar) into a longer run. The cadence preparation in bars 16–17 not only has the auxiliary figure three times (the last as prefix to a trill, showing how even routine ornaments can be brought into the motivic web), but the second half of bar 16 also has a four-note figure which is in effect a sixteenth-note division of the leaping 3rds in the subject, and is used as such later in the fugue. The second half of the section then starts developing these ingredients. The block with the chromatic tetrachord is put end to end with itself in a rising sequence (from bar 18), contrapuntally inverted from bar 24. From bar 30 the sixteenth-note figurations in bars 13–17 are given a more concertante form. It would be unwise not to look closely at these seemingly non-thematic moments for concealed motivic development. First, there is a perceptible line of bass notes from bar 30 to bar 39: a' (bar 30), g' (32), f' (34), e' (35), d' (36–7), d♯' (38), e' (39). Whether by accident or design, this is identical to the harmonic formula noted in bars 1–2 of the Grave. More significant for the Fuga is the line in the top notes: c''' (bar 31), b'' (32), b♭'' (33), a'' (34), which is picked up again at bar 39 and taken down to g♯'' (end of 39), g♮'' and f'' (40), and e'' (41). The chromatic descent therefore extends to form a countersubject for the climactic bass entry of the subject in bar 39, explaining the purpose of the harmonic deformation of the subject here, and revealing that the motivic agenda of bars 30–45 has been to unite these originally separate elements of the exposition.

The second paragraph (to the dominant cadence at bar 73) begins in the style of a concerto solo break, the slow harmonic rhythm and echo effects contributing to the sense of expansiveness. The auxiliary figure is now worked in bariolage, and the descending scale in bar 46 can be derived from the rising scale segment outlined by the subject. Bar 49 is particularly pleasing, having the auxiliary twice recto and once inverso in the space of a single bar. Otherwise, the chromatic quarter notes in the top part in bar 64 make explicit the use of this chromatic figure; and bar 65 introduces a new sixteenth-note diminution of the subject's 3rds. The object of the third paragraph (bars 73–103) is to move to C major. We have a new development of the chromatic block from bar 73, now in a descending sequence, and inverting every time the unit repeats. Just as C major was emphasised in the opening section, so it is here with an entry at bar 81 that extends the leaping 3rds up to g'' in bar 84, and subsequently with tiratas up to b'' at bar 87, all this supported by a rising bass scale from a in bar 82 to g' at bar 87. The importance of C major as a point of arrival is marked by a complete exposition, with an arpeggio decorating the tonal answer in bar 89, and by a bass entry of the subject proper in bar 91, complete with descending chromatic countersubject.

The remainder of this half of the Fuga, to bar 137, returns to a longer stretch of concertante solo style. This is a large expansion of bars 13–17 of the first section. The four-note division of the subject's leaping 3rds is given recto in bar 94 and inverso in bar 95, separated by the inverted auxiliary. It is used in the actual subject in bars 104–5. These two shapes are then treated to the most brilliantly virtuoso rhythmic manipulation from bar 110. Bach sets up a pattern from bar 112 of having the auxiliary motif as notes 3–5 of the bar, though sometimes on top, sometimes in the middle of the texture. But in bars 117–18 he has it not only in notes 3–5 of both bars, but across the barline as well, giving an effect of intensification that is further enhanced in bars 121–3, where it occurs in the usual place, but irregularly, and across the barline as well, with dizzying, destabilising effect.

The Phrygian cadence in A minor at bars 124–5 can hardly be a main marker cadence, and in any case it would be unusual, in terms of this type of fugue, to end a main section with an episode rather than at least one entry. From bar 125 the subject is introduced in inversion and transposed around, but it is not a proper exposition. On the other hand there is a full dominant cadence at bar 137 which corresponds better to the binary mid-point. It is less emphatic than the mid-point cadence in the C major Fuga, but that is a substantially longer piece than this and benefits from a clear structural break. From bar 137 there is a complete exposition, with the subject twice recto and twice inverso in a symmetrical pattern, in accordance with the custom in some binary dances of inverting the principal motif after the double bar.

There is no need to cover every detail of the second half of the fugue. Melodic inversion prevails, in the subject from bar 137, and in the chromatic block from bar 149. The seeming respite from the all-pervasive auxiliary figure in the calm 6ths in bars 157–61 in fact includes its augmentation, while the 6ths themselves link this fugue further to those in G minor and C major. It must be significant that the subdominant colouring towards the end climaxes at bar 257 on the same agonised dominant minor 9th, followed by sighing pairs, that was the crisis of the Grave. Thereafter there are the usual concluding gestures of a dominant pedal (bars 262–4), and the Neapolitan 6th (bars 269–70). The coda from bar 280 begins with what are effectively inverso entries over a tonic pedal, until the harmony swings to D minor at bars 285–6. Here the sensitive melodic sixth degree (f") again unleashes a shower of florid decoration, but one that still manages to include the auxiliary both recto and inverso, as well as decorating a series of rising and falling 3rds.

Every detail of this Fuga is so carefully thought out, and the effects so well placed, that adding ornaments could hardly improve it. The keyboard version is nonetheless worth comparing since it is skilfully done. Some of the additions seem more fussy than enhancing, such as the bass imitation from bar 18, and the *brisé* 6ths in bars 157–61, rather undermining this as a moment of respite from constant sixteenth notes. There are nonetheless some cadential decorations that might be considered.

Bach has written very few slurs, and numerous suggestions have been made.[77] The subject has no slurs until it is inverted at bar 126, but this does not necessarily mean that the slurs should be read back to the beginning. The slurs for the inversion may be part of a programme of varied articulation, since the move to legato is further intensified to fully notated super-legato at bar 130. Bar 66 is the unique occasion when Bach slurred the first two sixteenths of the auxiliary motif, which looks as if it was done without thinking since they are not slurred in the bars before or after. It has to be borne in mind, though, that composers at this time, even when they seem to be taking most care with notation, are always more interested in the total effect than in consistency of every detail.[78]

3. Andante

After such a lengthy and elaborate working of the binary sonata plan, this third movement is just about as simple and straightforward a working of the same plan as it is possible to imagine. Two four-bar phrases, with a half close at bar 4 answered by a full close at bar 8, followed by a brief modulation to the dominant constitute the entire first strain. The second strain continues the four-bar pattern, giving this movement a Lied-like simplicity of structure. Apart from that, the stylistic reference is to a type of Venetian concerto slow movement in which the solo is supported by repeated chords on the upper strings, as is the case in Vivaldi's Op.3 No.7 (arranged by Bach for harpsichord as BWV 972), and the oboe concerto in D minor attributed to Alessandro Marcello (BWV 974). While these two concerto movements are in an abbreviated concerto ritornello form, though, Bach's movement is binary, so there may be another conflation of prototypes (concerto texture in binary form) here. Binary slow movements are common in Vivaldi's sonatas and concertos generally.

The keyboard version is transposed down a 5th so the effect of the solo violin original is changed, and the keyboard's repeated-note bass is down a further octave, probably to fill out the keyboard in a rich, low tessitura. The arranger has also added little comments in an inner part in the manner of the Air from the D major Overture-suite BWV 1068. There are variants in rhythm and ornaments in the keyboard version that violinists might consider for repeats.

In line with its policy of exact note values, NBA has changed the prefix to the trill in bar 25 to ♩♬ from Bach's ♩ ♬ which better represents the free ornamental nature of this standard figure. It is worth noting that there is no fermata at the end of the Andante, suggesting that, like the Presto of the G minor Sonata, the Allegro breaks in suddenly on the reflective mood, and that there may be a tempo relation between the two movements.

4. Allegro

This movement picks up again the concertante style of the episodes in the Fuga. As in the Fuga, the echoes give a sense of expansiveness and large scale, enhanced here by the long stretches of static harmony at the beginnings and ends of strains (see the figured bass digest Ex.3.11). A very lively surface over static harmony is a feature that this movement shares with the Preludio of the E major Partia, perhaps suggesting performance in a largish building such as a church or the hall of a palace, as do, for example, Corelli's very spacious sonatas Op.3 No.12, or Op.5 No.1.[79] The echoes in this Allegro certainly suggest Baroque *trompe l'oreille* if played from a gallery, as does the very unexpected chromatic *piano* ending. This may refer back to the chromatic tetrachord that played such a prominent part in the Fuga. It also provides just the special touch needed to finish such a long and demanding journey as we have made in this Sonata, dying away to the foundation note a that started the Grave and ended the Fuga.

As previously noted, the main conceptual aspect needed to comprehend moto perpetuo pieces of this sort is to sense the underlying harmonic rhythm. A broad grasp of tension levels is vital for projecting Bach's long paragraphs. Thus, from bar 21 onwards is one long dominant pedal which is finally released into tonic at the very end (see Ex.3.11).[80] A performance that makes shapes out of the surface without feeling this tug of the groundswell is missing the point. The underlying principle is of static harmony at the main centres, and more rapid change in transitions. The main harmonic event in the first strain is the confirmation of the dominant modulation in the cadence at bars 13–14. Thus, the first strain starts with four bars of a single chord, then harmonic change at the speed of half-notes (bars 5–6), quarter notes (bars 7–8), quarter notes and eighth notes (bars 9–10), slowing to half notes again at bars 11–12, and with a whole bar of dominant of E minor at bar 13. Similar observations could be made about the second strain, with the addition that the chromatic passage from bar 56 to the middle of 57 needs to be felt as fundamentally a decoration of a tonic pedal.

The Simrock edition (1802) standardised the figure in the second beat of bar 53 to have the 32nds on the second note (♪ ♬ ♪ ♪), and this was followed by BG and most older editions. The autograph is quite definite that they are on the third note, confirmed by the fact that Bach wrote no slur, but did for the figure on the third beat.[81]

Ex.3.11 Allegro of BWV 1003, figured-bass abstract

Partia Seconda BWV 1004

As noted in the discussion of the B minor Partia, each of these suites is of a different type. In the B minor the variation element is prominent in the form of Doubles. In the D minor it is more subtle, and relates to the type of partita in which each dance is a variation on the same theme.[82] The common elements vary between movements in the D minor Partia, generally with first strains using the same type of ingredients, and second strains concentrating on different individual ones. The original *partite* of Frescobaldi, published in the 1610s, were also free in their treatment of common elements. After this more subtle form of variation, the Ciaccona crowns this suite with one of the greatest of all variation movements.

1. *Allemanda*

Having noted the similarity between movement openings in this Partia, it has to be said that there is a strong family resemblance between Bach *soggetti* in D minor, many of which alternate the tonic triad with the diminished 7th on the leading note. The same alternation runs through the French Suite in D minor BWV 812. Perhaps the most useful example to compare with this Allemanda is the subject of the D minor Fugue from Book I of *The Well-tempered Clavier* (Ex.3.12), which may have been written around the same time as this Partia. As we have noted in previous pieces in these Solos, the minor sixth degree (b♭' here) is the most expressively sensitive note of the minor scale, and the D minor Fugue seems designed to demonstrate the character of that interval as expressing sadness, pain, or exclamations.[83] To emphasise the exclamatory quality, Bach has put one of François Couperin's affective ornaments (the 'aspiration') on the b♭' of the subject in the form of a dot, normally used by Bach for emphasis as well as separation. The subject ends on the fifth degree of the scale, giving a curious questioning quality since it implies the Phrygian cadence traditionally used in word setting for questions. The opening of the D minor Allemanda is one of Bach's most original and subtly expressive uses of the diminished 7th, often a tired cliché when directly outlined. By not ending on the outer notes c♯' or b♭', but on e", he has given the same expression of questioning exclamation as the D minor fugue subject. In which case there should not be an accent on the e" (tempting because it is the highest note and dotted, but to be avoided since it is in the weakest part of the bar), but on the c♯', with the rest of the diminished 7th chord lighter and dying away.

Ex.3.12   Subject of the D minor Fugue from Book I of *The Well-tempered Clavier*

Otherwise this Allemanda contrasts with the B minor Allemanda in being German-Italian rather than German-French, and in this respect is similar to the Allemande of the D minor English Suite. The first strain is a classic example of Bach's structural principles in this vein. Allemandes usually have some reference to the typical French two-bar opening phrase. There is a slight feel of this in the first two bars, with a caesura after the e", and a cadence into bar 3. But the music is more continuous than is usual in French style, which normally has clear-cut phrases, and there is no clear phrase ending at the beginning of bar 3. Bach takes the figure in the second half of bar 2, the end of the two-bar opening phrase, and makes it the first unit of a sequence that continues as a modulation to the relative F major: an *enjambement* from the balanced French-type phrase into a sequential Italian-type one. There are nonetheless some elements of French style lurking beneath the continuous sixteenths.[84] The first harmonic accent after the opening is F major in bar 6, part of Bach's usual minor-key scheme of having a visit to the relative major on the way to the dominant. Having the 3rd rather than the tonic on the downbeat of bar 6 makes this a weak phrase ending, similar to the French *coulé de tierce*, and enables the sixteenths to proceed seamlessly. This is an important if momentary point of repose, though, and the phrase ending needs to be felt after the third note (f'). The figured-bass digest (Ex.3.13) shows the sequence in bars 6–7 that achieves the modulation to the dominant. Of the two sharpened notes, the g♯ is the more important since it is the note that makes the modulation, and so is the more accented of the two. As in the Allegro of the A minor Sonata, a feeling for harmonic rhythm is vital for the tension levels of this piece. In bars 9–10 the BG divides the slur that covers the second half of bar 9 and the first half of bar 10 (bar 9 comes at the end of a line in the autograph, but the way Bach has drawn the slur makes clear that it is to be continued into the next line). The point of Bach's long slur is to spin out the tension over a long dominant effect from the middle of bar 9 to the beginning of bar 11, where tension is released into much quicker harmonic movement in the new key of A minor. Dividing the slur could imply a subdominant effect at the beginning of bar 10, a relaxation of tension or even a sort of echo, at a moment which in fact is increasing the tension from the 7th to the much stronger 9th.

Ex.3.13   Allemanda of BWV 1004, figured-bass abstract

Overall there are two scale descents in this strain: one to the dominant 9th (bar 10) and one to the Neapolitan 6th (bar 12). The sequence in bars 11–12 tumbles down the scale until it hits the d' of the Neapolitan 6th in the middle of bar 12. We then have a corresponding bar and a half of tension building, followed by Bach's favourite resolution of the Neapolitan 6th onto a last-inversion dominant 7th (bar 14), with the affective interval of the diminished 3rd (b♭"–g♯") outlined from the end of bar 13 to the beginning of bar 14. There is thus an implied common bass note from the middle of bar 12 to the end of bar 14 (see Ex.3.13). Old methods tell string-bass continuo players to crescendo into a tied subdominant note since it normally becomes the 7th of a dominant 7th after the bar-line, in the strongest and most directional version of the dominant chord.[85] The ability to feel the harmonic tug of this bass note through these two and a half bars is a crucial part of the ability to project this sort of piece in a single compelling sweep, the point of the sonata style with its long, complex phrases. The remainder of the strain is a winding-down of tension, with Bach's favourite tonic pedal effect from half-way through bar 15 to the double bar (see Chapter Two section 7).

Second strains in minor tend to move from the dominant at the double bar, through the tonic to the subdominant. There is therefore a *coulé de tierce* weak ending in D minor in the first beat of bar 18, and a full close in G minor into bar 23. There is another weak ending in F on the third beat of bar 27. As can be seen from Ex.3.13 the chords in the middle of bars 28 and 29 are suspended dominant 7ths, a strong dissonance requiring an accent and a light resolution onto the 5/3.[86]

The notation of triplets at this period can be ambiguous. It normally entails a slur over the three notes plus the number 3, but sometimes it is just the slur. Bach is more consistent in the Allemanda than in the Corrente. But a slur can also be just to indicate that the group is a triplet, without necessarily implying an articulation. A common effect in galant style, particularly in flute music, is to articulate each note of the triplets separately.[87] In the large pedaliter chorale prelude on 'Vater unser' BWV 682 in *Clavier-Übung* III Bach systematically wrote dots over each note of the triplets, meaning separate and with equal emphasis rather than staccato, an articulation that should certainly be borne in mind for pieces in the very galant, Potsdam style of this chorale prelude, such as the Adagio ma non tanto of the E major flute Sonata BWV 1035. Whether it is appropriate at this earlier stage is a matter for experimentation and taste.

2. Corrente

The rubric 'Segue la Courante' at the end of the Allemanda in the autograph is a warning against taking Bach's exact terminology too seriously. This is nonetheless an Italian style of corrente with the character of a triplet division of the Allemanda. Perhaps the triplets here should have a tempo relation to the triplets there.

There are several types of dotted notes in courantes. Sometimes they seem to be just written-out *notes inégales*, not uncommon in German mixed-style repertory such as Graupner's clavier *Partien* (Darmstadt 1718) and some of Schenck's viol Sonatas, but even in French repertory such as the first book of viol pieces by Marais's pupil Jacques Morel (Paris 1709).[88] There is also a more Italianate type with dotted rhythms throughout and the Italian profile of broken chords and sequences, which corresponds more to this Corrente, which would normally imply a sharper dotting than ordinary French *notes inégales*. The general consensus of commentators on this Corrente, though, is in favour of assimilating the dotted notes to the triplets, and that certainly matches its triplet-division nature. Perhaps the most germane piece to compare it with is the last movement of the Fifth Brandenburg Concerto, where Bach in the autograph fair copy (1721) aligns the sixteenth with the third note of the triplet.[89] A similar effect is in the Corrente of the first clavier Partita BWV 825 (published 1726).

The figured-bass digest (Ex.3.14) shows how similar the first strain is to that of the Allemanda. Both have a rounded opening phrase using the same harmonic formula (bars 1–5 in the Corrente), a rising scale pattern (6–11), a series of sharpened notes to get to the dominant (A minor; 13–17), and the bass note of the Neapolitan 6th becoming the 7th of a last-inversion dominant 7th (21–2). Further similarities may be found in the second strains of both pieces. The digest shows internal cadences and phrase endings that are concealed under the moto perpetuo, particularly the important F major cadence into bar 12, and which should provide a point of relaxation. It also shows the agenda of the second strain to develop the feature of accented 7ths on sharpened notes, intensifying to two successive ones in bars 51–2.

Ex.3.14 Corrente of BWV 1004, figured-bass abstract

Related to the harmonic structure is the motivic working. Bach's purposeful and integrated use of triplets, as opposed to their looser, more decorative use by contemporaries such as Telemann and Veracini, are noted in the discussions of the B minor Allemanda, and the E flat major cello Courante.[90] Triplets are more pervasive in this Corrente and are one of only two rhythmic effects, the other being the dotted rhythm, so one would expect significant use of patterns involving the two. A useful comparison is with the E flat major cello Courante (see the commentary in Chapter Four). The opening phrase of the D minor Corrente (four bars) has two contrasting rhythms: triplet in bars 1 and 2; dotted eighth–sixteenth in bars 3 and 4. The technique here, which goes back to the earliest Italian sonatas of the 1620s, is to alternate the two units until you want to build a climax, when you take the more active one and put it end to end with itself in a succession of bars, as Bach does from bars 16–20, building to the highest note of the strain (b♮"). The dizzying, spiralling effect thereafter, filled with melodic dissonance of diminished 3rds and 4ths, down to g♯, the lowest note, is something Bach may have got from the very striking opening of Vivaldi's Op.4 No.8 (*La Stravaganza*, Amsterdam c.1714). But where Vivaldi is interested in the bizarre and surprising, Bach builds the effect into a logical expressive scheme.

3. *Sarabanda*

It is difficult to think of a French sarabande as *navrée* as this one. If the B minor Sarabande is elegiac and processional, the D minor is passionate and tragic. This is due partly to the rhythm, partly to the rich decoration, and partly to the harmonic language. Sarabandes normally have two four-bar phrases in the first strain, the first divided in some way (1+1+2 here) with an off-beat phrase ending, the second straight through with an on-beat phrase ending. The dotted notes (though surely not accents) on the second beats of the first two bars, far from being steady and processional, have the effect of grief-stricken lurching, helped by the diminished 7th at the beginning of bar 2 but also by the two sharply dissonant major 7ths, at the end of bar 3 and the beginning of bar 4. The second of these must be a uniquely tortured use of the *coulé de tierce* weak phrase-ending formula. As in the G minor Adagio, a tirata takes the line up to the sensitive minor sixth degree (b♭') at the beginning of bar 5, supported by the subdominant note in the bass which, as in the Allemanda and Corrente, is held to become the 7th of a last-inversion dominant 7th in bar 6. This and the harmonic formula of the opening four bars are the elements from the preceding movements that are being varied here.

In the second strain there is a more conventional version of the *coulé de tierce* at the beginning of bar 12. Since that is a phrase ending, the b♭" on the second beat is enhanced by, as it were, taking a breath before it. It is not only the sensitive note in this piece, but structurally important in leading the modulation to the subdominant G minor, achieved at bar 16. A yet more elaborately prepared and accented b♭" is in bar 17, leading the phrase that takes us back to D minor. Bars 21–4 are a varied reprise of the metre of the first four bars, but with heightened anguish, partly created by the tension in the half-note chord in bar 21, and partly by the fact that it proceeds to the Neapolitan 6th in bar 25, whose bass note g now stays, not as the seventh of a dominant 7th, but as the 5th of the more dissonant diminished 7th on c♯. The jagged figurations in bars 22–3 and elsewhere are of a type used in the Baroque period to represent tortured anguish: Monteverdi, in the madrigal 'Mentre vaga Angioletta' from his eighth Book (Venice 1638) goes through a useful catalogue of such affective *figurae*, using this sort to demonstrate the words 'ritorti giri' (twisted turns). The *petite reprise* from the second-time bar reinforces the effect in a continuous sixteenth-note division.

In spite of the elaboration, the sarabande's decorative level of note value is still the eighth-note, with sixteenths and 32nds as progressively lighter and freer values. Standard French inequality would be quite out of place, but eighths do need a feeling of on-beats and off-beats, particularly after a dot. A long and heavy b♭' at the end of bar 1 greatly detracts from the force of the diminished 7th chord at the beginning of bar 2. Sensitive rhythmic placing of decorative note values is all-important for the maturity of expression latent in this piece.

4. *Giga*

The Giga continues the variation principle of this Partia, working the common ingredients in yet another way. Not all these were present in the Allemanda, but one principle of variation, and a technique much used from Haydn to Brahms, is to add some new element to an existing one as a way of building up one's material.[91] The Giga starts with a shape we have not had so far, the usual ritornello in its simple form (i.e. without a closing motif as such, see Chapter Two section 5). As can be seen in the figured-bass digest (Ex.3.15) it starts with a balanced two-bar phrase in a closed shape, with a prominent 6/5-chord on the leading note (other movements used the diminished 7th here, though the 6/5 was also prominent later in the Corrente). Then an open-ended circle of 5ths sequence takes us round the key of D minor in bars 3–5, and there is a cadence in bar 5. The dotted eighth note in the middle of bar 5 is Bach's way of writing a full stop: the Allemandes of the first two cello Suites use it for the same purpose. The circle of 5ths sequence did not play a part in the Allemanda, which concentrated on ascending and descending scale sequences, but it made an appearance in the second strain of the Corrente, and now in the Giga becomes a principal element. To the opening ingredients the rest of the Giga adds the rising and falling scale sequences we had in the Allemanda, and a new element of falling thirds (Ex.3.15 bars 8–9 etc). This is the Giga's own new contribution and clearly derives from the arpeggio outline of the first two bars. Another feature of the opening that is very prominently featured throughout the piece is the 6/5–5/3 progression in bar 2, played on notably in the echo passages at bars 10–11 and 25–6. It is combined in a kind of diminution with the circle of 5ths progression in bars 36–7. At bars 37–8 the feel of the harmony is of the Neapolitan 6th resolving onto a last-inversion dominant 7th, a progression that is a kind of signature for this Partia.

Ex.3.15   Giga of BWV 1004, figured-bass abstract

Dörffel in BG, and many other editions, gave the slur in the opening figure over all three eighths, following the very approximate slurring of Anna Magdalena Bach, rather than just over the first two, as in the autograph. Bach's bowing is livelier and springier, and typical of the Baroque style of bowing.[92] Bach's omission of the *forte* at bar 27 is probably not an oversight but an assumption that, after bars 11–12, nobody could possibly think of not returning to *forte* at bar 27.

5. Ciaccona

This is such an achievement, and the subject of profound meditation by the best musical minds over the past three hundred years, that one quails at the prospect of writing about it. There is no point in trying to match it in words, I shall stick to my brief of style and structure from a performer's point of view.

Bach in these Solos frequently conjures up imaginary large-scale forces from a single violin: the concerto in the A minor Fuga and Andante, and the spacious grandeur of organ music in the chords and flourishes of the G minor Adagio or the implied long long-held pedal notes in the E major Preludio. The Ciaccona is perhaps the ultimate Baroque oxymoron, exploiting the tension of opposites inherent in the solitary violin recreating not only social court dance, but the final, or close to final, number of a Lully opera, involving orchestra, chorus, soloists, corps de ballet, in a form that is not conventionally limited but (in theory at any rate) infinitely extensible. The chaconne or passacaglia in the seventeenth century could mean two opposite things: either the individualistic, solo, personally anguished operatic lament; or the suave, rounded, courtly social dance. Bach used both of these expressive associations in his vocal works, the second one notably in the opening chorus of Cantata 78 (1724, a movement with striking similarities of key and motifs to the *Passacaille* from Lully's opera *Armide* of 1686), where the genre represents a social emotion expressed by the whole Church embodied in a four-part chorus.

Within that broad reference, there are many other cross-references. In Lully's terms, the chaconne begins on the second beat while the passacaille begins on the first.[93] So Bach is right for a chaconne in that respect, but Lully's chaconnes are normally in major keys and passacailles in minor ones. In the German tradition, however, the term Ciaccona was used for various types of ground-bass piece. In Italian terms there were two traditional ground basses. The ciaccona bass outline was (in notes of the major scale) 8563451; the passacaglia, in notes of the descending minor scale, 8765, which could also be filled out with chromatic steps by using the major and minor alternatives for the seventh and sixth degrees. By this token, the C minor Passacaglia for organ BWV 582 is more like a ciaccona.[94] One of the most original uses of the ciaccona bass is in Purcell's Chacony Z 730, where its essentially major-key outline is not only put into G minor but also filled with tortured chromatic dissonance. Bach has contrived in a way to combine both basses in the Ciaccona. A version of the actual ciaccona bass is at the beginning, but more obviously at the opening of the D major section (Ex.3.16.m^1).[95] The passacaglia bass in its most usual form is in Ex.3.16.f^2, and with chromatic steps in Ex.3.16.b^1. Terminology was fluid in the German tradition: Georg Muffat changed the title of the Pasagaglia in his *Armonico tributo* (1682) to Ciacona in the revised and expanded version of 1701, changing also the time signature from $\frac{3}{2}$ to $\frac{3}{4}$.[96] Constant fluid and flexible remoulding of a ground bass is as typical of Frescobaldi's keyboard *passacaglie* as it is of Lully's orchestral chaconnes and passacailles. If Bach, in this most virtuoso demonstration of the principle of developing variation, moulds the bass fluidly from chaconne to passacaglia and back it is no more than we would expect, given his exhaustive 'research' of musical materials, genres, and styles.

The descending chromatic tetrachord has an obvious technical advantage for invertible counterpoint in double stops, which no doubt explains its presence as a countersubject in the A minor and C major fugues, and elsewhere. It is an inevitable linking feature within the Solos and between them. Spitta expressed a commonly held view that since the Ciaccona is longer than all the rest of the Partia put together, it is not really part of it, but appended.[97] This view was really the product of the circumstances of nineteenth-century concert giving, where the Ciaccona was normally played as an individual item, and it would not have been advisable to inflict the entire Partia on an audience. The other common nineteenth-century view, voiced by Ferdinand David, that the Solos were essentially for teaching and study, is probably nearer the mark, though not quite in the way that David intended. The *senza basso* pieces fit best into Bach's programme of speculative works, where he is presenting what he considers to be his ultimate versions of things. The intended audience was not a concert public in the modern sense, but more probably what he said on the 1722 title-page of *The Well-tempered Clavier*: for those eager to learn, and for the delight of those already advanced in the art.

The Ciaccona is not separable from the rest of the Partia; it summarises and brings together on a large scale what had previously been specific to individual movements. We have noted that this Partia is in the tradition of the variation partita, but in the broadest sense. It is what in nineteenth-century terms is called 'symphonic variation', where each succeeding variation takes things from what has gone before and adds something of its own. This process in the preceding movements is then summed up and fulfilled in the Ciaccona. The elements can easily be seen from the figured-bass digests for the preceding movements, and these may then be related to the variant forms of bass in the Ciaccona:

Ex.3.16.a: cf. Corrente bars 1–5; for the element of falling 3rds in bars 3–4 of the Ciaccona cf. Giga bars 14–15

b: cf. Sarabanda bars 9–11

c: cf. Allemanda bars 12–15 etc. This progression of a Neapolitan 6th moving to a last-inversion dominant 7th is something of a signature of the Partia, e.g. Corrente bars 21–3, Sarabanda bars 22–3, Giga bars 37–8.

Ex.3.16 Ciaccona of BWV 1004, bass variants: numbers refer to variations (in four-bar units)

e and m: cf. Giga bars 33–4, 36–7
f. cf. Allemanda bars 11–12
g: cf. Sarabanda bars 17–19
n: cf. Giga bars 14–15; this element of falling 3rds is greatly extended in Ciaccona variation 57 (bars 225–8).

No doubt these connections could be pursued further. They are of course standard coinage in Bach's version of the tonal system, which is why he was able to make such discreet and unselfconscious links between movements.

Not least of the large-scale features of the Ciaccona is the range of stylistic references it traverses. The initial reference is to Lully, who used a standard formula for building up the rhythm in this type of piece, that was followed even more systematically by Germans such as Buxtehude and J.C.F. Fischer. Bach follows roughly this pattern for the first ten variations. Lully normally begins with a group of eight-bar phrases in the characteristic chaconne rhythm. Then, to be completely systematic (which he rarely is), the rhythmic build-up consists of eighths in the violins, then in the bass, then anapaest rhythm (♫ ♪) in the violins, then in the bass, then sixteenths in the violins, then in the bass, then a relaxation to the opening rhythm again.[98] The opening eight-bar phrase normally consists of two four-bar phrases, each of which begins in the same way (rather like antecedent-consequent phrases), and the second of which is recast to have a hemiola. A straightforward example is in the F minor Ciaccona by Georg Böhm in the Möller manuscript (Ex.3.17a). Böhm, organist in Lüneburg, is one of the people from whom Bach may have learnt connoisseurship of French style. Bach's Ciaccona does not have a hemiola, but the second phrase is still an intensification of the first. Given that the opening plainly refers to the Lully style of chaconne, the dotted rhythms in variations 3–6 are probably written-out *notes inégales*, just as Bach wrote them out in Cantata 78. They are therefore meant to be closer to a graceful triplet rhythm than to apoplectic goose-stepping. Particularly the isolated eighths in bars 1–3 need to be light, as in the Sarabanda: the notion in some older editions that the chords are meant to be repeated is based on a misunderstanding of Bach's practical notation. The feeling of beginning on the second beat of the bar, rather than the downbeat, is an important feature of the genre, and has the effect of drawing the listener into the unstoppable, mesmeric impetus of the chaconne. The Ciaccona cannot be played at the tempo of a Lully chaconne, but the all-important *allure* of the dance can still be preserved at a slower tempo. Variation 7 moves to the anapaest rhythm. Lully's rule was that, when eighths are mixed with sixteenths, they are all played equally, as Bach has notated them.[99] Variation 8 goes into sixteenths on the division principle, just as Lully would, but now Bach begins to move away from Lully's smooth, stepwise French style into more arpeggio shapes, and specially into a level of melodic dissonance more usual in the operatic lament than in suave courtly style. The diminished 3rd interval in the third beat of bar 31, which has figured so prominently in the preceding movements as part of the signature progression from the Neapolitan 6th to the dominant 7th (Ex.3.16.c), is taken up again in variation 10 where it appears no fewer than four times, twice in bar 39 in a cross-rhythm. It occurs once more in its usual harmonic situation in bars 43–4. The technical control and unerring sense of placing that enables Bach to take a detail of this sort and make it significant is an important factor in the gripping expressive power of this music.

Ex.3.17   Georg Böhm, Ciaccona in F minor: a) bars 1–9

b) bars 25–37

The remainder of the first section (to variation 33) leaves Lully far behind, and moves through the Corellian sonata style of moto-perpetuo sixteenths, to something closer to the German virtuoso tradition of Biber (from variation 17). In variation 16 one might derive the arpeggio pattern from the end of bar 63 to bar 64 from the Sarabanda (bar 6), or the Giga (bar 35), while the 32nds that start to appear in bar 65 have been in the Allemanda. The most extraordinary part of the movement is from variation 21, where directly stated dissonant intervals recall Vivaldi's more bizarre and capricious moments, to variation 22 where ecstatic, dervish-like swirling figures at the highest pitch show how Bach can build in, and control, the irrational as part of his total view. He capitalises on the unifying impetus of the chaconne, that enables him to include such extremes. In the autograph he wrote the word Ciaccona in a curious way, with a circle instead of a capital C, as if this piece is a microcosm that can include a whole world of styles and emotions.[100]

From this mystical height we come down to its opposite in an arpeggiated passage with rational imitations. Lully's chaconnes include trio sections as moments of relaxation between full sections, and the arpeggio episode from variation 23 may be intended to represent one of these. Again a standard version of the effect is in Böhm's Ciaccona (Ex.3.17b), where a three-note figure is treated to a quasi-fugal exposition. The plot of Bach's arpeggio section is similar, with the three-note figure in the bass at variation 24, in the cantus at variation 25, and in the alto at variation 26. It is then treated to two chromatic extensions: as descending paired-note sighs (*Seufzer*) in the cantus of variation 27, inverted as the rising pentachord (used by Lully as an alternative to the descending tetrachord) with chromatic steps in variation 28. This recto/inverso pair of variations is answered by a second pair, with a chromatic inverso in the bass of variation 29 and a diatonic recto in the bass at variation 30. Whether all this can have the effect of a relaxation is arguable, but this group of variations does seem to build up in texture to the return of 32nds in variation 31 and the fully chorded reprise of the opening chaconne rhythm, complete with hemiola in bars 131–2, that ends the section and sets up the sublime contrast of D major.[101]

Many things contribute to the effect of the *maggiore* second section. One of them is the prominence of the interval of the 6th. The expressive importance in these Solos of the sensitive sixth degree of the minor scale has been noted. At the end of the first section, with the return of the chaconne rhythm in variation 32, the opening pair of variations is recast to put the emphatic minor sixth degree b♭" with its wide-spaced G minor chord (bar 128) in the first of the pair (in bar 8 it was in the second of the pair), followed by a declining set of chromatic sighs in variation 33. A large part of the sweetness from variation 34 onwards stems from the predominance of the interval of the major 6th: there are three in variation 34, and another three in variation 35, while this whole group of variations builds up to a climactic major sixth degree (b♮") in variation 37, before going into sixteenths for the next group. The first major 6th (on the second beat of bar 134) is particularly lovely, being the first-inversion of the mediant as a substitute for the dominant, a chord used at this time by Veracini and others, and most effectively by Handel in the variation second movement of his concerto Op.6 No.12.[102] Bach wastes no detail in his pursuit of economy of materials and expressive cogency. At the return to

D minor, variation 52 ends on a bare octave and the first chord of variation 53 is a startling minor 6th with b♭'.

There is no need to go into every detail of the third and final section, except to say that there are correspondences between the second and third sections in that they both involve large-scale pedal effects based on the two middle strings of the violin.[103] Variations 41 to 44 build on this in repeated notes; variation 55 then has a tonic pedal decorated with an auxiliary; and variations 58 to 60 have a dominant pedal in bariolage. In what is perhaps the greatest commentary on this Ciaccona, the Finale of Brahms's Fourth Symphony, Brahms obviously felt the effect of this bariolage to be one of winding down since he uses it for that purpose at bars 69–80 there.[104] The move to triplets at variation 61 is a standard one near the end of variation sets. Finally, in the eight-bar reprise (variations 63–4), the little flourish that starts the concluding hemiola at bar 255 recalls the questioning phrase at the beginning of the Allemanda that opened the whole Partia, and perhaps gives its answer.

Structural aspects of the Ciaccona have been much written about. Various commentators after Spitta have wondered what the actual theme is that is being varied.[105] Though Lully uses a variety of related bass patterns within chaconnes (as Bach does), in his practical, danced chaconnes the most important thing is the *mouvement* of the genre, which includes aspects of tempo, rhythmic character, and the magnetic forward impetus characteristic of this dance, rather than the feeling that a particular theme is being varied. In a way the genre is itself the theme. There is nonetheless Bach's adherence to the Invention principle, where the fundamental material for the whole piece is exposed in the opening bar or so. It has been pointed out that by subtracting the first eight bars as the theme, the remaining four-bar units are roughly in the Golden-Section proportions 31:19:12 between the three sections, by which token the first eight bars constitute the theme and variations start at bar 9.[106] On the other hand, the total number of bars, including the first eight but excluding the last bar, is 256, which is neatly the product of 4^4, in which case variations start at bar 1.[107] Proportions do not work out exactly, and all one can say is that, taking the total number of four-bar units, the proportions 33:19:12 are very roughly in the harmonic proportions 3:2:1, proportions that were commonly used by Bach.[108] Johann Peter Kellner's copy lacks bars 89–120, 126–40, 177–216, 241–4. While this may reflect an earlier version, and has a logic in omitting both of the arpeggio sections (variations 23–30 and 51–2), it is difficult to think that the omission of bars 126–40 is original since it makes for a very awkward transition to D major and picks up the maggiore section in its eighth-note phase.[109]

Many strands of tradition contribute to this Ciaccona, and in order to get a perspective on Bach's achievement it is well worth exploring the hinterland.

Closest to Bach are the organ Ciaconas and Passacaglia of Buxtehude. If the D minor Passacaglia BuxWV 161 has much in common with Bach's C minor Passacaglia BWV 582, the two Ciaconas BuxWV 159 and 160 represent a German version of the rhythmic build-up described above. The G minor Passacaglia in Georg Muffat's *Apparatus music-organisticus* (Salzburg 1690) is often cited as a notable example not only of this, but also of a rondeau structure, though Muffat's refrain is a simple repeat while Bach continually varies and develops his reprises.[110] More typical of the immediate antecedents of Bach's Ciaccona in string repertory is the Ciaccona in the second of Johann Schenck's *Scherzi musicali* for bass viol (Amsterdam 1698). As Bach does, Schenck starts with the usual Lullyesque phrases before going into more soloistic dotted variations, running bass ones, chordal ones, and periodically returns to a simpler movement before beginning the next build-up. In violin repertory Bach is more likely to have known a piece such as the 'Paβacagli' from the sixth of Biber's 1681 *Sonatae* than the fifteenth 'Mystery Sonata'. The Ciacona in Partia 3 of Biber's *Harmonia artificiosa-ariosa* (1696, reprinted Nuremberg 1712) is an excellent example of this genre in the German virtuoso violin tradition. Biber uses a minor-key version of the ciacona bass, in A minor 17♯1563451, of which Bach's 17♯16451 seems to be a condensed version that can also easily relate to the passacaglia bass. In the seventeenth-century manner Biber builds up to a climax of virtuoso figurations in 32nds, via chords, and ends with triplets. The seventeenth-century aesthetic of contrast, and ranging over many manners in separate sections, typically represented in this repertory by J.J. Walther's *Scherzi* (Leipzig and Frankfurt 1676), is where Bach started at the very beginning of his career. He later used many of the same ingredients, but sought to create larger, unified structures as a way of retaining traditional values while moving to new formal principles and expressive possibilities.[111] Virtually every detail of the Ciaccona has antecedents in the rich brew of overlapping traditions that constituted Bach's musical environment. His contribution was to bring them together into an all-encompassing unity that undergirded a new, large-scale expressive power.

Sonata Terza BWV 1005

1. *Adagio*

This is one of the most extraordinary demonstrations of what can be achieved in making a whole piece grow from a tiny cell. Two notes must be the smallest possible unit for this: to start in this way with a single note would give the effect of a mere accompaniment, as in the slow movement of the Alessandro Marcello oboe concerto that Bach arranged for keyboard as BWV 974. In the

Adagio of the Benedetto Marcello C minor concerto (BWV 981), which also begins with repeated notes in a single part and adds an extra part in each succeeding bar, the repeated notes are dotted, which already gives a grouping of two notes, albeit on a single pitch. Bach in the C major Adagio gives character to his two notes by means of the dot and slur.

As so often with Bach, the nature of that character has been subject to a wild variety of interpretations. Spitta has a wonderful purple passage about this Adagio and its keyboard version (BWV 968), and comparisons have ranged from French overtures to the Grail music from *Parsifal*.[112] There is a common type of slow movement, generally in $\frac{3}{2}$-time with the rhythm ♩ ♪ ♩. ♪ ♩. ♪, in ensemble works of Telemann and others around 1710 to which this may have some relation.[113] The slurred auxiliary figure without the dot is the basis of the second movement of the Fourth Brandenburg Concerto, and a similar figure comes in here at bar 5 etc. If one takes a late-Romantic view, the sixteenth-note will not be light, but in terms of *c*.1710 it almost certainly would be, and in fact is often related to the ornament known as the *accent*.[114] This is described by Montéclair as 'a sorrowful raising of the voice, mostly in plaintive airs . . . a sort of sob at the end of a long or accented note, sounding a little the step above the accented note'.[115] As ever, the truth probably lies somewhere between these two extremes and, as with dotted rhythms generally, the degree of dotting, accentuation and lightness is subject to the feeling of the expressive moment.

The 'sorrowful' implication is another remarkable aspect of this piece. Bars 1–3 seem to begin the common four-chord opening formula I II$^{6/4/2}$ V$^{6/5}$ I (see Chapter Two section 7), but the unexpected b♭ in bar 4 pulls the leading note down in the manner of the *lamento* bass. In the very ordinary key of C major, Bach here pursues to a logical extreme his usual tendency to move to the flat side of that key, and the Adagio soon turns to the anguished mood of previous movements in D minor and G minor, a mood reinforced by the left-hand additions in the keyboard version.[116] The mood in this case is nonetheless more elegiac than tragic on account of the steady, processional tread of three quarter notes per bar, as noted in the B minor Sarabande. Flourishes are reserved to mark the closing bars of the two main sections: the cadence in G minor into bar 15, and in C minor (with *tierce de Picardie*) into bar 44. As can be seen from the figured-bass digest (Ex.3.18), the surface elaboration of these closing bars is supported by an increase of chromatic, even enharmonic, harmony (bars 7–15 and 39–45).

As implied by the similarities to Marcello and Telemann movements mentioned above, the reference here is to the concerto, and therein lies another remarkable aspect of this Adagio. Bach treats each string of the violin as a separate voice, or instrument in a string ensemble, with each part coming in on a new string in the first four bars, from the bottom string up. This is matched at the end by each string in turn beginning a little flourish before the final cadence (bars 39–42; e" d' g a'), in the manner of the equivalent recorder flourishes in the slow movement of the Fourth Brandenburg Concerto.

Ex.3.18   Adagio of BWV 1005, figured-bass abstract

The consensus of opinion about who made the keyboard arrangement BWV 968 is more in favour of Bach in this piece than was the case for BVW 964.[117] It certainly makes a remarkable keyboard piece, whose quality was much admired in the older literature, specially considering that the logic of string layout on the violin is lost on the keyboard. As in the arrangement of the A minor Sonata BWV 964, the right hand generally has the original violin part while the left hand adds accompaniments. Symptomatic of the loss in violin logic is the omission in the keyboard version of bar 17. Harmonically, since we are in G minor at this point, one would expect the 7th (g') in bar 16 to resolve onto f#' in bar 17. The f♮' in bar 17 seems on the contrary to be moving away from G minor, but then in bar 18 we get the expected f#' after all, in an effect that is sometimes called 'regressive' harmony. The keyboard version solves this anomaly by omitting bar 17. In the violin original Bach begins this second section (from bar 15) with the same agenda across the strings as at the beginning, with entries of his main motif in successive bars on the G, D, and A strings, giving bar 17 a logical function not present on the keyboard.

As with the A minor Grave, this Adagio ends with the Phrygian cadence. Bach wrote no fermata, but added the ¢ time signature of the Fuga as a kind of direct at the end of the last stave of the Adagio, indicating that the player is to go straight into the Fuga without a break. It was customary, when the prelude ended on the dominant, for the fugue subject to begin on the fifth degree, as happens here.

2. Fuga

This is the longest and most elaborate fugue of the three and has therefore often been seen as a companion to the Ciaccona, as the longest dance movement. Both represent disciplined forms: one a specific contrapuntal genre, the other a variation type. Both are based on the descending tetrachord, implied in its diatonic form by the fugue's subject in bars 1–3 etc., and stated in its chromatic form by the countersubject in bars 4–7 etc. (Ex.3.19). The chromatic tetrachord has already been hinted at in the bass of bars 1–5 and elsewhere in the Adagio (see Ex.3.18), which treats chromatic steps in a strongly expressive way. The Fuga, on the other hand, with its hint of *stile antico*, treats the tetrachord as an expressively neutral building-block in invertible counterpoint.

Ex.3.19 Fuga of BWV 1005, abstract of subject and countersubject

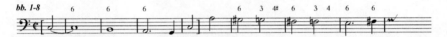

Andreas Moser thought that this fugue was too complicated to have been conceived for solo violin and probably originated as an organ piece. Spitta also took it to be an arrangement of an organ piece, though Schweitzer thought it had little in common with Bach's organ works.[118] There may be some historical justification for the view that it originated on the organ, and Bach did use similar materials in organ fugues, but in fact the fugue is fundamentally conceived in terms of the violin and would need a great deal of recasting, not to say recomposition, to make it idiomatic for the organ.[119] It is not even quite clear how many parts the fugue is in, though the exposition seems to have four entries in the pattern subject–answer–subject–answer (bars 1, 4, 10, and 16). The entry at bar 24 cannot be part of the exposition since it is in F major and forms a pair with the tonic entry at bar 30. The tendency for pieces based on the falling chromatic tetrachord to move to the flat (subdominant) side of the key has been noted in the Adagio, and is a link between this prelude-and-fugue pair of movements.[120] A particularly ingenious implication of four parts, in a passage that does not go beyond the sort of double-stopping common in Corelli's sonatas, is the stretto on the tail of the subject in bars 137–42. All this is in no way to underestimate the technical skill needed for performing this fugue on the violin.

The evidence for an organ original is circumstantial and based on several publications of the Hamburg composer and writer on music, Johann Mattheson. In November 1720 Bach was in Hamburg to take part in a competition for the post of organist at the Jakobikirche. As things turned out, Prince

Leopold apparently summoned him back to Cöthen before the competition took place and Bach evidently withdrew his candidature. The official church account gives no indication that Bach played in Hamburg on that occasion.[121] Later (1728) Mattheson published a vaguely worded description of what seems to be this event, though without mentioning any names. His accusation that the candidate who was finally chosen had bought his way into the post ('was better at preluding with his thalers than with his fingers') in spite of the excellence of 'a certain virtuoso, whose merits have since brought him a handsome Cantorate' (which makes it fairly certain that this virtuoso was Bach), does not seem to have any basis in fact. Mattheson does, however, say that the virtuoso (*sc.* Bach) during that visit to Hamburg played 'on the most various and greatest organs, and aroused universal admiration for his ability', which is likely to be true.[122] Much later (1754), in the obituary for Bach written by C.P.E. Bach and others, there is an account of Bach in Hamburg 'about the year 1722' playing for two hours on the organ of the Catharinenkirche 'to general wonderment'. His programme included a half-hour improvisation on the chorale 'An Wasserflüssen Babylon' in the presence of the very distinguished and aged organist of the church, Johann Adam Reincken, who had written a large-scale chorale fantasia on that melody, a piece that Bach knew well.[123] Reincken died in November 1722 so this event must have taken place before then, perhaps during Bach's 1720 visit to Hamburg.

The possible relevance of all this to the C major Fuga is in a later description by Mattheson of the skills necessary for playing in competitions for organist's posts. In a competition for the post of organist at the Hamburg Domkirche in 1725, Mattheson tells us, one of the tests was to improvise a fugue on a subject and countersubject which he quotes, and which are virtually identical to those of Bach's G minor organ Fugue BWV 542/2.[124] In 1727 a test for the same post had a subject very similar to that of the C major Fuga, though in G major and there is no mention of the violin (Ex.3.20a). Mattheson gives this as an example of an 'easy fugue subject, best played on full organ in such a way that the inner parts also have their share of it, not just the outer ones'. He then gives various combinations, including the chromatic countersubject of Bach's fugue (Ex.3.20b–g). It can be seen that Bach does not use Mattheson's form of the answer (b), nor of the subject inversions (d–e), nor the triple stretto possibility (g).

One important point that Mattheson makes about his subject is that the first eight notes are part of a chorale melody, though he does not say which. The chorale that best corresponds is 'Komm heiliger Geist, Herre Gott' (Ex.3.21a), of which the first phrase is identical to the first eight notes of Mattheson's subject. The fact that Bach's subject may therefore derive from a chorale melody has given rise to large speculations about a religious

Ex.3.20 Johann Mattheson, *Grosse General-Baß-Schule* pp.36–9, subject with possible combinations: a) subject; b) answer; c) with chromatic countersubject, and inversion; d) inverted with different semitones; e) inverted with the same semitones; f) simultaneous recto and inverso; g) triple stretto

programme in the violin Solos. Whatever about Mattheson's subject, Joel Lester has proposed 'An Wasserflüssen Babylon' (Ex.3.21b) as the chorale basis for Bach's subject, on which Bach apparently improvised 'for almost half an hour' before the aged Reincken.[125] Could the C major Fuga be a relic of that improvisation? Mattheson makes no mention of Bach in this discussion, though just before it he does mention a father, whose son was to play for an organist's post, sending his son 'to L— to the famous B—, to prepare him' (a plain reference to Bach in Leipzig).[126] It has nonetheless to be said that both subject and chromatic countersubject, and their combination, are utterly standard materials in this tradition. The classic demonstration of them is in Sweelinck's Fantasia Cromatica, based on a block of triple counterpoint (Ex.3.22a) in which the top part would be identical to the sequence in Bach's subject if the 4th leaps were filled in by steps.[127] Nearer to Bach is a Fugue in D minor by Johann Pachelbel, in which a similar block of counterpoint has the 4th filled in (Ex.3.22b).[128] In these examples, if one imagines the leaps of a 4th also filled in, one can see how suitable this subject is for stretto. That these were standard building blocks for improvisation is shown by the extract from a partimento fugue from Bach's environment (Ex.3.22c) which has both subjects inverso first (without the 4ths filled in) and recto second (with them filled in). Partimento fugues are written mostly as just a single-line figured

Ex.3.21 Cognate chorale melodies: a) Komm, heiliger Geist, Herre Gott

b) An Wasserflüssen Babylon

bass, though with brief passages in two parts (as here) to let the player know the precise shape of subject and countersubject. They were standard teaching material for improvising fugue. As William Renwick says, an organist who had mastered the patterns embodied in these partimenti would have excelled at this part of Mattheson's exam.[129] A fully worked-out fugue by Bach on these materials is the early keyboard Canzona in D minor BWV 588 (Ex.3.22d).[130] But the C major Fuga is not an early work and it is surprising to find Bach using such very ordinary materials in a fugue of around 1720, though he did in his educational works sometimes set out to demonstrate that very ordinary traditional materials still had unsuspected possibilities, and there is a strong speculative element in the violin Solos as a collection.[131] Bach would hardly have used such standard materials in their basic form in a large-scale organ work at this stage of his maturity. At the time when Sweelinck was writing his demonstration Fantasia Cromatica, Monteverdi was showing what highly original and expressive counterpoints could be combined with chromatic steps in the final madrigal ('Piagn' e sospira') of his *Quarto libro dei madrigali* (Venice 1603). Bach himself, in other works, was endlessly inventive of new ways to treat the chromatic tetrachord.[132] Mattheson, when he first quoted this subject and countersubject, was more likely citing common materials for practice in improvisation than remembering a particular work or improvisation of Bach's. The answer to why Bach used them in the violin Solos must be the potential of these materials for working on the violin in double-stopping, as shown by the Gigue of Westhoff's first Suite for violin *senza basso* (1696; Ex.3.22e–f). Here, as at the equivalent point in Bach's Fuga, both subject and countersubject are inverted after the double bar. Bach must assuredly have used these materials in keyboard improvisations, but for a fully composed fugue of his maturity he is more likely to have chosen them specifically because of their suitability for the violin.[133]

Whatever Mattheson knew of Bach's Fuga in 1731, by 1737 he certainly had seen it, or something like it, since he now gives the subject, countersubject, and answer in Bach's form.[134] But he still gives it in G major and with the soprano entry first, followed by the alto, unlike the violin Fuga. Mattheson does not mention Bach here, but does on the next page where he discusses the

Ex.3.22 Traditional counterpoints for the chromatic tetrachord:
a) Jan Pieterszoon Sweelinck, Fantasia Cromatica, bars 21–5

b) Johann Pachelbel, Fugue in D minor, bars 21–3

c) Langloz partimento Fugue 25 in F minor, bars 4–8

d) Bach, organ Canzona in D minor BWV 588, subject and countersubject in bars 15–20

e–f) Johann Paul von Westhoff, Gigue in A minor for unaccompanied violin, beginnings of first and second strains

subject of the Fuga of the A minor Sonata. It is possible that Mattheson knew a G major keyboard version of the C major Fuga—the keyboard version of the Adagio (BWV 968) is in G—or it may be that somebody who knew both his *Grosse General-Baß-Schule* of 1731 and the Bach fugues told him about them. It is likely that Mattheson knew no more than the subjects, and that by hearsay. If he knew the originals it is odd that he does not mention that they are for unaccompanied violin, surely the most remarkable thing about them.

We have already noted that the three fugues in these Sonatas have different types of subject: the G minor a canzona type, the A minor a dance type, and this a kind of *stile antico*. It is hardly strict *stile antico* since it is based on half notes and quarter notes rather than whole notes and half notes, one of the most important identifiers of true *stile antico*. In addition, the leap in the cambiata in the first full bar (a' g' e' f') should strictly not be filled in with an eighth note, and the chromatic tetrachord in the countersubject is a mannered, seventeenth-century feature.[135] Bach rarely wrote in pure *stile antico*, generally preferring to use it in conjunction with some more modern component. There is a seventeenth-century tradition of learned contrapuntal works for keyboard, represented for example by Froberger, where some expressive *moderno* feature such as a dissonant leap in a subject is used in the general context of the emotionally cool *stile antico*. This expressive combination of opposites evidently appealed to Bach, as can be seen in the Fugues in C sharp minor and B flat minor in Book I of *The Well-tempered Clavier*. The chromatic tetrachord fulfils something of that function in the C major Fuga.

Another possible *antico–moderno* combination is of *stile antico*-type fugue with concerto-style solo episodes, as in the third movement of the Fourth Brandenburg Concerto. This is certainly one of the formal elements in the C major Fuga. In the Fourth Brandenburg Concerto, the subject is sometimes brought in by the ripieno instruments underneath the concertante figurations of the solo violin. One of the brilliant effects in the C major Fuga is the way in which Bach counterfeits this effect on a single violin by building the notes of subject and countersubject into the soloistic figurations in the episodes (bars 171–5 etc.). If the concerto element of 'tutti' expositions alternating with 'solo' episodes in a quicker note value is common to all three fugues in these Sonatas, the C major is not only the longest, but also the most complex in its formal combinations. This is the most elaborate of Bach's combinations of fugal and concerto-ritornello principles not only with the binary sonata—the dominant cadence at bar 201 represents the double bar, after which the subject and countersubject are inverted (*al riverso*) just as in Westhoff's binary Gigue—but also with the da capo principle, something he used also in the concerto-style Preludes of the English Suites. Johann Peter Kellner, in his copy (P 804), simply writes the words 'Da Capo' at the equivalent of bar 288, as Bach did in the English Suites.[136] This may reflect an earlier stage of composition since the binary division (bar 201) is roughly at the Golden Section point of the Fuga without the da capo (288 bars).[137] It would not work in the final version since Bach has filled out the texture of the reprise from bars 289–96. The purpose of this is to make the reprise emerge from what has gone before and not be too crudely obvious. In the large-scale da capo fugues he wrote at Leipzig, Bach tended to make the reprise grow out of the final episode as a logical climax (as in the E minor 'Wedge' Fugue for organ BWV 548/2, and the lute Fuga in BWV 998) rather than stopping, then having a literal da capo.

In the following discussion I have for convenience divided the fugue into six sections plus a reprise. This is purely for ease of reference and is not intended to force the piece into a formal straitjacket. The Fuga could be interpreted as: tutti (bars 1–66)—solo (66–92) | tutti (92–165)—solo (165–201) | tutti (201–245)—solo (245–288) | reprise. But Bach is more subtle than that and makes the cadences at the end of tutti sections more final than those at the ends of solo sections, so the pattern could be: tutti | solo—tutti | solo—tutti | solo—reprise. Apart from the binary proportion mentioned above, there does not seem to be any particular numerical proportion between sections, other than that each tutti-solo group is roughly the same length, the second slightly longer, the third slightly shorter (92–109–87 bars, with the reprise 66 bars).[138]

The problem of writing such a long piece, based on an economical amount of material and for an instrument of restricted pitch range (rarely more than three octaves for Bach), is how to maintain impetus and make events significant.[139] Bach has contrived to solve this partly by masterly handling of texture and pitch levels, and partly by a most sophisticated blend of formal prototypes. The virtue of the concerto format in this respect is that the contrast of 'tutti' passages, based on one texture and set of note values, and 'solo' passages, based on another texture and note values, marks out the broad areas. The binary element, emphasised by the inversion of subject and countersubject after the 'double bar' (bar 201), then gives a yet larger division, and the da capo rounds it all off. Within these general formal principles Bach has built large sections with clear objectives and cadential markers.

Each succeeding fugue in the Sonatas has a more complex organisation of its opening section. The G minor Fuga shows that the fundamental model for this section is the usual ritornello shape (see the commentary above). In that fugue the exposition of the four voices corresponds to the character head; there is then a sequential tail that introduces 'solo' figurations; a full-voiced version of the subject, with a chromatic tinge, corresponds to the closing motif; and there is a decorated cadence. The A minor Fuga expands this into a binary dance/sonata shape, with a dominant cadence, after which there is a great deal more development and introduction of new figurations before the tonic cadence that ends the section. The C major, with an opening section of 66 bars, is the most elaborate of the three. As in the A minor Fuga, the C major's exposition contains in compressed form much that will be developed more expansively later in the opening section, and yet more so later in the fugue. The exposition, as already outlined above, has four entries and a dominant cadence at bar 20, as is usual in a regular exposition when the fourth voice has the answer. We would then expect a short codetta to bring the exposition to a close in the tonic, perhaps with a final tonic entry. There is nothing abstruse about this expectation, the plan would have been familiar to every organist who prepared for the tests described by Mattheson, and to anybody else who had gone through the usual figured-bass study with partimento fugues.[140] The expectation gives Bach the opportunity to project expansiveness not only in terms of length, but also in the diversity of figurations he derives from the exposition, and of the tonal ground covered. Before we get to the expected C major entry there is, very unusually, a subdominant entry (F major) at bar 24 that gives the C major entry at bar 30 the effect of being the second of a pair. This leads to a tonic cadence into bar 34 that answers the dominant one at bar 20.

The unusual inclusion of the subdominant at this stage has already been hinted at in the first bars of the Adagio, and is a symptom of the range and scope of the piece to come. It also sets up the first of two tonal axes that are fundamental to this fugue, of the 5ths (G major, F major) on either side of the tonic C major. The subdominant entry therefore balances the dominant answers in the initial exposition. But this is not only an indication of tonal scope, it is the result of Bach's realisation of how rich the implications of the very ordinary subject and countersubject actually are. It can be seen in the answer (in G major, bars 4–7) that the subject, far from being the simple diatonic thing it seemed on its own in bars 1–3, when it is combined with the countersubject ranges unexpectedly widely around the key. Answer and countersubject start three 5ths away from G with E major (bar 5 downbeat; it is actually the dominant of A), then outline two cadences: of D (end of bar 5), and of C (end of bar 6), before the tail of the subject cadences on G (into bar 8; i.e. in G major: V of V, V of IV, V of I). The basic material itself thus balances a cadence on the dominant with one on the subdominant before cadencing on the tonic. When the subject enters in the tonic (bar 10ff) all this is transposed into C, except that the expected cadence on F at the end of bar 12 actually goes to D minor instead (bar 13), and there is a hovering around the triads of D minor and A minor before a strong cadence on D into bar 16. The reason for this is that the answer and countersubject actually start with an implication of A minor (directly in bar 4; represented by its submediant F major in bar 16). This feature is not wasted either, and A minor and D minor are important tonal centres later in the fugue.

Harmonically the chromatic tetrachord can be interpreted in two ways. One is as a series of cadences, as here. The other, simpler, interpretation is as a series of changing 3rds, from major to minor. The first allows Bach to imbue C major, the ultimate diatonic key, with rich chromatic harmony that embraces much of the circle of 5ths. The second yields a composite major-minor mode, containing all the major and minor alternative notes of the scale, therefore most of the semitones. Bach makes dramatic use of this composite mode to extend the final cadence of the section by means of an interrupted cadence to A flat major (bar 62), submediant of C minor. This move is normally associated with the later Haydn and Beethoven, but here it already fulfils the same function of extending tonal range.

In the codetta of his extended exposition (bars 20–3) Bach has begun to break up this material into more aerated and concertante 'solo' figurations. Motivically the pairs of eighth notes are clearly derivable from the subject, while harmonically the series of cadences outlined by the codetta continue the implications of the countersubject. The function of the remainder of the section (bars 34–66) is to expand on elements of the exposition and move towards a more concertante style. Bach first picks up the codetta figure (bars 34–7), which has a chord on the downbeat and something involving eighth notes afterwards, extends the eighth-note element on the division principle (bars 38ff), and introduces a diminution of the dactylic ♩♫ element of the subject (♩♫♩) which will contribute much to the 'solo' character of the episode that follows. This builds up at bar 44ff to a concertante version of the subject and countersubject, based on the codetta's pattern of chord followed by eighth notes. (The a' given by NBA in the chord in bar 48 is a mistake for g', compare bar 336 and the autograph). The concertante dissolution of subject and countersubject into eighth-note figurations will be carried much further in the 'solo' episodes. The codetta pattern is inverted and further developed in bars 52–5, while the 'continuo' passage in bars 57–9, in which the bass is a decorated version of the chromatic countersubject, is a development of the 7–6 suspensions in bars 8–10. All this is supported by a harmonic groundswell whose waves correspond to events in the motivic working. From the point where eighth-note diminutions begin, the bass ascends from a (bar 38) to f' (bar 44), leading up to the climactic C major entry of subject and countersubject for this section. Thereafter the inherently descending nature of subject and countersubject is greatly extended in a long bass scale that descends from f' (bar 44), breaking back an octave from g to f' (bars 48–9), down to g (bar 60), the goal note for the final cadence of the section. These large harmonic shapes are a vital part of the sense of large scale and coherence in the fugue.

Several factors contribute to the sense of contrast and relaxation of the 'solo' episode that constitutes the second section (bars 66–92). Bach had not used arpeggio outlines in the first section until the final cadence in bars 64–5. The zig-zag arpeggios from bar 66 are linked to the opening material by the diminution ♩♫♩ of the subject's dactyl. It is worth noting that Bach does not seem to want any break at the end of the first section since the slur begins on the first note of bar 66 (given correctly in NBA but wrongly beginning on the second note in BG). The texture of single-part arpeggios is freer in effect than the constant multiple stops of the first section. This effect is supported by a broader harmonic rhythm, with a long g pedal (bars 67–72). The goal of this section is A minor, which has in fact been reached in two steps by bar 76. Thereafter there is a bass descent of one note every two bars from e' (bar 78) to a (bar 84), then a faster rise (one note per bar) from a to the dominant pedal on e' (bars 88–92) that prepares the entry of the 'tutti' in A minor. A feature of this section, and one that demonstrates yet again Bach's remorseless exploitation of every element that arises, is his use of the 7♯/5/4/2 chord (i.e. dominant 7th above tonic pedal) in bar 70. It recurs in a sequence every two bars as far as bar 84, then becomes the basis of the rising scale (with g♯' pedal) in bars 84–6, leading to a climactic version as the more dissonant 7♯/6♮/4/2 (i.e. diminished 7th over pedal) at bar 91.

Strange as it may seem, these first two sections are in one sense a mere prolegomenon to the main business of the fugue, which is now worked out in two large 'tutti' sections with two matching 'solo' episodes. The business of these 'tutti' is to 'research' the subjects in terms of contrapuntal devices: the first (from bar 92) in stretto, the second (from bar 201) in melodic inversion. Within that broad plan there are further layers of agenda being worked through. First of all, the key of A minor introduces the second of the two tonal axes, of 3rds on either since of C major (A minor, E minor). This large 'tutti' block accordingly begins in A minor and ends (bar 165) in E minor. On the way there are two main cadences: on G as dominant of C (bar 137), and on D as dominant of G (bar 147). We are therefore moving to the sharp (dominant) side of C major overall. Initially, though, there is a visit to the flat side since the A minor stretto in bars 92–3ff is answered by a stretto in D minor in bars 98–9ff, and so builds on the importance of these two triads in bars 13–16 of the first section. It may be noted, on the way, that the subject in the bass at bar 99 migrates to the middle part half-way through bar 101, a common feature in this fugue and part of the art of fugue for violin. These stretti at the 5th below (*in hypodiapente* to use the learned terminology that delighted Bach in *The Art of Fugue*) are matched towards the end of the section by stretti at the 4th above (*in epidiatessaron*, bars 147–8ff).

A further objective in this third section is the sequential extension of the tail of the subject. The precedent for this is in bars 12–16 of the exposition, and in this section it receives its dramatic development. It begins in the middle part in bar 105, and migrates to the top part in bars 107–8. After several entries of the subject and answer, it is taken up again in the middle part from bar 123. An ingenious compression of head and tail is in the top part from the second half of bar 130, with imitation in the middle part from 133. The dramatic dimension is in the very full-textured tonic entry from bar 135. Most unusually this has a strong half close in the middle of the subject, almost with the effect of a section ending, that leaves the tail suddenly unsupported in mid air in bar 137. This surprising effect brilliantly highlights the ingenious stretto of the tail from bar 148, which, as we have already observed, manages to imply four voices without ever going beyond double stops.

The general shape of the following 'solo' episode (section four) is an arch, from the bottom string (bar 168) to almost the top of Bach's violin compass (e''' in bar 194), subsiding then into the section cadence (bar 201). It is briefer than the first 'solo' episode (section two) and has more active figurations, representing a more rapid rate of chord change, and reflecting the fact that it comes after a yet more strenuous 'tutti' section than the first one. It picks up the zig-zag arpeggios from the first 'solo' episode (bars 165–6) and develops the shape into a rapid rising figure (bars 168–70) with a chord change on every quarter note. The purpose of this is to get from g (bar 168) up to g' (bar 171), which turns out to be the first note of the subject in a complete C major entry of subject and countersubject in, as it were, *style brisé* (bars 171–6; the end of the tail is somewhat sketchy but the main notes are there). This is the end product of the process of aerating the subject in concertante fashion that began with the entry in bar 44 of section one.[141] From e' in bar 176 we carry on up, now yet more actively with chromatic steps, to d" in bar 179, the first note of an equivalent *brisé* entry of subject and countersubject in G major (bars 179–84). If the tail of the subject had been occluded in these *brisé* versions, the purpose of the whole section is to build up to its ultimate extension, when it comes out radiantly over the long pedal d in bars 186–200.

The dominant cadence into bar 201 corresponds to the binary division of the piece, after which subject and countersubject are melodically inverted, as was common in some dances such as allemandes and gigues. The principle of this type of inversion is to take the 3rd of the triad as the axis and rotate around it.[142] This is best seen in the entry in G major from bar 205: if the original subject has the notes 56543 of the scale, the inverted version will have 17123, as here. The first entry (from bar 201) is therefore not the subject in G, as one would expect after such a strong G major cadence, but a sort of tonal answer on C. The first note is d' not c' since it must follow logically from the G major chord before moving into C. The strategy of the entries here is to return to the first tonal axis, of 5ths around C. So we have entries in C major (bar 201), G major (bar 205), and F major (bar 209). There is then a series of imitations that plays on this axis: the figure to be imitated starts in the top part at the end of bar 216 and runs to the beginning of bar 220. During its course it manages to include the leading note of C major (bar 216), the B flat of F major (bar 217), and the F sharp of G major (bar 218). It is imitated in the middle part from the end of bar 219, and in the bass from the end of bar 222.

One further objective in this section is worth noting. The melodic inversion of the chromatic tetrachord lacks one chromatic step (the e' in bar 207 has to be repeated, and the d" in bar 211). A detail such as this is the grit in the oyster for Bach, who makes the whole section work to a climactic, full-textured entry (bar 235) in which all the chromatic steps are present in the bass (bars 235–9).

The last 'solo' episode (section six) provides the ultimate pitch climax of the fugue. The section therefore starts low (bar 245), inverts the zig-zag figuration of bars 165–6, and works up to the pitch climax in two waves. The first moves up from c' (bar 245) to c''' (bar 256, crucial notes are basically the scale notes on the downbeat of each bar), which is the first note of the countersubject (now recto) in a *brisé* entry that runs from the end of bar 255 to 259. Where the equivalent entry from bar 171 was at a low pitch, this corresponding one is at a high pitch and the parts are inverted, i.e. the countersubject is above the subject. From this plateau we ascend in a further wave from c''' to the peak of g''' (bar 263). In spite of being on the weak beat of the bar this note deserves some nuance of emphasis as the extreme pitch of this very long piece. From it we tumble back down to c''' at the end of bar 265, the first note of another *brisé* subject entry, this time in F major (the *brisé* entries in section four had been in C and G, in this section they are in C and F).

The C major Fuga must be one of the very strictest examples according to Marpurg's definition of strict fugue (see Chapter Two section 8). Mattheson, discussing the subject of the A minor Fuga, marvelled at Bach's ability to develop such a substantial piece from such a brief subject. The C major Fuga is even more worthy of admiration in this respect, in the tightness of its motivic working, and in the infinite variety it achieves without ever straying from the subject. Bach's perspicuity in assessing the implications of this combination of subject and countersubject, and his ability to explore its potentialities on every level, make a fugue such as this an object that amply repays long contemplation. Just as Sweelinck found rich developments for the chromatic tetrachord in his Fantasia Cromatica, so Bach has found them here in terms of the tonal system. No wonder that Sweelinck's grand-pupil Reincken congratulated Bach on being the living embodiment of these old traditions.

3. *Largo*

In the scheme of third movements in the Sonatas we have a Siciliana in the style of a trio sonata slow movement (BWV 1001), an Andante in the style of a concerto slow movement (BWV 1003), and this Largo in the style of a solo sonata slow movement (i.e. violin and continuo). The very familiar ciacona-bass outline of the first sentence (to the middle of bar 4) dictates a euphonious, diatonic sound-world, no doubt designed to contrast with the chromatic language of the Fuga, in the relaxed subdominant key. This bass seems to have had a special significance for Bach since it is one of the three themes of the canon he is holding in the Haussmann portrait (see Chapter Two section 7). There it is in the form 87653451; in this Largo it has one extra note. All but one of the movements of Corelli's Op.5 No.10 are based on it, and a comparison with the melodic line of Corelli's Adagio is instructive for Bach's techniques of ornamentation (Corelli gives only the essential melody note over each bass note; Ex.3.23). Bach has exploited the familiarity of the bass formula by setting it off with a rather broken-up melodic line, made coherent by the impetus of the bass.

Ex.3.23   Corelli, Adagio of violin Sonata Op.5 No.10, bars 1–4

After the supreme formal sophistication of the Fuga, the Largo is in a straightforward binary form, with a dominant cadence into bar 8, and a second 'strain' that re-runs the material of the first, with developments, back to the tonic F major at bar 18. On the way the second section visits the subdominant in the form of its relative minor (G minor, bars 10–13, a better key for the violin than B flat since Bach wants to expand the texture to bar 13), and after the section cadence there is a coda with some cadenza features. The extension of the final cadence by means of an interrupted cadence onto a diminished 7th in the middle of bar 20 may link with the similar effect noted in bars 61–3 of the Fuga.

Within this simplicity there is, as one would expect, a great deal of art in the construction of the piece. The first section (to bar 8) seems to have an irregular structure of 3½ bars followed by 4½ bars. The figure in the third beat of bar 4 is the *coulé de tierce* intermediate phrase-ending formula onto the third note of the scale, which is answered by the more final downbeat onto the tonic note of C in bar 8. If one imagines the piece barred in $\frac{2}{4}$, the first sentence would be eight bars in the standard pattern 2 + 2 + 4. There are then two bars which are units in themselves (end of bar 4 to the last beat of bar 5 in Bach's barring), followed by a gradual return to the more regular shapes of the opening. The second section (bars 8–18) continues more or less in a single sweep, in which even the G minor cadence into bar 13 has not the effect of an ending but is the climax of the piece, after which this long phrase subsides in bars 16–17 into a transposition of the closing material of the first section.

The slow movements of the Sonatas are among the best demonstrations of Bach's integration of ornamentation into composition. The ornamental level of note value not only provides the motivic surface, but is indispensable to the expressive force of the music. It is unlikely that a soloist could improvise so cogently and coherently. The most obvious motif is the cambiata figure in the second beat of bar 1 etc. Its inversion provides the accompaniment at the end of bar 4 etc., and as the movement progresses it becomes ever more prominent and expressive. In the first beat of bar 3 the leap of a 3rd is expanded to a 4th, and from the end of bar 9 it decorates what were originally two separate units and grows (from the second half of bar 10), with inversions and expansions of the leap, into the very expressive run of sixteenths that leads up to the climax. It is therefore probably not appropriate to phrase off too much the decorated 4–3 resolutions in the first and third beats of bar 10 since the point here is the development to a longer line. Less obvious is the use of the group of three rising notes (a' b♭' c") in the first beat of bar 1. It takes many forms recto and inverso in bars 2–3, and, as Heinrich Schenker has shown, also provides the basis for larger shapes since the sixteenths from the last beat of bar 3 to the middle of bar 4 outline the three notes f' g' a'.[143]

The main problem of notation in this piece is whether or not to make the slurring uniform. Should the sixteenths in the first beat of bar 14 be slurred as in the third beat of bar 1, or did Bach intend a difference? Should the closing material of the first section (bars 6–7) be articulated differently from when it reappears at the end of the second (bars 16–17), or did Bach think of the slurring when writing bars 16–17 and neglect to go back and enter it in bars 6–7? The answer is by no means clear-cut and there are ways in which variant articulation may reflect underlying subtleties of the music itself. This has been sensitively discussed by John Butt, who makes apt comparisons with Bach's practice of notating bowings in related works.[144]

Allegro assai

This is Bach's only use of the tempo marking Allegro assai in an autograph.[145] According to Quantz, Allegro assai is a general term covering Allegro di molto, Presto etc., so not a moderate but a true Allegro.[146] J.G. Walther (1732), also close to Bach, gives a more nuanced view: for some it means very quick, and for others not too quick, and he sensibly concludes that it is slow or quick as appropriate to the character of the movement.[147] Given the concertante, virtuoso character of this movement it would seem to mean as quick as is brilliant, without glossing over the rhythmic variety and subtlety that lies beneath the stream of sixteenth notes.

Like the Giga of the D minor Partia this movement has a character rhythm at the opening of each strain, and then goes into a moto perpetuo for most of the rest of the movement. As one would expect from Bach's 'invention' principle, the fundamental materials of the movement are given in the first four bars. They are constructed from two basic motifs: the five-note scale at the beginning of bar 1, and the auxiliary figure at the end of bar 4. Figures of the second type are sometimes called 'messanza' since they mix conjunct and disjunct movement.[148] The five-note scale is developed throughout the first four bars. Even in the very first bar it takes three different forms: as a downbeat figure in the first beat, the leap of a 5th in the second beat, and an upbeat figure in the third beat. The whole bar adds up to a triple time with a very light second beat and a rather stronger third beat, a configuration that returns strategically at bars 16–19 etc. In bar 2 the scale is extended upwards, and in bar 4 extended downwards. Bars 5–8 then develop new patterns from the *messanza* figure, the key to which is the fact that the last two beats of bar 8 are an augmentation of the original figure in the last beat of bar 4, which then explains bar 6 as its inversion.[149] Another form of *messanza*, combined with the 'groppo' or turn figure, which also involves auxiliaries, is in bars 5 and 7 etc. The scale principle is further extended in the second strain, finally up to the climactic highest note g''' (bars 88–9), after which the crucial pitches slowly descend scalewise to g' in bar 97. This unusually high passage for Bach picks up again and emphasises (in bars 91–2) the pitch climax of the Fuga.

This movement continues Bach's tendency to emphasise the subdominant side of C major, already noted in the Adagio and Fuga, and in the Largo (whose tonic is F major). Thus the first harmonic accent outside C is on F major in bars 5–8 (see the figured-bass digest in Ex.3.24). The G minor that is the goal of the long pedal from bars 29–40 might also be seen as an accent on the flat side, though Bach quite often accented the minor mode at section ends, a tendency also of Corelli's.[150] The flat side is again represented in the second strain by the very long section in D minor, relative minor of the subdominant, from bars 55–77, representing the subdominant emphasis customary in the second strain of Bach's binary pieces although, as in other places in the violin Solos, one cannot help feeling that the key scheme here has in fact more to do with pitch levels on an instrument with a range restricted to three octaves than to any particular philosophy of key relations.

Any work on this movement should be based on the autograph, NBA, or careful recent editions since the bowings given in BG, and so in many older editions, are almost entirely wrong.

Ex.3.24 Allegro assai of BWV 1005, figured-bass abstract

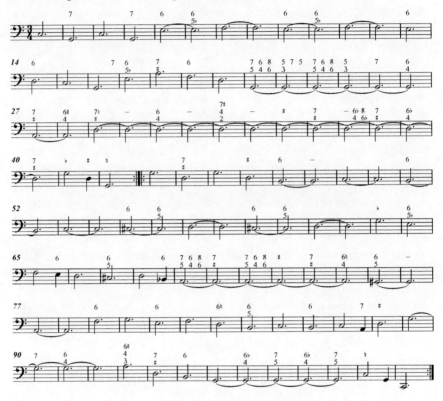

Partia Terza BWV 1006

The E major complements the other two Partias, and completes the cycle of Solos as a whole, in various ways. The B minor, because each movement has a Double, distributes the weight of movements fairly equally throughout. The D minor is end-weighted, the Ciaccona being longer than all the other movements put together. The E major is front-weighted, having the most substantial movement first. It also relates to a different type of suite. The allemande–courante–sarabande type of suite was developed in solo instrumental music in France around the 1620s. The chaconne/passacaille was part of that suite type, but more like a sarabande *en rondeau* than the large-scale orchestral version that Lully developed from the 1670s. The Lully type was that cultivated in ensemble works by German composers such as J.C.F. Fischer from the 1690s, and it is this type that Bach used as the main background reference in the Ciaccona, so including an orchestral-style item in a solo instrumental suite. The Ciaccona nonetheless also includes elements from the German virtuoso solo violin tradition, as well as from Vivaldi, so covers a wide stylistic range. In the E major Partia we move on to the type of ensemble overture-suite of which Telemann wrote a large number in the first two decades of the eighteenth century. In them dances from the solo instrumental suite such as the courante are rare, while dances such as the loure, popularised by post-Lully French composers in the 1690s, notably André Campra, are common.

It is perhaps odd that Bach did not begin this Partia with an overture, since he shows how that can be done on a four-stringed instrument in the C minor cello Suite. In choosing the Italian concerto allegro style instead he may be developing a line of thinking represented in the English Suites for clavier, which have expansive Preludes in the concerto ritornello format. In the German mixed style, the second section of the French overture had in any case often taken the form of a large-scale combination of concerto and fugue. An interim combination may be seen in the Prelude of the G minor English Suite, which has a very brief 'subject', with entries from the treble downwards as is standard in Lully's overtures, but which then develops into the ritornello of a concerto-style movement. Having said that, the E major Preludio is not really a ritornello-type movement either, though a comparison with the orchestral versions shows that there are quasi-tutti and quasi-solo elements. This type of piece has been related to the concept of *perfidia* such as is found in Torelli's concertos, i.e. the rapid alternation of a motivic figuration between two solo violins over a pedal bass.[151] Such passages occur also in Vivaldi's concertos, and we may have here yet another echo of the 'Great Mogul' concerto RV 208 (which Bach arranged for organ as BWV 594). The last movement of that concerto (Allegro in $\frac{3}{4}$-time) has two substantial cadenza-like episodes involving bariolage over a pedal. Bach had already used the concerto ritornello plan in the three large fugues of the Sonatas, and in this Partia he may have wanted something different in concerto style to complement that. The title Preludio does not imply any particular form or genre, so it allowed him to exploit ambiguities.[152] The Italian concerto allegro is at an opposite stylistic pole from the dances of the overture-suite, and this contrast seems to have appealed to Bach. He later used this modern-style Preludio, arranged for organ and orchestra, in Cantata 29 to introduce a *stile antico* choral fugue.[153]

The overall pattern of the Partia is of pairs of movements, with a progression of time-signatures: Preludio ($\frac{3}{4}$) and a slow dance (in $\frac{6}{4}$ time); two moderate dances ($\mathbf{\phi}$ and $\frac{3}{4}$); and two fast dances (2 and $\frac{6}{8}$).

1. *Preludio*

This movement is yet another example of Bach's fascination for suggesting large scale on a single small instrument with four strings, thereby expressing a fundamental paradox in the nature of the violin. We have seen this worked out in different ways in the Ciaccona and in the C major Fuga, and although this Preludio may seem to be a very different type of piece in fact the objective is the same. One facet of the suggestion of scale is the concerto reference. Another, noted in the Adagio of the G minor Sonata, is the reference to the organ, in particular to long-held pedal notes, implying a large instrument and building. This can be an actual held bass note on the organ pedal-board, as in the organ Fantasia BWV 542/1 (cited in Ex.3.1), or it can be implied by pedalised pitches in upper parts, as in the opening section of the G major *Pièce d'orgue* BWV 572, or in this Preludio. Apart from this organ reference, there are plenty of violin antecedents for similar effects in the *da chiesa* tradition, for example in the opening movements of Corelli's Sonatas Op.3 No.12 and Op.5 No.1, or in the German violin tradition in the A major Sonata from Biber's 1681 *Sonatae* (Appendix 1).[154] These string examples show that the manner is flexible and athletic, though the harmony is static, and that spaciousness in no way implies heaviness. In violin terms, the pedal effects are in long sections of bariolage based on the top two strings. In this we may see, over the Solos as a whole, a progression from darkness to light, from the G minor Sonata with its tonic and dominant as the bottom two open strings, to the E major with its tonic and subdominant as the top two.[155] Within this Preludio the desire to use the E string and A string as pedal notes may well have dictated both the ambiguity of genre and the unusual key scheme, with its heavy emphasis on the subdominant A major. As the figured-bass abstract shows (Ex.3.25), almost half the movement (62 of 138 bars) is taken up with pedal effects on E or A (the numbers in boxes are the number of bars on a pedal note; dotted whole notes represent two bars).

Ex.3.25   Preludio of BWV 1006, figured-bass abstract

The way in which Bach has exploited this objective is no less magnificent than his achievements in the Ciaccona or the C major Fuga. The very long E major opening pedal of 32 bars not only gives the desired sense of spaciousness, it is also bound ultimately to sound as if it is a dominant, rather like the Prelude to *Das Rheingold*. But instead of resolving onto A, it suddenly switches at bar 33 to the unexpected and remote key of C sharp major. This has the effect of greatly increasing the sense of spaciousness, like walking from one large hall of a palace into another. The effect is somewhat weakened in the Sinfonia of Cantata 29 since the added bass smoothes over the transition, though something of the frisson is preserved by the orchestral strings suddenly having a 'halo' effect of sustained chords. C sharp major functions as dominant of F sharp minor (relative minor of A major), but before we get to A major itself at bar 59 there is another long pedal on the dominant of C sharp (bars 39–50; G sharp as the 3rd above E balances C sharp as the 3rd below). This play on key expectations, and the delay in fulfilling them, greatly enhances the grandeur and sophistication of this movement at the same time as ensuring its coherence. For most of the movement the dominant B major is conspicuously absent. When it does eventually come as the goal of a cadential progression (bars 111–13) it immediately slips off to A again (bars 113–16), and does not arrive properly till bar 120.

This is another movement, like the D minor Giga, in which the character rhythm is limited to the opening bars and the rest is a moto perpetuo of sixteenths. Although there is no tempo indication, it is clearly allegro. Nevertheless, like the D minor Giga and the C major Allegro assai, it should not be so fast as to gloss over its variety of voices and metrical units. It is worth looking at the orchestration of the Sinfonia of Cantata 29 in order to see what the various areas and figurations suggested to Bach himself.[156] In the organ arrangement he dispenses with the *forte–piano* contrasts, but uses trumpets and timpani to give the effect of a tutti. On this basis, the material from bars 1–12 counts as tutti, and the bariolage passages generally count as solos. There are fundamentally two elements in the opening (as in the C major Allegro assai): the *messanza* figure in bar 3, which later develops into bariolage; and the scale figures in bar 4, which are essentially a division decoration of the arpeggios in bars 1–2. The orchestration of the opening bars (Ex.3.26) suggests that the *messanza* figure counts as solo, as indeed it turns out to be in most of the bariolage passages, and that the scale figure counts as tutti, as it is at bar 51ff and elsewhere. This distinction reveals that the equivalent tutti figure at bar 29ff is in fact an inversion of the scale figure. The use of short chords on the trumpets here makes the change of texture to sustained string chords for the C sharp major at bar 33ff particularly striking (the effect is repeated for C sharp major at bar 90ff). The figuration at bar 39ff, and the

Ex.3.26   Sinfonia of BWV 29, bars 1–11

equivalent at bar 102ff, is over a sustained bass pedal. At the long-delayed arrival at B major in bar 113 the trumpets begin a *Bebung* pattern normally used by Bach for a crescendo build-up, and from the final arrival at E major in bar 129 they play continuous lines for the only time in the movement.[157]

Both the Sinfonia of Cantata 29 and the arrangement in BWV 1006a begin with a downbeat chord or bass note in bar 1. BWV 1006a/1 also adds an extra bar so that the whole piece ends on a downbeat. All this emphasises the fact that the original violin version not only ends *ex abrupto*, with a short note and rest on the third beat and a fermata over the final bar-line, but begins *ex abrupto* as well.[158]

2. Loure

It may seem odd to pair this movement with the Preludio, they are such opposites, but that is in fact the point of the pairing. The Preludio represents the solo virtuoso Italian sonata/concerto style, the Loure the highly articulate and rhythmically profiled French dance style. The difference in playing technique is explained by Georg Muffat (1698), who gives two bowings for a minuet (Ex.3.27), one bowed out in alternate bows in the fluent Italian style, one with retakes, to ensure down-bows on main beats, in the 'lifted' French style. This is the only dance in the Partia that lacks any hint of Italianate sonata/concertante admixture.

Ex.3.27   Georg Muffat, bowings for a Menuet: a) Italian style

b) French style

The loure was one of the most fashionable dances in the first decades of the eighteenth century. As is often the case, it was the success of one particular example that set the fashion, in this case the loure *Aimable vainqueur* from André Campra's *Hésione* (Paris 1700; Ex.3.28), which was still being danced up to the 1770s. It has been described as 'a unique blend of gently expressed nobility, tenderness, and tranquillity', and this description seems appropriate also to Bach's Loure.[159] Matteson in 1713 testifies to the fashionability of the loure in Germany ('jetzund sehr *en vogue*'), and adds the important points that it is a type of slow gigue, and that the many dotted notes are over-held ('die *Puncta* wol ausgehalten').[160] This means that the dotted rhythms have the usual *inégal* lilt, noted also in the Siciliana of the G minor Sonata. In bars 6–7 Bach has written the appoggiaturas as full quarter notes because that is how he wanted them played. If he wrote them in the usual way as small eighth-note graces there is a danger of their being played too short. As the notation works out, in the rhythms ♩ ♪♫ ♩ ♩ and ♩. ♪♩ the eighth note and sixteenth note are clearly meant to have the same value, neither of which is exactly as written, but both coincide in the triplet feeling of *notes inégales*. This tallies with numerous other loures where ♩. ♪♩ has occasionally to coincide with ♩. ♫ ♩. ♫ in written-out *notes inégales*.

Ex.3.28   Campra, Loure 'Aimable vainqueur', bars 1–4

As usual, contemporary descriptions give wildly opposing characters. On one hand the loure is similar to the musette, i.e. of rustic character (Brossard 1705), on the other it is 'proud and arrogant' ('ein stoltzes und aufgeblasenes Wesen') and therefore beloved by Spaniards (Mattheson 1739). Variety of character is also apparent in examples, and the precise character of each one must be worked out within this spectrum. A crucial factor for the dance character is that quarter notes are lifted (i.e. slightly separated), as in the courante.[161] The suggestion by some writers that the trill in bar 1 should have a turn at the end, linking it to the following quarter, is against that character. In the Loure of Bach's G major French Suite the main sources have dots over the three quarter notes that lead up to the final chord of each strain, implying not only separation but also a certain weight on each one ('gravitätisch', as J.G. Walther says).

Given that this is in the purest French style, it is rather bare of essential ornaments. In the (lute?) arrangement that Bach made (BWV 1006a) he included numerous extra ornaments, perhaps because the person who commissioned the arrangement asked for suggestions.[162] In Ex.3.29 I have incorporated these into bars 1–4 of the violin version. In bar 10, Bach's re-notation of the first beat as ♪♩. ♪♩. ♪ clarifies the rather curious ♪♩. ♪♩♪ of the violin version, and there are other rhythmic variants elsewhere. A violinist wishing to vary the repeats could well consider this alternative version of the Partia.

Ex.3.29   Loure of BWV 1006, bars 1–4, with ornaments from BWV 1006a

3. Gavotte en Rondeaux

This and the Menuets form a pair (duple time/triple time) of moderate-speed dances. The Gavotte consists of a refrain and four couplets, and in this respect is similar to the last movement of the E major Violin Concerto BWV 1042, also a nine-fold rondeau.[163] The essence is for the couplets to have contrasting characters, yet develop facets of the refrain. The refrain (bars 1–8) is a neat example of one of Corelli's ways of mixing dance and sonata: to have the first half of a phrase in dance style and the second in sonata style (see Chapter Two section 2), and this is what happens in the first four bars. The neat feature is that the second four bars (the consequent) reverses the pattern and has the first half as an eighth-note division of the original dance rhythm and the second half back in the dance rhythm. The first couplet (bars 9–16) repeats this pattern, though with the eighth-note movement extended further into the second phrase. The second couplet (bars 24–40) takes the two 5ths from the refrain (e'–b' and b–f♯') and works them as drones, musette-style, in bars 25–6 and 29–30. It continues by taking the 7th, the defining interval of this movement, and plays on that as a drone (bars 32–6). The third couplet (bars 48–64) takes further the tendency of the first couplet to dissolve the dance rhythm into continuous eighths; and the fourth couplet (bars 72–92), after reversing the dactyl of the refrain (♩♪♪) to an anapaest (♪♪♩), as Bach also did in the second Gavotte of the D major Overture-suite BWV 1068, returns to the drone/pedal and develops it in the manner of a solo episode in a Vivaldi concerto, with the characteristic expansiveness expressed in slow harmonic rhythm and long slurs. The increasing length of the couplets (8–16–16–20 bars) reflects their increasing elaboration, and the development of eighth-note figurations from one couplet to the next repays study.[164]

Prominently featured is the 7–6 suspension/appoggiatura, common in solo violin music. A comparison with a contemporary movement based on the 7–6, such as the 'Bouré' of Vilsmaÿr's Partia V, highlights Bach's extraordinary ability to make every detail of his material significant by uniting the surface to the fundamental structure in successive layers. Rather than using the 7–6 in the ordinary way as a sequential formula, Bach has concentrated on the 7th as a characteristic sonority. The most prominent note in the first four bars is therefore a" at the beginning of bar 2, the fourth degree of the scale and the 7th of the dominant 7th.[165] The first two bass notes leap upwards from e' to a', and bars 3–4 fill in this interval with a descent of four notes (a" g#" f#" e"). This outline of the upward leap of a 4th and four steps down is an important building block in the Gavotte. It provides the first five bass notes of the first couplet (bars 8½–10), and the outline of the lowest notes in the second couplet (bars 25–8), transposed up into B major (the dominant, and goal of this couplet) in bars 29–32. A particularly neat touch is that the typical *coulé de tierce* phrase-ending formula of four steps down, slurred in pairs, at the beginning of bar 32, is a diminution of it. This intermediate phrase ending marks the end of the first half of the couplet; the second half concentrates on the fourth degree of B major (e") as its dominant 7th, with a final cadence in B (into bar 40). The third couplet fills in the upward leap of a 4th with steps (e' f#' g#' a' in bars 48½–50), so inverting the four steps down, and answers this with the four steps recto in F sharp minor (the goal key of this couplet) in bars 60½–62 (b' a' g#' f#'). The four steps upwards are again in E major as the lowest notes in bars 74½–76, answered in G sharp minor (the goal of this couplet) in bars 80½–82. Like the Preludio, the Gavotte has an axis of thirds around the tonic E major, with C sharp minor as the key of the first couplet and G sharp minor the key of the last, but the other two couplets have their roots a 4th apart (B major and F sharp minor).[166] In this way the characteristic sonority of the 7th in bar 2, emphasising the fourth note of the scale, provides a structural link that runs through all aspects of the piece.

The Gavotte does not offer much scope for extra essential ornamentation, and there are few extra ornaments in BWV 1006a. The trill at the beginning of bar 1 of the refrain is replaced by an eighth-note grace each time, and a trill is added to the g#" in the second half of bar 63. NBA has silently changed a couple of the bowings.[167] The slur in the first half of bar 33 should be over the first three notes only. It was changed to four notes presumably because of the assumption that the e" would have to be held, but few would now take such a literal view of Bach's notation in double stops. In the second half of bar 38 Bach made a correction, and what he wrote could be taken as two slurs (as in NBA), or as a slur over the first two notes extended to cover the f#", or to cover all four notes. The options are there to choose from in a bowing strategy. NBA also omits the unique fingerings in the autograph fair copy in bar 33: 3 on the e" and 1 on f#' (i.e. not to use the open E string; the fingerings are given in BG). Georg von Dadelsen thought that these are definitely by Bach, though others have been less certain.[168]

4. Menuets

Although there is not the usual 'da capo' instruction at the end of Menuet II, Menuet I is clearly intended to be repeated 'da capo' after Menuet II. Not only do the Gavotte and Menuets form a pair of duple-time/triple-time movements, but they also complement each other formally as rondeau/da capo structures in that there are not two gavottes but one 'Gavotte en rondeaux'. This is in line with Bach's policy of providing variety of types in his suite collections.

The combination of a courtly dance (Menuet I) with a rustic, musette-style one (Menuet II) is a common one with Bach.[169] Menuet II in itself alternates musette and sonata style. In spite of its seeming simplicity after the Gavotte en Rondeaux, Menuet I is in fact a sophisticated working of the minuet genre. Part of the sophistication comes from the variety of phrase units, including two unusually extended six-bar phrases (bars 12–18, 29–34). Another part is the function and use made of sonata/division eighth-note passages. The melodic outline of the first two bars is of a falling 3rd g#" to e", supported by a corresponding bass e" to c#". This progression is treated to an eighth-note variation in the eight-bar sonata-style return from C sharp minor to E major in bars 19–26: in bars 19–23, the first note of each two bars is g#' f#' e', with the e' supported by c#' to confirm that the figuration in bar 23 is C sharp minor as submediant of E major, as in bar 2. After the reprise of the first two bars (bars 27–8) the consequent of the first strain (bars 4–8) is treated to a six-bar sonata-style extension, adapted to cadence on the tonic (bars 29–34). This time the bowing of the eighths gives the typical minuet shifting accents:

| ♩ ♩ | ♩ ♩ | .[170]

Arnold Dolmetsch, following Quantz, suggested that the appoggiatura in bar 12 of Menuet I should be two beats long. One could argue that the appoggiatura in bar 2 etc. of Menuet II should be a quarter, corresponding to the last two beats of bar 4, but given the prevalence of paired eighths in this musette style, an eighth-note interpretation seems more likely to be intended.[171] Menuet I should be repeated after Menuet II since Bach has marked some pairs of this type 'alternativement'.

5. *Bourée*

The Partia finishes with a pair of fast dances. There is also a perceptible progression through the Partia from the purely dance-style Loure, via the mixed-style Gavotte-Menuet pair, to two movements in which the sonata style has virtually taken over from the dance. Sol Babitz's suggestion of *notes inégales* for this Bourée is therefore *mal à propos*.[172] Only the first four bars of the first strain, and the first two of the second, are in dance rhythm. The merest hint at the end of bar 32–3 neatly underlines the final reprise. The rest is in constant eighths, complete with concertante echoes. As usual the stream of notes of a single value overlies a variety of metric units, though this is not as complex as in the Double of the Tempo di Borea of BWV 1002.

The bowing in bar 12 of the autograph is problematic. The slur ends on the second last note, a pattern which should probably be read back to bar 10 also, otherwise the echo will have a different bowing from that which it echoes.[173]

6. *Gigue*

The Gigue completes the gradual return to the concertante style of the Preludio. Like the Bourée it has a predominance of long phrases in sonata/concertante style, based on a single note value, rather than shorter dance phrases. The echoes common to both Bourée and Gigue are also a link to the Preludio, as is the subdominant (A major) emphasis in both strains of the Gigue. As may be seen in Bach's own harmonized version in BWV 1006a, the first strain begins with a four-bar balanced phrase to establish the rhythmic character, and then has a single long phrase to the end of the strain. This corresponds to the sonata version of the common ritornello shape, with a sequence modulating to the dominant and a closing area with a pedal. The second strain has a half close on the dominant of F sharp minor at bar 20, a full close in the subdominant A major at bar 24, and ends with an equivalent sequence and pedal to those in the first strain. As often in these motoric movements, Bach uses a dotted eighth note as a punctuation mark (bar 4). This is a weak-beat phrase ending, with the goal of the phrase on the downbeat g♯', not the upbeat e'.[174] In the half close at bar 20 the phrase ends on c♯": the last eighth g#" is the upbeat to the next phrase, corresponding to the upbeats to bars 1 and 25.

This movement is an excellently clear example of the relation of surface decoration to structural function, and also for the importance of understanding harmonic structure in order to project tension levels. After the oscillation between E and A in bar 5, reinforced by its echo in bar 6, we expect the pattern to be repeated in bars 7–8 between B and E, with bar 8 an echo repeat of bar 7. But bar 8 turns out to be the first unit in a circle of 5ths sequence that modulates to B. Bach therefore expresses this change of function by switching from the oscillation pattern in bar 7 to the sequence pattern in bar 8. The change of function is emphasized in BWV 1006a by a change to a markedly new rhythmic pattern in the bass.

There is a bowing question in the autograph here similar to that in the Bourée. In the second half of bar 12 Bach ends the slur on the second last note, but in the second half of bar 28 it covers all six notes. NBA has the slur covering all six notes in both cases, though it could equally have been the intention to cover only five notes in both cases.

CHAPTER FOUR

The *6 Suites* for Cello BWV 1007–1012

Suite 1 in G major BWV 1007

1. *Prelude*

This Prelude has often been compared with the C major Prelude in Book I of *The Well-tempered Clavier*. They both belong to a tradition of broken-chord preludes/toccatas (various names have been used) that can be traced back to Italian lute and theorbo toccatas at the beginning of the seventeenth century.[1] The similarities are obvious, but the comparison is useful for showing what these Preludes have in common in their purpose and structure, and even more so for defining the individuality of this cello Prelude.

One function of the prelude as a genre was as an improvisation to introduce composed music such as dances, or to set the key for concerted music in church. In Bach's notes for the order of service in Leipzig in 1723, he begins by improvising ('*praeludi*ret') before the concerted music begins ('*musici*ret').[2] Such improvisations traditionally had two standard harmonic ingredients: scale sequences and pedal notes, and these are precisely the ingredients in the C major Prelude of Book I. The cello Prelude lacks the scale sequences, but exploits the pedal element with a great deal more sophistication. If the term prelude originally implied improvisation, the purpose of notating preludes was for instruction, both for models of improvisation and for instrumental technique. So, just as the first unaccompanied cello pieces, the *Ricercari* of Domenico Gabrielli, contain all sorts of situations that are common in continuo playing (see Chapter One section 3), in the same way Bach's cello Preludes may be partly intended to fulfil the same preparatory function. For example, the figuration in bar 1 might be seen as relating to the 'wave' motif Bach uses in cantatas.[3] The similarity of figurations in this Prelude to the (fragmentary) 'Pedal-Exercitium' BWV 598 for organ also points to an étude function, a function common in unaccompanied string music.[4] It is possible that the striking chromatic scale over a pedal, that builds to the climax of the

Prelude and brilliantly exploits the genius of the cello for wide leaps, first occurred to Bach as an organ pedal effect.

This Prelude is an extraordinary and classic example of Bach's ability to make his material grow from the inherent nature of an instrument, from the smallest motifs to the broadest structures. The open strings are crucial in this key since they provide the four most closely related key centres (tonic, dominant, subdominant, and dominant of the dominant). The use of the G and D strings as pedal notes is obvious (see the figured-bass abstract Ex.4.1). The A string functions as the 5th of a D pedal in the bariolage passage (bars 31–6). Most ingenious is the use of the C string, which seems to dictate the entire harmonic structure of the Prelude. Its most obvious use would be as the subdominant root, but in this Prelude the subdominant key is conspicuous by its absence. There is also a certain coyness about modulating to the dominant. After the opening four-bar pedal in G we are clearly meant to feel a pull towards D (as dominant) in the E minor triads in bars 5 and 8. Using E as chord vi in G, changing to chord ii in D, is one of the commonest ways of modulating to the dominant, so the E minor in bar 5 and the dominant 7th of D in bar 6, repeated in bars 8–10, seem to give a strong modulation. But Bach immediately cancels this with a move to A minor (chord ii in G) in bars 11–12, the c♮ in bar 12 countering any feeling of D major. Bars 16–19 are back in G repeating the opening formula, which leads us to expect that the low C♯ in bar 20 will finally get us to a pedal D, as the previous c♯ in bar 6 had failed to do. Instead, and most dramatically, the bass does not go up to D, but down to C♮, so when the open C string finally comes it is not as the subdominant, but as the 7th of the dominant 7th in its most dissonant inversion (6/4/2). This gives the C a very strong feeling that it must resolve downwards, which of course is impossible on the cello. Nonetheless, the feeling of gravitational

Ex.4.1   Prelude of BWV 1007, figured-bass abstract

pull runs all through bars 21–5 until the resolution finally comes two octaves higher than expected (b, and the rest of the chord of G major) in the second half of bar 25. Bach exploits the drama of the situation with wide pitch range and a fermata in bar 22, followed by a cadenza-like passage until the long-awaited modulation to D is finally achieved in bar 28.[5]

Bach articulates this harmonic strategy with a highly purposeful use of texture. The relaxed, open texture of the beginning gradually contracts to its tightest spacing in bar 11, the most dissonant chord so far and the diminished 7th that pulls away from D to A minor, before opening out again to the texture of the beginning at bars 18–19. The return to the opening four-bar harmonic formula in bars 16–19 articulates the structure of the Prelude as being in two sections, the second of which (from bar 16) greatly expands on elements of the first. Thus the C♯ in bar 20 corresponds to the c♯ in bar 6. The manipulation of texture is also more extreme in the second section, since in the bariolage it contracts to a series of repeated notes involving the A string in bars 33–6, before expanding spectacularly to the climactic 6/4 chord (bar 39) and a transfigured version of the opening four-bar formula. Here and throughout the Prelude tension levels are matched by the degree of strenuousness required in playing the instrument, just as in one of Bach's large canonic organ chorale preludes one's whole physical being, including feet, is engaged in realising an intellectual and emotional concept.

Manipulation of motifs also plays a part in the dramatic argument of the Prelude. There are two longer scales, both of which have particularly expressive notes as their goal. The first (bar 19) runs down to the low C♯ (extending the scale that ran down to F♯ in bar 14). The second (bars 22–3) correspondingly runs up, more dramatically since it breaks back twice to heighten the effect, to e♭'. This has nothing to do with C minor, but is part of one of Bach's most expressive chords, the dominant minor 9th, made here more sophisticated than usual by being over the implied last inversion of a dominant 7th.[6]

Most unusually in these Suites, the fermata at the end is over the final chord, rather than over the double bar-line. This is presumably because the climax comes right at the end of the piece in the last four bars, and the final chord needs to be dwelt on since it is the goal of it all.

2. Allemande

The Allemande uses much the same materials as the Prelude, yet provides a foil and complement to it. Both start with the same chord, but whereas the Prelude continues with broken chords, the Allemande draws it out into scales, which the Prelude uses only sparingly. As one would expect, scales then become an important structural unit in the Allemande (see the figured-bass abstract Ex.4.2a), whereas pedal effects had been the main structural unit in the Prelude The smoothness of scales is matched by a predominant sonority of euphonious 3rds, 6ths and 10ths, and indeed one could express the first strain entirely in terms of those intervals (Ex.4.2b). The concentration on 3rds also accounts for the prominence of 7th chords, being agglomerations of 3rds (7th outlines are notably in bars 7, 13, 25–29, and in the final bar of each strain). Smoothness and fluency are also implied by the ¢ time signature (the time-signature of allemandes is normally c), with two beats per bar rather than four.

The Allemande also complements the Prelude by taking Prelude's key scheme and fulfilling in the most radiantly straightforward way the moves that had been frustrated, and therefore had created dramatic tension, there. The Allemande has a different four-bar opening formula, though still with a strong pedal element. This is followed by the same move to an E minor triad (bar 6) as the stepping-stone in a modulation from G to D (vi = ii), and the same reinterpretation of E as the bass of a second-inversion dominant 7th in D (6#/4/3; bars 6–7). But where the Prelude slipped off D back to G, the

Ex.4.2 Allemande of BWV 1007:
  a) figured-bass abstract

b) abstract in terms of 3rds, 6ths, and 10ths

Allemande's momentary G major at bar 9 is simply to set up the strongest chord in the strain (4♯/2 in D; bar 10) whose highly directional 7th in the bass powerfully motivates the long bass scale down to the ultimate 6♯/4/3 in bar 13. The spacing of this chord is very striking, covering an even wider range than the chromatic scale at the end of the Prelude, and lasting for a whole bar after more rapid harmonic rhythm. The 6/4/3 chord is an important symptom of unity of surface and structure in the Allemande, and of its scale-based nature. It is the inversion of the dominant 7th chord in which the bass has no particular tendency, and so can regularly step either up or down. It is therefore the one most commonly used in conjunction with stepwise, scale basses. It may seem rather scholastic to apply such elementary harmonic analysis to this music, but the ability to project it requires understanding as well as feeling. Casals made some cogent remarks to this effect with regard to this Allemande. He pointed to the need to feel the pull of the d♯ from the beginning of bar 5 as part of the modulation, and to the importance of the c' in the third beat as part of the diminished 7th sonority, rather than an unconsidered passing note.[7]

The second strain starts with a narrow pitch range, and opens out into the most jagged texture in the piece, with dialogue between upper and lower strings and broken-up phrases, reflecting the increase in tension customary with the move to the minor mode after the double bar. For the projection of this section it is worth noting the very different uses made of the dotted eighth note in the rhythm ♩. ♩ . It can be the equivalent of a full stop (bar 4), or a lesser punctuation mark (bars 5 and 21); it can be a concluding cadence formula (end of bars 14 and 23), or a beginning (bars 15 and 24). In each of these the dotted eighth has a different weight. In this section the peak of tension is the Neapolitan 6th in bar 22, with its dissonant resolution to the 4♯/2 in bar 23 (noted in the commentary on the D minor violin Partia in Chapter Three as a favourite progression of Bach's), which colours the move to A minor.

Both the Prelude and the first strain of the Allemande made significant use of E minor, so Bach has avoided that key in the second strain. In the Prelude the subdominant C major was conspicuous by its absence. Since Bach's normal policy for second strains is to pass through the relative minor (E minor here) to the subdominant (C major), he has neatly combined minor-mode colouring with the subdominant by using A minor, relative minor of C major, to represent both. The concluding events of the second strain mirror those of the first. The two 6♯/4/3 chords in D major in bars 7 and 13 frame a descending scale of parallel 6s (see Ex.4.2a). The two 7/5/4/2 chords in the second strain (bars 25 and 29) correspond to these, and frame an equivalent scale sequence in G major, now in the form of a circle of 5ths. As a final *jeu d'esprit* Bach has worked in two further, very attractive, 6/4/3 chords at the end of bar 29 and the second beat of bar 30.

This is a typical sonata interpretation of the allemande genre, with an opening four-bar phrase, and in this case with an extra two-bar one, then a single continuous phrase to the double bar. French style is limited to a few trills, and the *coulés de tierce* in bars 19 and 20. In the music of François Couperin the grace note would be played before the second eighth, though slurred to it (see the discussion of Ex.2.7 in Chapter Two section 2). Bach, when he wrote this figure out in full notes, normally put the grace note on the second eighth (♩ ♫). Whichever interpretation is adopted, this is a conventional intermediate phrase-ending formula equivalent to a comma or caesura, so the accent is on the first eighth and the rest is phrased off, with a slight pause afterwards.

3. Courante

The Courante in turn complements the Allemande by featuring wide leaps, as opposed to the Allemande's smooth scales. It is also a classic example of Bach's use of his ritornello shape in its sonata guise (see Chapter Two section 5), and of his endless ingenuity and resourcefulness in handling it. Little remains of the dance genre other than the time signature, the upbeat to bar 1, and the binary structure. Such dance character as it has is in the first eight bars, after which it goes into irregular, sonata-type phrases.[8] The usual four elements are marked in Ex.4.3. Element 1, which sets the character, has two balancing four-bar phrases, with a half close at b.4 answered by a full close at b.8; element 2 modulates to the dominant; element 3 is the closing motif and in this case has a pedal; and element 4 is the cadence. The formula is clear, but Bach rarely uses a standard formula without playing on it in some novel and striking way. In this instance he makes the second four-bar phrase of element 1 contain a sequence (X), which he uses again in the continuation (element 2) where it naturally belongs. He also interrupts the cadence (element 4) of the first strain. At the end of the second strain he plays magnificently on this feature by inserting the sequence (X) again before the final cadence. The sequence therefore, normally the material of the continuation (2), becomes part also of the character head (1) and the cadence (4), where it points to the fact that the closing pedal (3) is in fact its inversion. One element has thus come to permeate all other elements of the scheme, expressing Bach's ceaseless urge to unify and integrate.

As usual in these binary pieces, the peak of tension is in the minor-mode area of the second strain, in this case E minor as one would expect in G major (bars 23–8). Here tension is expressed in jagged, dissonant leaps, exploiting

Ex.4.3 Sonata structure in the Courante of BWV 1007

the feature of leaps in the opening material: an augmented 4th into bar 26, an augmented 5th into bar 27, and a major 7th into bar 28. In which case the e' grace note to the d♯' in bar 26, given in the later eighteenth-century Sources C and D, detracts from this climactic note. The point is that the d♯' never does resolve to e'; only two bars later does it finally resolve, and then not to e' but to E two octaves down. The force of the d♯' might be better served by a discreet amount of viol-type vibrato (i.e. close shake) than by an appoggiatura or trill.

4. Sarabande

The sarabande as a genre is the one in which Bach keeps closest to the dance character, and at the same time has one of his subtlest blends of stylistic elements. The fundamental note values in the usual French sarabande are half notes and quarter notes. Eighth notes are the decorative level, so in a French sarabande would be *notes inégales*. The French level of rhythmic inequality is mostly inappropriate for Bach, but eighths are still a light note value. The *coulés de tierce* in bars 2 and 4 are written out here in full notes, but still represent an intermediate phrase ending on a weak syllable (see the commentary on the Allemande). Sixteenths are an extra level of decorative note value, therefore lighter and more fluent than eighths. They represent the division/sonata element here and are not melodic as such.[9] The first strain is a typical sarabande structure with two four-bar phrases, the first of which is in the shape 2+2 bars and the second goes straight through as a 4. Overall there is a gradual move from fundamental to division note values. Bar 3 moves to eighths and bar 5 to sixteenths, which become continuous in bar 7. The pattern of antecedent phrase in the dance rhythm and consequent phrase in division note values is common in lighter dances such as gavottes and bourrées, and this sarabande shows how the same principle can be applied in a more refined and subtle way in the sarabande genre. The second strain echoes this progression towards shorter note values, though starting with a higher ratio of sixteenths.

Bach particularly liked to use the second-beat accent feature of the sarabande, though in French terms that is only one of a number of characteristics of the sarabande.[10] As here, he often ends phrases and even strains with an accent on the second beat. In French sarabandes this is unusual, since they normally end the first four-bar phrase on the weak third beat of the bar, and the second on the strong first beat. When the strain is repeated this gives the effect of a lyric verse form with an ABAB rhyme scheme. Bach has retained something of this effect here by making the seventh bar of each strain continuous sixteenths, thereby masking the second-beat accent in those bars.

Several of Bach's sarabandes have Doubles that can be used as repeats. One would think twice before interfering with the delicate rhythmic balance of a sarabande such as this, but it is worth looking at the Sarabandes of the A minor and G minor English Suites for clavier, probably written at around the same time as, or slightly before, the cello Suites, to see the amount of decoration Bach thought appropriate. The Sarabande Double of the D minor English Suite is a constant eighth-note division, and that of the B minor violin Partia is unusual for being a triplet division.

The rhythm ♩. 𝅘𝅥𝅰𝅘𝅥𝅰𝅘𝅥𝅰 in bar 3 is a case of Bach's notation being more accurate that accurate notation. Schwemer and Woodfull-Harris have added a triplet sign to the three 32nds, not present in any of their five sources. This urge of some editors to make the 32nds 'add up' removes the sense of decorative lightness and freedom, as in a tirata, that Bach intended.

5. Menuets

Each of the movements so far begins with a version of the four-chord formula at the opening of the Prelude. The Sarabande is closest to giving it exactly; the Allemande and Courante are not quite so obvious, but both have an initial top line that outlines the notes b c' b in the first phrase, and so does Menuet I. Otherwise this Menuet has a very similar agenda to the Sarabande in the arrangement of four-bar phrases and the use of the division note value (eighth notes here). Bar 3 of the opening phrase is a division of the rhythm of bar 1. In the second strain the eighth-note movement gradually takes over. Bars 9–12 have a similar shape to bars 1–4, though with some extra eighths. In bars 13–16 the eighths take over entirely. The last eight bars are in the standard pattern 2+2+4, and the rhyming of bars 21–4 with bars 13–16 has a similar effect to the rhyming of the second-last bars of each strain observed in the Sarabande.

Menuet II is based on the descending diatonic tetrachord, a common element in *minore* minuets. Its most obvious use is in the *minore* of the little G major Menuet in Anna Magdalena Bach's 1725 *Clavier-Büchlein*.[11] In countless elementary keyboard selections, these two Menuets must be the best-known 'Bach' pieces that Bach never wrote since they are by the Dresden court organist Christian Petzold.[12] In which case they are an even better example of the prevalence of the tradition than if they had been by Bach. The cello Menuet II, like the Sarabande of the C minor cello Suite, manages to imply a great deal of harmony in a single line, including the 7–6 suspensions conventionally associated with the tetrachord (if one imagines the e♭ in bar 1 resolving to the d in bar 2). There is some doubt about the Es at the ends of bars 3 and 7. They have flats only in Sources B and D. The Bärenreiter variorum again does not give the full picture: Sources A, C, and E have no accidental the first time, but a natural the second time. BG spells out the implications of this by putting a flat in bar 3 and a natural in bar 7. This brings variety, and subtly underlines the move onto the dominant at the double bar. The phrases of the second strain form two antecedent-consequent pairs, each again in the pattern 2+2+4. Within their seeming simplicity these two Menuets, both individually and as a related pair, are a perfect example of the possibilities in the mixed style for varied, yet unified, moulding of motifs and phrases.

In P 269 Anna Magdalena has written a fermata over the final chord as well as over the final bar-line of Menuet II. This is either a mistake, since none of the other sources has it, or Bach meant that the final G of Menuet II should not to be cut short, and that there should be a slight a gap before the return of Menuet I 'Da Capo' (see also the comment on this in section 3 of the Introduction)

6. *Gigue*

This Gigue has been compared to the third movement of the Sixth Brandenburg Concerto.[13] The slurred pairs certainly give a similarity of feel, but the $^{12}_{8}$ of the concerto implies a fleeter movement than the $^{6}_{8}$ here. Formally they have little in common; and this Gigue has an indefinable quality of robust 'hunting gigue', perhaps given by the unslurred arpeggio in bar 2 and implication of horn 5ths in bars 3–4. More striking is the variation element that runs throughout this Suite, in which each successive movement takes elements from preceding ones and develops them in a new way. The features common to this Gigue and Menuet I are: four-bar phrases; an identical half close in bar 4 of each piece; and particularly the use of the dactyl figure (♩ ♫) in the Menuet, converted to an anapaest (♫ ♩) in the Gigue, for moulding phrases. Its absence from the minor-mode phrase that ends each strain (bars 9–12, 25–8) sets off the smooth quality, with small intervals, of that phrase. In the extension to the second strain (bars 28–34) Bach uses a time-honoured technique for building a climax, of alternating two rhythmic units (in this case ♩ ♫ ♩ and ♩ ♩ ♩) for several bars, then increasing the pace by concentrating on one. In bar 32 he concentrates on the second, getting as far as the leading note, then releases this into the tonic, and makes up for the missing sixteenths in bar 32, by having two pairs of sixteenths in succession in bar 33. This 6-bar phrase gives a perfect sense of climax and conclusion and there is no need to imagine that it must originally have been eight bars long.[14] The elision of the last two phrases, and the expansion of the last one from four to six bars, are crucial to the effectiveness of this climax.

In common with several pieces by Bach in G major, this Gigue has a minor-mode phrase at strain ends. This feature is common in Corelli, and therefore in many early eighteenth-century sonata composers, and can be traced back in Italian vocal music at least to Cavalli in the earlier seventeenth century.[15] In its flattening tendency it is related to the use in minor keys of the Neapolitan 6th at cadences

Suite 2 in D minor BWV 1008

1. Prelude

This Suite seems to have been conceived as a pair with the G major, so much do the two suites complement each other. This is particularly so in the D minor Prelude, which contrasts with the G major in structure and in mood. Where the G major uses the ringing chordal resonance of the cello, the D minor speaks with its lonely, melancholy lyrical voice. The triad at the opening is melodic, rather than harmonic/chordal as in the G major, and the first phrase (bars 1–4) develops with small intervals in a narrow compass, concentrating on the sensitive notes of the minor scale. Whereas in structure the G major is fairly tight, the D minor is more expansive, and in fact it can be difficult initially to see quite what the argument is, particularly in the long second section. The key to the Prelude is in the opening triad. There can be no doubt that in the same impulse that Bach thought of the close-spaced D minor triad in bar 1 he also thought of the possibility of the dramatic, open and sonorous version at bar 40. The argument of the piece is how he gets from one to the other, and the masterly and dramatic way in which he exploits bar 40 for the rest of the piece.

There are three broad sections, each marked with a strong perfect cadence at the end, as is usual with Bach (bars 1–13, 13–36, and 36–63). A grasp of the figured-bass outline (Ex.4.4) is important since the first two cadences are elided, i.e. the last note of the old phrase is also the first note of the new. Section 1 is in Bach's customary sonata shape, with a closed four-bar phrase to begin, then an open-ended sequential continuation to the cadence. In view of his ultimate objective, it is significant that he has avoided having any sharpened notes in the bass in this opening section, other than the c♯ in bar 2. The sensitive notes in bars 2–3 are c♯ b♭ and e' (see the commentary on the Allemanda of the D minor violin Partia in Chapter Three). Another noticeable feature of this opening phrase is the descending eighth-note tetrachord at the end of bar 4, which stands apart from the usual flow of sixteenths. The two 4ths (rising from b♭ in the second beat of bar 2 to e' in the second beat of bar 3, and falling from d to A at the end of bar 4) provide the threads on which Bach hangs the rest of the section. From bars 3–9 the augmented 4th interval is stepped out in the highest notes of every other bar, the process underlined

Ex.4.4 Prelude of BWV 1008, figured-bass abstract

by each of the steps being a dotted eighth note. Meanwhile 3rds and 10ths are also important, as noted in the commentary on the Allemande of the G major Suite. From the beginning of bar 5 the bass notes of every other bar outline a falling 4th from B♭, to G at bar 9, and ultimately to F at bar 13.[16] On a local level the broken 3rds in bars 6 and 8 (see Ex.4.4) reflect this larger progression of 10ths.

Having avoided sharpened bass notes in section 1, Bach features them in section 2. The reason why this section can seem diffuse is that it has a feinted modulation to the expected dominant, but Bach works here on a larger scale the same dramatic avoidance of the dominant as he did in the G major Prelude. In Ex.4.4, the point of the rising scale in bars 13–21 is to get to the dominant of A minor, and we would expect this rising wave to cadence in that key. But the next four bars or so swing the harmony down again to D minor, and a second rising wave (from bar 25) peaks in bar 30 on the dominant of D (with the 7th in the bass). The expectation of A is held back, and so is all the more fulfilling in the climactic pedal in section 3 (from bar 43).

The harmonic implication of bar 32 can be puzzling. Norblin in 1824 gives the bass note on the second beat as G♯. In a way this would be very neat since the figured bass would then have d, instead of A, tied over the bar-line, with a 4♯/3♮ inversion of the diminished seventh on the first beat of bar 32, intensifying the 4♯/2 dominant 7th at the equivalent place in bar 30. But all the eighteenth-century sources have A, and we have noted on many occasions in the violin Solos Bach's fondness in single-part music for the dominant or diminished 7th-over-pedal effect (7/5/4/2 or 7/6/4/2).

Section 3 (from bar 36) then sets up the dramatic C♯ chord in bar 40 by plunging down from the most effective note to set it off (B♭). In a way one should be able to find in any piece the single most important note, to which everything builds up in a series of waves and from which the piece ebbs away, and it would be gratifying to be able to do so here. But Bach's mind is more complex than that, and in section 3 we have a whole area with a series of climactic points. Both pitch extremes of the Prelude (reserved until now) are used in rapid succession (C♯ in bar 40, g' in bar 44); there is dramatic use of the most dissonant version of the dominant 7th, with fermata, in bar 48 (this together with bar 40 correspond to the two positions of the diminished 7th in bars 2–3); and the chord at bar 40 is repeated (in heightened diminished-7th form) at bar 54. The high-pitched pedal build-up, and the placing of the chord in bar 48 with fermata and dramatic silence, make it difficult to avoid thinking of it as the ultimate climax of the Prelude. The scope of this long climactic section is further emphasized by the fact that the Neapolitan chord at bar 49 is laid out to suggest as much as possible a root-position E flat major, therefore sounding much more distant than the normal version of the progression suggested by the figured bass. This hushed moment, and the gradual return to *forte* (there will have to be an intermediate accent on the F♯ in bar 52), make the chord in bar 54 hardly less of a climax than bar 48. Meanwhile our augmented 4th has not been forgotten. It is outlined rapidly in bar 43 in the form of a diminished 5th from c♯' to g', after which it gradually declines at the rate of one note per bar from g' back to c♯' in bar 48.[17]

It can be seen that the note C sharp is structurally and dramatically important, in bars 2, 40, 48, and 54. Its final manifestation is set off by the dissonant diminished 3rd outline, prefigured *piano* in bars 49–50 (e♭ d c♯), and given full dramatic impact in bars 53–4. It is echoed in bars 58–9, so it would seem reasonable that any arpeggiation pattern for the final bars should be from the top down, along the lines of the final bars of the G major Prelude. Opinions differ about whether to arpeggiate or not. Some play the chords as written, some add small flourishes between, and there have been many suggestions for arpeggiation patterns.[18] Whichever solution is chosen, these final bars are a mere cadential formula, therefore a winding down, not a climactic, transfigured version of the main material of the Prelude, as at the end of the G major.

2. Allemande

The special qualities of this Allemande, and of Bach's style generally, are highlighted by a comparison with the D minor Allemande and Double from Marin

Marais's First Book of viol pieces (Paris 1686) in Ex.4.5. I have given only the solo viol part since Marais said they could be played without accompaniment and the *basse continue* does little more than duplicate bass notes that are already in the solo part. Allemandes can range from an Italianate sonata allegro, with little of a dance phrase structure, to a more French type with clearly defined phrases. Bach's D minor Allemande is already more French in its time signature c, rather than the more fluent ¢ in the G major Allemande.

Ex.4.5   Marin Marais, First Book of Pieces for bass viol, Allemande and Double in D minor, first strain

Bach's Allemande has a French-type first phrase, in two halves with a caesura on the last beat of bar 1. Marais in this instance is irregular in having an extra bar, but playing with phrase lengths is part of the art of the solo instrumental dance. Both have a similar pitch strategy: in Bach's case each half of the phrase has a descent of a 5th, from a to d in the first half of bar 1, matched by A to D from the end of bar 1 to the middle of bar 2. Similarly Marais has a descent from a to f in bar 1 to the beginning of bar 2, completed by a to d in bar 3 to the beginning of bar 4. Marais also has a caesura, after the falling 3rd in the first beat of bar 2 (which is basically the same as the *coulé de tierce* intermediate phrase ending). It is worth noting where this figure comes in Bach's Allemande, since it implies a slight break and is often masked by continuous sixteenths (compare Ex.2.7d). Bach has the figure in the third beats of bars 3, 4, 6, and 14, and in the first beats of bars 20 and 22. Awareness of this articulation point greatly enhances the feeling for Bach's variety of phrase shapes. It is essential for projecting the play on phrase lengths in the second strain, with a short phrase from bar 13 to the third beat of bar 14, then a very extended phrase that runs into the subdominant (G minor) reprise at bars 17 to the third beat of bar 18 (see the figured-bass abstract Ex.4.6).

Ex.4.6   Allemande of BWV 1008, figured-bass abstract

Apart from a similar pitch strategy in the first phrase, both Bach and Marais use the common key scheme in the minor mode of moving from tonic to dominant with a visit to the relative major on the way (Marais bars 7–8, Bach bar 4). But the similarities do not go much further than this and the differences are marked. Marais is fundamentally melodic in intention, and the sixteenths of the Double do little more than form elegantly balanced patterns in the old division variation tradition. Bach, on the other hand, has a tightly worked and developmental motivic surface, more in the sonata than the dance tradition. In spite of two full phrase endings and several intermediate ones in bars 1–6, from the end of bar 6 Bach spins out a very long and powerful continuous phrase to the end of the strain. In this piece he uses the augmented 4th to push the movement forward (in bars 5, 8, and 10; see Ex.4.6). Given that this is his technique here, he makes a dramatic point of it in bar 9 (in the form of a diminished 5th).[19] This node of tension is then released in a shower of 32nds, a characteristic of sonata movements we have already noted in the Adagio of the G minor violin Sonata (see the commentary in Chapter Three).

As one would expect, Bach does not waste the feature of the descent of a 5th in the opening phrase, and he structures the latter part of the long final phrase of the strain on a slow descent from e (second beat of bar 9) to A (half way through bar 11), with dramatic interruption. A further point of connection is the plunging arpeggios from e' (end of bar 6) to G♯ (middle of bar 7), which is varied in bar 21, and recast to end on A for the final cadence in bar 23.

In Marais's Allemande one would normally expect sixteenths to be played unequally, though the degree of inequality is variable according to circumstances. His Double, on the other hand, is a division in constant sixteenths where marked inequality is out of place. In the mixed style, Bach uses some French features, as outlined above, but in a sonata context. The point here is the subtlety and variety of bowing patterns, however one interprets the sources, and anything like conventional French inequality would be quite inappropriate.

3. *Courante*

This Courante has even less of French style about it than the Allemande. It is a very moulded version of the usual ritornello type, with a four-bar opening phrase, an open-ended section that modulates to the dominant, and a closing motif (bars 13–15) with a pedal. Within this scheme the objective seems to have been to blur the boundaries by an almost total lack of full cadences within strains, a continuity the Courante shares with the Prelude, whereas the Allemande had relatively more cadences. The Allemande also made strategic use of the last (4/2) inversion of the dominant 7th whereas the Courante, like the Prelude, uses the first (6/5) inversion with crucial, sensitive leading notes in the bass (see the figured-bass abstract Ex.4.7). Thus we have c♯ in bar 2, matched by a in bar 6 (first inversion of F major and part of the relative major area on the way to the dominant); and c♯ in bar 10 matched by d♯ (confirming the dominant modulation) in bar 15.

Ex.4.7 Courante of BWV 1008, figured-bass abstract

There are numerous features in this Suite that recall the D minor violin Partia, probably because they represent Bach's associations with the key of D minor rather than for any more particular reason. The final bars of each strain of their allemandes use the same progression, and the first strains of the two courantes have a very similar organization. The opening phrase of the cello Courante uses the simplest version of the Ciaccona bass. Since that outlines the diatonic tetrachord d c B♭ A, and Bach is particularly interested in building short-term and longer-term links from his opening material, one would expect tetrachords to play an important part in the piece as a whole, which indeed they do. Mostly they occur in broken intervals on the second and third beats of the bar, as in the groups d–g in bar 7, and f–c in bars 12–13, which then becomes the bass of the pedal effect c–f in bars 13–14. At the end there is b♭–f in bars 28–9, which in turn becomes the bass of the closing pedal f–b♭ in bars 29–30.

4. Sarabande

This Sarabande also is comparable to the Sarabanda of the D minor violin Partia. Both have phrases with the typical rhythm ♩♩ ♪ in the first two bars, and three quarter notes in the third bar, and both use a variety of note values. If the violin Sarabanda is somewhat tragic in mood, the cello Sarabande is more brooding. For variety of note values, a look at a similar piece in the background tradition is useful for defining Bach's style and therefore for performance issues. The Sarabande from Demachy's D minor suite for unaccompanied bass viol (Paris 1685, the first such viol publication; Ex.4.8) is a good example of the sophistication of style in French lute and viol repertory of the later seventeenth century. Each note value has its own relative weight. Generally in a French dance genre there are two fundamental note values and one decorative one (see Chapter Two section 3). In the $\frac{3}{4}$ sarabande, fundamental note values are half notes and quarter notes, with eighth notes as decorative, therefore susceptible to rhythmic inequality. In a sophisticated solo piece such as this Demachy example any inequality is clearly meant to be subtle and varied expressively. The group of four eighths from bars 4–5, for example, has a special weight since it elides the end of the first four-bar phrase very expressively, and

Ex.4.8   Demachy, *Pieces de Violle*, unaccompanied Sarabande in D minor, first strain

leads to the chord on the second beat of bar 5. Standard triplet inequality would quite undermine the subtlety and expressiveness of this so the group needs to be treated as a whole, perhaps with a lingering on the first note, part of the meaning of the bowing slur. A further sophistication is the use of sixteenths as an extra level of decorative notes: more decorative, therefore meant to be played yet more freely, than eighths.

An example of this lightness and freedom is in the sixteenth-note flourishes in even-numbered bars of the Sarabande from Bach's E major French Suite. Sixteenths in the D minor cello Sarabande have yet further subtlety in the variety of bowings: as a group in bar 3, in pairs in bar 7 and so on, a variety of bowing patterns typical of the oncoming galant style with its many levels of decorative note values. Not to differentiate between the relative weight of different note values loses the rhythmic character and also the true expressive nature of these pieces. In view of its close relation to a French sarabande, the eighths here could perhaps be 'un tant-soit-peu' more unequal than those in the B minor violin Sarabande, or at least have a nuance of differentiation between on-beats and off-beats. The groups of three eighths at the ends of bars 2, 4 etc. are in fact a motivic use of the *coulé de tierce* figure, and should preserve a hint of that.

In comparison with Demachy, Bach uses a very regular pattern of two rhythmic/chordal bars followed by two bars with a single line, similar to the layout of lighter dances which often have an antecedent in dance rhythm and a consequent in a division note value. The eighth-note patterns at cadences derive from the viol *style brisé* (as at the strain cadence in Ex.4.8). Bach's regularity of patterning is untypical of seventeenth-century French composers, but very typical of Germans writing in French style, such as in the lute suites of Esaias Reusner. A mannered feature used by French composers, particularly in sarabandes, is to begin with a closing gesture such as a cadence. Bach does that here, and the rhythmic subtlety of the first bar, which could be read as the second half of a cadential hemiola, is entirely typical of the sophistication of French solo instrumental suite. The trills in bar 1 etc. are complex, with an anticipation and a termination that are part of the compound ornament. Even though written out in full values, these notes are free and by no means to be played exactly as written. According to Quantz, such trills should be continued into the termination.[20] Georg Muffat, on the other hand, has a sort of trill that dies away on the dot and stops before the termination, a type used by Bach in the E minor Prelude of Book I of *The Well-tempered Clavier*.[21] Trills in this movement need to be played luxuriantly and with a longish appoggiatura.[22] As the Sarabande proceeds, the chords become more dissonant, from the major 7th in bar 9 to the diminished 7th in bar 22. The major 7th is an important sonority and would be lost if decorated with an appoggiatura and trill. Perhaps a viol-type vibrato could be used instead.

5. *Menuets*

Menuet I states more explicitly the descending tetrachord that lay behind the first phrases of the Courante and Sarabande.[23] The commonness of this formula for *minore* minuets has been noted with reference to the Menuets of the G major Suite. In the D minor, the second four bars of the first strain invert the pattern to go up five notes from d to a (breaking back an octave in the second last bar), a neat consequent and equally traditional. The main issue is the marked contrast of character between *minore* and *maggiore*. Menuet I is in the overcast key of D minor, with the same close-spaced tonic triad at the beginning as began the Prelude, though now as a chord, and small intervals moving in a narrow compass, whereas Menuet II is in the very open key of D major with expansive leaps and long, freely flowing runs.[24] The double stops and chords in the D minor contribute to a feeling of effort, where the D major is open and free. Less obvious is the use of phrase structure in this expressive agenda. We have noted in the Sarabande the alternation of dance rhythm in fundamental note values, and continuous divisions in decorative note values. In the Menuets, the D minor alternates these on a very small-scale level, every bar. The D major, by contrast, alternates them in a much broader way, with the antecedent four bars of the first strain in dance rhythm and the consequent in flowing eighths. In the second strain this tendency is taken further, with the eighths of the consequent (bars 13–16) flowing on through the final eight bars, pausing only for the widest leaps in the piece.

Notes inégales, as might be played in a minuet by Lully, are not appropriate in this mixed style. The decorative level of note value here is less melodic than part of the motivically-oriented sonata style, expressed in a great variety of articulations (however one interprets the often ambiguous sources).[25] There is, though, a strong contrast in Menuet II of long, flowing bars and bars broken up into phrased-off pairs. The fermatas at the end of both minuets are probably conventional in this instance, to show the end of the piece rather than indicate a gap. In Anna Magdalena Bach's copy (P 269) Menuet II begins on the same line as Menuet I ends, so the fermata at the end of Menuet I is probably only meant for the end of the Da Capo.

6. *Gigue*

This Gigue has many links with the previous movements of this Suite. Its $\frac{3}{8}$ time signature and many double stops and chords continue the mood of

Menuet I in a more energetic vein, in contrast to the lighter $^6_8$ and more fluent movement of the Gigue of the G major Suite. It is in the usual ritornello form in its sonata guise, but very strikingly has two contrasting pedal effects, rather than just one closing-motif pedal. The first pedal is in the bass (bars 21–4), while the second is in the upper part (bars 25–8), as was the closing pedal in the Courante (see the figured-bass abstract Ex.4.9, also Ex.4.7). The first pedal is not actually part of the closing motif since it is in the section that achieves the modulation to the dominant. It does this by converting the bass of the tonic (d) into the 7th of the dominant of A in a 4#/2 chord (bar 24). Precisely this method had been employed in the Allemande (see Ex.4.6 bars 8–10) with its concentration of 4/2 chords. The really clinching use of this chord is in the second strain, where Bach reverses the order of pedal types and has the upper-part pedal first (bars 61–4) and the bass pedal second (bars 69–72) so that the 4#/2 when it comes in D minor (bar 72) is in precisely the form it was at the climactic moment, with fermata, in bar 48 of the Prelude.

Ex.4.9   Gigue of BWV 1008, figured-bass abstract

The phrase structure of the first strain is very regular, but it is always worth seeing what expressive use Bach makes of this. The first section (to bar 16) is 4+4+8 bars, ending on a half close that prefigures the pedal patterns (bars 15–16). The modulating section (to bar 24) is 2+2+4 bars, and the closing section is 8 bars. In the second strain Bach does again what he did in Menuet II and makes the division note value (sixteenths here) more continuous. So we have 4+4+8 again, but now the 8 is in virtually continuous sixteenths. This trend continues until from bar 57 all the pedal effects and linking material are in continuous sixteenths, giving a single long phrase to build up to the climax in bar 72. This last section therefore (from bar 49) has larger units of 4+4+16 to finish the suite, in a type of gigue ($\frac{3}{8}$) that inherently tends towards more broken-up than continuous phrases.

Suite 3 in C major BWV 1009

1. Prelude

We have noted several times that certain shapes seem to be associated with certain keys (see also the discussion of the Praeludio of BWV 996 in Chapter Five). In keyboard music this probably comes from natural-feeling shapes on the keyboard in improvising. The initial gestures of preludes and toccatas very often are based on these shapes. In D minor, for example, Bach has a preference for a shape based on the tonic triad, with the semitones on either side (C sharp and B flat), as can be seen in the violin Partia and the cello Suite. In C major there is tendency towards scales in Bach's tradition, as in Buxtehude's organ Praeludia BuxWV 136 and 138, or in Bach's three-part Sinfonia BWV 787. Bach also has a tendency towards arpeggio shapes covering two octaves, as at the openings of the organ Praeludium BWV 545 and the organ Sonata BWV 529/1. In cello terms C major has of course a great natural, open resonance since all is based on the C string which has a particularly rich overtone series (the opening scale and arpeggio are identical to the notes of the natural trumpet, two octaves down). Bach uses the open C and G strings to great effect in this Prelude.

Bach sometimes uses a chromatic version of C major, perhaps to avoid the ordinariness of the key, or perhaps because of its very centrality and the possibility in moving in either sharp or flat directions. This is particularly so in the C major violin Sonata BWV 1005 where he uses a version of C major that also includes the notes of the minor mode. In the C major cello Prelude he seems to have gone in the other direction and written a particularly diatonic piece. In fact the structure of this Prelude is considerably more straightforward than the Prelude of the G major Suite, in spite of the C major being over twice as long. In contrast to the overcast mood of the D minor Suite, with its narrowly spaced triad at the beginning of the Prelude, Menuets and Gigue, Bach in the C major has aimed for broadness, openness and generosity.

The harmonic scheme is simple (see the figured-bass abstract Ex.4.10) even in comparison with the equally broad-paragraphed Preludio of the E major violin Partia (Ex.3.25). Secondary key centres are only suggested, in a brief move to the dominant (G major, bars 7–13), then to the relative minor (A minor, bars 18–27), and there is no reprise. The main point of the Prelude is the long dominant pedal from bar 45, lasting for 17 bars. Transitions are also

Ex.4.10 Prelude of BWV 1009, figured-bass abstract

effected with the minimum of elaboration. The move from C to G is achieved by turning the tonic of C in bar 6 into the subdominant of G in bar 7. As noted in the Gigue of the E major violin Partia and elsewhere, a change of harmonic function normally carries with it a change of surface figuration, so here the scale in bar 6, which belongs to the opening figurations in C, changes in bar 7 to the pattern that will decorate the circle of 5ths in G. On a broader level, given Bach's 'invention' principle and the opening bar's scale and arpeggio, it is hardly surprising to find that the first part of the Prelude (from bar 2) concentrates on scales, though with a gradual admixture of broken intervals, and that when the tonal centre starts to move back to C (from bar 28) for the build-up to bar 45, it concentrates on arpeggio figures. In a way the long dominant pedal combines both, by implying stepwise polyphonic parts in the broken chords.

There are also, as usual, balancing equivalents at various stages. The falling circle of 5ths, that goes down from c in bar 7 to G in bar 13, is balanced by a rising sequence, of falling 3rd followed by rising 4th, that comes up from C in bar 37 to the G pedal in bar 45. The rising progression is used again later to cover almost the entire octave of C (bars 72–6), with Bach's favourite device of halting dramatically on the leading note (b in bars 76–7), which does not fully resolve to c' until bar 82. Another point of balance is the way in which the unstable dominant pedal of A minor in bars 20–24, which falls away in bars 24–6, prefigures and sets off the very solid dominant pedal of C major from bar 45.

Given that the main event is the long dominant pedal, David Watkin has pointed out the close resemblance of this to the final 'Arpeggio' pedal in the second movement of Corelli's C major violin Sonata Op.5 No.3 (Ex.4.11).[26] The fundamental progression of Bach's pedal is identical to Corelli's, including the touch of C minor towards the end, though Bach has expanded on it with decorative part movements. If one objective of these Suites is to provide the cello with a repertory equivalent to that of the violin, this is surely a case in point. But as important for the cello is its function as continuo instrument, particularly in the many seventeenth- and eighteenth-century sonata collections (including Corelli's Op.5) that specify the accompaniment as for harpsichord *or* (rather than *and*) cello, in which case the cello would sometimes have to add chords and parts. We have noted in connection with the G major Prelude the fact that early Italian unaccompanied cello pieces seem to have been conceived as practice repertory for continuo playing. An instructive function is also typical of Bach in his more speculative collections, which include the violin Solos and cello Suites, a function continued from the first publication of the Suites around 1824 as *Six . . . Etudes* until today, though without the continuo-playing dimension. Watkin uses the term 'lateral harmony' for the scale at the opening of this Prelude, as a demonstration of how in a decorated accompaniment a chord can be represented by a scale. The final two bars of the Prelude demonstrate all three ways of representing harmony: by a scale, by an arpeggio, and by the chord itself.

Ex.4.11   Corelli, first Allegro of violin Sonata Op.5 No.3, final bars

Bars 80–1 form a common type of hemiola, in which the second beat (end of bar 80) is a rest, an effect also hinted at in the first bar of the D minor cello Sarabande. The trills in bars 85–6 do not seem related to the wavy lines at the

end of the A minor violin Grave BWV 1003/1, but rather to the ribattuta ornament that starts with slow repetitions and gets quicker. Only Kellner (P 804) puts a trill sign also on the lower note in bar 86, but the trill is obviously meant to be continued. The effect probably derives from *doigt couché* viol technique, and the method of performing it is described by Leopold Mozart in terms of the violin.[27]

2. Allemande

As usual in his suite collections, Bach in these Suites is working through a campaign of dance types. The G major Allemande is in flowing sixteenths, similar for example to that of the A major English Suite. The D minor uses more dance phraseology, and much more detailed articulation. It also introduces a flourish of 32nds. In some Allemandes Bach introduces 32nds only in the second strain as an ornamental element (E minor English Suite, D minor French Suite), but sometimes he uses them as a fully integrated motivic element throughout the piece (C minor French Suite, A minor clavier Partita), as he does in this Allemande. They are essentially a decorative note value that moves by step, and this enhances the fact, obvious from their first bars, that the Allemande takes up the scale element of the Prelude, while the Courante takes up the arpeggio. The scale aspect also permeates the structure of the Allemande much more than in the Prelude, as the figured-bass abstract in Ex.4.12 shows. The prelude had used progressions related to scales, such as the falling circle of 5ths and the rising progression where the bass goes down a 3rd and up a 4th, but the Allemande uses straightforward scale patterns in parallel 6s and 7–6s (bars 7–11, 19–21).

Another feature continued from the Prelude both here and in the Courante is the multiplicity of pedal effects, particularly using the open C and G strings.

Ex.4.12 Allemande of BWV 1009, figured-bass abstract

The pedal pattern from the end of bar 6 into bar 7 recalls the rising chromatic scale at the end of the G major Prelude. The pattern from bars 9–10 and 22–3 is a reworking with 32nds of the type in bars 22–3 of the C major Prelude. Apart from pedals, the Allemande takes a pattern used in bars 37–41 of the Prelude in which figurations go alternately over and under the main harmony notes. In the Allemande, the first time the descending scale sequence of 7–6s appears (from the end of bar 7), the figurations are all above the bass notes, but when it is repeated an octave lower (bars 10–11) they are alternately over and under. The figuration on the third beat of bar 7 directly refers to this moment in the Prelude.

As is common with Bach in dance genres, the opening has a regular shape with balanced dance phrases, but thereafter there is a single long phrase to the double bar, sonata-style. In the long c-time bars the shape of the opening section may seem odd, ending on the third beat, but thinking them in $\frac{2}{4}$-time gives the standard pattern 2+2+4 bars. As usual, the second strain is more continuous, other than the customary full close in the relative minor (bar 17). The dotted eighth-note A minor chord here is the equivalent of a full stop, and corresponds to the chord in the middle of bar 5 of the first strain where it was not part of a full close so did not break the continuity. At the end, the second half of bar 23 refers to the opening of the Prelude, including both scale and arpeggio elements, preparing for the arpeggio that begins the Courante.

3. Courante

The Allemande begins with a two-octave extension of the Prelude's scale, and ends with the same chord as the Prelude; the Courante begins with a two-octave extension of the Prelude's arpeggio, and ends with the same chord. The Courante has an eight-bar opening phrase (ending with a dotted quarter-note in bar 8 as a full stop) which has the same harmonic structure as first eight bars of the Prelude. Both have the same number of tonic and dominant chords, and both go straight to the dominant with f♯ as soon as the phrase is over. Otherwise the Courante has in common with the Prelude some pedal effects, such as the minor tinge in bars 31–4 etc (compare bar 58 of the Prelude) including the 6/4/3 on the flattened sixth degree in bars 33–4 (compare bar 79 of the Prelude).

The first strain is in Bach's usual sonata version of the ritornello shape, with a closed eight-bar phrase, an open-ended phrase that moves to the dominant, a pedal with minor-mode tinge, and cadence, very much like the G major Courante though without the ingenious juggling of elements we noted there. There is nonetheless a substantial development in the second strain of elements in the first. As may be seen from the figured-bass abstract (Ex.4.13)

Ex.4.13   Courante of BWV 1009, figured-bass abstract

the scale segment in bars 3–5 is extended in bars 25–8. In the second strain these scale sequences are very much extended in bars 48–53, and especially in a new rising version in bars 65–72 that climaxes on the final dominant pedal in a way comparable to bars 37–45 of the Prelude. In the first bars of the Courante Bach sets up a pattern of a smoothly stepping figure alternating with an arpeggio rocketing around the instrument. He does not use this regular alternation again until the rising scale from bar 65 that builds up to the final pedal. Other neat correspondences are the pause on the relative minor (A minor) in bar 56, corresponding to the pause on the tonic in bar 8 (and indeed to the A minor pause in bar 17 of the Allemande); and the arpeggio in bar 79 that goes up to d' as the 5th of G, and corresponds to the arpeggio in bar 35 that goes down to D as the root of D. Dotted quarter notes here have an important function in articulating the structure behind the continual stream of eighths.

4. Sarabande

At the end of the Prelude Bach has three ways of representing C major: by a scale, by an arpeggio, and by a chord. The scale and arpeggio have been worked in the Allemande and Courante; the Sarabande takes the chord, which frames the movement at start and finish. This must be the richest and most sonorous chord on the cello, based on the combined overtone series of the two lowest open strings, and Bach has conceived a wonderfully expressive agenda to set it off. In the Prelude he develops the expansive, diatonic aspect of C major, rather than the expressive, chromatic aspect he explores in the C major violin Sonata. The expansiveness is still in the Sarabande, in the large, sonorous chords and the range to g', but it also has a greater tonal, and hence expressive, range than we have had so far. This is the first movement in this Suite where the first accidental is B flat rather than F sharp, and the flattening tendency of the first bars provides the key to what is to come. At the end of the first strain the B flat returns as part of G minor, continuing the minor tinge that we have had at cadences in the other movements. After the double bar this expressive chromatic feature is developed much further. The f' on the second beat of bar 9 corresponds as minor 7th to the b♭' in bar 2. Its tendency to cloud the serenity of the major chord is strongly reinforced in bar 10 where it is reinterpreted as the minor sixth degree of A minor, the most expressive degree of the minor scale, and part of a diminished 7th chord. This move is much intensified in the following bars when the c♯ at bar 13 throws the line up into the lonely, melancholy world of the D minor Suite, where the chords fall away and the plaintive high pitch is far from the comforting warmth of the C string. In returning, Bach takes the chromatic step in the bass in bars 9–10, which had moved to A minor, and extends it in the final phrase (from bar 20) in a chromatic ascent from G to c, again developing the minor-key tinge from the end of the first strain. The Sarabande thus adds an expanded range of moods to the other aspects of expansiveness of the preceding movements.

As always, the motivic working is inseparable from the expressive narrative. In the first bar the most noticeable rhythmic element is the dotted eighth note. In the first phrase as a whole one can follow its development from ♩. ♪ , to ♪♪♪ in bar 3, and ♪♪♪♪ in bar 4. Further developments are easily seen, but worth noting particularly is the very expressive use of all of these for the crucial expressive f♮s in bars 9 and 10.

In working on an interpretation of this piece, it is important to consider the extra ornaments in Sources C, D, and E, both here and in the Bourrées, which may reflect a revision by Bach. It may also be worth noting the Largo tempo indication in Source E, which well reflects the expansive character.

5. Bourrées

The contrast between these two Bourrées is so finely judged that it hardly needs to be brought out further than the colour change for Bourrée II implied by Kellner's '*pian*[o]' (alone of the eighteenth-century sources).[28] Bourrée I has energetic chording, two-in-one melody (i.e. a single line implying two parts), and broken intervals and arpeggios, whereas Bourrée II moves almost entirely in scale steps, continuing the contrast of scale and arpeggio that has been worked in virtually every movement so far in this Suite. Bourrée I plays on a very regular phrase structure to exploit the contrast of bars in dance rhythm (bars 1–4) and bars in a division note value (eighths in this case, bars 5–6). The first strain is in the pattern 2+2+4 bars, in which the 4 moves into the division note value. After the double bar the division note value gradually takes over. There is another 2+2+4, where the second 2 is mostly in eighths and the 4 is entirely in eighths, then (from bar 16) a similar 2+2, but the 4 is now extended into a long, continuous phrase of eight bars in which the eighth-note motifs are extended and developed. The expectation of regularity, answered by a sudden expansion of phrase, is typical of sonata style.

The highly articulated phrase structure of Bourrée I is rounded out and masked under smooth eighth-note scale figures in Bourrée II, which almost entirely avoids the implication of more than a single line. The balanced *coulé de tierce* equivalents in bars 2 and 4 of Bourrée I are replaced in bars 3–4 of Bourrée II by a phrase that runs down to the tonic of the scale, then bounces off that in a rising scale. This provides a classic example of one of the simplest methods of changing key, by running up or down a scale and simply switching to the notes of the next key. The d' in bar 18 is another example of Bach dramatically pausing on a leading note, as he did towards the end of the Prelude, in this case with the implication of an augmented 4th (a♭–d♮') that recalls the similar effect in the second strain of the G major cello Courante.

6. *Gigue*

The first phrase of the Gigue inverts not only the melodic direction of the opening of the Prelude, but its expressive associations as well. Rather than recalling the harmonic series of the natural trumpet, the broken-chord element of the Gigue (bars 3–4) has bucolic suggestions of yodelling, or the Dudelsack. This is carried further in the large amount of the piece given over to drone effects: in the Prelude, pedals accounted for exactly one third of the piece; in the Gigue the proportion is just under 40 per cent. Bars 35–6 etc. add typical bagpipe semitone appoggiaturas over the drone. As well as the general mood of good humour, there is an element of comic humour in the scale that tumbles down after the double bar, and the conversion of the yodelling figure into an enormous leap in bar 52.

There is no knowing the order Bach in which Bach composed these Suites, but the C major Suite does seem to complement the D minor, as we noted in the Prelude. The same time signature and very similar materials in the D minor Gigue suggest that, after composing the D minor, Bach decided in the C major to bring out opposite expressive possibilities inherent in these materials, which would not have been appropriate to the sombre mood of D minor.

Suite 4 in E flat major BWV 1010

1. Preludium

This is the only Prelude in Anna Magdalena Bach's copy entitled 'Preludium', which makes one wonder if it did not originally belong to a different series, or was an isolated piece brought in to fill a gap.[29] It goes against the grain of the cello inasmuch as the harmonies are obviously meant to ring on, particularly the bass notes, yet the key allows little use of the resonance of open strings. The lute, with the open diapason courses in the bass, would seem to be a more suitable instrument. Those places where descending bass scale shapes break back an octave would also be less noticeable on the lute since the bass courses are octave strung (i.e. with one string at 8' and one at 4' pitch). The cello necessarily gives a more melodic impression since notes are individually created rather being part of resonant chord groups, as they would be in the equivalent type of keyboard prelude. On the other hand, all this may be exactly the point of the piece for the cello. Given the partially étude nature of these Preludes, and the importance of E flat and its relative keys even though they do not lie ideally on the instrument, this may be a study in the viol technique of *tenues*, i.e. holding the notes of chords as long as possible 'to sustain the harmony and the cleanness of the sound'.[30] This would explain the choice of a key where almost all notes have to be fingered, and also the zig-zag shape of the figurations, together with their bowing implications. Altogether this Prelude makes more advanced technical demands than the preceding ones.

The shape of the Prelude is led almost entirely by the bass. The argument of the first half is to get down the small interval from E♭ in bar 1 to C♯ in bar 49, the expressive interval of the diminished 3rd that we have noted as a Bach favourite on numerous occasions, particularly in the resolution of the Neapolitan 6th. After the C♯ the harmonic bass leaps back up to E♭, as a preparation for the D pedal from bar 52 (see the figured-bass abstract Ex.4.14), confirming the agenda. A large part of the attraction of this Prelude is the effect of the passing 7th in the bass. The bottom octave is therefore filled out with descending scale shapes, that sometimes break back an octave in order to keep descending (as at bars 11–12 etc.), and sometimes run into a circle-of-5ths pattern (as in bars 11–19). This latter pattern has the advantage of giving a broadly descending effect while using relatively few notes of the octave. The

Ex.4.14 Prelude of BWV 1010, figured-bass abstract

shape is also present in the top notes of the chords of bars 1–8.[31] This Prelude therefore concentrates on the scale shapes that we noted as missing from the G major Prelude, which concentrated on pedal effects.

The strongest use of C♯, in terms of Bach's harmony, is as the leading note to the dominant of G minor, and in fact G minor is the most important secondary key centre in the Prelude. It is also marked by highly dramatic treatment. The more expected C minor had been reached at bar 27, and its conversion to the dominant of F minor in bar 29 is the first time one feels a definite move away from E flat. The feeling of moving away harmonically is matched by a change in surface patterning. The pattern of one bass note per bar is broken (from bar 31) and changed to one every other bar, and further changed (from bar 41) to shifting the stress from bass notes to the top notes of broken chords, until we reach G minor itself in bar 45. The importance of this is marked by having the straightest scale shape so far in the bass, down from G to C♯ (bars 45–9), tension being increased by the insistent repetition of the G minor triad.

The cadence in G minor that we expect after the C♯ is dramatized by a large cadenza section, and does not resolve until bar 62 (see Ex.4.14). The C♯ is another case of Bach's liking for pausing dramatically on a leading note. He uses the effect again on the leading note to E flat in bar 88, the d repeated an octave higher in bar 90 and not resolved until the final chord. Each of these crucial leading notes is followed by a flourish covered by a very long slur. This is more likely an invitation to improvisational freedom than an indication of articulation (compare the enormous slur in bars 22–5 of the lute version of the C minor cello Prelude, BWV 995/1). There are many ways of dividing it up. Erwin Grützbach has analysed the two flourishes (bars 49–51 and 88–9) in terms of rhetorical *figurae* (various types of *tirata*, *circolo* etc) and suggested bowings based on them.[32] Alternatively one could take more general shapes, for example the flourish from bar 49 is in two waves, the first up to b♭ and the second further up to e♭'. The second wave involves a change of chord in bar 51 (see Ex.4.14), again with the diminished 3rd progression in the bass. Whatever the solution adopted, the feeling of freedom is paramount. The cadenza section in bars in 49–62 is a large expressive expansion of the opening pedal from bars 1–9. At its climax (bar 59) Bach reinterprets the tonic e♭' as an agonised dominant minor 9th, the furthest he goes in his reinterpretation and 'researching' of this note, strongly suggesting that this is his reason for choosing G minor as the main secondary key.

2. Allemande

Within the uniformity of genre in these Suites there is a great variety of treatments. This Allemande is the most complex so far in its variety of elements. The opening sentence refers to the typical French allemande opening phrase with caesura (end of bar 2 here), but the answering second part of the phrase is twice the length of the first. As in some of the preceding Allemandes, the barring makes this phrase look irregular but in $\frac{2}{4}$ barring it would be a regular 4+8 phrase, and the half-bar phrase ending cuts the finality of the full close. The remainder of the strain is a single long phrase, made more complex than usual by an extension (from the second half of bar 13) that repeats the fundamental harmonies of the cadence (bars 14–16 correspond to the end of bar 11–13½; see the figured-bass abstract Ex.4.15).

The ¢ time signature and smoothly running scales of the first two bars recall the G major Allemande. What makes the E flat Allemande more complex is the significant admixture of another note value (eighth notes) to

Ex.4.15 Allemande of BWV 1010, figured-bass abstract

the usual sixteenths, a process taken further in the Courante. This gives Bach the opportunity to 'research' different rhythmic combinations, which in turn are related to harmonic function. The pattern in bars 3–5 decorates a rate of harmonic change in half notes; the more rapid alternation in bars 9–12 decorates a harmonic change in quarter notes in the climbing sequence that moves to the new centre of B flat (see Ex.4.15). This reflects the customary moulding of harmonic rhythm, in having static harmony at the main key centres and more rapid change when moving from one key centre to another.

The extension (bars 13½–16) introduces two new features which are then developed in the second strain. The first is the palindromic pattern in bar 14, extended in a sequence in bars 36–7. The second is the harmonic formula of bars 15–16, in which the bass note changes function to be the 7th in a 4♮/2 chord. This formula is varied four times in a series of cadences from bars 21–30 (see Ex.4.15). The fact that so much of the second strain is taken up with exploring possibilities of this formula accounts for its not returning at the end, and the final cadence corresponds to bars 12–13.

All the eighteenth-century sources have the paired slurrings in bars 23–4, and most in the equivalent places in bar 27 and bars 29–30. Richard Efrati suggests Leopold Mozart's instructions for slurred pairs of sixteenths: 'the accent falls on the first of the two, and it is not only played somewhat louder, but it is also sustained somewhat longer, while the second is slurred on it quite smoothly and quietly, and somewhat late'.[33]

3. *Courante*

This carries the Allemande's mixture of note values further, and has the most sophisticated mixture of note values we have yet had in a courante in these Suites. The D minor violin Corrente had triplets; the G major cello Courante had a mixture of eighths and sixteenths; the E flat Courante has all of these. The use of triplets, and of the galant-style mixture of note values, has been discussed with reference to the Allemanda of the B minor violin Partia (see the commentary in Chapter Three). For some reason triplets are more common in courantes than in allemandes before 1720. In Corelli's Op.5 No.7 triplets have a division/variation function, to decorate a repeated phrase, or to intensify a line as it worked to a climax. Telemann uses them in the A major Corrente of his *Six Sonates* (1715) in a more structural way to articulate a series of thematic motifs.[34] The E flat cello Courante is Bach's closest equivalent to this. Characteristically, however, Bach brings in the triplets not just once for a particular local function, but builds them into the basic materials. The opening eight-bar phrase has an antecedent of four bars with eighth notes and sixteenths, and a consequent with triplets. This sets up a rhythmic contrast at the beginning that Bach later exploits very purposefully. The triplets in the consequent phrase have a relaxed effect because they decorate a falling sequence. Their climax-intensifying inversion in the closing motif in bars 18–21 is therefore all the stronger in effect. In the second strain, Bach develops this contrast in bars 42–7 by alternating relaxed triplets with the upward rushing sixteenths of the antecedent. The closing motif in bars 56–9 is now at a lower pitch, so less tense than originally: he therefore runs the triplets further up to e♭' in the second last bar so that the end of the Courante spans the full two-octave pitch range outlined at the beginning of both the Prelude and the Allemande of this Suite.

There are links between movements in this Suite similar to those observed in the C major Suite. The Allemande concentrates on smooth scale figures in sixteenths, as in the Prelude's cadenza passages, whereas the Courante starts with the Prelude's broken chord outlines in eighth notes. This relationship goes deeper than the motivic surface in that the first bar of the Courante is in fact a condensed version of the harmonic formula that opens the Prelude (compare Ex.4.16 bars 1–2 and Ex.4.14 bars 1–9). Apart from the Prelude, the figured-bass abstracts also show the strong variation element between the Courante and the Allemande. Both use the falling circle of 5ths sequence in their second strains (Allemande bars 33–5, Courante bars 31–41). Such a common progression is not necessarily significant, but other progressions are much more obviously related in shared structural function at equivalent points in each piece. Bars 9–16 of the Courante and bars 7–11 of the

Ex.4.16 Courante of BWV 1010, figured-bass abstract

Allemande have the identical function of increasing harmonic momentum in the move to the dominant. The progression in bars 14 and 36–7 of the Allemande recurs in bars 50–4 of the Courante, also at an equivalent structural point.

Two details of variant readings are clarified by reference to the figured-bass abstract Ex.4.16. Kellner's reading in bar 9 of f rather than g for the third eighth note looks plausible from the motivic point of view, but the harmonic sequence here differs from that in bar 1 so g is preferable. In bar 34, all the eighteenth-century sources other than Anna Magdalena Bach have d♭' as the last note of the bar. Again this sounds plausible in terms of surface patterns, because of the a♭ in the following bar, but is not justified in terms of the underlying harmonic sequence. The E flat in bar 10 is not in the figured-bass abstract since it is preferable to represent the sequence here. As a 7th in the bass it resolves to D in bar 12.

4. Sarabande

Bach generally prefers the rhythmic/chordal type of sarabande represented in the G major and D minor cello Suites. There is a move in the C major Suite, and yet more in the E flat major, towards the lighter, more aria-like type preferred by other composers in the galant style such as Bach's friend the lutenist Silvius Leopold Weiss. This Sarabande continues the variation principle between movements by having a melodic interpretation of the outline of bar 1 of the Courante, in a line that moves up through notes 5–6–7 of the scale (see Ex.4.16). Through this link the opening of the Sarabande is ultimately related to the opening of the Prelude (the harmonic progression of bars 1–4 of the Sarabande is fundamentally the same as in bars 1–9 of the Prelude). The sonority of the 7th chord is also important, as it was in the Prelude.

The main rhythmic feature of the C major Sarabande was the use and development of the dotted rhythm ♩. ♪. Like the C major, the E flat Sarabande introduces the dotted rhythm gradually (once in bar 2, twice in bar 4), but then makes consistent melodic use of it, often combining it with a suspension across the bar-line. The interpretation of the dotted rhythm is the main point at issue in this Sarabande. Many composers in the German mixed style notated conventional French *notes inégales* with dotted rhythms in sarabandes. The melody here, however, is not of the usual stepwise French type, but consists of decorated harmonic outlines. The structure is also very mixed, and provides a classic case of the sonata version of the ritornello shape worked in terms of sarabande four-bar phrases. It starts with a rounded 2+2 phrase; then has a phrase that develops the dotted rhythm and moves to the dominant; and finally has a closing motif with an upper pedal. In which case the dotted rhythms here are not written-out triplet *notes inégales* but a decorative character rhythm. The rhythmic intention is probably best seen by comparing this with the E flat major Adagio in the Sonata for obbligato harpsichord and violin BWV 1017 (Ex.4.17). This also uses the galant variety of note values, but in a multi-layered rhythmic texture and with a consistency typical of Bach. The essence is that the violin's dotted rhythm and the equal eighths in the bass are not assimilated to the triplets, but that each of the three lines forms a separated and contrasted rhythmic strand, played more or less as written. The violin's dotted rhythm could be slightly over-dotted in the usual lilting way, and forms an elegant contrast to the harpsichord's triplets. Knowing the violin movement it is difficult not to feel the dotted rhythms of the cello Sarabande in the same way.

Ex.4.17 Adagio of Sonata in C minor for obbligato harpsichord and violin BWV 1017, bars 1–5

5. Bourrées

The most obviously individual feature of Bourrée I is the upbeat run of sixteenths, unique in Bach's *senza basso* bourrées. This may be a continuation of the galant mixing of note values we have had other movements: the flourishes in the Prelude, and the mixture of two note values in the Allemande, extended to three in the Courante. It is a decorative feature, but for Bach it is also part of the *inventio* of the piece and he builds on it in very much the same way as he built on the dotted rhythm in bar 2 of the Sarabande. Its occurrence increases as the piece develops: once at the beginning, twice in bars 6–7, four times in bars 8–10, eight times in bars 26–30, and extended into a continuous run in bar 34 that links the sixteenths to the flourishes of the Prelude.

The echoes are in the two later eighteenth-century sources. They are not in Anna Magdalena Bach's copy, and Kellner only has *piano* at the end of bar 45 and *forte* at the end of bar 46. Bach did write echoes in the Fuga and Allegro of the A minor violin Sonata, and in the Preludio and Bourrée of the E major violin Partia, which Anna Magdalena is erratic in reproducing in her copy of the violin Solos (P 268). In these pieces the echoes contribute to the spaciousness of the concertante style, and the same seems true of Bourrée I.

After the bustle of Bourrée I, Bourrée II provides one of the most effective contrasts in all of these suites. It uses a very modest lower tessitura, with a simplicity of note values matched by a masterly simplicity of structure, basically a favourite Vivaldi cadence formula played four times. All the eighteenth-century sources other than Kellner have c rather than ¢ as the time signature for the second Bourrée, which may imply a relaxation of tempo, though perhaps the contrast of note values already achieves this sufficiently. The dance-like simplicity and lack of sonata features make a slight French swinging of the eighths seem appropriate here in a way it would not be in Bourrée I.[35] A further aspect of French performance style that might be considered is Demachy's fourth way of playing the bass viol, i.e. plucking (*pincer*) in imitation of lute and theorbo.[36] It has to be said, though, that the associations of pizzicato nowadays are not primarily with French seventeenth-century viol repertory. Whatever the details, in all the variety and complexities of these Suites this Bourrée in its simplicity must be the favourite movement of many.

6. Gigue

This piece gives the lie to the notion that there are any steady key characters in Bach's music. Organists would probably associate the key of E flat major with meditative warmth (as in the chorale prelude 'Schmücke dich, o liebe

Seele', BWV 654) or a lively majesty (as in the Prelude and Fugue from *Clavier-Übung* III, BWV 552). This Gigue seems to have more in common with an earthy Beethovenian sense of humour. $^{12}_{8}$ is the most fluent of Gigue time signatures, in stark contrast to the $^3_8$ of the Gigues in the two preceding Suites. The first phrase is short, does nothing but decorate the E flat arpeggio, and ends with an unusually emphatic full stop in the middle of bar 2, subtly giving the impression of landing on the wrong foot. The possibility of opposite characters being created with similar materials is demonstrated by the structural similarity of the first strain here to that of the Sarabande. After the opening phrase, there is one that moves to the dominant, and (from bar 7) a closing motif with an upper pedal (compare the figured bass abstract Ex.4.18 with bars 9–11 and 25–8 of the Sarabande). Upper pedals in this Suite may be traced to bars 45–9 of the Prelude; those in the Sarabande and Gigue may also be related to the Vivaldian cadence formula noted in Bourrée II.

Ex.4.18 Gigue of BWV 1010, figured-bass abstract

In the second strain Bach plays with witty good humour on this sonata/ritornello shape. After the double bar he runs it in B flat, but replaces the closing motif by a falling sequence (bars 15–18) that runs straight into C minor at bar 19. The C minor version exploits the emphatic full stop of the original first phrase by landing instead on a dramatic diminished 7th (in the middle of bar 20) that swings the tonal direction round to G minor, also the Prelude's goal as a secondary key. It has the pedal closing motif from bar 22, and a full close with pause in G minor before the final tonic reprise from the end of bar 26. The E flat reprise then has all these ingredients, including both the falling sequence (from bar 35) and the pedal closing motif (from bar 39).

The knowing simplicity of the opening phrase is matched by the broad simplicity of harmonic movement, with a great deal of repetition (see Ex.4.18). With Bach repetition in itself does not necessarily imply an echo. Particularly in the Vivaldi tradition its function may be to intensify, what Arthur Hutchings called 'kinetic recurrence'.[37] There is no suggestion of echoes here, and the character of this Gigue is thrown into relief by comparison with the $^{12}_{8}$ Giga in the D minor violin Partia, in which most of the movement is in sixteenths in brilliant concerto style and the echoes are part of this concertante expansiveness. The E flat Gigue is hardly in concerto style in this sense, and the repetitions are part of its humorous, headlong character.

Suite 5 in C minor BWV 1011

The background to scordatura has been discussed in Chapter One. The scordatura that Bach uses here is a common one for both violin and cello. The most notable use of it on the violin must surely be in the sixth of Biber's 1681 *Sonatae*, where the violinist has to tune the E string down to d" in the course of the piece (see Chapter One section 2). The 'Crucifixion' sonata of Biber's 'Mystery' sonatas, with the tuning a e' b' e", has effectively the same grips. On the cello, as on the violin, there will be a change in sonority, with the two Gs giving added resonance for C minor and G minor. Other chords also change colour, for example E flat major (as in bar 17 of the Prelude) now has an open string, and further chords become possible. This scordatura also gets around the potential awkwardness of a♭ on the D string. Of course many play this Suite without the scordatura (Kellner notates it in normal tuning). Scordatura notation nonetheless shares the advantage of tablature, of telling the player which string the composer wishes to be used at any moment. In bar 27 of the Prelude, for example, the chord at the beginning of the bar that ends the first section has g on the D string, whereas g as the first note of the fugue subject at the end of the bar is the open top string. Bach builds strongly on the foundations of the three lower strings, with pedals on C and on G, and sometimes on C and G, or G and d, combined.

Some editions in scordatura do not give the correct key signature, and of the eighteenth-century sources only P 289 (from the second half of the century) does. It should have the usual three flats and also a natural sign on the top line. In fact the top string is notated with two flats fewer than the others. Neither the A flat nor the E flat in the key signature applies to the top string. Thus the note that is written a (without flat) will be the open top string and sound g. Otherwise notes above a need to be read a tone down in a one-flat signature, so the note that is written b♭ will sound a♭, c♯' will sound b♮, e' without a flat will sound d♮', and so on; but the note that is written a♭ will sound a♭ and be taken from the D string, as will the note written g. Look out also for notes around a♮ that must be taken from the D string (bars 7–8 of Gavotte I, for example). All this will be obvious to those familiar with playing in scordatura, but those reading the score may need some starting help. With only one string detuned there is little difficulty, but readers are not helped by editions that give the key signature incorrectly, and sometimes also try to indicate the sounding pitches as well as the written ones.

Anybody working on this suite would be well advised to look also at Bach's autograph lute arrangement BWV 995 (see the commentary in Chapter Five), from which the many errors in Anna Magdalena Bach's copy can be corrected, and further information about slurrings and ornaments may be deduced. The changes that Bach made in the rhythmic notation of the Allemande are also important. There is no doubt that the cello version came first since there is evidence in the lute arrangement that he was working from a copy in scordatura.

In terms of instrumental ensemble music, neither this nor the E major violin Partia is a regular overture-suite. The E major has the right sort of dances, but an Italian concerto-style Preludio; the C minor cello Suite has a Prelude in the form of a French overture, but the dances of the solo instrumental suite. A further mixture, with dance movements of both types, is in the French Overture for harpsichord in *Clavier-Übung* II (BWV 831). The C minor cello Suite relates less to the ensemble overture-suite than to the suite for solo bass viol or lute, in which a French overture was one of a number of prelude options.

1. *Prelude*

The Prelude is ostensibly in the form of a French overture, with a first section in duple time and a second, imitative, section in triple time, but it is far from the original Lully model (see the discussion in Chapter Two section 6). Bach's Prelude fully represents the late-Baroque development of the overture to include elements of Italian style, such as motivic working in the first section and a fully developed fugue, often combined with the concerto ritornello pattern, in the second. The stylistic markers of the first section of an overture are dotted rhythms and tiratas. To these Bach adds his own predilection for weaving long runs of sixteenths.

Two important aspects of the first section are already present in the first bar. The first is that the time signature is ₵, not c as given by Dörffel in BG and hence other older editions. Of the eighteenth-century sources, only the Vienna MS has c. It was compiled at a time when the ₵ signature was falling out of use, and it changes all ₵ signatures in the Suites to c.[38] So, although

Heinichen describes the first section of the late-Baroque overture as 'normally slow and expressive ['pathetisch']', slowness is relative.[39] In the first section of this Prelude most bars have a chord at the beginning and a decorative second half, as one might expect with only one downbeat and one upbeat per bar. Where there is a chord in the second half of the bar (as in bar 5) some rhetorical emphasis is clearly intended. The second aspect concerns the long slur in bar 1. In most instances these slurs are bowings, but other possibilities should be kept in mind. The very long slurs in the Prelude of the E flat cello Suite can mean a sense of improvisational freedom. Slurs can also on occasion mean that notes are to be played equally (the runs of sixteenths in the overture Variation 16 of the Goldberg Variations have dots over the notes to indicate equality of emphasis, and similar runs, though not marked with dots, are in the Overtures in C major and D major BWV 1066, 1068, 1069). In the C minor cello Prelude they most probably mean that the notes form a single upbeat group, an extended tirata. An identical group of eleven sixteenths in bar 5 of the bassoon part of the D major Overture BWV 1069/1 has a more detailed slurring, with a slur over the first three sixteenths, and the rest slurred in pairs. A similarly detailed slurring is given in the anonymous lute tablature version of BWV 995, though mainly with pairs across the beat (but see also the commentary on BWV 995). The likelihood that slurs in the cello Prelude mean bowings is borne out by bars 23–4, which are slurred in groups of eight in the cello version, giving a slight accent at the beginning of each group, whereas Bach's autograph lute version has a single enormous slur from the middle of bar 22 to the middle of bar 25.

Related to the interpretation of these longer groups is that of the groups of three sixteenth notes. In revisiting works around 1730 Bach seems to have sharpened his notation of dotted rhythms. The best-known case is the French Overture BWV 831, which exists in a copy in C minor by Anna Magdalena Bach (made before mid-1733) and in a printed version in B minor (1735), from copy provided by Bach.[40] What in the C minor version was written ♩ ♫♫ was changed in the B minor version to either ♩. ♬ or ♩ ♩ ♬ , there being no evident difference between these two. Bach made a similar change in the lute version of the Allemande from this cello Suite: where Anna Magdalena Bach has ♩ ♫♫ , Bach's autograph lute version (written 1727–31) has ♩. ♩. ♬ . This is important in that it takes the groups of three sixteenths out of their relation to the longer runs, and makes them purely decorative tiratas. There is no such difference in the notation of the Prelude, except that where Anna Magdalena wrote ♩♬ in bar 7, Bach wrote ♩. ♬ in BWV 995. The fact that bar 7 of the cello version is written with 32nds shows that the groups of three sixteenths elsewhere should probably be played more or less as written, in the spirit of the longer groups. Such things are never quite cut and dried, though, in that the group of three sixteenths in bar 16 is no more than the prefix to a trill and can hardly be meant to have more than a freely decorative function. The notation is therefore to a certain extent free and conventional, rather than exact. On the question of over-dotting, it is part of the range of *notes inégales* in which a background feeling of compound time takes the squareness off the written duple notation. Whatever players decide, it is by no means to be applied mechanically, but a resource to be moulded expressively.

After the broad impetus of the first section, the $\frac{3}{8}$ section brings a much more detailed movement in a light dance metre. There are no tempo indications in any of the eighteenth-century cello sources, other than time signature and rhythmic character, but Bach has marked this second section *tres viste* in the lute version BWV 995. This is Bach's only use of this tempo indication, and is his quickest French tempo.[41] It may be that Bach envisaged a faster tempo for the lute than the cello. If one compares the two $\frac{3}{8}$ Gigues in the cello Suites, the C major has a broad harmonic movement and is clearly quicker than the D minor, whose denser working is closer to that of the C minor Prelude. Although the succession of ¢ and $\frac{3}{8}$ is typical of Lully, the $\frac{3}{8}$ here is in the metre of a passepied, a favourite metre of Bach's and one that became fashionable in the decade after Lully's death. Johann Philipp Kirnberger, a pupil of Bach's with a particular interest in Bach's connoisseurship and command of variety of metres, describes the $\frac{3}{8}$ passepied metre as 'performed in a light but not entirely playful manner'.[42] There are a number of pieces in which Bach plays with the combination of binary dance structure in passepied metre and fugue.[43] In the C minor Prelude he uses his favourite combination of fugue with the concerto ritornello pattern, using the subject as the ritornello, and having modulating episodes that develop elements of the subject in the manner of Marpurg's 'strict' fugue (see Chapter Two section 8). The aspect of dance structure that he has kept is the length of the subject, which at eight bars corresponds to the normal length of first strain of a passepied.

This fugue is an even greater tour de force than the violin fugues in being essentially a single line throughout. The few double stops are mostly to emphasize structural cadences and play no part in the contrapuntal argument. Within this constraint Bach manages to give the impression of a four-voice exposition. He does this by the ingenious way in which he has devised his subject, by the placing of entries, and by their type. As Casals pointed out, the subject in itself gives the effect of having two voices, the first consisting of the first two notes, the second by the next three, and so on.[44] It therefore has two units that can be separated and recombined in different ways. This gives the illusion of different tessituras within the pitch range of two-octaves-and-a-3rd in the exposition (see Ex.4.19). The first entry (end of bar 27, Ex.4.19a) is in the 'alto', with its answer (end of bar 35, Ex.4.19b) in the 'cantus'. There is then a short codetta that develops the tail of the subject (compare bar 34 with bars 43–5), followed by a scale up and a scale down (bars 46–7). These motifs will be further developed in the episodes. The codetta leads to a 'bass' subject entry (end of bar 47, Ex.4.19c) in which Bach has inverted the pitch relationship of the two units of the subject so that this entry uses the lowest octave of the instrument (down to C), with its answer in the 'tenor' (end of bar 55, Ex.4.19d), also with its units inverted. One might ask how it is possible to distinguish alto and tenor entries since both use more or less the same notes. They can be distinguished according to the customary layout of a four-voice exposition in which, if the alto and bass have the subject, then the cantus and tenor have the answer. This is by no means invariable, but it is the background theory.[45] Bach has made a seamless line of his exposition by not having a definite cadence at the end of the subject, so that it can run on into the answer (bars 34–5). The most definite cadence comes at the end of the exposition (in bars 62–3). Further subtleties are the hint of hemiola in the last two bars of each entry, and the hint of the head of the subject (in a sixteenth-note division) in the codetta (bars 44–5), two features that will be richly exploited later.

Ex.4.19 Prelude of BWV 1011, subject entries (at sounding pitch):
a) alto subject, bars 27–35

b) cantus answer, bars 35–43

c) bass subject, bars 47–55

d) tenor answer, bars 55–63

The argument of the rest of the fugue is to have two main entries, one in G minor (end of bar 101–8) and one back in C minor (end of bar 149–57), both with the intervals between the two 'voices' of the subject greatly expanded. At the beginning of the fugue Bach uses the two-unit subject to give the effect of a four-voice exposition; now he exploits the larger dramatic possibilities of this same feature. The G minor entry has the two units the original way up, the C minor has them inverted. On the way, the rising and falling scales of the codetta are expanded into a substantial episode (bars 63–70) that modulates to the relative major (E flat major), as Bach normally does on the way to the dominant in a minor key. In the original subject the tail ran into continuous sixteenths, and this note value now gradually takes over the whole subject, just as the division note value commonly does in the second strains of dance movements in these Suites. This gives endless opportunity for the organic development of motifs. The process begins in the E flat entry (end of bar 71 to bar 79), and is carried further in an allusion to the subject in C minor (end of bar 87) that builds on the hint of the subject in continuous sixteenths noted in the codetta (bars 44–5). This is an allusion, rather than a subject entry: its end is indeterminate and runs into sequential development of the hemiola figure at the end of the subject (bars 92–6). After the G minor entry there is a visit to the subdominant (F minor), with an entry (end of bar 129 to bar 137) equivalent to the E flat one, but now entirely in sixteenths. After the C minor entry with expanded intervals (end of bar 149ff) there is a series of pedals: an upper one from bar 166, and a dominant one in the bass from bar 171 that prepares the final subject entry—a reprise of the 'alto' entry at the beginning, though now ending with a full close (bars 182–3). What seems like an entry from the end of bar 195 is in fact just some motifs taken from the subject, continued as a sequence. The long tonic pedal from bar 209 leads to a final ascent of bass notes from C (bar 214) to G (bar 220). This is an extension of the two, then three, scale steps in the first bar of the subject, which have motivated much scale activity in this fugue. The cadenza in bars 220–2 recalls the similar cadenza for pedals in the organ Fugue in A minor BWV 543/2, a fugue of similar rhythmic character to this (see Ex.2.9a).

2. Allemande

Of Allemandes with a decidedly French *allure*, this makes an instructive comparison with the Allemanda of the B minor violin Partia. There, Bach has a typical allemande opening phrase, has written out the *notes inégales*, and mixed in galant-style triplets. The structure of the piece is nonetheless a sonata one, with long spun-out phrases of indeterminate length, on which he has worked a surface of French-style ingredients. The same applies to the C minor cello Allemande, though the ingredients here are different ones.[46] In this piece Bach has taken two characteristics of a French *entrée*, or first section of an overture: the dotted rhythm, and the tirata or *trait*. To these he has added his own favoured ingredient of extended runs in even sixteenths, and applied these surface ingredients to a sonata structure. It all has the neat effect of picking up again the features of the first section of the overture-style Prelude. Often in French overtures the duple-time of the first section returns again after the second section, so there is an expectation that the first section of the Prelude will return again after the *tres viste* fugal second section. But it does not, and the Allemande answers that expectation instead. In this there is another point of comparison with the French Overture for harpsichord BWV 831. There the ¢-time section does indeed return at the end of the overture, which may account for the fact that the dance movements do not begin with an allemande, but go straight into the Courante.

The C minor Allemande shares with the first section of the Prelude more than just the general features of dotted rhythms, tiratas, and runs of sixteenths. The opening figure in bar 1 is identical to that from the end of bar 5 of the Prelude, which Bach had particularly emphasised there by having a chord in the middle of bar 5, the only time he does so before the final cadence of the section. Both Prelude and Allemande develop this figure in endless rhythmic variants, used for extended phrase building. The variable length and elaboration of upbeat figures give a great variety of emphasis to the downbeats. Another feature in common with the Prelude is the implication of different voices. The opening phrase of the Allemande has an Invention-type 'exposition', much favoured by Bach, in which the figure in the cantus in bar 1 is imitated in the bass in bar 2. There are further developments between voices later on, as when the melodic line in the cantus in bar 23 migrates to the bass in bar 24 and to the middle voice in bar 25.[47] There are further layers here in that these bars are bound together by a top line in which the note a♭ (bar 24) increases in tension to become a minor 9th in bar 25, before resolving to g in the second half of the bar, the g in turn being rendered dissonant by the D♭ in bar 26, and drawn down to e♮ in bar 27.

One writer has commented that this Allemande 'seems to many players to be in danger of falling apart structurally'.[48] This may be in part because of the excessively slow tempi chosen by some, in view of the fact that the time signature of the Allemande, as of the Prelude, is ¢.[49] The middle of the bar is therefore an upbeat and, as in the Prelude, there are very few chords other than on the downbeat. It may also be because of the sophistication with which Bach has dealt with his mixed dance/sonata genre. The opening phrase is an irregular shape of five bars. Within that it has the Invention-type imitation in bar 2, and a hint of a very irregularly placed *coulé de tierce* caesura at the beginning of bar 4. The argument of the phrase is to mould the rhythm of the opening bar expressively, with different groups of sixteenths that climax on an expressive dominant minor 9th in the middle of bar 4. The long sixteenth-note upbeat in bar 5 then begins the move away from the tonic. In accordance with his usual harmonic scheme for a minor-key movement, Bach passes through the relative major (E flat) on the way to the dominant (G minor) at the double bar. In this piece, though, he has a policy of avoiding cadences in intermediate keys. In his desire to keep the phrase from touching the ground harmonically between bar 5 and the double bar, he approaches an E flat major cadence (bars 11–13), but immediately slides off it to C minor (bars 13–14), the note C in turn becoming the bass of a last-inversion dominant 7th (6/4/2) in G minor (see the figured-bass abstract in Ex.4.20). Bach similarly deflects the customary subdominant (F minor) cadence in the second strain (bars 28–9). This avoidance of intermediate cadential punctuation is clearly intended to make sections as continuous as possible, and an understanding of the strategy is necessary for feeling the coherence of the piece.

Ex.4.20 Allemande of BWV 1011, figured-bass abstract

In the version for lute, BWV 995, Bach has consistently written his *inventio* in dotted rhythm (♩. ♪ ♫ instead of ♩ ♪ ♫ ♫). This applies to the second quarters of bars 1, 2, 6, 7, 13, 20, 22, 27 and 29, and to the first quarter of bar 13, but not to bars 11–12. The imprecise notation of the lute version indicates the ornamental quality of the figure. Quantz (1752) describes the traditional way of playing this figure in overtures and *entrées*: the dotted note should be played with emphasis and the bow detached during the dot. If three or more 32nds follow a dot or rest they are not always played in their literal value, especially in slow pieces, but executed at the extreme end of the time allotted to them, with the greatest possible speed. Each 32nd is bowed separately and slurring is seldom used.[50] Whether or not this should be applied back to the Prelude is for players to decide. All that can be said is that Bach did not notate it there. It may be significant that the lute intabulation (not by Bach) consistently lacks the tie to the second quarter note in the *inventio* of the Allemande (Ex.4.21).[51] Evidently the intabulator felt that the note was too long without repetition, whereas in the equivalent figure in bar 6 etc. of the Prelude the note

Ex.4.21 Allemande of BWV 995, bars 1-4, anonymous lute intabulation

is not repeated and the three sixteenths come after a sixteenth-note rest (see Ex.5.2). Particularly in this movement it is worth looking at Bach's lute version, especially for ideas for ornamental variants that might be useful in repeats.

3. Courante

The Allemande and Courante in this Suite are a tightly related pair. Both are superficially in French style (this is the only Courante of these Suites in $\frac{3}{2}$-time), yet both are masterly examples of the mixed style, in which a collection of surface features clothe what is essentially a sonata structure of long spun-out phrases with developmental motivic working. A sonata dimension that is perhaps less obvious is the relationship of these two movements to the type of sonata Adagio represented by the first movement of the G minor violin Sonata BWV 1001, in which a chord is followed by a flourish. The difference is that the flourishes in this Allemande and Courante are cast in the motivic language of their respective dance genres. Like the Allemande, the Courante has a five-bar opening phrase, but with a bass in the manner of an organ pedal part that regularly goes up five notes of the scale before the cadence (see the figured-bass abstract in Ex.4.22). There is an identical move away from the tonic in bars 5-6 of both pieces. A further detail that connects them is the $\frac{6}{4}$-time bar at the end of each strain of the Courante, whose sixteenths and rhythm refer to the *inventio* of the Allemande. These are the only $\frac{3}{2}$-time bars here, which differentiates this Courante from ones by, for example, François Couperin, with their typical shifting between $\frac{3}{2}$ and $\frac{6}{4}$ (see Ex.2.6a). Instead of this Bach exploits a regular metre, with its possibilities for motivic working.

In other respects this Courante complements the Allemande rather than resembles it. Spitta has a poetic description of the subject rising from the depths in the first phrase (as does the Prelude), with a corresponding sinking down again at the end.[52] The Allemande, by contrast, works from the top down. A less obvious difference is that the Courante is broken up into smaller phrases. The phrases are marked off by the figure of four descending eighth notes, which is one of Bach's equivalents to the *coulé de tierce* phrase-ending formula. The campaign of these in the first strain is the key to the argument

Ex.4.22   Courante of BWV 1011, figured-bass abstract

of this Courante. They come at the beginnings of bars 7 and 9, and are a formula for a weak, indeterminate phrase ending, fading out as on a mute vowel at the end of a French poetic line, with a slight pause afterwards and a new impetus on the note that begins the next phrase on the second beat of the bar. If we take the first three bars of the Courante as having three separate rhythms (the first with two beats of eighth notes, the second with a dotted note on the third beat, and the third with quarter notes); then the phrases from bar 5 extend and develop these (the first in bars 5–6, the second in bars 8 and 10, and the third in bars 9 and 11). This is held together by the successive rise in crucial pitches, from b♭ in bar 6 to e♭' in bar 10. As usual in these binary pieces, the division note value (eighths here) becomes more pervasive in the second strain, so in bars 17 and 21 there is an *enjambement* in which the phrase-ending eighth notes run on into further eighths in the following phrase (compare Ex.2.6b).

Separate quarter notes are one of the prime rhythmic characteristics of this type of French courante, and according to Quantz the bow is to be detached on each quarter, each quarter being a separate pulse.[53] This explains the dots over the quarter notes in the second beat of bar 3 in P 289, meaning equality of emphasis as well as separation, and the articulation is obviously meant to be continued with subsequent quarters. With regard to eighth notes, there is the usual problem of locating the piece in the spectrum of mixed styles. In spite of the bowing in fours it is difficult for anybody familiar with the keyboard and chamber music of Couperin to feel the eighths here as absolutely equal. In the spectrum of Courante types (see Chapter Two section 2), this Courante comes with Courante I of the A major English Suite and the Courante of the D minor French Suite, not quite at the extreme French end represented by the Courante of the C major Overture-suite BWV 1066, but with enough French characteristics to justify a slight tug of pairs. This would apply to broken chords (as in bar 11) as well as to melodic steps, as it does in *style brisé* lute music. The combination of detached quarter notes and slight inequality of eighths gives a natural moderate tempo and poise to the movement.

4. Sarabande

This Sarabande is a thoroughgoing stylistic paradox. In its phrase structure it is a typical French sarabande, yet its surface is worked entirely in the division note value of a sonata movement. Its eighth-notes have therefore nothing to do with French *notes inégales*. Bach worked the sarabande structure in many different ways but they all have in common the four-bar phrase units without which they would have no connection with the genre. In spite of the surface working, this Sarabande is in fact more typical than many in that it has two four-bar phrases in the first strain, the first in the standard pattern 1+1+2 bars, ending on the weak third beat, followed by 4 bars that go straight through, ending on a downbeat. In a French sarabande the second phrase would have a hemiola, which is hinted at in the figurations here, though hardly noticeable.

There are a number of contributory factors in the stylistic background to this piece. In Italian sonata terms there is a typical Corellian type of sarabande with the usual structure in the melody, but with a bass accompaniment that moves in continuous equal eighths (see Ex.2.3). This way of combining dance and sonata/concertante styles was used by many, including Bach, in various dance genres. In the tradition of division variations, which is related to the sonata style, the Sarabandes in Johann Schenck's *Scherzi musicali* Op.6 for bass viol (1698) are mostly followed by a *Variatio* in eighth notes (see also Chapter One section 4 for German lute and keyboard examples). In Bach's own practice, we have noted on many occasions his tendency to increase the proportion of division note values in the second strains of binary pieces. The Sarabande of the D minor cello Suite, for example, goes into very similar movement to this in its second strain. Bach's originality in the C minor is to apply the principle from the very beginning, and see how it can be developed as an *inventio*.

Having decided to restrict himself to a single line throughout, Bach's main expressive resources are melodic dissonance and tessitura. One phenomenon of *senza basso* instrumental music is that the lone instrument can make even the simplest things sound highly expressive, a phenomenon characteristic of the repertory from Domenico Gabrielli to Telemann. In a sensitive performance even such a simple idea as going up the plain notes of the A minor triad followed by a major 7th leap down, at the beginning of Telemann's A minor

Fantasia for transverse flute, can be extraordinarily moving (see Ex.6.2). In the C minor Sarabande Bach goes much further, with a large proportion of dissonant intervals either approached directly or implied by proximity, as in the implication of the augmented 2nd B♮–A♭ in bar 1. He also concentrates on one of the most melodically expressive devices, the appoggiatura. This can be expressive of well-being in a warm major key (as in the prelude on 'Wachet auf' BWV 645 in the 'Schübler' organ chorales), or the extreme of chromatic anguish (as in the subject of the B minor Fugue from Book I of *The Well-tempered Clavier*). In the C minor Sarabande Bach ranges over this expressive spectrum, from the stark C minor opening to the warmth of E flat major in the second phrase.

Tessitura and density of movement are then important for development. In the first phrase, bar 2 expands the pitch range, and bars 3–4 expand it yet further, the expansion being matched by extension of the group of eighths from one bar to two. As one might expect, this is in miniature the argument of the whole Sarabande. The second strain again has a phrase of 1+1+2 bars, but then a continuous phrase of eight bars, building up to the climactic e♭' in bar 17. It seems sacrilegious to provide a figured-bass abstract for this, but it is worth doing to see quite how powerfully Bach has made his single line imply strongly dissonant harmony (Ex.4.23; the abstract also takes into account the autograph lute version, which gives Bach's own interpretation of the harmony). The first two bars seem to do what Telemann did in his A minor flute Fantasia, i.e. add an expressive note below a triad: the major 7th below g in bar 1, the diminished 7th below a♭ in bar 2. As one would expect, the second strain brings a higher level of dissonance: first the D♭ in bar 9, but then the extraordinarily expressive and complex 11th chord in bar 11. The fact that these figured-bass progressions lie behind the single line is what gives the solos their solidity and power. Few of Bach's contemporaries could match his ability to conjure up such rich harmonic effects from so few notes.

Ex.4.23 Sarabande of BWV 1011, figured-bass abstract

5. Gavottes

Whatever the technical feel of Gavotte I, the intention can hardly be one of dramatic, effortful chordal playing. It must be in the light, dance nature of the gavotte, with the cello played 'lyra-way' as one might expect in scordatura. Chordal gavottes are endemic in French viol music from Demachy to Marais.

This is another good example of the principle in lighter dances of having a dance-metre antecedent and a sonata-style consequent in a division note value (eighths in this case). The consequent does nonetheless continue the chordal nature of the antecedent by being *style brisé* chords rather than melodic decoration. The appoggiaturas added in bars 1–3 in the two later eighteenth-century sources mask the distinction of styles between the two types of phrase and should perhaps be reserved for a repeat or da capo. The remarks made with regard to the Courante about the *coulé de tierce* intermediate phrase-ending formula, in the form of four descending eighth notes, hold good here as well. The phrase endings in bars 4 and 8 are both of this type. In the second strain there are again cases of *enjambement* to give greater continuity: in bar 16 the formula is repeated in sequence to lead into the next phrase, and in bar 30 also the eighths continue.

The lute version (BWV 995) clarifies Bach's view of the harmony, particularly in places such as in bars 17–19 where the solo cello figurations are slightly oblique. It also has a very attractive sequence of 7ths in bars 1–4, and a particularly neat feature is the effect of dialogue between upper and lower courses in this phrase.

Gavotte II is unusual in being in the same mode as Gavotte I, so has to achieve contrast by other means. It raises the division note value from eighths to triplets, though it is by no means a division on Gavotte I (a very clear idea of the underlying harmony is given by Bach's lute version). It also harks back to the Sarabande in being exclusively in a single line, without double stops other than the unison in bar 8 that hardly affects the integrity of the line. In the lute version, Bach heads it 'Gavotte 2nde en Rondeaux', indicating its combination of binary and rondeau structures, another contrast with Gavotte I (see also the commentary on the pair of Gavottes in the D major cello Suite).

Being almost entirely in its division note value one expects sonata-style phrase extensions. Most of the second strain is accordingly taken up by the long extended phrase from bar 13 to the double bar, with two avoided cadences, the second of which runs into a reprise of the opening motif (bar 20). One may, though, see a connection with Gavotte I in one of the basic figures of Gavotte II (Ex.4.24a, given from the lute version), in which a 3rd alternates with a diminished 5th. This progression is in bars 5–7 of Gavotte I in the cello version (Ex.4.24b); since it is part of the *soggetto* of Gavotte II, it recurs many times in the course of that piece.

Kirnberger comments on the difference between $\frac{9}{8}$-time (as for example in the Double of the B minor violin Sarabande) and $\frac{3}{4}$-time with triplets (as here). $\frac{3}{4}$ triplets are 'quite light and without the least accent on the last note',

Ex.4.24 a) Gavotte II of BWV 995, bars 4–8

b) Gavotte I of BWV 1011, bars 5–8 (at sounding pitch)

while $^9_8$ is 'heavier, and with some weight on the last note'.[54] In other words $^9_8$ often has a change of harmony on the last of the group of three eighths, but not triplets, so triplets are more fluent. Anna Magdalena Bach has two pause marks in the final bar of Gavotte II, one over the first note of the bar (c) and one over the double bar-line. This may be to show that Gavotte II should stop on the upper c after the second-strain repeat, before repeating Gavotte I da capo.

6. Gigue

This movement has caused some puzzlement. The incessant dotted rhythm has been found 'heavy', the long notes have been thought to prove that the lute version came first since it has imitations under them, and in spite of the typical canarie rhythm it has been found to be 'not a true canarie' because of its phrase structure.[55] Bach, unusually, has three Gigues in these Suites with the same $^3_8$ time signature, but he still preserves his usual objective of representing different types. We have already noted the difference between the D minor Gigue, dense and serious, and the C major, more open and fluent. The C minor Gigue carries this trend further. It seems to pick up the swirling triplets of Gavotte II and intensify them to a wild, ecstatic quality, a quality that is in the tradition of the canarie.[56] It lacks the typical canarie upbeat ♫ ♩ | ♫ ♩ | (used in the canarie/gigue of the C minor French Suite, a movement worth comparing with this), but the simpler upbeat contributes to the headlong impetus. The wild quality is in the hypnotically insistent rhythm, and the swirling effect of having so much built on falling thirds (again like Gavotte II). It is also in the fact that the entire first strain can be read as a single phrase, whose climax note is emphasized by length, and by the extraordinary rhythmic effect of falling away from it in a series of what Little and Jenne call 'megameasures', with only one downbeat in three bars (bars 15–17, 18–20, 61–3, 64–6).[57] In comparison, the lute version, with its 'Invention' interpretation of the opening bars and little imitations, seems tame. There is no point in using length as such to emphasise a climax note on the lute or harpsichord since they cannot sustain it. This is true *senza basso* writing.

The ultimate ecstatic moment is in bars 55–6. The later eighteenth-century sources put a trill sign on each note; Anna Magdalena Bach has a wavy line running from the (sounding) e♭' to just before the f' in bar 57. In the lute version Bach just has a trill sign on the equivalent of the e♮', with a written-out turn at the end. The options for this sign have been discussed with reference to the Grave of the A minor violin Sonata BWV 1003/1. Suggestions range from bow vibrato (Frederick Neumann) to continuous trills (as in equivalent places in Bach's organ Sonatas).[58] An appealing possibility, given the ecstatic moment, is to use French viol technique, with an accelerating left-hand vibrato on the e♭', glissando up the semitone, turning into a trill on the e♮', perhaps with the lute's turn at the end.[59] The anonymous lute intabulation has a vibrato sign at the beginnings of bars 16 and 32.[60]

Suite 6 in D major BWV 1012

1. Prelude

The question of the instrument for which this Suite may have been written is discussed in Chapter One section 3. The principle of structuring a piece around bariolage on the open strings is an obvious one. As we have noted in Chapter One, gigues featuring campanella/bariolage are endemic in lute, viol and violin music of this time. The Giga of the second of Telemann's 1715 *Six Sonates* for violin provides a straightforward example. In D major and $\frac{12}{8}$-time it inevitably shares material with Bach's Prelude, though the comparison is perhaps unfair since Telemann intended no more than a light-hearted movement to finish a suite, whereas Bach was conducting profound 'research' into the principle. Telemann's headlong gigue tempo would also not suit Bach's sixteenth-note cadenza in bars 83–9.

In Bach's own works the obvious comparison is with the Preludio of the E major violin Partia, and indeed there are many points of contact between the two movements, even allowing for Bach's agenda of representing different types rather than repeating them. Both are the sixth of their respective sets. Both use a slightly unusual harmonic structure (for Bach) because of the necessity of having open strings as tonal centres: the E major Preludio has an unusually heavy emphasis on the subdominant A major; the D major Prelude emphasises the supertonic E minor (i.e. the top string of the five strings). Their time signatures ($\frac{3}{4}/\frac{12}{8}$) are complementary (triple simple/duple compound), and both make use of harmonic pedals and echoes to evoke largeness of scale. Yet the effect is somewhat different in each case. The violin Preludio is in a very extrovert concerto style, whereas the cello Prelude is in a more meditative, sonata style, perhaps providing an opposition of church and chamber between these two pieces. In spite of having virtually the same number of bars (102/104), the cello Prelude is substantially longer because of its four beats per bar and tempo. The areas, as the Prelude develops, are correspondingly broader.

Five strings offer more scope for bariolage than four, and this may explain the curious bracket around the top four strings in Anna Magdalena Bach's copy. Each of them provides an important structural node in the Prelude. The C string is by no means dispensable. Its use is always part of an important line, and especially as the climax to the long bass descent from a to E in bars 75–82 (see the figured-bass abstract Ex.4.25): a climactic use of the 6/4/3 chord similar to that in bar 13 of the G major Allemande. In transposing the Prelude down to G major for a four-string instrument lines can be adapted, but the spaciousness of the effect is undermined.

Apart from bariolage, the opening *inventio* features echoes. As noted in the E major violin Preludio, and elsewhere in the violin Solos, these can give a concerto-style spaciousness, particularly when combined with long harmonic pedals. In the D major prelude they have spaciousness, but they also contribute a structural effect of isolating bars 1 and 3 as two concentrated blocks of material from which the rest of the Prelude will develop.[61] This intensifies the effect of opening out from a repeated unison. Most of the echoes are in the two later eighteenth-century sources; Kellner has none, and Anna Magdalena Bach stopped writing them after bar 15. One wonders if later in the Prelude they do not sometimes become a mannerism that interrupts the flow, particularly when the 'echo' does not repeat the bar before, as in bars 46ff. The climbing figures from bars 66–9 are important in building up to the very long A pedal that begins (in the figurations) in bar 70, and the gradation would be better served by a crescendo than a *piano*. It may be noted that there is no echo indication in bar 11 in any eighteenth-century source; the *piano* in the equivalent place in bar 22 is in the later sources only.

The Prelude, as so commonly with Bach, is based on his usual ritornello shape in its sonata version, repeated with expansions and developments in ever larger sections. The first section is of twelve bars, starting with a closed shape of four bars, then a sequence that modulates to the dominant (bars 5–9), and a closing motif with a pedal (bars 10–11). The opening and closing elements present, as it were, a list of three pedal patterns, arranged in order of increasing elaboration. Bar 1 grows from a single note, adding the other factors of the tonic chord one by one, similar to the way in which composers of the time constructed phrases for the natural trumpet; bar 3 has a simple

Ex.4.25 Prelude of BWV 1012, figured-bass abstract

harmonic alternation of 5/3 and 6/4 chords, and adds passing notes; bar 10 has both rising and falling shapes. This is a simple example of the ability to arrange ideas into significant form, part of the rhetorical technique of *dispositio*; the other aspect of the technique is to develop them. Within this section there is already significant development in that the sequence in bars 5–7 develops the three-note shape in the first beat of bar 3, putting it end-to-end with itself and expanding the intervals; and the rising arpeggios with passing notes in bars 8–9 develop the shape from the second to the sixth notes of bar 3. The closing motif in bars 10–11 is ambiguous since it is itself a pedal on the A string, so could be regarded as the beginning of the A major 'answer'. The real beginning in A major has nonetheless to be the bariolage figure in bar 12, corresponding to bar 1. Bach exploits this ambiguity later.

From bar twelve the opening section is repeated, based on the A string, with the modulation now bringing us up to the top string (bars 12–22). At this point it is time for more development, so pitches now open up into expanding intervals around a repeated e' (bars 23–30) until they grow into the sequence material (as at bar 5ff) that modulates up yet another 5th to B minor (bars 30–3). The bariolage in E minor is subtly varied by having a mixture of whole-bar patterns (bars 23–4, 27–8) and half-bar patterns (bars 25–6, 29–30), reflected in the dynamic markings of the later sources. B minor, relative minor, is a more important related key than E minor, so it has a longer and more importantly developmental section (bars 33–46), with a higher melodic dissonance level and greater pitch range. This section does not modulate in itself, but ends with the closing motif still in B minor (bar 46), exploiting the ambiguity of the figure by leaving us wondering what its function is now that it no longer marks the arrival at a new key centre. In the event it moves towards the next important tonal goal, G major (subdominant; bars 54ff), where we return to the opening material with bariolage on the last string where it is possible. The emphasis given to the subdominant (a 5th below the tonic) by the reprise is important to balance the preceding move up three successive 5ths to B minor.

Most of the rest of the piece is a long dominant pedal. This looks as if it begins at bar 68, but here again we have ambiguity since bars 68–9 have the function of the closing motif, introducing the new pedal section that runs from 70, essentially to bar 86. In the figured-bass abstract I have notated the movement of the parts in order to show the structure of scales with 7–6 suspensions, accelerating in bar 81 to the climactic 6/4/3 which covers a wide range of the instrument, then filled in by the sixteenth-note cadenza. In bars 90–2 the bariolage moves down from the A string back to the D string, and in bars 97–8 intervals get smaller and more chromatic, continued in skeletal form in the chords in bars 98–9. The final tonic pedal is an expansion of the pattern in bar 3 to Bach's normal five-chord pedal formula, similar to that at the opening of the G major Prelude. Bach has infinite ways of decorating this formula according to the motivic working of the piece. At the beginning of the G major Prelude he uses the same arpeggiation pattern for each chord; at the end of the D major he has a different pattern for each chord, as he had used different pedal patterns at the opening. As a whole this Prelude is a compelling study and 'research' of the idea of the pedal. It is one of the most effective demonstrations of Bach's growth principle, in which seemingly endless diversity on the broadest scale can develop naturally and logically from the simplest possible unit of a repeated note.

2. Allemande

At the end of the Prelude J.P. Kellner has the instruction 'Sequi Allemande adagio', and indeed this movement is perhaps the ultimate marriage of the sonata adagio and the allemande. The obvious comparison is with the Adagio of the G minor violin Sonata, which has the same scheme of large chords on main beats, separated by flourishes. This manner has been seen as related to the 'Agréments' for Corelli's Op.5 Sonatas published by Étienne Roger (Amsterdam) in 1710.[62] It was not an uncommon one in adagios and allemandes, and the same manner is shared by the Adagio of Sonata IV and the Allemand of Sonata V of Johann Schenck's manuscript sonatas for unaccompanied bass viol.[63] Less obvious is the comparison with the Allemande and Courante of Bach's C minor cello Suite, where in the Allemande the flourishes are replaced by the dotted rhythms and tiratas of the French *entrée*, and in the Courante they take the form of typical French courante groups of eighths in $\frac{3}{2}$ metre. Since all the other Allemandes of these Suites, with the possible exception of the D minor, are of the sonata allegro type, it may be that this and the C minor are intended to represent other possible sub-genres. The D major cello Allemande has also been compared to the Allemande of the D major clavier Partita BWV 828 (published 1728).[64] That comparison serves only to underline the difference between the manner of this cello Allemande (whether originated by Corelli or not, it stems from the Corelli era), and the rhythmically highly organised decorative surface, including triplets, of the galant adagio of the 1720s, as represented in the clavier Partita. As in the G minor violin Adagio, the continuous beaming of notes in the eighteenth-century sources is highly suggestive of the improvisatory freedom of these flourishes, a freedom that is undermined in the *c.*1824 edition by crudely chopping them into eighth-note groupings. The compromises adopted in the Bärenreiter variorum and, less so, in BG are still inhibiting to freedom.

Adagio, as in the cognate opening movement of the G minor violin Sonata, is probably a fairer expressive pointer that the 'molto adagio' of the two later eighteenth-century sources. The direction 'Molto adagio' is rare in Bach's works and something of a special effect.[65] Adagio better implies the steady tread of harmonic progression, with the freedom of flourishes in highly decorative note values. A very slow tempo loses the necessary duality of slow movement made expressive by a surface of fast-moving notes. Given this duality, the decorations have an ecstatic quality, helped by the radiance of D major and the brightness of the E string, that Bach supports by masking the main structural cadences. As the figured-bass extract (Ex.4.26) shows, the structure is the usual one of a closed phrase in the tonic (to bar 3), followed by a move to the dominant: first to its relative minor (F sharp minor, bar 4), then to A major. The harmonic structure of this second element is particularly neat since bars 5–6 have the same progression as bars 1–3, but reinterpreted in A major. Bar 7 has the effect of a closing motif, repeated in bar 19. Within this, the main cadence into bar 3 is elided by the decoration of the *coulé de tierce* phrase ending. In the equivalent effect in bar 5, the trill is only in the two later sources and would normally be on the g♯' as a *tremblement lié* in this formula. Having it on the f♯' may well be intentional, though, since it slightly detracts from the phrase-ending feel of the formula. In both cases the formula puts an irregular accent on the chord on the second beat, dramatically emphasizing the beginning of the new phrase.

Ex.4.26   Allemande of BWV 1012, figured-bass abstract

Phrases are extended in the second strain, with more continuous 32nd movement. The long implied bass descent (bars 9–12) leads to F sharp minor, representing the minor mode. This is normally the point of maximum dissonance, as is the case in the dominant minor 9th in bar 13, resolved in expressive second-practice style by leap to the 3rd. After the F sharp minor cadence in bar 14 there is a single long harmonic period to the end. Both strains end with the same five-chord pedal formula that ended the Prelude.

3. Courante

After the ecstatic meditation of the Allemande, the Courante seems designed to provide maximum contrast in its broad, athletic movement. It takes up again the spacious planning of the Prelude, and also details of figuration: the arpeggiated pedal at the opening, and the sixteenth-note patterns in bars 49–50 etc. (compare bars 84–5 of the Prelude). There is spaciousness also in the opening phrase, continuous for eight bars, and which covers the total pitch range (D–b') used in this piece. After that we have to wait unusually long for the g♯ (bar 12) that will take us to the dominant.

Comparison with the C major cello Courante shows what a difference just a pair of sixteenths in bar 1 can make. Although the C major is longer (84 bars) there seems to be a great deal more going on in the D major's 72 bars. Comparison with the E flat major cello Courante shows Bach using a different principle of development for sixteenths here. They begin to grow in the dominant pedal (of A major; bars 12–14), the tension generated by the pedal being then released in the stream of sixteenths cascading down a sequence of falling 3rds (bars 15–18). If these sixteenths are relaxing, a correspondingly more intricate and busier rising version is part of the closing material (bars 23–5).

As one would expect, the opening phrase contains in microcosm the materials of the piece. As the figured-bass abstract shows (Ex.4.27) there are two progressions: a rising 4th in the progression d–g implied by bars 2–3 (g represented by its first inversion), and falling 3rds (bars 3–6). The rest of the abstract shows how sequences of rising 4ths and falling 3rds, moving at different speeds, control the pace of the movement. There are the usual three elements in the first strain: a closed phrase of eight bars at the beginning; a

Ex.4.27 Courante of BWV 1012, figured-bass abstract

modulating section (bars 9–19); and an expansive closing area (bars 20–8), defined as such by its repetition at the end of the second strain (bars 64–72). After the double bar, the second strain inverts not only the arpeggios of the opening, but also the stream of sixteenths of bars 15ff (bars 59–63), now decorating a series of rising 3rds. A further element of the first strain that is developed in the second is the 4#/2 chord in bar 26. This motivates the falling chromatic progression in bars 43–6, answered by a rising one in bars 51–5.

Bach normally has a pitch strategy based on the total range used, and this is another binding and focusing factor. Of the pitch range outlined in the opening phrase of the first strain, the b' (bar 3) is energetically built up to and emphatically repeated at the relative minor area (B minor; bars 39–41), the area that normally has maximum tension; while the D that concludes it (bar 8) returns again only at the very end (bar 72).

4. Sarabande

Sarabandes in $\frac{3}{2}$ time are not necessarily slower than those in $\frac{3}{4}$, nor necessarily more grave (this Sarabande could hardly be described as more grave than the $\frac{3}{4}$ Sarabanda of the D minor violin Partia).[66] It seems rather to imply a broadness of movement, in this case the extension and expansiveness that Bach evidently associates with the five-string cello. Other sarabandes with this time signature share this quality. That of the D minor English Suite for clavier has an elaborate Double in eighth notes; that in the E minor Suite 'aufs Lauten Werck' BWV 996 has decorative note values up to 32nds. These two are certainly grave in the sense of minor-key seriousness, suggesting that the D major cello Sarabande may have the affect of a major-key lament, in the sense of Handel's 'Lascia ch'io pianga' from *Rinaldo* (1711).[67] This would account for the prominent leap to the subdominant in bar 2, and the long development of falling paired notes ('Seufzer') in the second strain, and makes the sweetness of the D major 3rd in the first chord particularly poignant. On the other hand, the leap to G may have more to do with the convenience of open strings in a heavily chordal texture. Perhaps all these things coincide. Either way, this very beautiful and expressive piece has been much loved, and frequently arranged for other media.[68]

Of the Sarabandes, this most nearly approaches the aria type cultivated by contemporaries such as the lutenist Silvius Leopold Weiss. The structure of the first phrase (1+1+1+1 bars) is Handelian, as noted above. Bach's constant agenda in these binary pieces, of development through the common decorative note value, is nonetheless present here too. The first phrase introduces the two main ingredients: the falling 3rd and cambiata shape (i.e. 3rd leap down and step back; bar 2), and the slurred step down (bar 4). In the second strain the quarter-note movement gradually becomes all-pervasive, on the principle of short dance phrases being extended into longer sonata phrases. Bach's ability to integrate every decorative detail into the motivic scheme is well illustrated in bars 13–14, where what looks like ordinary part movements in *style brisé* (from the middle of bar 13 to the middle of bar 14) can also be read as a palindromic version of the cambiata shape, with expanded intervals. This intellectual element is not just incidental. It focuses and refines the other gifts of melody and rich harmony and textures, which are all the stronger for being controlled.

This is another Sarabande for which Arnold Dolmetsch has suggested conventional French *notes inégales*, and notated it in $\frac{9}{4}$ time, though with the caveat that 'this lengthening and shortening of notes is not bound by mathematical divisions of time'.[69] As we have seen with reference to the D minor cello Sarabande, in sophisticated French solo instrumental music rhythmic inequality is variable and depends on the expressive moment. Anything approaching ordinary French inequality would be out quite of place in the aria style with sonata features of the D major Sarabande. But emphasis in the sense of 'good' notes and 'bad' notes is clearly needed.[70] With sensitive placing, the second-beat pauses and various types of paired quarter notes in the first strain can be made to express great maturity of emotion with seeming simplicity, opening out into longer, eloquent phrases in the second strain.

5. Gavottes

The time signatures ¢ and 2 (𝟤 in Kellner's copy) are tantalising since they would seem to imply some distinction of tempo or affect between the two Gavottes. Of writers in Bach's environment, neither Quantz nor Kirnberger have anything relevant to this situation. In Lully's dance music the two time signatures appear to have been interchangeable.[71] A number of early eighteenth-century French writers say there is no difference, though some say 2 is faster, without being specific. Saint Lambert (1702) is unique in saying that it is twice as fast. Georg Muffat (1698), who had known Lully and preached French style in Germany, says it is slower.[72] One can take one's pick. Given Bach's propensity for encyclopaedic demonstrations of different types and sub-genres it may be that he wanted to represent both signatures since they were both in common use for the Gavotte, there being no real difference between them. Or the difference may be one of affect or style: the courtly ¢, the rustic 2.

This can hardly be called a variation suite, yet Bach explores different characters of similar basic materials in successive movements. The Prelude uses open strings for architectural pedal effects (courtly virtuosity); the Gavottes use them for rustic drones (pastoral simplicity). Even Gavotte I has something of a drone effect at its opening, using the G, D, and A strings for a pair of open 5ths, while Gavotte II features a D-string drone. The first four movements alternate two types of beginning: the Prelude and Courante start by building up arpeggios from the tonic note; the Allemande and Sarabande begin with the same chord of D major with the 3rd on top, as do the Gavottes. Gavotte I and the Sarabande are very much a pair in the number of chords and grips they have in common, but used for quite different characters. Both move to the subdominant note for their second chord, but whereas the strong subdominant 7th at the beginning of bar 1 of the Gavotte is the movement's defining sonority, the Sarabande concentrates on smooth parallel 6ths, rounded out by appoggiaturas.

Apart from their inherent contrast of character, the two Gavottes also differ in phrase structure, representing two different combinations of binary and rondeau patterns. Gavotte I is a rounded binary structure, with a decorated reprise of the first strain at the end (bars 20ff). There is an element of rondeau in this, but it is very much strengthened in Gavotte II, which is properly a combination of binary form and rondeau (the eighteenth-century sources do not write out the repeat in bars 21–4, but direct the player back to a *segno* ⁒ at the beginning, as in a regular rondeau). This matches the contrast between the two Gavottes in the C minor cello Suite, the second of which Bach headed (in his autograph lute arrangement) 'Gavotte 2nde en Rondeaux'. There are, as it were, two couplets: bars 4–8 which adumbrate a drone pedal, and bars 12–20 which have the drone fully presented. Repetition of the first strain *en rondeau* gives this Gavotte something of the sublime simplicity of Bourrée II of the E flat cello Suite.

Although the cello Gavottes are less influenced by sonata style than the violin ones, they nonetheless increase the division note value (eighth notes here) after the double bar. Kellner's rhythm for the drone in Gavotte II (quarter notes continued in bar 15, half notes in bar 16) underlines the elision of the phrase ending in bar 16, but hardly matches the eighth-note figurations above, or the antecedent/consequent structure of bars 14–20 as a whole.

6. *Gigue*

Whatever the order in which Bach wrote these Suites, there is a feeling that we have made a journey from the G major, and now return in the D major Suite to elements of that, but having arrived at a more advanced playing technique, greater variety of material, and a more elaborate way of dissecting and developing it. As in the G major Suite, the Prelude and Courante open with arpeggiations of the tonic triad, starting on the tonic note; the Allemande,

Sarabande and Gavotte I (Menuet I in the G major) with a three-note chord with the 3rd on top, and the Gigue with the 5th leaping to the tonic. It is as if all the movements were growing from the opening of the Prelude, outlining successive notes of the tonic triad, and completing it with the Gigue. Both Suites have a Gigue with a hunting flavour, this character more pronounced in the D major. A further aspect of cyclic completion in the D major Suite is in the fact that whereas the Sarabande and Gavotte I outline notes 3–2–1 of the scale melodically in their first bars, the Gigue inverts this to 1–2–3 and adds 5. Pedal effects are again important: the pastoral musette of Gavotte II becomes a hunting-horn call in the Gigue (bars 5–8). The Gigue of the D major is also more complex than that of the G major in continuing the binary/rondeau combination of Gavotte II. After the second phrase with its pedal (bars 5–8) there is a phrase that moves to the dominant where, unusually, the opening theme returns (end of bar 17–21), followed by a different, more elaborate pedal-type effect, corresponding to the closing motif with pedal usual in Bach's binary sonata movements.

The second strain is in two main sections, with the sequence of elements reworked. The first section, concentrating on large leaps, uses the first pedal effect (end of bar 36–40); the second, a condensed reprise (end of bar 52–68), uses the second pedal-type effect (bars 65–6). The second runs its elements continuously into one another, finally covering the full three-octave range d"–D (bars 65–8) that has been the home pitch range of this Suite.

CHAPTER FIVE

Works for Lute/Lautenwerk BWV 995–1000, 1006a

Suite in G minor BWV 995
(arrangement by Bach of the C minor cello Suite BWV 1011)

For detailed comment on each movement of this Suite, see the commentary on the C minor cello Suite in Chapter Four.

The sources for this are: an autograph manuscript by Bach, in staff notation on two staves (*B-Br* Ms.II 4085 Mus.); and a version in lute tablature made from it by an unnamed lutenist (*D-LEm* Sammlung Becker, Ms. III.11.3).[1] Bach's autograph has the dedication 'Piéces pour la Luth à Monsieur Schouster par J.S. Bach' on the title-page; the tablature version has the same title, though without the dedication 'à Monsieur Schouster', and with 'la Luth' changed to 'le lut'. Bach's mistake with the gender of 'le luth' stems from the fact that in German 'die Laute' is feminine. The term 'Pièces' was traditionally used for French suite collections for lute, keyboard, or other instruments: Bach heads the first page of music with 'Suite pour la Luth'. This is therefore the only one of the putative lute works that is unequivocally assigned to the lute by Bach himself. Bach's autograph is not a careful fair copy, but shows him making the arrangement as he went along. It dates from somewhere between 1727 and 1731; the tablature version must be subsequent to that.

There are various puzzles presented by these sources. One is the identity of 'Monsieur Schouster'. Given the time and place of Bach's preparing the arrangement, he is most likely to have been Jacob Schuster (?1685–1751), a Leipzig bookseller with several circumstantial connections to Bach.[2] It is unlikely that Bach made the arrangement for Schuster himself to play, and more probable that Schuster was looking for lute works to sell, since he advertised 'Lauten-Partien' among musical items for sale. He therefore may have commissioned Bach to make the arrangement, or asked Bach if he had anything for the lute. This in itself would be curious since Bach was not known as a lutenist and Schuster would have been much better off selling keyboard music by Bach. The autograph, in spite of being a dedication copy, is not in Bach's fair-copy handwriting, but in his drafting hand. After the Prelude, bass notes and rests in particular are very cursorily written, as are performance indications. There is no doubt that the cello version came first since many of the corrections show that Bach was working from the cello scordatura.[3] The title-page with the dedication may have been added later, in which case the arrangement may originally have been made for some other purpose in Bach's musical activities, and subsequently offered to Schuster. Taken all together, it looks as if Bach made this roughish copy as a basis for an experienced lutenist to make an idiomatic intabulation. The fact that he wrote none of these works in lute tablature strongly suggests that he did not play the lute to any extent himself. Lutenists were expected to be able to play continuo parts from staff notation, but its use for solo music is very unusual.

The anonymous tablature version is just such an intabulation. The writing and ornament signs suggest that it was prepared in the circle of the lutenist Adam Falckenhagen (1697–1754), perhaps by Falckenhagen himself.[4] Falckenhagen moved in the same geographical area as Bach (Leipzig, Weissenfels, Weimar) though not directly overlapping with Bach at any stage. Also suggestive is Falckenhagen's close connection to Johann Christian Weyrauch (1694–1771). From 1707 Falckenhagen was educated by his uncle, Pastor of Knauthain, a village near Leipzig where Weyrauch was son of the Cantor, and both later went on to Leipzig University. Weyrauch was living in Leipzig at the same time as Bach, is known to have been a friend of Bach's, and made the intabulations of BWV 997 and 1000 that form a group in the Becker collection with the intabulation of BWV 995.

Another problem is the instrument Bach had in mind. In these works there is always the suspicion that Bach was thinking in terms of lute-like textures on his favoured keyboard instrument, the Lautenwerk, rather than of the lute itself. Here the intabulation is a useful critique by a contemporary lutenist of Bach's feeling for the lute. A close comparison of the two versions yields the impression that Bach was indeed imagining lute effects, and in accordance with his sound grasp of instrumental practicalities was making allowances for what was possible technically. Given the sort of devices of arpeggiation and emphasis that violinists use to project the polyphony in unaccompanied violin works, the result is possible to play as it stands. There are nonetheless awkwardnesses, and what lies well on the instrument will always sound better than what does not. The most pervasive change in the tablature version is transposing bass notes down an octave onto the diapason courses for ease of playing.[5] Since the diapason courses are octave strung (one string at 8' and one at 4' pitch), the written note will in any case be sounded.

The main instrumental problem about Bach's arrangement is that it goes down to GG, so requiring a 14-course lute. The normal lute in use in Germany from the 1690s was the French 11-course lute (usually in D minor tuning, with doubled courses from the third course down, as follows: f' d' a.a f.f d.d A.a, and five diapason courses going down from G.g to C.c). 12-course lutes were also not uncommon. The German 13-course lute (also in D minor tuning, with two extra diapason courses going down to AA.A) was developed by the Dresden virtuoso Silvius Leopold Weiss around 1718, and this is the lute required by the tablature version.[6] Jakob Adlung, organist in Erfurt who knew Bach, mentions a 14-course lute, and a few instruments with the extra course to GG survive by German makers, including Bach's friend the Leipzig lute and violin maker Johann Christian Hoffmann, which is the most likely solution to the problem of the instrument.[7] The intabulator adjusts the bass to the 13-course lute with a bottom note AA. This can be sensitively done, but it is clear from Bach's arrangement that, in his imagination at any rate, the pitch GG plays a crucial role. Bach in his mature works had a strategy for the highest and lowest pitches on whatever instrument he was writing for, part of his practical mentality, and pitch levels are an important part of the structural and expressive shaping of the piece. This is particularly obvious in the works he wrote for clavier with a four-octave compass, and in the works for unaccompanied violin and cello. In the Prelude of this Suite the bottom note, GG, is very prominent in the ¢-time section, tolling away in the tonic pedals at the beginning and end of the section, and giving it much of its *gravitas*. In the $\frac{3}{8}$ section Bach does not use the bottom note again until the very end (bars 209–13), where it returns as an insistent tonic pedal, with the important function of binding this quick section to the ¢-time opening. All the subsequent movements end with this bottom note, in very much the same way that the cello Suites generally have a spacing of the tonic chord that links successive movements with a characteristic sonority. In a way similar to the Prelude, the Sarabande uses GG at the end of its first phrase and not again until the very end, a clearly audible strategy given the isolated nature of the bass notes in this piece.

The amount of adjustment the intabulator felt it necessary to make varies between movements. The Courante has fewest alterations. In Bach's delightful chordal additions to Gavotte I (bars 1–8) a few notes have been changed for greater comfort, but then the intabulator has sensitively reorganized the entire bass pattern to make an equally logical one to Bach's. Even in Gavotte II, seemingly one of the trickier moments, only a few bass octaves have been changed, mainly putting down the bass in bars 18–22 to correspond with 1–4. Occasionally we see Bach putting a note up an octave to avoid having to finger a diapason course (the e♮ in bar 70 of the Prelude, the f♯ in bar 190; F♯ is no great problem and is used elsewhere, notably bar 2 of the Sarabande, but in bar 190 the octave switch conveniently gives the first fret on nearby courses).[8] These are cases where Bach was avoiding notes not available on the open diapasons. Elsewhere the intabulator shows a closer practical knowledge of the lute than Bach's, for example in bar 136 of the Prelude where Bach has written octaves that are redundant since the e♭ and g will in any case sound on the octave strings of the diapasons and can simply be omitted. A reverse situation is in bar 15 of the Allemande, where the intabulator has omitted the F and avoided Bach's parallel octaves. Bach was obviously thinking of the F as resolving the sonorous 6♮/4♯/2 chord at the beginning of the bar, but here the octave of the G diapason can be taken to be resolved by f in the middle of the bar. The most radical change the intabulator has had to make for playability is in bar 25 of the Allemande, where Bach has written a chord at the beginning of the bar that is unplayable unless arpeggiated. The intabulator has accordingly rewritten the first beat so that the notes c' and a are not played simultaneously (Ex.5.1a–c).

Ex.5.1 Allemande of BWV 995, bar 25:
a) anonymous tablature version

b) transcription (author)

c) Bach's staff-notation version

Sometimes the intabulator has put basses down an octave to impress with dexterity on the rich lower courses, as at bars 89–91 and 120–2 of the Prelude.[9] On the other hand, the bass has been put up an octave at the end of bar 31 of the Allemande, since the dotted rhythm and 32nds are clearer on the fingered courses than on the unstopped diapasons. In one instance (bars 167–70 of the Prelude) the intabulator has actually changed the bass line (to BB♭ C D E♭, and also omitted the first notes in the top part in bars 169 and 170) since the convenience of the lower octave was wanted but C♯ was not available. Although this smoothes over the force of Bach's cross relations (c/c♯' and e♭'/e♮) in bars 168–9, the substitution is perfectly logical and appropriate. In spite of numerous extra bass notes, however, the lute arrangement adds little or no real counterpoint and hardly compromises the cello original's tour de force as a single-line fugue in four 'voices' (see the commentary on the C minor cello Suite).

Some signs in the tablature are useful pointers for performance. *Ensemble* signs (a vertical stroke between two tablature letters) are frequently used to counteract the tendency to break chords. This is particularly important in the Courante, where the quarter notes need separate emphasis as part of the character of the genre (see the commentary on the C minor cello Suite). Elsewhere the *séparé* of breaking chords may have performance implications for the cello version. In bars 2 and 4 of the Prelude (see Ex.5.2) the breaking of the intervals involving f♯ means that the melodic line is effectively double-dotted. The tablature has also much to offer as regards ornaments and slurs. In the matter of ornaments it is difficult to know quite how much Bach himself would have added when playing. His works in manuscript tend to have few, perhaps because he reckoned to be present at the performance or lesson where the copy would be used. His printed works have considerably more performance detail. A useful indicator is the Sarabande of the G major clavier Partita BWV 829. Here, most of the piece is unornamented except for the first four-bar phrase, where he has notated a number of appoggiaturas at two different speeds. This was common practice in the early eighteenth century, to give an indication of performance details at the beginning and leave it to the player to continue them for the rest of the piece, necessary if a piece was printed for general distribution, but not necessary if the composer was present to demonstrate or advise.[10] There can be no doubt that he and his contemporaries did add many graces. The intabulator has added appoggiaturas/*ports de voix* in this Suite to most accented notes, from below if approached from below, and from above if approached from above (as can be seen in Ex.5.2); a comma before a note is an appoggiatura from below, after a note it is from above; two parallel strokes after a note are a short trill.[11] The tablature offers useful ornaments for the ¢-time section of the Prelude, but the ornamentation of the ⅜ fugue subject, if played in the usual way with the appoggiatura taking half the value of the main note, undermines the rhythmic character of the subject. Perhaps something snappier is intended, such as would give an accent to the main note rather than rounding out the rhythm. A particularly lute version is

Ex.5.2 Prelude of BWV 995, bars 1–35, transcription (author) of anonymous tablature version

the *port de voix* where the main note is sounded on one course and the appoggiatura on another, giving a characteristic semitone sting effect, as in the middle of bar 13 of the Prelude (Ex.5.2). The signs at the beginning of bars 3 and 16, and also on the final melodic notes of each strain of the Sarabande are for mordents. In places the galant filigree of Falckenhagen's generation can undermine the grand simplicity of the original, as in the cadence in the final two bars of the Prelude. This ending is analogous to several others of Bach, notably the final bars of the organ Toccata in F major BWV 540/1, and of the C sharp major Prelude in Book I of *The Well-tempered Clavier*. The addition of a trill and anticipation to the dominant chord seems fussy at the end of this imposing piece.

Bach's slurs in the cello version seem to have the practical function of indicating bowings. In his lute arrangement they seem to have a more general function of indicating groups or harmonic shapes. It would not be right to draw conclusions for cello performance from the slurs in the intabulation. They are purely practical in terms of the lute, normally involving two or three notes on one course, generally either to or from an open course. Thus, the slur in bar 1 of the cello Prelude is to show that the whole flourish is a decorated upbeat to bar 2, whereas the tablature's slurs are technical advice to the player as to which notes can conveniently be grouped together. This being the case, the difference in bars 68–70, where sixteenths are paired within the beat in bars 68–9, and across the beat in bar 70, has little significance other than that the pairing will be different according to the layout of the figurations in relation to the open courses. The result nonetheless gives a stimulating variety of articulation. Very long slurs do occur in contemporary lute music, but Bach's slur in the Prelude from bar 22 to bar 25 is surely to indicate that this sixteenth-note cadenza is a large extension of the upbeat figure in bar 1.[12] The fact that this cadenza creates a charming campanella effect involving the open f' d' a and f courses can hardly have escaped Bach. Further harmonic slurs in the autograph are in Gavotte I (bars 28–31), and particularly in the Sarabande. In the latter case, Bach's slurs show harmonic groups, but they also separate the fingered notes from the bass progression on the diapasons, an idiomatic lute effect not present in the cello version (Ex.5.3). They also point up the fact that the figuration in the first four-bar phrase is reversed in the second. The tablature slurs, on the other hand, are melodic, slurring adjacent notes and at the same time expressively accenting melodically dissonant intervals.

Ex.5.3 Sarabande of BWV 995, first strain:
a) anonymous intabulation

b) Bach's staff-notation

Suite in E minor BWV 996

The earliest source of this Suite is a manuscript copy made by Bach's Weimar colleague and distant relative J.G. Walther (*D–B* Mus.ms.Bach P 801), copied some time between 1714 and 1717 while Bach was at Weimar, and with the title 'Praeludio—con la Svite da Gio: Bast. Bach'.[13] To this has been added 'aufs Lauten Werck' by the organist Johann Tobias Krebs (1690–1762), who studied with Walther from about 1710 to 1714, and with Bach himself from about 1714 to 1717. Krebs, together with Walther, compiled a large manuscript collection (P 801–803) of keyboard works by Bach and other contemporary keyboard composers that gives a revealing insight into the works in circulation in Bach's environment at that time.[14] A second important source (private collection of Wolfgang Wiemer) was copied by another keyboard pupil of Bach's, Heinrich Nicolaus Gerber (1702–1775), probably in 1724 when Gerber was in the early stages of his studies with Bach.[15]

This is both the earliest of Bach's 'lute' works and the one that is most problematical for performance on the lute. Various scordaturas and transpositions have been suggested, but nothing can get around the fact that it is almost certainly intended for keyboard.[16] Its range (three octaves C–c") is precisely that described by Jacob Adlung for the Lautenwerk, and in May 1715 Bach's Jena relative, the organ builder Johann Nicolaus Bach, built a Lautenwerk which was bought for the household of Duke Ernst August of Sachsen-Weimar.[17] Ernst August was not directly Bach's employer (Bach was employed by the elder Duke Wilhelm Ernst), but Bach not infrequently provided music for him, much to the elder Duke's annoyance. This Suite is therefore most likely to have been composed around 1715 for the Lautenwerk, and Krebs added the phrase to the heading to explain its unusual compass and texture in a collection of keyboard works.

Much can be learnt about the development of Bach's concept of the suite and its dance genres, and also his concept of the lute, by comparing this Suite with the G minor BWV 995. In the G minor the Invention principle is fundamental to all aspects; the E minor shows Bach at the very end of his earlier style, on the brink of assembling the suite collections of around 1720. While the G minor shows Bach imagining playing the lute and making allowances for lute practicalities, there is little evidence of concern for lute practicalities in the E minor other than a generally thin and low-lying texture, in comparison with his other keyboard suites. Paradoxically, it is the 'lute-like' low tessitura that makes for too much business on the diapason courses and is one of the main problems for playing this Suite on the lute.

1. Praeludio

Like the Prelude of BWV 995 this is, to a certain extent at any rate, in the manner of a French overture, with a duple-time section (c here, rather than ¢) featuring dotted rhythms and tiratas; and a triple-time section (also $\frac{3}{8}$) featuring fugal imitations. But the genre is not quite in focus. The first section, marked *Passaggio*, is not like a French *entrée*, but like the sort of improvised keyboard Praeludium described by Friedrich Erhardt Niedt (1674–1708) in the second part of his *Musicalische Handleitung* (published Hamburg 1721). Niedt had studied with J.N. Bach in Jena, and his precepts may represent something of a Bach family tradition for teaching improvisation.[18] Whether that is so or not, his recipes plainly represent standard practice in the central- and north-German keyboard traditions around 1700, to judge by the repertory. Niedt recommends beginning a prelude with 'a *Lauff* [i.e. a run or *Passaggio*, that] starts in the discant, goes down into the bass and then comes to rest on a full chord'.[19] Some of Bach's clavier Toccatas start in just this way, with a pattern that runs from near the top of the keyboard, repeating the pattern in each octave until it reaches the bottom octave, as happens in the E minor Praeludio. These flourishes, which were improvisation gambits, tend to have slightly different shapes in different keys, based on the way the shapes on the keyboard lie under the hand, as may be seen in the organ Praeludia of Buxtehude and others, and in the initial ideas of many of Bach's keyboard works generally. C major and F major tend to concentrate on scales; G minor tends to bounce off the accidentals B flat, E flat and F sharp; D minor tends to move in a circle between B flat and C sharp. E minor has a tendency to be shaped around the tonic triad and the accidentals F sharp and D sharp, with a strong tendency towards the minor sixth degree (C natural), whether as an expressive melody note or as the bass note in an interrupted cadence, which can then be the first inversion of A minor (another strong centre of gravity) in the Phrygian cadence in E minor. A fairly typical example from the seventeenth-century keyboard tradition is in the opening of the Toccata by Matthias Weckmann (c.1616–1674) given in Ex.5.4.[20] Niedt continues his instructions for improvising a prelude with a Chaconne, since he is demonstrating how different genres may be improvised on the same figured bass. Other common prelude types are demonstrated in the first *Clavier-Übung* (Leipzig 1689) of Bach's Leipzig predecessor, Johann Kuhnau (1660–1722). Closest to the Praeludio of BWV 996 is the Praeludium of Kuhnau's Partie II in D major. This has a flourish that runs all over the keyboard; a chordal section; a lightly imitative ('fugal') section; and a return to chords at the end. Parallel with these keyboard examples, such flourishes were also standard at the beginning of instrumental works generally and may be traced back to the early seventeenth century in keyboard toccatas of Frescobaldi, lute and theorbo toccatas of Kapsberger, and sonatas for various instruments. Biber's violin sonatas commonly begin with a flourish of this sort over a pedal, as do many of Weiss's *stylus phantasticus* lute pieces.

Ex.5.4   Mathias Weckmann, keyboard *Toccata 3i Toni*, bars 1–7

The copy of BWV 996 made by H.N. Gerber is particularly relevant here since Gerber copied out this Suite together with the E minor clavier Toccata BWV 914. This Toccata is in four sections: an opening that corresponds to the flourish but in this instance is more like an organ pedal effect; an imitative second section; an Adagio in free, recitative style; and a substantial Fuga that seems to be a reworking of a fugue attributed elsewhere to Benedetto Marcello.[21] Gerber, in his copy of the Toccata, has headed the Adagio section 'Praeludium', which implies that Bach initially conceived this Adagio as the prelude to the fugue, and indeed the flourish in bar 7 of the Adagio returns in extended form at the end of the fugue. As a prelude, the Adagio has largely the same hand-shapes as those in the *Passaggio* of BWV 996, and with the same gravitational pull towards A minor (Ex.5.5).[22] Seen in this light, the *Passaggio* is a very effective and original gesture that manages to combine in a single line many of the traditional ingredients. It is also decidedly from the keyboard tradition.[23]

Ex.5.5 Bach, keyboard Toccata BWV 914, third section bars 1–8

As regards the dotted rhythms and tiratas, they do not necessarily come from the French overture, but are also a common manner in accompanied recitatives and hence can feature in improvisational adagios such as one finds in the trio sonatas of Buxtehude.[24] BWV 914 and BWV 996 are in Bach's earlier style, and one may well ask why Bach gave them to Gerber to study at a time when he had finished putting together a whole educational series of mature works including the English and French Suites, the two-part Inventions and three-part Sinfonias, and Book I of *The Well-tempered Clavier*, some of which Gerber was subsequently also to copy. The answer must be that these are examples of improvisation. As Niedt says, students 'should save their own *Inventiones* until they can improvise a proper prelude alone' (i.e. on his figured bass).[25] The Presto section of Bach's Praeludio is like the equivalent section of a French overture in its time signature and in the fact that the voices enter from the top down. Otherwise it is in fact a very basic demonstration of how to improvise a keyboard piece in fugal style, using a common contrapuntal formula in which 3rds and 6ths alternate (Ex.5.6a and b). The ability to decorate such formulas up into figural counterpoint in characteristic textures was part of the stock-in-trade of organists' improvisations.[26] This is a particularly minimal example since the 'fugue' is rarely in more than two real parts, with a lot of repetition at different pitches. When it is in more than two parts the subject is in the bass, with continuo-player's chords over it. This Praeludio would be an excellent and very traditional model from which Gerber could learn the fundamentals. The Adagio and Fuga of BWV 914 are somewhat more sophisticated. Neither has anything like the concentrated technical accomplishment and expressive force of the Prelude of the G minor Suite BWV 995.

Ex.5.6 Praeludio of BWV 996, formula for fugal improvisation in bars 17–22:
a) simple

b) more elaborate

2. Allemande

This type, in flowing sixteenth notes without special rhythmic characteristics, appears also in the A major English Suite for clavier and the G major cello Suite, with both of which it may usefully be compared. The A major was probably the earliest of the English Suites to be written, perhaps not long after BWV 996, yet it has already moved much more in the sonata direction in long phrases that rarely touch the ground harmonically in a cadence. The Allemande of BWV 996 is much more like French examples by, for example,

François Couperin in that it's main business is playing with irregular phrase lengths (see Chapter Two section 2). Thus it has the usual two-bar opening phrase (to the beginning of bar 3), with a caesura after the first note of bar 2. Then there is a one-bar phrase to the beginning of bar 4, followed by a longer phrase of five bars to the double bar. The second strain, again like Couperin, has longer, sonata-like phrases, with sequences. Although not as thoroughgoing in its adoption of sonata principles as Bach's later allemandes, this is still in the mixed style. It differs from a purely French-style allemande by not being melodic, but based on chords decorated in the standard division note value of the genre (sixteenths). A French manner of performance, with unequal sixteenths, would be as inappropriate here as it would be in a sonata allegro by Corelli. The Allemande of the G major cello Suite, unlike that of the A major English Suite, does have intermediate cadences, but it combines the traditional allemande with the usual ritornello structure in its sonata guise, which by around 1720 had become Bach's standard structural principal for many types of composition. Attractive as the E minor Allemande is, it is not as artful as that of the G minor Suite BWV 995, which clothes the sonata structure with the external characteristics of an *entrée*.

3. Courante

The Courante, by contrast, is one of Bach's most purely French in style. The phrase structure is irregular (as usual in a courante) but quite clear, and the eighth notes are decorative rather than motivic. It is therefore comparable to the Couperin Courante discussed in Chapter Two section 2, and a similar manner of performance would be appropriate. In fact the combination of unequal eighth notes, and quarter notes played in a slightly detached way gives most of the characteristic movement of this genre. Comparison with the Courante of the C minor cello Suite/G minor lute Suite is useful for defining the blend of styles and hence performance criteria (see the commentary on the Courante of the C minor cello Suite in Chapter Four). The eighth notes in the C minor/G minor Courante are not just decorative. They are much more pervasive than in the E minor, and carry much of the argument of the piece. They therefore have more of a division/sonata function and are at a remove from those of French dance music, in a way similar to the Courante of the D minor French Suite. In the E minor Courante Bach achieves more density of movement in the second strain, not by increasing the sonata element as he was later to do, but by extra levels of decoration, and a chromatic climbing sequence (bars 20–1).

4. Sarabande

This well represents Bach's preference for the low-lying, rhythmic/chordal type of Sarabande over the lighter, aria type with a higher tessitura favoured by, for example, Silvius Leopold Weiss. The $\frac{3}{2}$-time Sarabande of the D major cello Suite manages to combine the two. As we pointed out in the commentary on that, the broader time signature allows Bach a wider variety of decorative effects: in the Sarabande of the D minor English Suite he has a Double in flowing eighth notes; in this E minor Sarabande he has decorative note values up to 32nds. The Sarabande is in one way a demonstration of how the language of essential and florid ornaments can articulate and intensify the expression, one could even say that to a large extent they are the expression. Of things that bind the movements of this Suite together, one might note the accent on the minor sixth degree in bar 2, and the Phrygian cadence at the end of the first strain, both typical of E minor; also the climbing chromatic progression that builds up the final phrase of the second strain (bars 17–21) just as its equivalent did in the Courante.

5. Bourrée

Little more need be said about this than that it is one of Bach's most straightforward melodic dance movements, without any of the move to sonata style (such as spun-out and elided phrases in division note values in the second strain) that is typical of his later bourrées and other lighter dances. For all that, its classic stylistic focus makes it one of his most attractive examples of the genre.

6. Giga

The heading of this movement in P 801 is Italian (Giga, not Gigue as in NBA V/10 p.100), and indeed it returns to the more abstract, less dance-based manner of the beginning of the Suite. Traditionally there was a close relation between the genres of allemande and gigue in the seventeenth-century suite, and this Giga takes up again, as part of its *inventio*, the descending scale of the Allemande, to which it adds (in the second half of bar 1) a broken chord figure. These two elements are then dissected separately and together, and extended sequentially, in the first strain on the old sonata principle. As is customary in imitative allemandes and gigues, the opening figure is inverted after the double bar, and the climbing chromatic sequence noted in both the Courante and Sarabande reappears in bars 15–16. Here again, the layout presupposes a keyboard player's hands and gives rise to severe difficulties on the lute.

Suite in C minor BWV 997

The sources for this closest to Bach are: a copy in staff notation (*D-B* Mus.ms.Bach P 650) made by Johann Friedrich Agricola (1720–1774), who was a pupil of Bach's from 1738–1741; and a version in lute tablature (*D-LEm* Sammlung Becker III.11.5) by Johann Christian Weyrauch (1694–1771), lutenist and friend of Bach's. Agricola's copy has on its title-page: 'C moll Praeludium, Fuge, Sarabande und Gique fürs Clavier Von J.S. Bach', written not by Agricola but by C.P.E. Bach in his later Hamburg period. Agricola's movement titles in the body of the manuscript are Prelude, Fuga, Sarabande, Gique, and Double. All the staff-notation versions are designated for keyboard. Weyrauch's tablature version, entitled 'Partita al Liuto', has only the Prelude (which he calls Fantasia), Sarabande and Gigue (which he calls Giga). It has been suggested that this reflects an earlier version of the work, lacking the Fuga and the Double of the Gigue, and dating from around 1730, but the source situation does not support this and the work most probably originated in the form of the staff-notation copies during the time when Agricola was with Bach, 1738–1741.[27] This would put it within a few years of BWV 998 and 1006a, around the time when Bach received the famous visit from the Dresden lutenists Silvius Leopold Weiss and Johann Kropfgans in August 1739.

Bach normally used the C1 clef for the upper stave in keyboard music, but all the staff-notation sources use the G2 clef with the same layout as Agricola's copy, so that is almost certainly Bach's original notation. This makes the texture very odd for a keyboard piece, with hands far apart, and at one stage it was thought that it might be an arrangement of a violin piece.[28] Closer inspection reveals that the upper stave is notated an octave higher than sounding (clear, for example, from the part-writing of the Fuga). Bach used this way of notating a lute part when it is transferred to keyboard in the Arioso 'Betrachte, meine Seel' from the Saint John Passion, where the organ and harpsichord options notate the upper line an octave higher than the lute original, with the direction to play it an octave down.[29] Conversely, in his arrangement for harpsichord and violin of a lute Sonata by Weiss (BWV 1025) Bach transposed the top line of the lute part up an octave for the harpsichord, this time without the intention of its being played at the lower octave. Like BWV 997, BWV 1025 also dates from around 1740.[30] The extant source of Weiss's Sonata lacks the initial Fantasia of BWV 1025, but it is almost certainly also by Weiss.[31] In it the right-hand part is a single line at a distance from the bass, with the same wide-ranging, swooping shapes as in the Prelude/Fantasia and other movements of BWV 997. The harpsichord part of BWV 1025 also uses the G2 clef, and it may have been the clarity achieved by separating the lines here that encouraged Bach to use the same system in BWV 997.

A further puzzle in BWV 997 is that the Double must be played as written since the figurations flow from one stave into the other. The range of the other movements, with the upper stave transposed down an octave, is AA♭–e♭'', a typical 13-course lute range, also probably viable for the Lautenwerk that J.F. Agricola saw at Bach's house around 1740 (see Chapter One section 4); but the Double has a range of C–f''', far beyond the lute, and notes above d''' are very rare even in Bach's keyboard works.[32]

The three movements intabulated by Weyrauch are suitable for the lute in that they are mostly in just two parts, with a florid top line and generally slow-moving bass. Weyrauch has done little other than alter the bass octave in places, generally down so as to put the bass notes onto the unfingered diapason courses. To make a lute version of the Double would not be so straightforward. It does not present problems of texture, but would need quite a lot of adjustment to condense its pitch range to that of the lute. The main problem is the Fuga, whose intricate textures and active bass need to be adapted.[33] One is tempted to think of the Lautenwerk as the ideal instrument here, were it not that certain parts of the Fuga are unplayable even on the keyboard as written (bars 63, 79, 87).[34] The bass also avoids GG (bar 64), which seems to have been available on at least one Lautenwerk, if we consider that an option for BWV 995. Kirnberger in his copy (P 218) seems not to have understood the intention of transposing the upper stave down an octave. He has passages in the lower stave transposed up an octave in order to avoid the unplayable moments, and also to rectify anomalies when a part migrates from one stave to the other.[35]

Weyrauch is our one real evidence for the piece being conceived for lute. Otherwise we have only the curious manner of notating it, and the textures and pitch range that result when the upper stave is transposed down. But that still leaves the mystery of the Double. Although none of his original lute works survive, Weyrauch was evidently a skilled lutenist whose own works were technically demanding. In 1732 the most prominent literary figure in Leipzig during Bach's time, Johann Christoph Gottsched, sent lute pieces by Weyrauch and keyboard pieces by Bach to his fiancée, who was an accomplished lutenist and keyboard player. In her reply she described them as 'as difficult as they are fine', and that 'anything by these two great Masters would please me better than their Caprices, which are impenetrably difficult'.[36] Caprice at this stage normally meant technical studies, or technically demanding 'lessons' (as in Locatelli's *Concerti . . . con . . . Capricci* of 1733, or Franz Benda's undated *Capricen*, for violin).[37] The Bach works may have included the C minor clavier Partita (BWV 826, published 1727 and 1731) which contains a Capriccio with much leaping of 10ths. Weyrauch's competence is borne out by his intabulations, particularly in his subtle interpretation of the opening of the Prelude in ringing campanella, an effect he uses also in the Sarabande (bar 4 etc.).

1. *Prelude*

The main difference between Weyrauch's intabulation and Agricola's staff-notation copy is that Agricola lacks the campaign of dynamics throughout Weyrauch's version. There is no knowing whether this was Bach's intention, or Weyrauch's assumption that any repeated figuration must be an echo. Where the repetition is fairly exact, from the middle of bar 30 to the middle of bar 31, and in bars 40–4 (where Weyrauch has marked the second half of each bar *piano*), it seems natural enough. The *piano* in bar 2, and the equivalent in bar 18, however, are more questionable since the bass is progressive. The *inventio* of a figure repeated insistently over this bass, building up the tension inherent in a pedal effect, which is then released into a descending scale (bar 4) is used equally effectively in the Gigue of the C major trio Sonata by Johann Gottlieb Goldberg (formerly BWV 1037) where there is no question of an echo effect. This seems more likely to be another case of kinetic, intensifying repetition rather than an echo. If there is to be dynamic nuance, one of the main advantages of the lute, it is surely that the c"s at the end of each of bars 1–3 should fade after the accent on the b♮' appoggiatura.

Comparison with other pieces of around this time, such as the *Fantaisie über ein Rondo* for clavier BWV 918, or the introductory Fantasia of BWV 1025, shows how tightly constructed and purposeful is this Prelude. It uses the expanded form of the ritornello shape in its sonata guise much favoured by Bach in Book II of *The Well-tempered Clavier* (also compiled around 1740).[38] There is a closed first phrase of five bars; then a spun-out section that passes through the relative major (E flat, bars 6–8) to the dominant (G minor, bars 9ff); and a closing phrase with a chromatic tinge and cadence (end of bar 14 to bar 17). All through this, new figurations are developed cumulatively from the opening *inventio*. The G minor section (from bar 17) moulds these shapes further, now with phrases modelled on the first one (a short version in bars 21–3, followed by a much extended one in bars 23–9), and modulating to the next expected goal, the subdominant (F minor, bar 33). The final section begins with a new, broken up and intensified development of the *inventio*, concentrating on the expressive appoggiatura (bars 33–4). Weyrauch adds expressive appoggiaturas also to the chords in bars 53–4 (g–f♯ in bar 53, c'–b♮ in bar 54). Altogether this Prelude compares very favourably in its maturity of structural control and development with cognate Preludes in Book II of *The Well-tempered Clavier.*

2. *Fuga*

This remarkable fugue is of a sort rare in Bach, where subject and countersubject are exposed at the first entry. The combination here is not only highly ingenious contrapuntally, but it is also perfectly geared to the technical and expressive resources of the lute. C.P.E. Bach tells us that his father's practice in composing keyboard works was to find ideas by improvising, then to work them up away from the keyboard.[39] This fugue, like the Prelude of BWV 995, seems to show Bach imagining playing the lute, perhaps improvising on the Lautenwerk, then getting carried away by the ingenuity of his ideas and taking less care for practicalities when he was away from the instrument. Although the fugue is in three parts, in the earlier stages it is rare to have more than two notes struck together.

The subject in itself is a commonplace, going up to the fifth degree of the minor scale, then, instead of continuing on up the semitone to the minor sixth degree, jumping down a major 7th. It is the shape at the opening of Telemann's A minor flute Fantasia, mentioned in the discussion of the Sarabande of the C minor cello Suite in Chapter Four (see Ex.6.2).[40] The form in which Bach gives it is nonetheless highly characteristic of his mature fugal style, starting off the beat so that the whole of bar 1 is an upbeat to the expressive leap down to a♭. He immediately exploits this off-beat beginning by making the countersubject seem to grow out of the accented a♭ in bar 2. The material is extraordinarily concentrated in that the countersubject is itself an inversion of the subject's first bar. One can hardly imagine a more neatly effective and expressive arrangement of these common materials, perfectly fitted to the lute.

Bach seems to have had a particular interest in music-rhetorical theory in the later 1730s, perhaps partly because of the attack made on him in 1737–8 by Johann Adolph Scheibe, for overloaded textures and a lack of elegant learning, and perhaps partly on account of the publication in 1739 of Johann Mattheson's *Der vollkommene Capellmeister*, which contains one of the classic eighteenth-century expositions of rhetoric in music.[41] The inversion relationship of countersubject to subject here corresponds to the rhetorical device of synonymia (presenting the same idea in different forms and contexts), and this device is richly used throughout this fugue.[42] To what extent Bach really thought in this way is debatable. What is certain is that showing the fundamental materials in different lights is historically one of the objectives of fugue. In his 'research' of the materials here, Bach extracts two elements from bar 1. One is a group of three notes (the first three notes of the subject); the other a group of five notes (the first five notes of the subject). Motifs of three notes, whether stepped out or expressed as the leap of a 3rd, are exploited in many different ways throughout the fugue. The motif of five notes changes colour as it is presented in different contexts. It starts on the first degree of C minor (bar 1); then appears in shifting harmonic situations: on the third degree of E flat major (bar 23); on the second degree of F minor (bar 27); on the sixth degree of G minor (bar 55); and on the fifth degree of C minor (bar 75). In addition to this there are all sorts of inversions of it along the way.

The total *inventio* of the fugue is not just the subject, but both subject and countersubject to the beginning of bar 5.[43] Given that bar 1 has the character of an upbeat, the *inventio* forms a four-bar phrase and corresponds to the first phrase of a dance movement, which also usually contains the elements that will be developed later. Bar 4 introduces a decorated suspension figure that provides the basis for subsequent extensions. Bar 5 immediately inverts this figure contrapuntally and adds a device known in contemporary contrapuntal theory as *inganno* (i.e. deception, where the seventh degree is suspended into a cadence and does not rise to the tonic, the ear being thus deceived of the expected cadence; in this case the seventh degree is also flattened).[44] Bar 6 then extends the decorative pairs of sixteenth notes to a group of four, motivating much subsequent development. Bars 1–6 (i.e. the opening phrase as far as the answer in bar 7) therefore present in embryo all the materials of the fugue, as well as the beginnings of their development. One can hardly imagine this being done with a technical and expressive concentration of greater maturity.

After the answer of both subject and countersubject in bars 7–10, the *inganno* is expanded into the delightful asymmetrical series of imitations from bar 10 to bar 16, all standard counterpoint but worked with the feeling of natural rightness that comes from mastery. Each approach to a perfect cadence is deflected by a 7th hanging on into the chord of resolution. This leads to a second exposition (from bar 17), also in the tonic. Having two expositions in the tonic corresponds to Vivaldi's practice in his Op.3 Concertos (a number of which Bach arranged for keyboard) of having an opening ritornello in the tonic, then a short solo break, then all or part of the ritornello again in the tonic, then a solo break that modulates to a new key. Bach uses this pattern with great resourcefulness and variety in fugues. If he has an entire second exposition it generally does something new with the material.[45] Here the second exposition inverts the subject and countersubject contrapuntally: in the first exposition the subject is above the countersubject (from bar 1), as is the answer (from bar 7); in the second exposition the subject is below the countersubject (from bar 17), as is the answer (from bar 23). After more playing with the *inganno* (bars 31–3) there is an episode that develops the motif of 3rds: as leaps in the bass (bars 33–4), antiphonally between parts (bars 35–6), put end-to-end in an extended line (bars 38–9), and at twice the speed in the division note value of this piece (sixteenths, bar 41), which will become the predominant note value in the middle section. The first section ends with a series of stretto entries (from bar 42) and a hemiola (bar 48).

Around 1720 Bach had written fugal movements in the concerto manner that have a reprise of the opening section at the end, as do most of the English Suite Preludes and the Fuga of the C major violin Sonata. Around 1740 he wrote several da capo fugues (the most obvious one apart from this being the Fuga of BWV 998) which differ from the earlier ones in that the second section is more or less the same length as the first, and systematically contrasts with it in being predominantly in the division note value of the piece. In the Vivaldian concerto the contrast between tutti ritornello and solo episode is often marked by a contrast of note value: for example, if the tutti are mainly in eighth notes, the solos may be mainly in sixteenths. In Bach's earlier concerto-style fugues this contrast of note values is usually exploited continually throughout the piece. In these later fugues, on the other hand, the contrast is used more broadly to distinguish the two main sections. The attraction of this later form is that it combines principles and effects from both the concerto and the da capo aria, and, more importantly, the second section has something of the effect of a Double on the materials of the first, thereby intensifying the impetus and opening up new possibilities for development. The subsequent return of the first section, with its slower note values, is hardly an anticlimax since its musical substance is sufficiently dense to benefit from repeated hearing, and its materials will now have acquired greater significance in the light of what Bach has revealed in them.

The second section accordingly begins (bar 49) with the suspension from the end of the subject (bar 4) in the bass, and a sixteenth-note figure based on the three-note motif in the cantus. It goes on to explore new developments of the basic motifs in ways that are sufficiently obvious not to need further explanation. More fascinating is the structure of this section. It consists of a group of three blocks that repeats in an ingenious palindromic formation, with the first appearance of each block in the dominant key G minor, and the second in the tonic C minor. Block A (bars 55–9) returns to finish the section (bars 105–9); Block B (bars 75–83) returns in bars 98–105; Block C (bars 83–8) returns in bars 93–8. When repeated (from bar 93) the blocks are contiguous, without linking episodes. They are also condensed in that the repeated version of Block B (from bar 98) elides the head of the subject (compare bars 75–6) since it had already appeared towards the end of Block C (bars 95–6). The exchange of parallel 6ths (bars 93–4) for parallel 3rds (bars 83–4) in Block C is precisely the example given by Forkel for the rhetorical device of synonymia.[46] The skilful dovetailing of this scheme, the asymmetry of linking episodes, and the effect of continual organic growth mean that in spite of its logic any feeling of schematic stiffness is avoided—yet further evidence of the maturity of this fugue, and fully justifying its being singled out as the greatest Baroque fugue for the lute.[47]

3. *Sarabande*

This sarabande may usefully be compared to some others in order to define the individuality of Bach's style. The Weiss Sarabande that Bach arranged in BWV 1025 is an example of a contrasting type of Italian influence. Both have a substantial amount of sixteenth-note movement, not usual in a French sarabande, but in Weiss's case the sixteenths are decorative in the manner of an aria, and the piece is essentially melodic. In Bach's case the movement is mainly harmonic, as we have noted before in Bach's sarabandes, and the sixteenths either pattern out chord progressions or are motivic and developmental, in the manner of a sonata. A further comparison might be made with the Sarabande of the seventh of Christoph Graupner's clavier *Partien* of 1718. This lies somewhere between Weiss's aria type and a French sarabande. It begins with a similar rhythmic figure to Bach's, but it stays strictly within the four-bar phraseology of the genre and there are no secondary motifs for development. Each phrase has a similar rhythmic structure, and the piece is developmental in that it moulds this in different harmonic directions and brings it to a reprise at the end. Neat and attractive as this is, it has nothing like the scope of Bach's development, and of course Bach's Sarabande has in addition the enormous expressive resonance of recalling the final chorus of the Saint Matthew Passion.[48]

The nearest to an aria-like sarabande in Bach's unaccompanied instrumental works is the Sarabande of the D major cello Suite, but even that has a substantial element of sequential motivic development in its second strain. This C minor Sarabande brings that development into the first strain as well. The first strain has the pattern observed now in many of Bach's dance movements, of a four-bar phrase in sarabande rhythm followed by one in a division note value This leads into eight bars of continuous motivic sixteenths with sequential development. Meanwhile Bach's contrapuntal way of thinking is rarely absent for long. The rising 3rds in bar 9 double in speed when they fall in bar 10, and the pattern is inverted when it comes in the second strain (from bar 25). With this contrapuntal development goes expressive development in that the intervals between cantus and bass in bars 9–10 open out to a dissonant diminished 5th, whereas at the corresponding place (bars 25–6) they close in to a major second. All in all this movement could more justly be described as a sonata movement with sarabande characteristics than a dance.

Weyrauch has made slightly more changes here than in the Prelude. Apart from changing the octave of some bass notes he has added chord members at the beginnings of bars 4 and 9, and has broken the upper notes of the chord at the beginning bar 8 into sixteenth notes, continuing the sixteenth-note movement of the bar before and for the sake of playability. Keyboard players might do the same for the chord on the second beat of bar 3.

4. *Gigue and Double*

Again, Weyrauch has made few alterations in the Gigue other than occasionally changing the bass octave. He also repeats the figure in ornamental 32nds at the end of bar 40 at the equivalent place in bar 42. The main problem, if it is a problem, is the Double, which cannot simply be transposed to make it playable on the lute. Howard Ferguson has shown that, with judicious switching of octaves, it can be brought within the AA♭–f" compass.[49] Yet it does feel like keyboard music, and particularly resembles the sort of concertante writing that Bach was using in the harpsichord concertos he arranged in the late 1730s, and in such pieces as the last movement of the D major gamba Sonata BWV 1028.[50] Both Gigue and Double recall the Prelude in using a similar opening harmonic formula, and the Double also recalls the semitone appoggiaturas of the Prelude in the auxiliaries in bar 5 etc. Whatever about the lute, the Double makes a most attractive toccata-style piece for the clavichord.

Prelude, Fugue and Allegro in E flat major BWV 998

The only source is an autograph manuscript by Bach entitled 'Prelude pour la Luth. ò Cembal. par J.S. Bach' (Tokyo, Ueno-Gakuen Music Academy). Analysis of the paper and handwriting dates it to around 1735.[51] Judging by the corrections Bach made in the second and third movements, it is a primary score not a copy of an earlier piece.[52] This puts it at roughly the same time as BWV 997 for which it makes a good companion: the C minor pieces are rather densely composed, the E flat ones looser and more improvisatory. Both have what might be considered an irregular series of movements, but that is only because Bach is usually so methodical and consistent in his suite and other collections.[53] Groups of various types of movements under the heading of Sonata were common in lute and viol repertory in the earlier eighteenth century. BWV 997 and 998 seem originally to have had no other general heading than Prelude, much as Bach's overture-suites have no other general heading than *Ouverture*. Individual movements of BWV 998 are headed Prelude, Fuga, and Allegro.

The terms 'Luth. ò Cembal' should not be taken too literally. This certainly makes a fine work for harpsichord, from which one can deduce important things about Bach's harpsichord touch, and also for clavichord, but the Fuga and Allegro present substantial problems for the lute. The Prelude has been compared to pieces in similar style by Weiss, but even this has unidiomatic things that Weiss would have done otherwise.[54] With a range of AA♭–e♭" Bach has kept within the lute's compass, but when he ran out of space at the end of the Allegro he notated the last few bars in keyboard tablature, not lute tablature. All this points to the Lautenwerk as the most probable instrument. Both Weiss and Bach were specially noted improvisers, and according to J.F. Reichardt, whose father was one of the last generation of outstanding German lutenists and who himself played the lute, Weiss and Bach on occasion improvised and played fugues in competition with each other.[55] It is difficult to see how this could have been a worthwhile competition if Bach had used the full resources of the harpsichord against the limited technical possibilities of the lute. It would make more sense if Bach had imitated lute style on the Lautenwerk, and BWV 998 would make excellent sense as a souvenir of such an occasion.

1. Prelude

This has an idiomatic lute texture, also found in Weiss preludes, of sonorous low notes on the diapason courses struck with the right-hand thumb, and an arpeggiated upper part for the other fingers. If playing it on the harpsichord one ought not to take the rests in the bass too literally since the Lautenwerk was undamped, as are the lute's diapasons generally, and even the lute's upper part will have many notes that sound through succeeding ones. C.P.E. Bach recommends the undamped pianoforte as the most delightful medium for improvisation, so long as one takes care to use its resonance properly; the Lautenwerk must have given much the same pleasure.[56] A super-legato touch is therefore needed on the harpsichord, with many trailing chord notes. In the E flat major Prelude from Book II of *The Well-tempered Clavier*, which appears to be a harpsichord piece based on this texture, Bach has to a certain extent notated the effect. A large part of the attractiveness of the BWV 998 Prelude is this suggestion of resonance, perhaps ultimately more at home on the keyboard which can pour out streams of notes, than on the lute where each fingered note is more of a separate event.

Comparison with the more composed E flat Prelude from Book II throws into relief the improvised nature of this one. It is in Bach's favoured structure of an opening section (bars 1–6 here) repeated several times, each time developed and varied to modulate around different keys, and it shows how suitable this structure is as a model for improvisation. The key scheme is Bach's customary one of tonic—dominant (B flat major, bar 6)—relative minor (C minor, bar 14)—subdominant (A flat major, bar 25)—tonic (bar 42). Features that strongly suggest improvisation are the fact that most of the piece consists of common continuo-bass progressions, decorated with freely varied figurations in the upper part; and the very economical use of material, with much transposed repetition. The C minor section is a transposition of the opening six bars, and the B flat section is later repeated in A flat. Hermann Keller thought that the progression in bars 39–40 sounds so illogical that Bach could not have written it, and proposed J.L. Krebs (a pupil of Bach's who also played the lute) as the composer.[57] It is true that Bach would more normally resolve the Neapolitan 6th in bar 39 onto a 6/4/2 chord on A flat (i.e. onto the last inversion of the home dominant 7th), but he may have wished for once to avoid this habitual resolution. The resolution to a 6/4♮/2 on E flat is in fact another symptom of the improvised nature of the piece. To get this resolution on the keyboard one need only play a chord of F flat major, then move the upper parts a semitone up to F major, and the bass a semitone down to E flat. The result may sound more typical of Anton Bruckner than of Bach, but the origin in keyboard improvisation is probably the same.

2. Fuga

The subject of the Fuga, in its even slow notes, is also in the general manner of Weiss.[58] Like the Prelude it also has much in common formally with the equivalent movement in BWV 997, in this case having the same da capo structure and the same change of note value in the second section. But here all is worked in a much looser way that suggests improvisation, and with sensuous instrumental sonority in the foreground rather than ingenious contrapuntal working. In the first section, slow-moving shapes from the subject predominate in the bass with no more than decorated harmony above, notably the appoggiaturas in 3rds and 6ths that start at bar 13, a galant-style feature that Bach used elsewhere around 1740 in the F minor Prelude from Book II of *The Well-tempered Clavier* and in the three-part Ricercar from the *Musical Offering* (1747). These work particularly well on the lute, as shown by Weiss and others. Improvised as all this seems, there is a great deal of art behind it. As in the C minor Fuga, the countersubject (bars 3–4) seems to grow out of the subject and indeed to be a kind of inverted diminution of it. And as in the Prelude of BWV 995 there is a suggestion of a four-voice exposition, with cantus and alto subject and answer (bars 1–5), and tenor subject (bars 7–8) with bass answer (bars 11–12). The section as a whole centres on a series of subject and answer entries increasingly spaced out, so the remainder of the section has a bass subject (bars 15–16) and cantus answer (bars 21–2), separated by episodes based on the appoggiatura figure.

What Bach is really exploring in this section is the curious form of the answer (bars 3–4) which stays in E flat until its last three notes, thereby altering two of the intervals of the subject (a real answer would be: b♭ a♮ b♭ c' f g a♮ b♭; see Chapter 2 section 8, and Ex.2.13d). One could say that the answer in itself is a demonstration of fugal erudition, but that would be to falsify Bach's instincts as a practical composer. He does not want to move too quickly to the dominant, and the resulting form of the answer presents him with just the sort of anomalies that give scope for development. To 'research' this is the purpose of the fugue. By replacing the leap of a 3rd between the fifth and sixth notes of the answer with a step (as in bars 12 and 22), the answer will end a tone too low, swinging the harmony round to either A flat major (bar 13) or F minor (bar 23). The argument from bar 11 to bar 17 is that the answer in bar 11 ends a tone too low (beginning of bar 13), so is repeated a tone higher to end on B♭ (beginning of bar 15); this sequence is then clinched with an entry of the subject proper (bars 15–17). Further felicities are that the first episode (bars 17–20) is based on a sequence using the inversion of the auxiliary shape of the first four notes of the subject, and the conclusion of the section (bars 23–8) is based on the rising steps of the last four notes of the subject. At the end Bach has the parallel 3rds of the appoggiatura figure take over the entire texture (bars 25–8) so that all four parts move in contrary-motion parallel 3rds.[59] So beneath the surface expression of genial ease and repose there is a sharp mind and considerable contrapuntal genius at work, another manifestation of Bach's concern at this time to reconcile galant style with traditional contrapuntal skill.

Unlike the C minor Fuga in BWV 997, the introduction of sixteenth notes in the second section does not bring more intense impetus, rather a quiet susurration on the surface while the bass proceeds in steady quarter notes as before. Here again, sonority rather than contrapuntal ingenuity is the essence. The object of the section is to combine new material with the subject, and accordingly there is a middle-part entry in bar 35, with a bass answer in bar 39 in the version that ends on a♭. This motivates two sequences, one on the answer version of the first four notes of the subject (bars 47–50), and one on the last four notes but with a 3rd leap (bars 51–5). 3rd leaps then build the most intense part of the fugue (bars 55–60), leading back to a tonic entry of the subject (bar 61). The section ends in the middle of bar 75, the da capo neatly dovetailed in by a subject entry in the middle part on the second beat of that bar, and continuing with it decorated by the last of the sixteenth notes.

3. Allegro

The time signature $\frac{3}{8}$ with half bar-lines is to be distinguished from $\frac{6}{8}$ in that $\frac{6}{8}$ is a duple time with an upbeat in the middle of the bar, whereas $\frac{6}{8}$ here is a triple time with a second, lighter downbeat after the half bar-line (see the commentary on the Presto of the G minor violin Sonata). Bach generally uses $\frac{3}{8}$ in dance metres having small and detailed steps such as the passepied, which usually has a change of chord on the third eighth note. The tempo direction Allegro is therefore to be interpreted in terms of a metre with more weight on each eighth note than in $\frac{6}{8}$. Also in common with the passepied here is the almost exclusively four- or eight-bar phrase structure. This and the bass of repeated notes (bars 13–17 etc.) are features of the galant style that Bach cultivated in the 1730s.

The single exception to the four-bar phraseology is the very first phrase, which is of five bars. Without the bass note in bar 1, this bar would feel like an upbeat to bar 2, which would give us the ordinary four-bar phrase. But Bach is subtler than that. With the downbeat, and the downbeat of bar 2 being lighter, what we actually have is two pairs of $\frac{3}{8}$ bars. We then have the usual open-ended sequential move to the dominant, with a return of the opening phrase in the dominant (B flat major, bar 19). A feature peculiar to this movement is the fact that there are two closing motifs: bars 23–7 and bars 27–32. As one might expect, it is this unusual feature that provides the basis for the development in the second strain, which is almost entirely based on the second of the motifs. Bars 33ff have a development of it; bars 41ff have an inversion of it (with echo). This section has a continuous eight-bar phrase from bar 49, running into the first closing motif at bar 53 and a cadence in F minor. Bars 57ff have an inversion of the inversion. At bar 65 the inversion proper returns (with echo). There is no reprise as such, but a build-up from bar 73 that runs into the first closing motif from bar 87, and the strain is rounded off by the second closing motif from bar 91.

Altogether this differs from the two preceding movements in being more composed and intricate, less improvised, in effect. It nonetheless matches them in showing considerable art, if not in an improvised manner, in a light, galant style.

Prelude in C minor BWV 999

There is only one source for this, a manuscript copy in staff notation made by Johann Peter Kellner dating from after 1727 (*D-B* Mus.ms.Bach P 804), where it is entitled 'Praelude in C mol. pour La Lute. di Johann Sebastian Bach'. It is not known if Kellner was a pupil of Bach's, but he was at least acquainted with

Bach, was an enthusiast for his music, and we owe him many of the earliest copies of Bach works. P 804 is a bundle of miscellaneous manuscripts containing copies of some of Bach's very early keyboard works as well as ones close to the copying date (it also has Kellner's copies of the violin Solos and cello Suites) so gives little clue as to the date of composition. Kellner has the old 'Dorian' two-flat key signature for C minor, which Bach generally abandoned as he compiled the first book of *The Well-tempered Clavier*, finalised in 1722.

In terms of Bach's keyboard music BWV 999 belongs with preludes that pattern out chord progressions, such as the C major Prelude from Book I of *The Well-tempered Clavier* and the C sharp major Prelude from Book II (originally also in C major). Both of these Preludes were first written as plain five-part chords in half notes. They almost certainly had an educational intention as an elementary exercise in improvisation in that the pupil would pattern out the chord progressions in different ways, in the manner of the tradition recorded by Niedt of improvising different types of piece from the same figured bass.[60] Viewed from this point of view, BWV 999 looks very like a study in pedal effects. The four-chord formula that opens the Prelude (bars 1–7) is repeated in a more elaborate form at the end (bars 37–43); bars 8–12 have an upper pedal; and bars 17–33 are a long dominant pedal of G minor, with a sequence of descending diminished 7ths. The pupil who had absorbed this prelude would be ready to realise the continuo part in the opening chorus of the Saint John Passion. From a keyboard-technical point of view the Prelude could be said to focus on the use of the thumbs, something that Bach is said to have developed. David Schulenberg, noting that Kellner's copy ends with a quarter-note chord (changed to dotted half notes in NBA), suggests that the Prelude is incomplete and originally either returned to C minor, or went into a fugal section, as does the C sharp major Prelude of Book II of *The Well-tempered Clavier*.[61] Normally, if the prelude ends on the dominant, the fugue would begin on the fifth note of the tonic key. Alternatively, since the fermata is over the final chord, not the final bar-line, a cadenza or flourish may have been envisaged to conclude the Prelude, in the same way that Bach added a cadenza-style conclusion to the C minor Prelude from Book I of *The Well-tempered Clavier*, though without marking it with a fermata.[62]

The demonstrational aspect may have attracted Kellner to copy the piece, since he was an organist and composer who is not known to have played the lute, or he may just have been collecting anything he could lay his hands on. There is nothing in the prelude that necessarily suggests the lute other than the restriction of the upper compass to c" and Kellner's heading 'pour La Lute'. The designation almost certainly stems from Bach, who regularly mistook the gender of *le luth* (see the commentaries on BWV 995 and 998). There was no lutenist as such employed in the court music at Cöthen during Bach's time there. Even though Bach had access to a Lautenwerk at Weimar, the evidence for his having had one made at Cöthen is questionable.[63] This type of patterned-chord prelude nonetheless seems to have originated on the lute and theorbo. It appears in toccatas of Girolamo Kapsberger (Venice 1604), and there are many examples from Bach's time.[64]

Fugue G minor BWV 1000
(intabulation by J.C. Weyrauch of the Fuga from the G minor violin Sonata BWV 1001/2)

The only source for this arrangement is a lute tablature version by J.C. Weyrauch, entitled 'Fuga del Signore Bach' (*D-LEm* Sammlung Becker III.11.4). It is likely that Weyrauch made the arrangement himself. How much involvement Bach may have had, if any, or when the arrangement was made, cannot be said for certain. André Burguéte, noting that the alterations to the exposition significantly change the fabric of the music, suggested that such a level of recasting must have involved Bach, who may have provided a 'lute-esque' staff-notation version for an experienced lutenist to intabulate, making any necessary adjustments to take account of the possibilities and refinements of lute technique.[65] Bach did, after all, provide just such a version of the C minor cello Suite in BWV 995. It has to be said, though, that while the intabulation is skilful from the point of view of lute technique, it is not as accomplished from the point of view of composition as the organ version BWV 539, in which Bach's involvement is equally uncertain.

There are many minor adjustments throughout the Fuga, but the main recasting is in the exposition. In a fugue of this concerto type, the exposition could be defined as just the amount of the piece that exposes the subject in each of the four voices (to the middle of bar 5 in the violin version), or the entire tonic first section (to violin bar 14, lute bar 16). The lute alterations concern only the subject exposition. As we observed in the discussion of BWV 1001, Bach's violin exposition is very compact and ingenious in its suggestion of four voices within the pitch range of an octave (g'–g"). He has made a circle of entries in the sequence: subject (d")—answer (g')—answer (g")—subject (d"). The ingenious aspect is that, although the first and last entries are at the same pitch, the last is quite different in effect. The little addition at the beginning of (violin) bar 4 shifts the entry onto the second half of the bar, and whereas the first entry was solo, the last is surrounded by full chords involving the highest and lowest pitches so far. The organ version keeps this sequence, but expands the constricted pitch range by putting the fourth entry up an octave, and adding an extra tonic entry in the pedals (the entry of the subject in the pedals often provides the climax to the exposition in Bach's organ fugues). The lute version goes quite a lot further than this, evidently with a concern to 'regularise' the exposition. If the effect of the violin exposition is to have voice entries in the sequence tenor–bass–cantus–alto, the lute version changes this, and also the sequence of subject and answer, to: subject (alto)—answer (tenor)—subject (bass)—answer (cantus). This scheme is then superimposed on Bach's scheme in that we also (lute bar 6) have the subject repeated at the same pitch as the first entry, but this is now an extra cantus entry after all four voices have entered. Since the recasting has added a bar and a half to Bach's exposition, there is an extra answer (bar 7) to make up the half bar. This all means that the lute exposition ends up as two bars longer than the violin one.

The recasting is not technically gauche, and is skilful in replacing some of the original effects. In spite of repeating the pitch of the first entry, the entry at bar 6 is enriched by having a 'peregrinus' tenor entry on c in the second half of bar 5.[66] This gives the bar 6 entry the effect of being piled on top of an existing one in stretto at the 2nd, an effect common with this sort of subject with repeated notes (the best-known example is probably the first chorus of Cantata 21). Bach does not use this effect in the violin Fuga, probably for violin-technical reasons. This entry on c has been constructed from the bass notes in bar 4 of the violin version, just as the bass entry of the answer in (lute) bar 7 is constructed from the hint in the second half of (violin) bar 5. All of which gives the impression of a skilled lutenist looking at the violin version with a view to expanding the pitch range and enriching the texture to take advantage of the greater contrapuntal possibilities of the lute.

Skilful as it is, there are still weaknesses that make one doubt Bach's involvement. The main one is the way in which the recasting undermines the violin version's very purposeful use of pitch levels, a strategy typical of Bach's mature style. The lute's bass entry in bar 3 uses the very lowest notes of the instrument right at the beginning of the fugue, whereas the violin version saves this up for the last entry of all (violin bar 82). The violin version tops the fourth (repeat) entry with the highest note so far (b♭", violin bar 5), which leads into the passage of concertante sixteenth notes. This pitch is then taken up again towards the end of the section (violin bar 11) and brought down the scale to the tonic g' (violin bar 14), very neatly binding the whole first section, with its contrasting elements, together. In the lute version one might say there is an equivalent effect in the bass, from the entry on c (lute bar 5) down to G (lute bar 7), then on down to D (dominant, lute bar 8) that binds the exposition to the sixteenth-note passage. But other details are weak, such as the repetition of the middle of bar 1 into the beginning of bar 3 (hardly saved by substituting b♮ for b♭), a symptom of the more diffuse, less tightly organised nature of the lute version.

Other weak points, not really necessary from the lute-technical point of view, are the way in which the bass gets lost in (lute) bars 35–6; and bar 58, which lacks the different version of its countersubject and merely repeats the effect of the bar before. This intabulation is nonetheless a view of the piece by, at the very least, a contemporary and friend of Bach's and it is always open to modern performers to adjust it to their concepts. As far as shedding light on the performance of the violin version, the intabulation is not a great deal of help. Lute slurs are a particular aspect of lute technique, as noted in the discussion of BWV 995, and cannot be taken as a guide to performance on other instruments. In the pedal section (violin bars 38ff, lute bars 40ff), where violinists commonly arpeggiate, the lute version generally retains the eighth-note movement: the syncopated 3rds in (lute) bar 41 seem to be a *brisé* variation of bar 40 rather than a general instruction.

Suite in E major BWV 1006a
(arrangement by Bach of the E major violin Partia BWV 1006)

The main source is an autograph fair copy by Bach (Tokyo, Musashino Music Academy, Littera rara vol. 2–14) which has been dated on the grounds of paper and handwriting to 1736–7.[67] This is perhaps the most mysterious of Bach's 'lute' works since no instrumental designation has come down to us from Bach himself: the autograph part of the manuscript has nothing other than individual movement titles. There is, however, a nineteenth-century title-page with the title 'Suite pour le Clavecin composé par Jean. Sebast. Bach' that may or may not reflect an original title.

Any estimate of the intended instrument has to be deduced from internal factors. The most suggestive is the range AA–e", which just fits the 13-course lute, and that has been the most popular candidate. But E major is not natural to the lute in D minor tuning, and the Suite is quite unplayable in that key.[68] On the lute it is most frequently played in F major and is mostly possible in that key, though hardly idiomatic.[69] Klaus Hofmann has suggested the theorbo, which kept its Renaissance tunings until at least the mid eighteenth century (he suggests a e' b g d A, with diapasons tuned to the scale of E major, as favouring the bariolage of the prelude).[70] Of keyboard instruments, the restriction of compass would hardly make sense on the harpsichord. The clavichord is perhaps more likely since Bach is said to have 'often' played the violin Solos on it, 'adding as much extra harmony as he thought necessary'.[71] The simple transposition down an octave would account for the upper pitch limit, and German clavichords with a bass range to AA and GG are known from before 1750.[72]

Perhaps this is another sketch from which a lutenist might work up an arrangement. Apart from that, the most obvious candidate is again the Lautenwerk: André Burguéte went so far as to say that this is Bach's only surviving work for that instrument.[73] While the dances make good keyboard pieces, the Prelude with its long sections of bariolage can hardly be considered idiomatic. We have from Bach an excellent keyboard arrangement in Cantata 29 where these have been converted into much more keyboard-friendly Alberti-type figurations such as he used in his Vivaldi concerto arrangements. On the other hand, the long trill and general recasting in bars 82ff of the Gavotte en Rondeaux definitely suggest a keyboard. In view of this, a further keyboard instrument that might be considered is the Bogenclavier (also called Geigenwerk, or Claviergamba). This was a keyboard instrument designed to get around the fact that the sound of the harpsichord dies away. When a key is pressed, instead of a quill plucking the string a rosined wheel rubs against it like an endless bow. J.F. Agricola recommends it for cantabile melodies of violin, flute, or oboe: 'On this instrument much that sounds too dull and empty on the harpsichord would make its good effect'.[74] Agricola was thinking of the organist and inventor Gottfried Hohlfeld, a friend of C.P.E. Bach's who demonstrated a Bogenclavier in Berlin in 1753.[75] But instruments of this sort were being made from the later sixteenth century: one is illustrated by Praetorius (1619); another organ builder known to Bach, Johann Georg Schröter, inspected one at Dresden; and Clavier-Gambas, as well as Lauten-Claviers, were being made by Johann Georg Gleichmann at Ilmenau (near Arnstadt) from the early 1720s.[76]

A further instrument that has been suggested is the harp. Harpists are listed in inventories in Bach's environment, and his precursors in Leipzig wrote works with harp. Simon Hochbrucker (1699–c.1750), who demonstrated the pedal harp in Vienna in 1729 and later popularised it in Paris, visited Leipzig in the late 1730s; and the elder Petrini (after 1710–1750, his first name is not known) was in the court music of Crown Prince Frederick of Prussia at Ruppin and Rheinsberg in the 1730s; C.P.E. Bach wrote a sonata for him in 1740. According to Marpurg he could play equally fluently in all 24 keys.[77]

For detailed comment on style and structure, see the commentary on BWV 1006. The dance movements are suitable for keyboard, particularly the clavichord on which the thin textures work particularly well. Several of the original movements, such as the Loure and Menuet I, are in a two-part texture anyway and need little extra other than some filling out of chords. The Gavotte en Rondeaux and Menuet II are the most altered, the low tessitura of Menuet II being particularly akin to Bach's Lautenwerk style. The Bourrée, on the other hand, is almost entirely in a single part in the violin version, and has had a regular bass part added. In all these movements the violin's implied polyphony is frequently realised in a *brisé* texture.

Of particular value in BWV 1006a are the performance indications. While Bach is much more sparing of articulation slurs here than in the violin original, the much greater number of essential ornaments is very suggestive. Bach's own realisation of the harmonic implications of the original is also valuable.

CHAPTER SIX

The *Solo* for Transverse Flute BWV 1013

The unique source for this is a copy made by two of Bach's copyists (*D-B* Mus.ms.Bach P 968), entitled *Solo pour la Flute traversiere par J.S.Bach*. It comes at the end of a complete copy of the *Sei Solo* for violin BWV 1001–6 made by a copyist known as Anon.6. The flute *Solo* was started on the last, blank page of BWV 1006 by another copyist, until recently known as Anon.5, who made a number of good-quality copies for Bach at Cöthen and Leipzig, and whose handwriting was at one stage erroneously thought to be Bach's own.[1] Anon.5 stopped copying at bar 19 of the Allemande and the rest was copied by somebody whose handwriting is known only in this one source, so is no help in dating the copy. The NBA Critical Report dated the Anon.5 part *c*.1722–3, but more recent analysis has shown that the writing characteristics are in fact from a later stage, after 1725.[2] This means that BWV 1013 is not necessarily a Cöthen work, but could equally well date from Bach's early Leipzig years, perhaps around the time when he wrote a spate of cantatas with virtuoso solo flute parts in 1724 (see Chapter One, section 5).

The exceptional technical demands of this piece have encouraged the notion that it must have been written for an exceptional player, perhaps the great Dresden virtuoso Pierre-Gabriel Buffardin, just as it has often been suggested that the violin Solos must have been written for the Dresden virtuoso Johann Georg Pisendel. The notion that a demanding piece must have been written for a particular virtuoso is the product of modern concert giving and is a misunderstanding of the way Bach worked within his environment. For him the educational and speculative aspects were part of a unity with his duties as a performer, and a demanding piece could be 'for the use of youth eager to learn' as much as 'for the delight of those advanced in the art'. Bach says as much the 1722 title-page of *The Well-tempered Clavier*, and Forkel much later singled out the instrumental Solos as particular examples of this. It has been suggested that the flute *Solo* may have been a step towards a *Libro Terzo* for flute, to go with the *Sei Solo* for violin (described by Bach on the title-page as *Libro Primo*) and the *6 Suites* for cello (as a putative *Libro secondo*), in which case part of its use was as a means 'to make an ambitious student a perfect master of his instrument'.[3] These works belong with the very best études, in which demonstrations of instrumental and compositional techniques are joined to the highest artistic values.

These objectives may provide the answer to what have been considered problematic aspects of this piece, in particular the unremitting sixteenth notes of the Allemande, and the fact that it goes to top a'''. Violin, keyboard, lute, even violoncello piccolo origins have been suggested.[4] Is the piece as we have it complete, or was there a bass part?[5] The title does not specify *sans basse*, though each individual violin Solo has *senza basso* in its title. The transmission of the piece certainly suggests that what we have is complete, copied close to Bach and following on as a flute *Solo* after the *Sei Solo senza basso accompagnato* for violin. Given Bach's speculative bent, the seemingly unidiomatic aspects may well be the point of the piece. The note a''' may be very rare before 1800, but it was listed as the top note by Praetorius in 1619 (as a '*Falset*' note), by Corrette *c*.1740, and by Quantz in 1752.[6] Bach can write just as unnaturally for strings, in the unrelenting B minor violin Partia with all its repeats and Doubles, or the arpeggiated Prelude of the E flat major cello Suite with its lack of open strings. Long runs of sixteenths are endemic in Bach's more demanding flute parts, and the Allemande may well be a study for economy of breathing, and hierarchy of articulations, after which anything else would seem easy.

It has been suggested that the *Solo* is a systematic tour of styles: a German Allemande, an Italian Corrente, a French Sarabande, and an English Bourrée.[7] The movements also explore different voices of the flute: an Allemande for strategy of shaping and breathing, endurance, and high notes; a Corrente for leaps and concertante 'across the strings' figurations; a Sarabande in the rich, low register, *soupirant*, inviting colours, and using cantabile divisions; and a Bourrée with fife character, in the context of a light English *contredanse*.

1. Allemande

Of all Bach's unaccompanied allemandes, this must be the one most abstracted into the sonata moto-perpetuo style.[8] Even the Double of the Allemanda in the B minor violin Partia, its closest companion in this, retains the defining allemande upbeat to the first bar. Lacking this upbeat, the opening of the flute Allemande points to a third genre, the prelude, particularly of the technical-exercise type such as the D major Prelude in Book I of *The Well-tempered Clavier*.[9] A further clouding of genre is that it is not clear in the source whether, or how, the second strain is to be repeated.[10] But apart from these surface matters this Allemande is formally in line with allemandes and preludes that Bach was writing in the early 1720s in that it uses the usual ritornello structure in its sonata guise, a favourite formula that Bach treated with infinite variety and resourcefulness. The designation Allemande may well be to indicate the moderate tempo of the allemandes in flowing sixteenth notes in, for example, the English Suites for clavier. The title Prelude for a piece of this appearance could seem to indicate a brilliant *solfeggio*.

There is little reason to doubt that this is a piece for transverse flute. It seems built around the particular capacity of the flute to give variety of nuance to auxiliary and chromatic notes, according to their nature and expressive weight. This is typical of other flute movements by Bach, such as the Adagio ma non tanto of the E minor Sonata BWV 1034, or the aria 'Bethörte Welt' from Cantata 94 (1724) where it expresses the fickleness of the world. The unremitting sixteenths are a flaming sword against glib fluency, and an invitation to intelligent musicianship. Physical aspects of breathing and tonguing must be at the service of a mind and heart sensitive to the structures and harmonic conjunctions provided by the composer, an integration of the practical and physical with the intellectual and emotional that is completely typical of Bach. In this the Baroque flute, with its variety of voices and colours, differs from the Classical one, designed for evenness. Beneath the surface of sixteenths there lies a complex web of units, and often the implication of two or even three parts.[11] The player needs to develop a subtle hierarchy of breathing and articulation to match the hierarchy of phrase types and divisions. Too headlong a tempo will result in a general lack of nuance and intrusive large gulps for air. There is no one perfect solution to the problem of breathing in this piece, and different players have different capacities. So long as there is good structural understanding, repeated playings will suggest different and equally workable solutions.

The best introduction to this is Quantz's chapter on breathing (1752 Chapter VII), which also has excellent advice on understanding the intentions of the composer.[12] The unusual (for an allemande) opening actually provides a useful clue for shaping throughout the movement. In this style, beginnings and endings are often elided (a note can be at the same time the end of one shape and the beginning of the next) and function is ambiguous. A keyboard player would probably treat bar 2 as a shape beginning on the first note of the bar, repeated in bar 3 (in his arrangements of the Preludio of the E major violin Partia BWV 29 and 1006a Bach put a left-hand chord or bass note on the first beat of bar 1). The fact that this Allemande begins off the beat shows that shapes begin after the first note of the bar.[13] The repetition in bar 3 is also an indication for shaping. Repetition, paradoxically, can be emphatic and intensifying, or it can be relaxing. In this case the similarity to the Allegro of the A minor violin Sonata BWV 1003, where *fortes* and *pianos* are marked, implies relaxation. Whether the repetition is articulated by a different dynamic, or a different tonguing, or just a feeling of relaxation, it does give an opportunity for articulative breathing before the argument is resumed in bar 4.

The remainder of the first strain follows Bach's usual pattern for a first strain in a minor key. There is a move to the relative major (C major, bar 9), followed by one to the dominant (E minor, arrived at in bar 14), and chromatic closing material (bars 16–17). Within that, the pace of harmonic change, reflected in the motivic surface, is crucial for the ebb and flow of the piece. Generally there tends to be slow harmonic movement at the main tonal centres, and more rapid movement at moments of transition. This articulates the dynamic nature of travel from one key centre to another, and the static nature of arrival. Accordingly, there is a whole-bar harmony in bar 5 (see the figured-bass abstract Ex.6.1), half-bar in bar 6, quarter-bar in bars 7–8, and a return to whole-bar harmony when C major is reached at bar 9. The accelerando from bar 5 through bar 8 is thus all one cumulative shape and any interruption of it should be unobtrusive. It is particularly important not to split bar 5 from bar 6 since the colour change to F major in the second half of bar 6 is a striking effect that works only if bars 5 and 6 are taken as a pair. The

Ex.6.1   Allemande of BWV 1013, figured-bass abstract

arrival in bar 9, on the other hand, gives ample opportunity for an articulative breath.[14]

In the remainder of the strain, bar 13 is not an entry of the *inventio* in A minor, but a varied repetition of the pattern in bar 12. Bars 12 and 13 are therefore another pair. The important point of arrival here is g" at the beginning of bar 14, which needs the emphasis of accent and perhaps slight delay, though hardly an interruption of the flow. Strain endings often have a chromatic tinge, and this begins at bar 16 with an intensified version of the static figure in bars 2–3. Chromatic intensification of motifs will be carried further in the second strain. In bar 17 the third last note is f♮" (in accordance with eighteenth-century convention the sharp on f♯" in the second beat applies only to that note). This matches the b♭" in the equivalent place in bar 41, and is part of Bach's favourite progression from the Neapolitan 6th to the last-inversion dominant 7th (see Ex.6.1; also, for example, the commentary on the Allemanda of the D minor violin Partia in Chapter Three).

In a binary piece of this sort the agenda for the second strain is normally to take the succession of events that had run in the first strain from tonic to dominant, and run them back from dominant to tonic, with extensions and developments, and usually with a visit to the subdominant on the way (see Chapter Two section 7). Within this scheme there is usually a point of maximum tension before the subdominant entry. Bach invariably handles this agenda with subtlety and originality, and this Allemande is no exception. The second strain starts in the dominant and duly moves to the subdominant (D minor, bar 25). On the way, he takes the harmonically static figure from bar 4, which had the flute leaning on a sensitive appoggiatura (g♯'), and greatly intensifies it in bars 23–4 with all sorts of chromatic conjunctions. The D minor entry of the *inventio* in bar 25 leads, unusually, to a further entry in the dominant of the relative key (G major, bar 28), probably with a view to using more major-key and flute-friendly material. It corresponds to the C major entry at bar 9. Having these two entries (bars 25 and 28) close together presents a problem for the reprise in A minor, which would now seem banal if it simply repeated the opening of the piece. So Bach elides it (bar 33), and in A minor neatly condenses the events of bars 1–7, with the colour change to F major in bar 34, and the bar 4 figure in its choppy, chromatic version (as in bar 23), now also in A minor. After this condensed and developmental reprise, he needs to straighten out into a plainer version of A minor, and also to justify the final a'". Accordingly, the chromatic closing motif (bar 41) is a 4th higher than originally (bar 17), and the tessitura is extended by wide leaps (bars 41–5), preparing the final ascent. These leaps, new in the Allemande, are a feature of flute writing in imitation of Venetian concertos (Telemann objected to them as 'zigzag jumps'—'*krumme Sprünge*') that will be taken up again in the Corrente.[15]

2. Corrente

One way of looking at this *Solo* as a whole is as a study in sixteenth notes, the note value that predominates at this time and which Voltaire famously said he could not see the virtue of in the flute playing of Frederick the Great. If the Allemande is for sensitive moulding of ever-changing and developing shapes at a moderate tempo, the Corrente is for fluency and brilliance. The sixteenths are all in straight runs, rolling passages, and concertante, 'across the strings' violinistic figurations. In this the main interval is the 10th (introduced at the end of the Allemande), whether filled out by a scale, as a direct leap, or in an arpeggiated figuration.

This piece has been compared to the Courantes of the G major and D major cello Suites, with both of which it has features in common. It shares with the G major cello Courante its dramatic build-up to a climactic D sharp via a dissonant leap (flute bar 17, cello bar 26), a leading note whose resolution is delayed for two bars, and then resolves in a different octave (flute bar 19, cello bar 28). There is an inversion of this effect in the second strain, where a very long build-up to a cadence in C major (bars 35–41) is suddenly and unexpectedly deflected to E minor by the d♯' at the beginning of bar 42, not resolved until the e" two bars later. There is less systematic use of motifs here than in the G major cello Courante. The second strain has no tonic reprise as such, but a return to A minor at bar 48, and a fluid development of motifs in long, unbroken runs of sixteenths, though no longer than some of the examples for breathing in Quantz's *Solfeggi*.

3. Sarabande

This is the languishing, sighing character of the flute, in the *air plaintif* and the *air tendre*.[16] There is nonetheless no reason why a sarabande should have to be dead slow. Eighth notes are the decorative note value in this genre, and if they are treated as fundamental the necessary flexibility for nuances and shaping is lost. The broken-chord outlines in bars 17–19 etc. are particularly unsuited to a very slow tempo, and the *coulé de tierce* patterns (straightforward in bar 34, slightly decorated in bar 20, more so in bar 4) also imply light off-beat eighths. Within this framework the sixteenths bring in from the sonata style a further level of decorative note value, needing yet freer treatment. In this movement they are clearly meant to be of cantabile type, in which the same scales and rolling figures as in the Corrente are used to very different effect, suggesting luxuriant shaping rather than brilliant fluency.

The need for flexible eighths is evident in the first two bars. We have already encountered this type of *soggetto* in the subject of the C minor lute Fuga (see the commentary on BWV 997 in Chapter Five). In its pristine, unadorned form it opens Telemann's A minor flute Fantasia (Ex.6.2). It goes up the minor triad to the fifth degree, then instead of stepping up the semitone to the expressive sixth degree, jumps down a major 7th. This greatly enhances the expressive accent on the sixth degree. In this Sarabande Bach, in accordance with the genius of the flute for expressive appoggiaturas, has worked in a g♯' that outlines the added melodic dissonance of the augmented 2nd with the f♮' in bar 2, and expressive effect also in the Sarabande of the C minor cello Suite. The f♮' in bar 2 is then an appoggiatura to the e', as the e" in bar 18 is the d". All this gives ample opportunity for colouring and dynamic shading in the rich lower register of the Baroque flute.

Ex.6.2   Georg Philipp Telemann, Fantasia in A minor for unaccompanied flute, bars 1–6

The very expressive leap down to the minor sixth degree in bar 2 is answered by the more conventional step up in bar 6 (though still helped expressively by the g♯') beginning the sequences that lead to the climax of the strain in bar 14. The main phrase unit is 2+2, with a 4 at the end of each main section (bars 13–16, 31–4, 43–6). Within this pattern the point of maximum tension after the double bar is expressed by an irregular phrase of 6 (bars 21–6). The very clear sarabande structure gives natural breathing places.

4. Bourrée angloise

English country dances (*contredanses*) became very fashionable around 1700 in France and elsewhere.[17] They are lighter and more informal than the usual court dances, though often called bourrée or menuet, and that may explain the 'angloise' here. This witty piece recalls some features of the Allemande (though with an opposite expression) such as the repeated bars, perhaps implying an echo, and what are here *faux larmoyant* chromatic touches (bars 51–2, 63–4). The wit lies in the reversal of the normally dactylic rhythm of the bourrée to an anapaest, the fact that bar 2 is an augmentation of the rhythm of bar 1, and the early return of the opening rhythm in bar 4 (compare the more regular pattern in bars 1–6 of the *Battinerie* of BWV 1067). Comparison with similar rhythmic play in lute pieces of around 1720 by Silvius Leopold Weiss emphasises the highly concentrated and integrated nature of Bach's style.[18]

Powell and Lasocki, noting the European vogue for extended foot joints around 1720, suggest middle c' for the fourth note in bar 50, continuing the sequence from bar 48. It has been observed, for what it is worth, that the top notes (bars 12–15) spell out BACH.[19]

Appendices

Editorial policy in the examples has been to interfere as little as possible. Accidentals have been modernised, with editorial suggestions in small print; original beaming has been kept; some purely notational illogicalities have been smoothed out.

Appendix 1

Heinrich Ignaz Franz von Biber, *Sonatae, Violino solo*, Sonata I, first main section

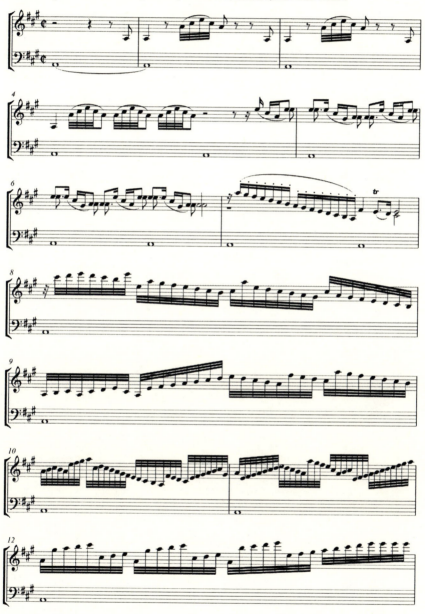

Appendix 2

Johann Jakob Walther, *Scherzi da Violino solo*, p.30.
© British Library Board. All Rights Reserved 29/12/2008 (Hirsch III 572)

Appendix 3

Nicola Matteis, a) *Fantasia* for unaccompanied violin (*D-Dl* Mus. 2045–R–1)

Nicola Matteis, b) *Alia Fantasia* (*D-Dl* Mus. 2045–R–1)

Appendix 4

Francesco Geminiani (?), *Sonata a Violino solo senza Basso*

Appendix 4

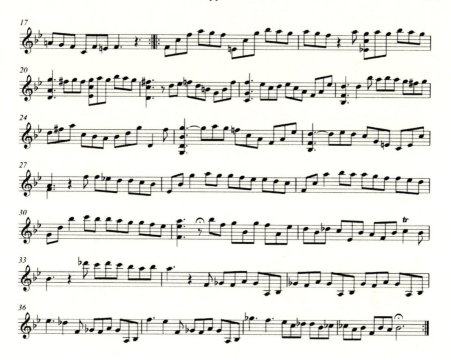

APPENDIX 5

Johann Georg Pisendel, *Sonata a Violino solo senza Basso* (*D-Dl* Mus. 2421–R–2)

Appendix 5

Appendix 6

François Couperin, Seventeenth harpsichord *Ordre*, [Allemande] 'La Superbe'

Notes

Introduction

1. See, for example, McVeigh and Hirschberg 2004.
2. This reflects the German title *Sonaten und Partiten für Violine allein* first used by Joseph Joachim in his edition of 1908; Joachim was also the first editor to have access to Bach's 1720 autograph.
3. Johann Krieger's 1697 keyboard collection has *Musicalische Partien* on the title-page, but 'Partita' for headings in the music.
4. The only exception is his keyboard arrangement of the third of Reincken's *Hortus Musicus* Sonatas (Hamburg 1688), with the movements Praeludium, Fuga, Adagio, and Allemande (BWV 966).
5. For full details, see KB VI/1.
6. See especially Dadelsen (ed), 1988; for an account of the transmission of the Solos before 1917, see Lester 1999 pp.19–22.
7. Other examples are *The Well-tempered Clavier* (1722) and the Inventions and Sinfonias (1723).
8. Dadelsen 1991 p.40.
9. For a discussion, with parallel facsimiles of selected bars from the violin Solos, see KB VI/2 pp.27–30 (partially reprinted by Schwemer and Woodfull-Harris 2000 pp.6–7); for an assessment of Anna Magdalena Bach's role as copyist, see Tomita 2007.
10. Schulze 1984 pp.96–8.
11. KB VI/1 p.28.
12. Stinson 1985; see also Stinson 1990 Chapter III, which has important further thoughts about Kellner's version of the Ciaccona.
13. KB VI/1 p.27.
14. Dadelsen 1991 p.42.
15. See Tomita 2007 p.60. She may have copied from a previous copy of her own. Possible evidence for this may be seen in the two fermatas (one over the final note and one over the double bar of Menuet II of the G major Suite). It could be that Bach added the second fermata to her original copy when he had proof-read it, when he felt that the piece was 'good enough' to copy (communication from Yo Tomita).
16. Martin Jarvis (2007) has proposed a more compositional role for Anna Magdalena Bach than most would consider likely. His proposals await publication and debate in an academic forum.
17. Stinson 1990 pp.60–1.
18. Beisswenger 2000 pp.78–80.
19. Leisinger 2000 pp.4–5 and 'Critical Notes'.
20. Eppstein 1976 p.47; KB VI/1 p.62.

21. Werner Breig in *MGG2* 'Bach, Johann Sebastian', column 1503.
22. Eller 1969 pp.132–3; also Eppstein 1976 p.37.

Chapter One: German Traditions of Solo Instrumental Music

1. See, for example, Boyd 2000 p.96.
2. Dok.III p.555, NBR pp.412–13; a similar quirk is recorded of one of Bach's last pupils, Johann Christian Kittel (see Herz 1985 p.40); for Kirnberger's retreat from practice into theory, see Borris 1933 pp.22–6.
3. Kirnberger 1771 p.176, Dok.III p.219.
4. NBR pp.323, 328.
5. Dok.III p.293, BR p.447.
6. For a comparison of Bach and Handel as violinists, see Scott 1935.
7. Dok.V p.117, NBR p.318.
8. KB VI/5 pp.64–5; Wolff 2000 p.133; Jones 2007 pp.203–5.
9. Dok III p.285, NBR pp.396–7.
10. Direction from the organ is usually written off too readily. Handel directed oratorio performances in London from a claviorganum, and Joah Bates directed the enormous forces for the Handel Commemoration in Westminster Abbey in 1784 from the organ, albeit with a greatly extended action so that the console was in the middle of the performers. Nearer to Bach is Johann Christoph Weigel's illustration of a 'Music-Director' (*c.*1722), who is conducting with two rolls of paper; Weigel in Nuremberg was the publisher of Bach's *Clavier-Übung* II (1735).
11. NBR p.136; for a full review of Bach as conductor, see M.M. Smith 1998 pp.71–3; also Dreyfus 1987 pp.31–2, and Köpp 2005 pp.222–3.
12. Report by J.F. Agricola, who was a pupil of Bach's from 1738–41.
13. Forkel 1802 pp.60–1, NBR p.472
14. Cartier 1798 pp.327–31, 'Fuga de la Sonate IIIe par Joh. Seb. Bach le manuscrit apartient [sic] au C[itoy]en Gavinies' (bar 269 is missing on p.330), see KB VI/1 p.51; for Salomon, see Dok.III p.478, also Philip Olleson in Kassler 2004 pp.300–1.
15. Pisendel, in a letter to Telemann of 1749, says that he was well aware of the merits of 'old Bach' (Dok.V p.172; see also Dok II p.513).
16. Of these, the first two are connected with Bach's career ambitions. The title-pages of the Inventions and Sinfonias (1723) and *The Well-tempered Clavier* (1722) may have been written to support Bach's application for the Leipzig cantorate in 1723 (Wolff 2003 pp.134–5).
17. Prinner 1677, quoted in Drescher 2004 p.109.
18. See Braun 1979.
19. Ruth Tatlow has proposed, on grounds of numerical proportions, that the *Libro Secondo* would have been the six Sonatas for obbligato harpsichord and violin BWV 1114–1119 (booklet notes for CD Homburger 2003, pp.11–12).
20. Bach is a great example of this, but he is by no means alone. The same could be said of Purcell's 'A Brief Introduction to the Art of . . . Composing Musick in Parts', published in Henry Playford's *An Introduction to the Skill of Musick* (London 12/1694).
21. Dok.III pp.292–3, BR p.447.
22. Apel 1990 p.51.
23. For a survey of German professional violin repertory in the early to mid seventeenth century, with editions of the more important sources, see Brooks 2002 (a concise survey concentrating on Étienne Nau is in Brooks 2004). Brooks concludes that native German repertory centred not on Italian sonatas, but consisted of dance tunes, divisions on popular tunes and polyphonic models, and fantasias that represent an essentially improvised tradition.

24. See Winternitz 1979 Plate 84a, also S.S. Jones 1995.
25. Some of Marini's Op. 8 'curiose e moderne inventioni' are recorded on CD Convivium 1998 (notes by Peter Allsop); a general view of Marini is presented on CD Romanesca 1998 (notes by Andrew Manze).
26. Ed. N.Harnoncourt (Wilhelmsavn: Noetzel Verlag, 1970); of many recordings that by Skip Sempé is a lively one (Deutsche Harmonia Mundi 1992).
27. See Allsop 2005 for a survey of musical relations between the Vienna court and Italian centres.
28. See Allsop 2005 pp.15–19 for examples.
29. Drescher 2004 p.10.
30. Apart from a mild version in a 'Cuckoo' sonata; he does use it in works preserved in manuscript (for a selection see DTÖ 93).
31. Ed. DTÖ 11; CD Manze 1994. In his collection of portraits of musicians, C.P.E. Bach had a series of famous violinists including Biber and Pisendel, which he may have inherited from his father (Leaver 2007 pp.125–6).
32. Thomas Drescher (1996 p.49) offers the following analysis of the first two sections of this Sonata, demonstrating its origin in a mixture of improvised and composed sections:
    1. Test of tuning, with frequent playing of the notes a, a', e" (bars 1–10);
    2. Improvisation ('Praeludieren') over a pedal, with insertion of a slow, composed episode (Adagio, bars 23–35), that prepares the change to the dominant (bars 11–43);
    3. Preparation on a dominant pedal (bars 44–6);
    4. Presentation of a contrapuntally elaborated set-piece composition (Presto) with imitative texture.
33. Drescher 2004 p.176; Marini also has the violin retuning in mid-movement, in the 'Sonata Seconda per il Violino d'inuentione' of Op.8, where the violin has to tune the E string down for a passage of double-stopped thirds, and up again afterwards (see Beckmann 1918, 'Anhang' No.5).
34. J.J. Walther 1694, 'Erinnerung an die Liebhaber deβ Violins'; see Thomas Drescher's thorough survey (2004).
35. Drescher 2004 p.23, p.108.
36. Webber 1996 p.50.
37. A number of references to this practice are listed in KB VI/1 p.64.
38. See Webber 1996 Chapter 8.
39. F-Pn Rés.Vm7 673; Fanselau 2000 p.23, p.58.
40. See Fanselau 2000 p.59.
41. For Pachelbel and Matthias Kelz, see Fanselau 2000 pp.59–60; for Pachelbel's chamber music, see Beckmann 1919.
42. Fanselau 2000 p.61; ensemble works of Furchheim and others are edited in Goebel 2006.
43. Hawkins's embroidery that Corelli spoke 'broken German' is a misunderstanding of Walther's word 'aus-gebrochen', i.e. exclaimed (Hawkins 1776, R/1963 p.676).
44. Dok.III p.288, NBR p.398.
45. Fanselau 2000 p.62.
46. Edited in Beckmann 1921 Heft 2; see Aschmann 1962 p.109, Fanselau 2000 p.62, also Robertson 2005.
47. See numerous references to Bruhns in NBR; also Mattheson 1740 p.26 for Bruhns accompanying himself. Pieces for unaccompanied violin by the Lübeck violinist Thomas Baltzar (?1631–1663) in Playford 1685 etc. probably owe more to the English lyra viol tradition than to a north German violin tradition (see Holman 1993 p.280).
48. CD Plantier 2006; the 1694 edition is entitled *Hortus Chelicus*.
49. 'Das ist Wohl-gepflanzter Violinischer Lust-Garten Darin Allen Kunst-Begierigen

Musicalis oder Liebhaberen der Weg zur Vollkommenheit durch curiöse Stücke und annehmliche varietät/gebahnet/Auch durch Berührung zuweilen zwey/drey/vier Seithen/auff der Violin die lieblichste Harmonie erwiesen wird.'
50. Henricus Albicastro (c.1660–c.1730), a Dutch violinist of German extraction whose real name was Johann Heinrich Weissenberg, published nine opus numbers of solo sonatas with continuo, trio sonatas, and concertos.
51. For the Klagenfurt MS see Nobes 1999.
52. Ed. in DEdM 17; CD Beznosiuk 2000.
53. Drescher 2004 p.117.
54. Chafe 1987 p.192.
55. Current location *D-Mbs* Mus. Ms. 4123.
56 Chafe 1987 p.6, p.187; Chafe points out that almost every instrumental work by Schmelzer has a counterpart by Biber, including the 'Ciaconna ohne ferneres accompagniomento'.
57. CD Plantier 2004.
58. Unique copy in *H-SG*; for details see the facsimile edited by W. Reich and M. Fechner. A reported copy in *B-Bc* (RISM W 959) was entered in RISM in error and has never existed (communication from Madame Wahnon de Oliveira, Library of the Royal Conservatoire, Brussels).
59. Edited by Beckmann (1921 Heft 5); there is also a heavily edited version by Gerhartz (1925).
60. For a useful listing of types of counterpoint in solo violin music generally, see Nobes 2000a pp.30–3.
61. Sole surviving copy, *GB-Lbl* b.48; facsimile and edition with full description of the source in Nobes 2000b; CD Nobes 1998. Unlike Westhoff's suites, Vilsmaÿr's are notated on the usual five-line stave with G2 clef.
62. Drescher 2004 p.117.
63. See the Preface to her facsimile (Nobes 2000b).
64. 'quae, cum una Chely exprimant, quod pluribus aliàs ludi solet Instrumentis. Magni Animi Tui Idea sunt, utpote qui unus collecta tenet, quae dispersa beatos efficiunt Principes.'
65. The Pisendel collection was preserved as an entity from 1760, was catalogued by Moritz Fürstenau in the 1850s, during World War II was stored with other valuable musicalia in a specially deep cellar of the Saxon State Library, which survived the bombing of February 1945 but was flooded to a depth of one metre, effectively destroying a number of items (Eller 1969 pp.61–2). There is also a possibility that some things marked as 'Kriegsverlust' may still be in Russia.
66. Dok.III p.189; BR p.452.
67. VBN p.101.
68. NBR pp.79–80, also Breig 1998; Pisendel had a high regard for Bach (see Dok.II p.513, also Dok.V p.172).
69. Hiller 1784 pp.188–9; Köpp 2005 pp.97–102.
70. The parts (now lost) were designated to be played by Volumier, Le Gros, Fiorelli and Lotti, who were all together in the *Capelle* only around 1710 (Moser 1966 p.133).
71. For example, by Goebel 1991 pp.139–42.
72. It is used by Froberger for his free, prelude-like lamentations.
73. See Ledbetter 2002 pp.222–3, p.334.
74. Studeny 1911 p.45; Moser 1966 p.134.
75. The series includes three pieces by Thomas Baltzar, Biber's Passacaglia, this Sonata attributed to Geminiani (wrongly headed 'g-moll'), Pisendel's A minor Sonata, and Westhoff's A major suite (Paris 1683). The series is still available from Fr. Portius-Verlag, A-Mauerkirchen. The Sonata attributed to Geminiani was in *D-B* Mus. 11764, now considered 'Kriegsverlust' (see Fanselau 2000 p.41). The attribution to Geminiani

has been questioned; the attribution is Pisendel's, and in style and details of notation the Sonata is similar to Geminiani's very Corellian *Sonate* for violin and bass of 1716.
76. A sonata in G minor for violin and continuo (*D-Dl* Mus. 2201–R–15, formerly 2201–R–10), which Moser (1966 pp.134–5) suggests may reflect Geminiani's studies with Lonati, is in fact in a later style and has been attributed by Kai Köpp to Pisendel (communication from Karl Geck).
77. The MS (formerly *D-Dl* Mus. 2020–R–1) was destroyed in 1945, but exists in a photocopy; ed. F. Giegling 1981; facsimile SPES 2005; CD Timpe 2004.
78. *D-Dl* Mus. 2767–R–3; ed. M. Talbot 2005.
79. CD Graulich 2003.
80. Proposed by Jung (1956 p.49), and others.
81. The Giga is on a theme also used by Handel (see Ledbetter 1995 p.41).
82. Fechner 1999 p.45.
83. The Capricci that Locatelli included in his Op. 3 Concertos (1733 but written during the 1720s), while technically the most demanding the Baroque has to offer, cannot be said to match Pisendel in musical substance and expression; the Caprices of Franz Benda (not published until 1804) are essentially short studies, each concentrating on some technical aspect.
84. Kahl 1948 p.118.
85. Quantz 1752 XVIII/58; Quantz attributes the fashion for the style to Vivaldi (trans. Reilly p.323).
86. For a more detailed discussion, with examples, see Ledbetter 2007 pp.211–19.
87. For instrument types, see Barnett 1998, and Wissick 2006; for bow-holds, see M.M. Smith 1995.
88. Cowling 1975, Markevitch 1989.
89. See the facsimile edited by M. Vanscheeuwijck (2006) who is convinced that the violin part is a subsequent addition (p.28).
90. RV 402, 416, 420; see Kotsoni-Brown 2000 p.29, p.251.
91. See Smit 2004 p.50.
92. Rampe and Sackmann 2000 p.34; Dreyfus 1987 p.134.
93. Kinney 1962 p.125; Biber played both 'violin-bass' and gamba at Kroměříž; for influence of viol technique on the development of the German virtuoso violin school, see Brewer 1997 pp.xi–xii.
94. Rousseau 1687 p.20.
95. CD Savall 2000.
96. See Milliot and La Gorce 1991 for a concise account of Marais's style.
97. See Hsu 1981 for details of French viol technique.
98. Kinney 1962 p.175, Cowling 1975 p.98, M.M. Smith 1995 p.47.
99. Étienne Loulié (1701) adds a further three; details in Hsu 1981.
100. '... *tic-tac*, par les coups d'archet enlevés, & tout en l'air, qui tiennent si fort du pincé de Luth & de la Guitarre, sur le modèle de quoi le Père *Marais* a composé ses Pièces, auxquelles, quoiqu'il les ait variées de six coups d'archet différens, on peut reprocher une partie du manque l'expression du Clavecin, qui en souffre une éclipse centrale, en ce qu'ils sont *Simples* (donnans leur coup sur la corde de la Viole, comme fait le Sautereau sur celle du Clavecin), & non pas *Complexes*, tels que ceux à l'Italienne, où l'Archet par le tiré & le poussé, unis & liés, sans qu'on apperçoive leur succession, produit des roulades de Sons multiples à l'infini, qui n'en paroissent qu'une continuité, tels qu'en formoient les gosiers de *Cossoni* & de *Faustina*.' (Le Blanc 1740 pp.23–4).
101. Le Blanc 1740 p.26. For a selection of quotations about the desirability of long bow-strokes in Bach's environment, see Grüss 1988 pp.331–2.
102. For a comprehensive survey, see Flassig 1998.
103. Edited in DEdM 67.

104. He may have been the father of the gambist and lutenist Johann Michael Kühnel, who in 1712 was in the Berlin court *Capelle* with Christian Bernhard Linike and later at the Weimar court of Duke Ernst August (Baron 1727 trans. D.A. Smith p.73; *MGG1* Bd.7 Spalt 1858; Flassig 1998 p.276).
105. 'weil die Viol d'gamba auß Engellandt her kombt', quoted in *MGG2* art. 'Kühnel, August'.
106. Friedrich Wilhelm II of Prussia (dedicatee of string quartets by Haydn and Mozart) only changed from the viol to the cello in the 1770s, and the last was the Elector Maximilian III Joseph of Bavaria (Flassig 1998 p.237).
107. '... le Theorbe, qui est propre pour accompagner toutes sortes de Voix, quand ce ne seroit que par la seule raison de sa douceur, qui s'accommode aux Voix foibles & delicates; au lieu que les autres Instruments les offusquent.' (Bacilly 1668 p.18).
108. For a detailed, if somewhat unsympathetic, assessment of Schenck's mixed style see Luttmann 1981.
109. CD W. Kuijken 1993.
110. Flassig 1998 pp.271–2.
111. Dok.III pp.116–17.
112. Hiller 1784 p.154.
113. Bononcini's Sonatas are edited by L. Lindgren.
114. See Davis 1986 pp.123–6 for possible relevance of viol techniques to the cello Suites; the viol underhand bow-hold continued to be used in Germany until *c*.1730 (M.M. Smith 1995 p.47).
115. '*Violoncello*, ist ein *Italiae*nisches einer *Violdigamba* nicht ungleiches *Bass-Instrument*, wird fast *tractir*et wie eine *Violin*, neml. es wird mit der lincken Hand theils gehalten, und die Griffe *formir*et, theils aber wird es wegen der Schwere an des Rockes Knopff gehänget und durch die rechte Hand mit einem Bogen gestrichen. Wird gestimmet wie eine *Viola*.' (J.G. Walther 1708 ed. Benary p.56).
116. Mattheson 1713 p.285, repeated in J.G. Walther 1732 ; early eighteenth-century descriptions of the violoncello are collected in Badiarov 2007.
117. Dok.II p.493, NBR p.252.
118. Dok III p.186–7, BR pp.451–2.
119. Dok III pp.312–13.
120. Dok.III p.349, NBR p.368.
121. Dok.III p.453.
122. Dok.III p.469, BR p.451.
123. Dok.III p.471.
124. See in particular Husmann 1936, Dreyfus 1987, Dürr 1990; the most recent summary of evidence and arguments is in Prinz 2005 pp.584–601; for a survey of types of bass violin, see Segerman 1995.
125. Schrammek 1977 p.347.
126. Wissick (2006 8.1) thinks that Corelli probably meant the B flat bass violin, in line with Corelli's general conservatism; it has to be said, though, that the parts do not go below C and are in places extremely agile.
127. Prinz 2005 p.585.
128. M.M. Smith 1998 p.75.
129. Recent iconographic evidence was presented by Gregory Barnett in a paper delivered at the Thirteenth Biennial International Conference on Baroque Music, University of Leeds, July 2008. Badiarov gives a very useful collection of quotations relating to the cello in early eighteenth-century Germany.
130. For a listing see Ledbetter 1987 Appendix B.
131. For a more detailed account of the development of French lute style in the seventeenth century, see Ledbetter 1987 Chapter Two.
132. '... sofern man die rechte Mensur wol nach itziger Art raußbringen wil, müssen die

gleichen Noten stets rückende oder springende, und nicht so gleiche weg gespielet werden.' (1676, letter to the reader).
133. Similar suite-like groupings are found in the printed arrangements (not by Reusner) for strings of Reusner's lute music; a selection of Reusner's suites is on CD Junghänel 1992.
134. The refrain of the Ennemond Gaultier Chaconne, together with a harpsichord arrangement of it by D'Anglebert, is given in Ledbetter 1987 p.82.
135. See Ledbetter 2002 pp.94–6.
136. These may arise from experiments with the theorbo, whose re-entrant tuning encourages them, with resulting campanella effects.
137. '... nach den Grund-Regeln der berühmtesten Meister Messieurs Du Faut Gautier, und Mouton eingerichtet ...' (Lesage de Richée 1695, 'Geehrter Leser').
138. 'Dieser hochberühmter Meister, hat schon die neue Italiänische und Frantzösische *Methode* dieses Instrument zu *tracti*ren, so glücklich *combini*rt, daß er nicht allein sehr anmuthig und *Cantable* ins Gehör, sondern auch Künstlich und Fundamentel *componi*ret hat.' (Baron 1727 p.74).
139. Dok.II p.179.
140. Dok.III p.125, BR p.444.
141. For some locations, see the article on Losy in *New Grove 2*.
142. 'eine nette, vollstimmige, mehrentheils gebrochene, frantzösische Art' (from a letter printed in Mattheson 1740 pp.171–2); for a general account of Losy's style see Vogl 1981, which should be read in conjunction with Crawford 1982.
143. For Weiss's date of birth, see Legl 1998 and D.A. Smith 1998; his complete lute works are currently being recorded by Robert Barto for Naxos.
144. Baron 1727 p.78, trans. D.A. Smith pp.70–1.
145. Dok.II p.366, NBR p.204.
146. Hoffmann-Erbrecht 1987 p.20.
147. *GB-Lbl* Ms. Add. 30387, *D-Dl* Mus. 2841–V–1.
148. The date 1706 is not in the London MS but in an autograph annotation to the Dresden copy; the *Tombeau* carries the date of Losy's death, 'arrivée 1721'.
149. See Crawford 2001; for the development of the German Baroque lute, see Lundberg 1999. The Sonatas in the Dresden MS are generally later though one (No.44) is marked 'composta a Roma', so must date from c.1710–14.
150. '...die in dem ächten und körnichten Geschmack geschrieben sind, wie ungefehr die Clavier-Arbeiten des sel. Joh. Seb. Bach....' (Dok.III p.351).
151. *GB-HAdolmetsch* MS II B 2 pp.83–4 (copied c.1760; the piece shows signs of having been converted to 13-course from 11-course lute; information from Tim Crawford).
152. *Oeuvres des Gallot* No.98.
153. A distant relic of this finale type may be in the D major string quartet from Haydn's Op.50 (the so-called 'Frog' quartet).
154. Dok III pp.492–3, NBR p.252; the lute was valued at 21 rtl, the Lautenwerke at 30 rtl; a Stainer violin was valued at 8 rtl. The lute was probably not an instrument bequeathed to Bach by the Leipzig *luthier* J.C. Hoffmann since Bach had already given the Hoffmann instrument(s) to J.C.F. Bach before he died (Dok II pp.449–50).
155. In volume II of his 1977 edition of the lute works Ernesto Cipriani proposes a special instrument called 'La Luth' (based on Bach's mistaking the gender of 'le luth') with 15 courses on the fingerboard, metal frets and levers to alter notes, *capo tasto* for all keys, and 77 cm string length (see North 1982 p.148, Grossman 1987 pp.31–3).
156. See Schulze 1966 for a detailed list, also Dreyfus 1987 pp.170–1.
157. Baron 1727 p.81, trans. D.A. Smith p.73.
158. Schulze 1966 p.35.
159. In 1743 Bach was godfather to Weyrauch's son, Johann Sebastian (Dok II p.407; see also Dok.I pp.135–6 and Dok.II p.223).

160. For a detailed account of the Lautenwerk and its possible relation to Bach's keyboard works generally, see Ledbetter 2002 pp.28–31.
161. For Hotteterre's time in Rome, see Powell 2008 p.120.
162. According to Ovid, Atalanta was famous for her running ability, and ran a race against her suitors in which the one who outran her would marry her, and she would kill the rest. She had an interesting life, being suckled by a she-bear, and she and her husband were turned by a vengeful goddess Cybele into a pair of lions on their wedding night.
163. See Ledbetter 2001 for this type of adagio as discussed by Hotteterre (1719).
164. For a detailed account of this development, see Castellani 1989.
165. According to Quantz (Kahl 1948 pp.116–17), Vivaldi's first compositions for traverso date from 1715–17 (Sardelli 2007 p.34).
166. See Castellani 1989 pp.569–70, also his introduction to the facsimile of Mattheson 1720.
167. Kahl 1948 p.116; for Buffardin in general see Kollpacher-Haas 1962; for the flute in the Dresden court music in the first decades of the eighteenth century, see Oleskiewicz 2005.
168. Telemann 1716, dedication letter; see also Rackwitz 1981 pp.71–2; Telemann's flute Fantasias (Hamburg 1732/33) are too late to have relevance to BWV 1013.
169. Buffardin apparently taught Bach's brother Johann Jacob in Constantinople before 1712 (Dok.III pp.287–8, NBR pp.289–90); Barthold Kuijken (1990, Postface) points out that there are no Bach flute sources in Dresden, nor are his flute works mentioned by Quantz. Bach's third son, Johann Gottfried Bernhard, played the flute (Dok.III p.408, NBR p.369), but since he was born in 1715 it is unlikely that BWV 1013 was written for him.
170. König 1959 pp.160–1.
171. A facsimile of *B-Bc* Ms.Litt. XY.15.115 is published as *Manuscrit allemand du XVIIIe siècle* (Raspe 1979); of sonatas attributed to Freytag three are for unspecified instrument, one for flute, one for oboe, and one for either flute or violin; for flautists and flute style in Bach's immediate environment, see Fanselau 2000 p.68; a list of flute players Bach knew or may have known is in Appendix 1 of Powell and Lasocki 1995.
172. Powell and Lasocki 1995 pp.14ff, Prinz 2005 p.244.
173. Dok.I p.128, NBR p.321; Dok I pp.54, 129.
174. Prinz 2005 p.259; Marcello Castellani has proposed 1724 as the date of composition of BWV 1013 (1989 p.573); the first version of the Saint John Passion was performed in April 1724 but the wind parts have not survived and the status of the flute (for example in the aria 'Ich folge dir gleichfalls' in the unfriendly key of B flat major) is uncertain (Dürr 1988 pp.134–8).

Chapter Two: Concepts of Style and Structure

1. Kahl 1948 pp.202, 205; an overture-suite by Telemann is in the Andreas Bach Book, a collection copied largely by Bach's eldest brother Johann Christoph (see Hill 1987 I pp.253–5).
2. Kahl 1948 p.108.
3. See Timms 2003 p.206.
4. VBN pp.308–9; Hill 1987 I pp.169–70; a selection of Pez's works is published in DTB Series 1 Vol.35; CD Les Muffatti 2007.
5. See Ledbetter 2002 pp.164–7.
6. For a possible connection between Bach and Couperin via Pisendel, see Delang 2007.
7. CD Les Muffatti 2005.
8. Muffat 1701 *Vorred*; a facsimile of the preface is in DTÖ 23; English translation in Strunk 1965 pp.89–92; all Muffat's prefaces are translated in Wilson 2001.

9. See Breig 1998 p.10 etc.
10. Dok.I p.63, NBR pp.149–50; for an overview of Bach's mixed style, see Siegele 1999.
11. For Corelli's knowledge of French style see Ferreira 1996; for the general diffusion of French dances in northern Italy from c.1660, see Klenz 1962 pp.106–22 and Barnett 2008 Chapter Two.
12. Allsop 1999 p.110.
13. Hotteterre 1719 p.59; for Hotteterre and Corelli, and *notes inégales* in Italian music, see Ledbetter 2001 pp.16–17; for Hotteterre's time in Rome, see Powell 2008 p.120.
14. For example in the Sarabande of the first *Concert Royal* (published in Paris in 1722, though written before 1715); Couperin does not use the effect throughout but as one element in a subtly mixed style.
15. For inequality in slurred pairs, see L. Mozart 1756 XII/10, also Collins 1967 pp.483–4.
16. For a more detailed account of *La Superbe* in the context of subtly varied inequality, see Ledbetter 2001 pp.17–18.
17. Evidence for the performance of the *coulé de tierce* is set out by Kenneth Gilbert in the Introduction to his edition of François Couperin's First Book of harpsichord pieces (Gilbert 1972 pp.xviii–xix); Gilbert calls it the *coulé de tierce mélodique* to distinguish it from the *tierce coulée* listed in many ornament tables as a harmonic dyad with added passing note.
18. See the tables in Boyvin 1690 and Dieupart 1701 (VBN I/D/1 and II/B/8); Boyvin gives it in the rhythm ♩♪♩); for a characteristic example of Bach's use of the *coulé de tierce* as a phrase ending (in each case followed by a rest), see the opening Sinfonia of Cantata 12 (1714).
19. The literature on Bach's knowledge of French style is very extensive: for the main points see Pirro 1907, Schulze 1985, and Horn 1986; for Bach's admiration for Couperin see Dok.III pp.4, 59, 77, 199, 215, 471, also VBN I/C/3, II/C/2, II/C/3.
20. Dok.III p.473.
21. See, for example, Oppel 1921 p.17.
22. Good advice for the performance of *notes inégales* is in Gilbert 1972 p.xx, also Mather 1973; the best eighteenth-century description is in the eleventh chapter of Hotteterre 1719, since it is clear and concise and he gives useful examples from repertory; for a detailed discussion see Hefling 1993.
23. For an attempt at a rationale for variable inequality in adagios, see Ledbetter 2001.
24. 'Il faut . . . distinguer sur tout les phrases qui sont dans le goût François, d'avec celles qui exigent le goût Italien.' (Mondonville 1748, *Avertissement*).
25. Edited by W. Michel and H. Teske; for a concise introduction to Quantz on variable inequality, see Fontijn 1995.
26. For a survey see Brown 1976, and Mather and Lasocki 1977.
27. See Ledbetter 2002 pp.59–61; for a nuanced account of Bach's reception of ritornello structures, see R. Jones 2007 pp.140–53; see also Fischer 1915, Dürr 1951 pp.106–7, Schulenberg 2008 pp.82–93.
28. Lutterman (2006) explores in detail the improvisatory background to Bach's cello Suites.
29. Lester 2001; see also Talbot 1971 for basic analytical concepts in the Italian concerto style.
30. For a wide-ranging discussion, see Dreyfus 1996.
31. Dok.I pp.220–1, NBR pp.97–8.
32. Dok.III p.87; for further applications of the terms 'arbeitsam' and 'laborieux' to the Italian style, see Telemann's autobiography in Mattheson 1731 pp.171–2.
33. Scheibe c.1730 III/iii/12.
34. Gaspard le Roux used a similar collection of entrée materials in the Allemande of his A major suite (Paris 1705, also Amsterdam 1707–8); pieces from this collection were copied by J.G. Walther in *D-B* Mus.ms.Bach P 801 (Gustafson and Fuller 1990

pp.255–6). The Menuet of Stölzel's Partia provides a good example of a first strain with a dance-style antecedent and a sonata-style consequent. In the *Clavier-Büchlein*, Stölzel's Partia and a suite in A major by Telemann come after the two-part Inventions and before the three-part Sinfonias. This suite element in the teaching programme may have been the spur to Bach's explorations in the French Suites.

35. See Ledbetter 2002 p.139.
36. Burney 1773 *passim*.
37. Marpurg 1753 pp.19–20, Mann 1958 p.156, also p.140.
38. For a detailed discussion see Chapter Four in Ledbetter 2002.
39. See Ledbetter 2002 pp.210–11.
40. For a very perceptive and detailed account see Lester 1999 Chapters Two and Three.

Chapter Three: The *Sei Solo* for Violin BWV 1001–1006

1. BWV 1046a; for BWV 542 and 594 see Williams 2003 pp.85–9 and 213–18; for BWV 903 see Schulenberg 2006 pp.147–52, 1992 pp.114–19.
2. See Rostal 1973 for comment on this manner of playing and on the 'Vega Bach bow' promoted by Albert Schweitzer and others.
3. Kahl 1948 p.219, Rackwitz 1981 p.94.
4. Dok III p.292, BR p.447; the organ version is BWV 594/2 (see Williams 2003 pp.70–4), the lute version is BWV 1000 (discussed below and in Chapter Five).
5. For a survey of views on the authenticity of 'Corelli's graces', see Urchueguía 2006 pp.15–16, 167, who concludes that Roger used a manuscript compiled by Corelli, or under his supervision.
6. See Zaslaw 1996.
7. As one of the manners in the opening movement of Op.9 No.6 (Amsterdam [1704]), and in the Adagio third movement of a manuscript Sonata (DEdM 67 p.64).
8. Quoted in Schroeder 1977 p.16.
9. Schulenberg 2006 pp.89–90.
10. For the Adagio, see Lester 1999 Chapter Two.
11. Beach 2005 p.33.
12. See the discussion of the E major Prelude from Book I of *The Well-tempered Clavier* in Ledbetter 2002 pp.64 and 183.
13. Did Bach really intend the bass note in the third beat of bar 3 of the Adagio to be e♮' (the note is also in Anna Magdalena Bach's copy and Kellner's)? While a 6-chord on e♮', with chromatic step down to e♭', then d', is theoretically possible the prevalence of the pitch e♭'' in the vicinity makes a bass e♮' most unlikely. The equivalent note in the reprise is a♭, and the major 7th features equivalently in other movements (see below). A recent recording using e♮' is CD Holloway 2006.
14. C.P.E. Bach 1762 xli/9.
15. Lester 1999 pp.49–50.
16. See endnote 13; e♭' is also missing from the third beat of bar 2 of the Fuga.
17. See Lester 1999 Chapter Three for a thorough analysis and discussion of many aspects of this fugue.
18. See Lester 1999 pp.65–8. A similar situation is in the G sharp minor Fugue in Book I of *The Well-tempered Clavier*.
19. Luttmann 1981 pp.110–11.
20. See the discussion of the C major Fugue of Book I of *The Well-tempered Clavier* in Ledbetter 2002.
21. The formal principle of successive 'rotations' of a block of material is discerned by James Hepokoski (1993 pp.24ff.) in the symphonies of Sibelius; for a related principle with reference to Bach, see Lester 2001.

22. See Stinson 1985 pp.204–7, 1990 pp.65–6.
23. Dadelsen (1989 p.72) proposes that Kellner's shorter versions of the G minor and C major fugues, and possibly also the Ciaccona, reflect earlier versions of these pieces than the versions in P 967.
24. Boyden 1965 p.439, Lester 1999 pp.63–4, J. Schröder 2007 p.67; for a critique of Boyden and Champeil, see Babitz 1972.
25. Rabey 1963/64 p.33, Efrati 1979 p.195.
26. Stinson 1985 p.211 footnote 27.
27. The slanting strokes in bar 41 of the lute tablature, interpreted by Kohlhase as *séparés* (NBA V.10 p.127), are syncopations since they do not come between the tablature letters (compare bars 37 and 39).
28. For Bach's version of RV 208, see Tagliavini 1986; also Williams 2003 pp.213ff.
29. Siegele 1975 p.87 describes it as 'schulmäßig'; Peter Williams (2003 pp.73–4) suggests that it was made by a pupil or friend under Bach's supervision.
30. Lester 1999 Chapter Four.
31. Quantz 1752 XIV/22.
32. Quantz 1752 XVII/iv/10.
33. See the discussion of the C sharp minor Prelude from Book I of *The Well-tempered Clavier* in Ledbetter 2002. Marion Scott (1935 p.199) sees the dot as a grace signifying beauty, as in the word 'beautiful' set in siciliano rhythm in Handel's *Messiah*.
34. L. Mozart 1756 VII/i/20.
35. Quantz 1752 trans. Reilly p.287.
36. Spitta II p.80.
37. Lester 1999 p.103.
38. Dörffel in BG omits almost all fermatas.
39. In the autograph the Presto begins on the same line as the end of the Siciliana, in which case the half-barring of the Presto may have some significance for a temporal relation between the movements (for continuation of the beat in successive movements where there is no fermata, see Franklin 2004 pp.113–14).
40. For the structural significance of bowing in this movement, see Butt 1990 pp.187–90; Dadelsen (1982b pp.50–3) gives telling examples in facsimile of Anna Magdalena Bach's untidy placement of bowing slurs.
41. Lester 1999 p.129 gives detailed comparative examples.
42. Spitta II p.93.
43. Siegmund-Schultze (1981 pp.97, 100) includes the concerto in the mix, but most of that overlaps with the sonata.
44. There are a few triplets in *second dessus* part of the Allemande in Couperin's trio sonata *La Piemontoise* from *Les Nations* (published in Paris in 1726), but the earlier, manuscript versions of this sonata (where it is called *L'Astrée*) do not have the dance movements so these may not date from before 1720; for details of the few in German keyboard suites 1710–20, see Ledbetter 2007.
45. VBN pp.338–9.
46. Suggested by Mansure 1992 p.159.
47. See Ledbetter 2001 pp.20–1, and the discussion of the G minor Prelude from Book II of *The Well-tempered Clavier* in Ledbetter 2002.
48. Ledbetter 1992 pp.68–9; notating inequality in allemandes was common in English Restoration harpsichord suites; an 'Alemand alla Franc[ese]' with dotted sixteenths throughout is in Sonata X of Lonati 1701.
49. See *New Grove 2* 'Notes inégales' p.191.
50. D-Dl Mus. 2413–R–12.
51. See Franklin 2004 p.114.
52. Tartini 1771, advice still being given in 1795 (Graves 1971 p.370).
53. See Fontijn 1995 pp.58–9 for Quantz's use of expressions for paired notes such as 'zwar

nicht egal, doch auch nicht zu unegal', and 'nicht zu gar ungleich wie sonst geschehen könte weñ dergl. Noten ohne Verbindung mit anderer Art vorkoṁen'; also L. Mozart 1756 VII/1/3.
54. For Bach's later use of these two notations, see Ledbetter 2002 pp.303–4.
55. Butt 1990 pp.200–6.
56. Kehr 1979 p.825.
57. See Introduction 1. Terminology.
58. Dolmetsch 1946 pp.86–7; Dolmetsch re-notates the D minor French Suite Sarabande in $^9_8$-time.
59. See Houle 1987 p.60.
60. Tarling 2001 p.120.
61. Dok.III p.627, BR p.447.
62. Dok.III p.124.
63. NBR p.323.
64. Spitta II pp.80–1.
65. See Dadelsen 1975 p.134, Siegele 1975 p.87, Eichberg 1975 pp.30–42, Schulenberg 2006 pp.356–9, Bartels 2004.
66. Each of the first movements of the clavier Partitas has a different genre title (see Williams 2007 pp.215–16).
67. Soderlund 1994 pp.79–80.
68. Quantz 1752 XVII/vii/58.
69. Hsu 1981 p.38, p.46; Moens-Haenen 1984 p.184.
70. Fuchs 1990 gives many Bach examples in facsimile.
71. Stowell 1987 p.254; Drescher 2004 p.222; Golan 2006 pp.19, 78.
72. Tarling 2001 p.154.
73. See the commentary on BWV 865/2 in Ledbetter 2002; for a fugue in $^2_4$-time see the commentary on the C major Fugue in Book II.
74. Dok.II p.264, NBR pp.327–8.
75. Dok.II p.295; Mattheson's term 'rücklings' does not mean 'backwards' but 'on its back': he explains it as melodic inversion in 1739 (Dok.II pp.375–6); see also Dok.III p.656.
76. I am taking rough proportions for practical reasons; for the significance of harmonic proportions in the *Sei Solo* and other works of Bach, see Ruth Tatlow's notes for CD Homburger 2003.
77. See particularly Rabey 1963/64 p.37, Whitman 1969 p.431, Golan 2006 pp.19–23.
78. See the section 'The myth of Couperin's "precision"' in Gilbert and Moroney 1987 pp.10–12.
79. Performance in church for the Solos was suggested by Forkel (see Chapter One section 1).
80. It may be that the lack of a slur on the last beat of bar 23 was not an oversight, but designed to put an accent on the beginning of bar 24.
81. Dadelsen suggests a slur on the 32nds to make the bowing come out; for this and very sensible general points about interpreting Bach original sources see Dadelsen 1982a pp.20–2. However, one cannot exclude the possibility that Bach made a mistake here: compare the situation in the London autograph version of the C sharp major Fugue of Book II of *The Well-tempered Clavier*, bar 29 fourth beat (I am grateful to Yo Tomita for pointing this out).
82. Amply demonstrated in Lester 1999 pp.143–4, 147.
83. '... les expressions de *Tristesse* ou de *Douleur*, dans les *Exclamations, &c.*' (Brossard 1705 p.128); this character was repeated by various eighteenth-century writers, see Wessel 1955 p.80; see also Ledbetter 2002 pp.171–2.
84. Often cited in support of this point is Anna Magdalena Bach's copy (in her *Clavier-Büchlein* of 1725) of François Couperin's *Les bergeries* from the eighth harpsichord

Ordre (1717); our not knowing what exactly she copied from does not invalidate the point that French ornaments often underlie Bach's sixteenth notes.
85. For example, Corrette 1741, Chapitre VI.
86. See Schroeder 1977 pp.15 and 23–4 for useful practical points for performing this piece.
87. Lohmann 1990 p.181.
88. See Schenck's Sonata V in DEdM 67 p.68, and Morel 1709, *La Dacier*.
89. Neumann 1966 p.450.
90. For a detailed discussion see Ledbetter 2007; for the bowing of triplets in this movement, see Tarling 2001 p.144.
91. Bach uses this principle already in the G minor Fuga for violin and continuo BWV 1026 (written sometime between 1712 and 1717), which combines its subject with successively new and varied counterpoints.
92. Dadelsen 1982b pp.52–3, Field 1999 p.92.
93. Montéclair 1736 pp.39–40.
94. See Williams 2003 pp.182–7 for background to BWV 582.
95. In the following discussion I have numbered the variations as four-bar units since not all units are in pairs, and groupings change constantly. Numbering starts at the beginning.
96. Allsop 1999 p.115. Mattheson (1713 pp.184–5) makes the usual distinction that the passacaille is more grave than the chaconne, and generally in a minor key; in 1739 (II/xiii/135) he, most unusually, reverses these characters, with the chaconne 'slower and more contemplative' than the passacaille, though still mostly in a major key.
97. Spitta II p.95.
98. A classic example of this pattern is the Passacaille from the G minor overture-suite in J.C.F. Fischer's *Le journal du printems* (Augsburg 1695), another piece that looks to the Passacaille from *Armide* as its model (CD Holman 1983).
99. See Hotteterre 1719, Chapitre XIéme.
100. Fancifully, one might see the letters A(llemanda) to O (alpha to omega) as the outer members of this Partia, there being 14 letters in the Latin alphabet between them, the cipher for the name BACH. It could also be simply that it occurred to Bach that, in the old time signatures, C implies imperfection (i.e. duple time, as in the Allemande), but the circle implies perfection (i.e. triple time, as in the Ciaccona). For Bach's way of writing capital C, see Lindley and Ortgies 2006 pp.614–15.
101. The arpeggio sections can have a relaxing effect on the lute: for the possibility of a lute origin for this piece, see Siegmund-Schultze 1981 p.100, and Altschuler 2005.
102. Another notable use is at the opening of the aria 'I know that my Redeemer liveth' from *Messiah*; the minor version is used equally expressively by Rameau in the refrain of the Act V Chaconne in *Dardanus* (1739).
103. Joel Lester (1999 pp.153–6) has written very perceptively about this and other aspects.
104. See also Knapp 1989 pp.6–8.
105. See Curti 1976 for a detailed discussion.
106. Lester 1999 pp.155–6, who has one of the most convincing numerical discussions.
107. Dammann 1967 p.91.
108. See Ledbetter 2002 pp.186–7 etc., and Tatlow 2007. For a highly evolved programmatic interpretation see Thoene 2002, and comments in Silbiger 1999 and Erickson 2002.
109. For comment on the omissions in Kellner's copy, see Stinson 1985 pp.202–3, and 1990 pp.62–4; the Poelchau MS (P 267) omits variation 61.
110. For other keyboard chaconnes, see Williams 1989, and 1997 p.95; for a thorough overview of chaconnes in Bach's background, see Silbiger 1999.
111. See the commentaries on the E flat major and B flat major Preludes from Book I of *The Well-tempered Clavier* in Ledbetter 2002.
112. Spitta II pp.81–2, Efrati 1979 p.250.

113. See for example the Adagio first movement of TWV 52.c1 (c.1708–1714), arranged by J.G. Walther for organ in *DdT* 26/27 p.336; also Dall'Abaco Op.5 No.3, fourth-movement Adagio in *DTB* Second Series Vol.1 p.73.
114. Compare the first beat of the Sarabande of Bach's E major French Suite with the first beat of the Sarabande 'L'Unique' from Couperin's eighth *Ordre* (1717); see also Ledbetter 2004 p.68.
115. Montéclair 1736 p.80: 'une aspiration ou elevation douloureuse de la voix, qui se pratique plus souvent dans les airs plaintifs que dans les airs tendres. . . . Il se forme dans la poitrine, par une espece de sanglot, à L'extremité d'une note de longue durée, ou forte . . . en faisant un peu sentir le degré immediattem[ent] au dessus de la note accentuée. . . .'
116. See the discussion of the C major Prelude in Book II of *The Well-tempered Clavier* in Ledbetter 2002.
117. Generally in favour are Schulenberg 2006 (pp.356–9) and Bartels 2004 (pp.11–17); against are Eichberg 1975 (pp.31–4) and Siegele 1975 (p.88).
118. Moser 1920 pp.31–2, Spitta II p.82, Schweitzer I pp.392–3.
119. A fairly literal organ arrangement in G major is in Schubert 1985 pp.152ff.
120. See also the commentary on the A flat major Fugue from Book II of *The Well-tempered Clavier* in Ledbetter 2002.
121. Dok.I p.27, Dok.II pp.77–9, NBR pp.89–91.
122. Dok.II pp.186–7, NBR p.91.
123. Dok.III p.84, also p.191 and elsewhere, NBR p.302; Dok.V p.172. Bach made a copy of Reincken's variations at the age of fifteen in Lüneburg (1700), his earliest surviving music autograph (facsimile and edition edited by M. Maul and P. Wollny).
124. Mattheson 1731 pp.34–5, Dok II pp.219–20.
125. Lester 1999 pp.85–6.
126. Mattheson 1731 p.33.
127. Sweelinck I/I No.I; see also Dirksen 1997 pp.384–98.
128. Pachelbel Organ Works No.18; see also Williams 1997 p.95, who points out that this fugue is in two manuscripts from Bach's circle.
129. Renwick 1999 p.151–2; see also Ledbetter 1995 pp.44ff.
130. See Williams 2003 pp.192–4, who cites further examples.
131. See the commentaries on the C sharp major and D major Fugues of Book II of *The Well-tempered Clavier* in Ledbetter 2002.
132. See for example the canons in the *Musical Offering*; also the commentary on the A major Prelude from Book I of *The Well-tempered Clavier* in Ledbetter 2002.
133. Telemann in *Der getreue Musikmeister* (1728 p.61) has the same materials worked for unaccompanied bass viol (see Lutterman 2006 pp.559, 563).
134. Mattheson 1737 p.146, Dok.II pp.294–5, BR p.442.
135. For *stile antico* see Ledbetter 2002 pp.85–7; for the cambiata see Heinichen 1728 p.339, and Buelow 1986 p.155.
136. For an assessment of Kellner's copy, see Stinson 1985 pp.208–10.
137. Taking the Golden Section point as a naturally occurring phenomenon, and not implying that Bach consciously aimed at an exact bar number.
138. For a discussion of numerical proportions in the *Sei Solo*, see Ruth Tatlow's booklet notes for CD Homburger 2003, also Tatlow 2007.
139. Bach's highest note for violin is a''' (Prinz 2005 p.463).
140. Ledbetter 1995 pp.45–7.
141. See Ernst Kurth in Rothfarb 1991 pp.83–90.
142. See Marpurg in Mann 1958 pp.185–90.
143. Schenker 1976 p.151; the progression of a third (*Terz-zug*) is a standard concept in Schenker's system. See also Lester 1999 p.107 for longer-term 3rd relationships.
144. Butt 1990 pp.194–7.

145. Marshall 1989 p.264.
146. Quantz 1752 XVII/vii/49.
147. 'in gehöriger Maße . . . es mag nun langsam oder geschwinde gehen . . . nachdem die verschiedene vorgzeichnete *Characteres* es erfordern', J.G. Walther 1732 'Assai' (taken, like many of Walther's definitions, from Brossard 1705)
148. See Bartel 1997 pp.318–19, also Butt 1990 p.193.
149. See Ernst Kurth in Rothfarb 1991 pp.93–4.
150. See the commentary on the G major Prelude from Book II of *The Well-tempered Clavier* in Ledbetter 2002.
151. Rampe and Sackmann 2000 p.75.
152. Dreyfus 1986 p.179.
153. See Ledbetter 2002 p.258 for further examples of this contrast.
154. Drescher 2004 p.224.
155. Lester 1999 p.8, also 52–3 and 117–22.
156. For details of the organ-concerto arrangements in BWV 120a/4 (probably 1729) and BWV 29/1 (1731) see Dürr 1995 pp.809–10 and 822–3, and Marshall 1972 I p.25.
157. For trumpet *Bebung* see Altenburg 1795 p.118; also Ledbetter 2002 p.210.
158. Ido Abravaya (2006 pp.95–6) points out that the first main downbeat in the violin version is in bar 4, but in the Sinfonia it is in bar 1.
159. Hilton 1997 pp.407, 437.
160. Mattheson 1713 p.192; Telemann used the loure to represent gout: 'Le Podagre' in TWV 55:D22/2 (see Zohn 2008 p.111).
161. Quantz 1752 XVI/vii/58.
162. P 1158; edited in NBA V.10.
163. Details of structural similarities are given in Klein 1970 pp.78–9.
164. See Lester 1999 p.160.
165. Carl Schachter makes a similar point, but treats a" as a neighbour-note since a descent in Schenkerian terms must begin with a note of the tonic triad (1987 p.12).
166. Schachter finds every detail of the Gavotte's structure prefigured in the Loure (1987 pp.23–4).
167. Discussed in Lester 1972.
168. Dadelsen 1988 p.10.
169. Lester 1999 p.140 lists some examples.
170. See Stowell 2001 pp.120–1, 128 for further details of the relationship of this to the danced minuet, and of bowings.
171. Dolmetsch 1946 p.105, Rabey 1963/64 p.45.
172. Babitz 1972 p.43; see also Stowell 1987 p.253.
173. Butt 1990 p.188.
174. See J. Schroeder 1977 p.28.

Chapter Four: The 6 *Suites* for Cello BWV 1007–1012

1. For details see the commentary on the C major Prelude from Book I of *The Well-tempered Clavier* in Ledbetter 2002; for the continuation of this tradition in lute preludes in Bach's environment, see K.-E. Schröder 2002 p.188.
2. Dok.I p.218, NBR p.113.
3. See Schweitzer II p.75.
4. Williams 2003 p.226.
5. Of the variants for bar 22, the readings g for the fifth sixteenth note (Source C) and b (Source E) are plainly mistakes, the notes do not belong to the V2 chord. The unanimous reading in Sources C, D, and E for the last eight notes of bar 27 as a c e f♯ g a b♭ c♯' may reflect a revision Bach made. The point is to emphasise the arrival on d' in

bar 28, and the emphasis by repetition (Sources A and B), or the touch of diminished 7th (Sources C, D, E) both achieve that. (Schwemer and Woodfull-Harris erroneously give b♮, not b♭, in the C, D, E reading).

6. For another highly expressive use of the dominant minor 9th, see the commentary on the Grave of the A minor violin Solo in Chapter Three.
7. Blum 1977 p.143.
8. Little and Jenne 2001 p.139.
9. Little and Jenne 2001 p.106.
10. For details see Ledbetter 1987 p.48.
11. Pointed out by Kinney (1962 p.358).
12. BWV Anhang II 114, 115.
13. Hulshoff 1962 p.95,
14. Proposed by George Pratt (1979, 1981), see also the review by George Kennaway (1980); Anna Magdalena Bach added a half-bar after bar 31, clearly through inadvertence.
15. See, for example, the Allemande of the G major French Suite, and the G major Prelude from Book II of *The Well-tempered Clavier*; Kinney (1962 p.360) proposes a Sinfonia by Francesco Conti (1721) as an example; for Cavalli, see Glover 1978 p.97.
16. For further comment on tetrachords see Hulshoff 1962 p.36.
17. Ernst Kurth in Rothfarb 1991 p.80.
18. Neumann (1994 p.27) points to the fact that Bach did not write 'arpeggio' as he did, for example, in the D minor violin Ciaccona, and in other places cited by Efrati (1979 pp.195–6); Bylsma (1998 p.50), who analyses the use of *figurae* and their development in this Prelude, has a good suggestion for arpeggiation; and Hulshoff (1962 p.96) has a useful series of examples giving arpeggiation patterns suggested by Alexanian, Klengel, Grützmacher, and Haussmann and Wenzinger, some of which incorporate the auxiliary figure in the second beat of bar 58; see also Pratt 1981.
19. Of the eighteenth-century sources only Kellner's copy (P 804) has the a as well as the d♯.
20. Quantz 1752 IX/7, endorsed by Pablo Casals (Blum 1977 p.125).
21. Ledbetter 2002 p.186.
22. See Grützbach 1993 p.61. For a Schenkerian view of this piece, and the bearing it might have on performance, see Tanenbaum 1980.
23. Kinney also sees a similarity between bars 14ff of Menuet II and bars 21ff of the Prelude (1962 p.368).
24. This kind of character opposition is common: in Act II of Purcell's *The Indian Queen* (1695) there is a dialogue between Envy and Fame, in which Envy is in $\frac{3}{8}$-time with small note values and intervals, while Fame is in $\frac{6}{4}$-time with large note values and intervals.
25. Little and Jenne suggest *notes inégales* in repeats (2001 p.78); they also talk of 'the actual bowings written in by Bach' (p.77), but unfortunately we do not know exactly what these were.
26. Watkin 1996 p.660, and see this article also for details of cello continuo playing.
27. L. Mozart 1756 X/31; also Grützbach 1993 p.62.
28. Little and Jenne (2001 p.45) suggest a faster tempo for Bourrée II.
29. Kellner's copy appears to be untitled, unless the heading was trimmed away at the top of the page; only the bottom of the letters of 'Suitte 4' are visible.
30. '*tenuës* qui conservent l'harmonie & la netteté du son' (Danoville 1687 p.9).
31. For the use of outlines common to the Prelude and successive movements, see Beach 2005 p.36; for a detailed Schenkerian approach, see Schachter 1994, who includes a theological interpretation of this Prelude.
32. Grützbach 1993 pp.56–8.
33. L. Mozart 1756 VII/3 and XII/10; Efrati 1979 p.39.
34. For a more detailed discussion with reference to courantes, see Ledbetter 2007.

35. Little and Jenne suggest a slightly slower tempo for Bourrée II to allow elegance and breadth in the syncopation, and *notes inégales* (2001 p.45).
36. Demachy 1685 p.4; Jordi Savall has made Bourrée II the basis of a very attractive series of pizzicato divisions (CD Savall 1998); Bach often uses pizzicato in continuo parts (Prinz 2005 p.576).
37. Hutchings 1978 pp.42–4.
38. See Saslav 1981 for the evolution of these two signatures in the later eighteenth century.
39. Heinichen 1728 p.348.
40. There is a large amount of literature that discusses the differences; for a basic presentation see Hefling 1993 pp.98–101; for details of the engraving of *Clavier-Übung* II see Boyd and Butt 1999 pp.462–3.
41. Marshall 1989 p.264.
42. 'Der Dreyachteltakt hat die lebhafte Bewegung des Passepieds; er wird leicht, aber nicht ganz tändelnd vorgetragen', Kirnberger 1776 p.130, translated in Beach and Thym 1982 p.397.
43. See the commentaries on the F major (Book I) and B minor (Book II) fugues of *The Well-tempered Clavier* in Ledbetter 2002.
44. Blum 1977 p.144; Reinhard Oppel found three voices, but did not explain how (1921 p.27).
45. See, for example, J.J. Fux in Mann 1958 pp.103–7.
46. Lutterman (2006 p.567) points to a similarity between the opening figure of this Allemande with that of the F sharp minor harpsichord suite in Le Roux 1705; there is also a similarity between Bach's Gigue and Le Roux's Gigue *La Favorite* from the same suite. Bach is, as usual, giving his own special development to traditional motivic elements.
47. Rothfarb 1991 p.82.
48. Vogt 1988 p.184.
49. An interpretation in the spirit of French viol music is on CD Savall 1998.
50. Quantz 1752 XVII/vii/58.
51. Grossman (1987 pp.85–6) gives a related example by Weiss, though his example has the repeated note as the top note of a chord, which would be less full without it.
52. Spitta II p.101.
53. Quantz 1752 XVII/vii/58, and see Chapter Two section 2.
54. Cited by Grützbach (1993 p.45).
55. Kinney 1962 p.396; Boyd 2000 pp.95–6; Little and Jenne 2001 p.152.
56. Mather and Karns 1987 pp.221–4.
57. Little and Jenne 2001 p.152.
58. Neumann 1994 p.29.
59. For a full discussion of the options see Moens-Haenen 1984, and 1988 Part II Chapter XI.
60. Grossman 1987 p.87; the sign # can also mean a trill (see *New Grove 2* 'Lute, para.7: Ornamentation', Table 5).
61. See also the discussion of the G sharp minor Prelude from Book II of *The Well-tempered Clavier* in Ledbetter 2002.
62. See the discussion of the Adagio of Sonata I in Chapter Three.
63. DEdM 67 pp.64, 68.
64. Mansure 1992 p.176.
65. Marshall 1989 p.264; possibly Bach's earliest use of it is in the D minor organ Toccata BWV 565, a piece around which there are all sorts of question marks but which itself has been proposed as originally for five-string cello in scordatura, with the top string tuned down to d' (Argent 2000; Williams 2003 pp.155–9; see also Altschuler 2005 pp.77–9, who proposes BWV 565 as originally for lute).
66. See Mather and Karns 1987 p.133.

67. 'Lascia ch'io pianga' is in *Il trionfo del Tempo e del Disinganno* (1707) with the words 'Lascia la spina, cogli la rosa', a comment on the passing of youth and beauty, and began life as an instrumental Sarabande in *Almira* (1705).
68. See Kinney 1962 p.406.
69. Dolmetsch 1946 p.85; see also the commentary on the Sarabande of the B minor violin Partia in Chapter Three.
70. Grützbach 1993 p.74.
71. Mather and Karns 1987 p.252.
72. Saint Lambert 1702 p.18; trans. Harriss-Warrick pp.36–7, and see also pp.xvii–xviii; Muffat has 2 as more moderate than ¢, though ¢ is less quick in gavottes than in bourrées (see Murata 1998 pp.138–9).

Chapter Five: Works for Lute/Lautenwerk BWV 995–1000, 1006A

1. KB V/10 p.108. The BWV numbers for these works reflect simply the order in which Schmieder catalogued them, they have no implications for chronology of composition.
2. See Schulze 1983.
3. KB V/10 p.107
4. Schulze 1983 p.246.
5. For a detailed account and assessment of the changes made by the intabulator, see Grossman 1987; a summary is in Grossman 1986.
6. Falckenhagen was a pupil of Weiss. For a survey of lute types in central Germany, see Lundberg 1999; and with particular reference to Weiss, see Crawford 2002.
7. Adlung 1768 p.133, probably based on almost identical wording in Kircher 1650 p.476 (see Grossman 1987 p.43); it is not clear that Kircher is not talking about the theorbo rather than the lute: 'Testudines, & Theorbae, ut plurimùm 10, sive 12, aut 14 chordarum ordinibus sunt instructae').
8. See Grossman 1987 pp.92–108 for fingering diapason courses here and in contemporary lute repertory.
9. Grossman (1987 p.93) cites examples of this from lute works of Straube.
10. Less systematic examples are in Handel's harpsichord *Suites* of 1720; a particularly clear example is the Allemande *La Couronne* from François D'Agincourt's *Pièces de clavecin* (Paris 1733).
11. See *New Grove 2* 'Lute, para.7: Ornamentation', Table 5.
12. Grossman (1987 p.72) mentions long improvisatory runs with long slurs in David Kellner's *Lautenstücke* (Hamburg 1747).
13. For the dating of Walther's copy, see Beisswenger 1992 pp.22, 27.
14. KB V/10 p.115; Schulze 1975 p.V; for the Lautenwerk, see Ledbetter 2002 pp.28–31.
15. See Wiemer 1987 pp.29–32, and Öhm-Kühnle 2006 pp.295–301; also Eisert 1994 pp.151–2. A third, less reliable, copy in A minor (*B-Br* II.4093) is thought by Kohlhase to have been made, possibly by a Weimar pupil of Bach's, in order to transpose the Suite into the middle of the keyboard (KB V/10 pp.116–20).
16. Difficulties for lute performance, and proposals for obviating them, are assessed in Burguéte 1977 pp.29–41; Jacob Lindberg (CD 1994) uses a scordatura from Reusner 1676 that helps to bring BWV 996 and 1006a within the range of the lute.
17. *New Grove 2*, 'Lute-harpsichord'; Schulze 1975 p.V.
18. Poulin and Taylor 1989 p.xxiii.
19. Niedt 1721 p.119; Poulin and Taylor 1989 p.157. *Passaggio* normally meant decoration of a melody; part of its nature was to have a mixture of *figurae* (Bartel 1997 pp.432–8).
20. Edited by S. Rampe 1991 No.6.
21. The version attributed to Marcello is edited in Eisert 1994 pp.172–6.
22. Dominik Sackmann (1999 p.35) has pointed to a similar *Passaggio* in Partita X of the

chorale partita 'Ach, was soll ich Sünder machen' BWV 770 (bars 21–5; possibly an Arnstadt work): in this case the flourish runs from the bottom to the top octave of the keyboard; see also the *Passaggio* that begins the organ Praeludium BWV 535a/1 in the Möller manuscript (edited in Hill 1991 p.1).
23. Such easily found 'hand shapes' play an equivalent role in lute music, particularly in improvised genres. It would be worth making a survey of lute repertory to see how they affect such flourishes there.
24. See for example the second (Lento) section of Op.2 No.3 (*DdT* 11 p.106); for a later Bach example, see the opening Adagio of the C minor clavier Partita BWV 826.
25. Niedt 1717 p.41; Poulin and Taylor p.260.
26. See the commentaries on the C sharp major Prelude and E flat major Fugue from Book II of *The Well-tempered Clavier* in Ledbetter 2002.
27. Schulze 1966 p.36; KB V/10 pp.140–1.
28. Spitta II p.160.
29. The lute was used in Version I (1724), the organ or harpsichord options in Versions III and IV (c.1730, c.1749; Dürr 1988 p.130).
30. See Wolff 1993.
31. Lute versions of parts of the Fantasia of BWV 1025 appear in the so-called Grüssau lute tablatures (see K.-E. Schröder 1995 pp.57–8, and Crawford 1999 pp.209, 236); see also KB VI/5 p.75.
32. See Dürr 1978.
33. André Burguéte (1977 pp.46–9) found the Fuga and the Double work perfectly on the lute; they may, but only after adaptation.
34. These may, however, be evidence of Bach's reported ability to play intervals up to a 12th in one hand (NBR p.369).
35. BG 45^1 pp.159–63 gives both versions in parallel, with the P 650 version in smaller type.
36. Dok.II p.223.
37. See J.F. Agricola's description in Dok.III p.293.
38. See, for example, the commentary on the F sharp minor Prelude from Book II in Ledbetter 2002.
39. Dok.III p.289, NBR p.399.
40. And of the subject of Handel's A minor keyboard Fugue HWV 609, also used in the chorus 'They loathed to drink of the river' from *Israel in Egypt*.
41. A rhetorical/expressive analysis of this Fuga is in Braubach 1986; see also the discussion of the D sharp minor Fugue from Book II of *The Well-tempered Clavier* in Ledbetter 2002.
42. See Bartel 1997 pp.405–8.
43. A block of material conveniently termed 'fugal complex' by Laurence Dreyfus (1996 p.182).
44. Mann 1958 p.91.
45. See Ledbetter 2002 pp.101–2, and the commentary on the G major Fugue from Book I of *The Well-tempered Clavier*.
46. Bartel 1997 p.408.
47. Burguéte 1977 p.46, who also says of Bach here that in many ways 'zeigt er uns eindrucksvoll die Faust' (p.47).
48. For a hermeneutic interpretation of this Suite, relating motifs from each movement to motifs in Bach's cantatas connected with Christ's Passion, see the booklet notes for CD Martin 2004 (e.g. BWV 56/i for the Prelude; the chiastic nature of the fugue subject, and so on).
49. Ferguson 1950. His octave transpositions are as follows: b.1 both staves down; b.9 lower stave at pitch; b.11 upper stave at pitch; b.16 (after double bar) upper stave down; b.21 lower stave down; bar 301/2 lower stave at pitch; b.321/2 lower stave down; b.41

lower stave at pitch; bar 43 upper stave at pitch; b.47 upper stave down. His correction of the last upper-stave sixteenth in bar 24 from c' to d' is clearly right.
50. That is, if Laurence Dreyfus is correct in suggesting c.1736–42 for BWV 1028 (1985 p.65).
51. KB V/10 p.153 suggests c.1740–c.1745; Kobayashi 1988 p.65, in a survey of late Bach sources, refines this to c.1735.
52. KB V/10 pp.153–4.
53. For a Trinitarian interpretation of how the movements relate to one another, see Leahy 2005.
54. André Burguéte (1977 p.49–50) quotes a prelude by Weiss that is actually more akin to the Prelude of the E flat major cello Suite. Konrad Junghänel (1988 p.98) points to bass shapes in bars 23–38 of the Prelude of BWV 998 as untypical of original lute music. See Dombois 1972 and 1973 for detailed comments on problems for the lute in this work, though he assumes that it must be played just as Bach wrote it. With the sort of adjustments that the intabulations of BWV 995 and 997 make it can work magnificently on the lute.
55. Hoffmann-Erbrecht 1987 p.20.
56. C.P.E. Bach 1762 XLI/4.
57. Keller 1950 p.179.
58. See for example the G major Toccata and Fugue in Weiss's Sonata 22, which also has broken-chord episodes, though scattered through the fugue in the manner of Corelli rather than in a special central section.
59. A similar use of climactic contrary motion parallel 3rds, based on very ingenious counterpoint inverted at the octave, 10th and 12th, is in bars 59ff of the G minor Fugue from Book II of *The Well-tempered Clavier*, another fugue of around this time (see the commentary in Ledbetter 2002). This passage in BWV 998 benefits from having the bass part on the diapasons, where it sounds both at pitch and an octave lower.
60. See the commentaries on these two Preludes in Ledbetter 2002.
61. Schulenberg 2006 p.176.
62. See Ledbetter 2002 p.152.
63. Henning and Richter 1982 p.477.
64. A keyboard realisation of Kapsberger 1604 is in Gilbert 1998, see in particular Toccata II arpeggiata; see also Burguéte 1977 pp.41–2, and Coelho 1987.
65. Burguéte 1977 pp.44–5.
66. A 'peregrinus' entry in this situation is an entry not on either the tonic or dominant.
67. Kobayashi 1988 p.39, which refines on Kohlhase's dating of 1735–40 (KB V/10 p.164).
68. It is a rare key for lute, though there is a concerto for lute and strings in E major by Karl Kohaut (1726–1784; *D-B* Mus. ms. 11834, see Grossman 1987 p.37).
69. Of recorded performances, Nigel North (Linn 1994) has recast BWV 1006 as an idiomatic lute piece in F major as Weiss might have done, whereas Hopkinson Smith (Audivis 2000) uses BWV 1006a transposed up to F major 'with only the slightest changes'.
70. Hofmann 1993.
71. Dok.III p.292.
72. See for example Henkel 1981 Nos 21 and 26.
73. Burguéte 1977 p.52; he later revised this opinion, proposing all of BWV 995–1000 and 1006a as minutely worked-out compositions, neither arrangements nor sketches, as important for the lute as BWV 1001–1012 are for violin and cello (1994 p.67).
74. Dok.III p.206.
75. Wiermann 2000 pp.162–4; C.P.E. Bach 1762 trans. Mitchell p.172.
76. Mattheson 1722 p.254; Sadie 1989 p.196; *New Grove 2* 'Sostenente piano. 1. Bows' erroneously gives the dates of birth of Hohlfeld and Gleichmann as the dates for their making these instruments.

77. Zingel 1964; KB V/10 pp.168–9; *New Grove 2* 'Hochbrucker', 'Petrini'; Zingel's article is essentially an apologia for playing the Suite on the modern harp.

Chapter Six: The *Solo* for Transverse Flute, BWV 1013

1. Numbering of unknown copyists as Anon.5, Anon.6 etc. is from Kast 1958. Anon.5 has been identified with the Cöthen organist Bernhard Christian Kayser (1705–1758); for a summary of Kayser's activities as a copyist for Bach, see Talle 2003 pp.155–71.
2. Kobayashi 1991.
3. Werner Breig in *MGG 2*, 'Bach, Johann Sebastian', col. 1503; Forkel 1802 p.61, NBR p.472.
4. Schmitz 1969 p.169.
5. Castellani (1989 pp.572–3) points out that this would lessen the difficulties of the piece.
6. That is assuming that the copy of Corrette *F-Pn* Rés. Vm^8 g.1 is the first edition advertised in the *Mercure de France* in December 1740; Hotteterre (1707 p.9) says that notes above g''' are unusable; see also Prinz 2005 pp.254–5.
7. Leisinger 2001, Preface.
8. For instructive comparison with other of Bach's unaccompanied allemandes, see Scheck 1975 p.185; for a complete facsimile, with detailed discussion of the Allemande, see Mather and Sadilek 2004.
9. The first bar of the Allemande might be seen as an extended allemande upbeat, or a typical Bach post-beat beginning (see Abravaya 2006 p.85).
10. Schmitz (NBA) has concocted first- and second-time bars; Leisinger (Bärenreiter) leaves it open to the player.
11. For analysis, see Mansure 1992 pp.189–90, and Schmitz 1958 p.75.
12. Quantz 1752 Chapter VII para.10; see also Quantz's *Solfeggi*: instructions for breathing are listed under 'Atem' in the Subject Index on p.95 of the Michel and Teske edition; an Allemande by Blochwitz that may be compared to Bach's is in Quantz's *Caprices* (No.45 in the edition by Michel and Teske; edited in Mather and Sadilek 2004).
13. Quantz 1752 Chapter VII paras.3 and 4.
14. Quantz 1752 Chapter VII para.4.
15. Mattheson 1731 p.176, also Telemann's dedicatory letter in *Die Kleine Cammer-Music* (1716; Rackwitz 1981 pp.72, 100).
16. '... les Flutes, que tant d'illustres sçavant faire gémir d'une maniere si touchante, dans nos airs plaintifs, & soupirer si amoureusement dans nos Airs tendres' (Mattheson 1722 p.114).
17. Mather and Karns 1987 pp.2–3.
18. See Weiss-Smith 1990, Angloise (p.17) and Bourrée (p.95). Movement 4 in Bach's early overture-suite in G minor for clavier BWV 822 has been headed 'Bourrée' in NBA V/10 perhaps on the model of this Bourrée angloise; according to Schulenberg (2006 p.28) it is closer to a rigaudon.
19. Powell and Lasocki 1995 p.13; Kuijken 1990, Postface.

Glossary

These explanations are summary. More detail will be found in the *New Harvard Dictionary of Music* and *New Grove 2*.

anapaest	a rhythmic unit consisting of two short notes and one long note
answer	usually the second entry of a fugue subject; at its simplest, if the subject moves in the 5th from notes 1–5 of the scale, a tonal answer adapts it to move in the 4th from notes 5 to 8 of the scale (for details see Chapter Two section 8)
antecedent–consequent	a pair of balanced phrases, usually at the beginning of a piece; most commonly the first phrase (antecedent) ends with a half close and the second (consequent) ends with a full close (*q.v.*)
bariolage	alternation of an open string with fingered notes on other strings
caesura	a pause about the middle of a verse line; in the classical French alexandrine line of twelve syllables it normally comes after the sixth syllable.
cambiata	a dissonance quitted by the downward leap of a 3rd; from this is extrapolated a melodic 'cambiata shape' covering e.g. notes 1756 of the scale, or inverted 1243; a classic example of the inverted cambiata shape is the very traditional subject that opens the Finale of Mozart's Jupiter Symphony
campanella	a passage in which adjacent or repeated notes are drawn from different courses of the lute so that they may continue to sound when the following note is struck
Capelle	ensemble, band; the musicians regularly employed by a court or church
chromatic tetrachord	see Lamento bass
close	cadence; half-close: usually an imperfect cadence (ending on the dominant); full close: perfect cadence (ending on the tonic)
concertante	in Italian concerto style
coulé de tierce	the falling interval of a 3rd, filled out by a light, rapid passing note usually played before the lower of the two notes, and slurred to it; it often articulates an intermediate phrase ending (see Chapter Two section 2 and Ex.2.7)
dactyl	a rhythmic unit consisting of a long note and two short notes
divisions	a technique of variation in which the beat is divided into successively smaller note values
enjambement	a term in French versification; when the sense of a line continues over the end of the line into the next line

Glossary

figura	a group of usually three or four rapid notes (often sixteenths) that may involve repeated notes, or steps (as in the *circulatio* or turn), or leaps, or mixed motion (as in the *messanza q.v.*)
galant style	introduced by opera composers in Naples after c.1710; generally has straightforward harmony, four-bar phrases often with dance rhythms, and a mixture of note values in the solo line (triplets, lombardic rhythm ♫., etc.)
golden section	the division of a line into two unequal segments, the lesser segment being to the greater as the greater is to the whole line; the section point is normally expressed as × 0.618 of the line
harmonic proportions	proportions from the harmonic series (2:1, 3:2, 4:3 etc.)
hexachord	a six-note scale devised for teaching pitch relations by Guido of Arezzo c.1000, based on the initial notes and syllables of each line of the plainchant hymn 'Ut queant laxis' (for the feast of St John the Baptist, relevant to singing since he is first mentioned in St Mark's Gospel as 'a voice crying in the wilderness'); each line begins on a successively higher note of the major scale, starting with C (Ut), and the initial syllables are Ut re mi fa sol la; hexachords also began with G (with 3rd degree ♮, a 'hard', square shape; or F (with 4th degree ♭, a 'soft', rounded shape) (cf. tetrachord)
inganno	Marpurg uses this term for flattening a leading note, thereby deflecting the effect of a perfect cadence
inventio	a term of rhetoric, used by Bach on the title-page for the 1723 fair copy of the Inventions and Sinfonias, for an initial idea that has possibilities for development; in complex pieces the *inventio* may include a whole block of complementary materials
inverso	a theme melodically inverted (see also recto)
inversion	1) melodic inversion: the direction of successive intervals in a theme is reversed, e.g. a 5th up followed by a 3rd down will invert as a 5th down followed by a 3rd up 2) invertible counterpoint: a complex of usually two, three, or four melodic strands which can be sounded simultaneously, each of which is usable as a bass so that each strand may be used in any voice
Lamento bass	a ground-bass pattern that steps down in semitones from the tonic to the dominant; the best-known example is probably Dido's Lament from Purcell's *Dido and Aeneas* (see Williams 1997)
messanza	a figure that mixes various types of conjunct and disjunct motion
Neapolitan	1) note: a feature of mid seventeenth-century Italian vocal laments; the expressive flattening of the second degree of the scale 2) 6th: an effect of subdominant harmony in which the 6th above the subdominant note is expressively flattened
ondeggiando	indicated by a wavy line, with or without a slur; it indicates a 'wavy' motion of the bow across two strings, back and forth; it can also mean vibrato
partimento	a fugal movement expressed mostly as a single-line figured bass (see Renwick 2001)
petite reprise	the final phrase of a dance is repeated again after all the normal repeats have been played
recto	a theme in its primary form (see also inverso)

scordatura	one or more of the strings/courses of an instrument is/are tuned to different pitches from their normal one/s; *discordable* in BWV 1011 is a French equivalent
second practice	a term used by Monteverdi (*seconda pratica*, 1605) for the free, expressive treatment of dissonance, as opposed to the first practice (*stilo antico*)
stile antico	Monteverdi's first practice (*prima pratica*); a continuation of the high Renaissance polyphonic style of Palestrina: alla breve ¢ time signature, white note values, fluid unsymmetrical lines, careful dissonance treatment, learned counterpoint
stretto	an Italian term meaning narrow; narrows the rhythmic interval between successive entries of a subject so that later ones enter before the previous one has finished
tetrachord	a series of four conjunct notes (cf. hexachord)
tirata	a group of rapid notes leading up to a beat
tremblement lié	literally, a tied trill; a trilled note in descending steps, where the step above the trilled note is tied to the notional note that begins the trill so is not repeated (sometimes indicated by a slur from the note above to the trill)
vieil ton	the standard Renaissance lute tuning in which the six fingered courses of the lute are tuned (from the top down) g' d' a f c G (or the same intervals down from a')

Bibliography

Only items cited in the text of this book are listed here. For a comprehensive listing of Bach literature see Yo Tomita's Bach Bibliography website:

music.qub.ac.uk/~tomita/bachbib/

In cases where the reference in the text is to editorial comment in a modern edition, the edition is listed under the editor's name in Literature after 1850. It would be too cumbersome to list all available editions and facsimiles.

Details of sources for BWV 995–1013 are given in the Introduction and at the relevant points in the book.

CD recordings are listed under composers.

1. Manuscript music sources

Biber, Heinrich Ignaz Franz von, [Rosary/Mystery Sonatas], *D-Mbs* Mus.Ms.4123; ed. G. Adler, DTÖ 25 (Vienna, 1905).

Gabrielli, Domenico, 'Ricercari p. il Violoncello di Dom:^{co} Gabrielli', *I-MOe* Ms.Musica G.79; facsimile ed. Vanscheeuwijck 1998.

Lonati, Carlo Ambrogio, [*olim*] *D-Dl* Mus 2020–R-1 (now lost); facsimile from photocopy, *XII sonate a violino solo e basso. Ms. Salzburg, Milano 1701*, intro C. Timpe (Florence: SPES, 2005); ed. Giegling 1981.

Matteis, Nicola (ii), [Fantasias for unaccompanied violin], *D-Dl* Mus. 2045–R-1.

Pisendel, Johann Georg, 'Sonata à Violino Solo Senza Baβo', *D-Dl* Mus. 2421–R-2.

[Various German woodwind and violin sonatas c.1720], *B-Bc* Ms.Litt. XY.15.115; facsimile ed. P. Raspe, *Manuscrit allemand du XVIIIe siècle* (Brussels: Éditions Culture et Civilisation, 1979).

Veracini, Francesco Maria, 'Sonate a Violino, o Flauto solo, e Basso dedicate all'Altezza Reale del Serenissimo Principe Elettorale di Sassonia', *D-Dl* Mus. 2413–R-12 [dedicatory letter is dated '26 Luglio 1716'].

2. Printed music sources

Albertino, Ignatio [Albertini], *Sonatinae XII. Violino solo* (Vienna, 1692).

Bach, Johann Sebastian, *Tre Sonate per il Violino solo senza Basso* (Bonn, 1802) [Simrock 1802].

Benda, Franz, *Études de violon ou caprices*, 2 vols (Leipzig, 1804); facsimile intro. J. Müller-Blattau, *Vierundzwanzig Capricen für Violine allein* (Stuttgart: Ichthys Verlag, 1957).

Biber, Heinrich Ignaz Franz von, *Sonatae, Violino solo* ([Salzburg], 1681); ed. G. Adler, DTÖ 11 (Vienna, 1898).

―― *Harmonia artificiosa-ariosa Diversimodè accordata* ([n.p., 1696]; Nuremberg, 2/1712); ed. P. Nettl and F. Reidinger, DTÖ 92 (Vienna, 1957)
Blavet, Michel, *Sonates melées de pieces, pour la flûte traversiere, avec la basse . . . Oeuvre II* (Paris, 1732)
Blochwitz, Johann Martin, *Sechzig Arien eingetheilet in Funffzehn Suitten . . . absonderlich aber vor Flute Traversiere nebst Basse Continüe* (Freiberg, [n.d.])
Bononcini, Giovanni Maria, *Arie, correnti, sarabande, gighe, & allemande . . . opera quarta* (Bologna, 1671)
Boyvin, Jacques, *Premier Livre d'Orgue* (Paris, 1690)
Campra, André, *L'Europe galante* (Paris, 1697)
Cartier, Jean-Baptiste, *L'Art du violon* (Paris, 1798)
Corelli, Arcangelo, *Sonate da camera a tre . . . opera seconda* (Rome, 1685)
―― *Sonate a tre . . . opera quarta* (Rome, 1694)
―― *Sonate a violino e violone o cimbalo . . . Opera Quinta* (Rome, 1700); . . . *Troisieme Edition ou l'on a joint les agréemens des Adagio de cet ouvrage, composez par M^r. A. Corelli comme il les joue* (Amsterdam, 1710)
―― *Concerti grossi . . . opera sesta* (Amsterdam, [1714])
Couperin, François, *Pieces de Clavecin . . . Premier Livre* (Paris, 1713)
―― *Second Livre de piéces de Clavecin* (Paris, [1716–17])
―― *Troisiéme Livre de piéces de Clavecin . . . Concerts Royaux* (Paris, 1722)
―― *Concert instrumental sous le titre d'Apotheose Composé à la mémoire immortelle de l'incomparable Monsieur de Lully* (Paris, 1725)
Demachy, *Pieces de Violle* (Paris, 1685)
Dieupart, François, *Six Suittes de Clavessin* (Amsterdam, 1701)
Farina, Carlo, *Ander Theil neuer Paduanen . . . benebenst einem kurtzweiligen Quodlibet von allerhand seltzamen Inventionen* (Dresden, 1627)
Fischer, Johann Caspar Ferdinand, *Le Journal du printems* (Augsburg, 1695); ed. E. von Werra and H. J. Moser, DdT 1/10 (Graz, 2/1958)
Frescobaldi, Girolamo, *Toccate e partite d'intavolatura di cimbalo . . . libro primo* (Rome, 1615)
Geminiani, Francesco, *Sonate a violino, violone, e cembalo* (London, [1716])
Graupner, Christoph, *Partien auf das Clavier bestehend in Allemanden, Couranten, Sarabanden, Giguen &c* (Darmstadt, 1718)
Höffler, Konrad, *Primitiae Chelicae* (Nuremberg, 1695); ed. K.H. Pauls, DEdM 67 (Kassel, 1973)
Hotteterre, Jacques, *Pieces pour la flute traversiere . . . avec la basse-continue . . . Livre premier, oeuvre second* (Paris, 1708)
―― *Deuxiéme livre de Pieces pour la flûte-traversiere . . . avec la basse . . . Oeuvre V^e* (Paris, 1715)
Krieger, Johann, *Sechs Musicalische Partien, bestehende in Allemanden, Courenten, Sarabanden, Doublen und Giquen nebst eingemischten Bouréen, Minuetten und Gavotten* (Nuremberg, 1697)
Kuhnau, Johann, *Frische Clavier-Früchte oder Sieben Suonaten* (Leipzig, 1696); ed. K. Päsler and H.J. Moser, DdT 1/4 (Wiesbaden, 2/1958)
Kühnel, August, *Sonate ô Partite ad una ô due Viole da Gamba, con il Baßo Continuo* (Kassel, 1698)
La Barre, Michel de, *Premier livre de pieces pour la flute traversiere avec la basse-continue* (Paris, 1702)
Le Roux, Gaspard, *Pieces de Clavessin* (Paris, 1705)
Lesage de Richée, Philipp Franz, *Cabinet der Lauten, In welchem zu finden 12. neue Partien* ([Breslau], 1695)
Locatelli, Pietro Antonio, *L'arte del violino: XII Concerti cioè violino solo, con XXIV Capricci ad libitum . . . Opera terza* (Amsterdam, 1733)

Marais, Marin, *Pieces de Violes* (Paris, 1686); *Basse-continüe des pieçes a une et a deux Violes* (Paris, 1689); ed. J. Hsu (New York: Broude, 1980)
—— *Pieces en Trio pour les Flutes, Violon, & Dessus de Viole* (Paris, 1692)
Marini, Biagio, *Affetti musicali . . . opera prima* (Venice, 1617)
—— *Sonate . . . con altre curiose & moderne inventioni, opera ottava* (Venice, 1626)
Mattheson, Johann, *Der brauchbare Virtuoso* (Hamburg, 1720); facsimile intro. M. Castellani (Florence: SPES, 1997)
Mondonville, Jean Joseph Cassanéa de, *Pieces de Clavecin avec voix ou violon . . . Oeuvre V^e.* (Paris, [1748])
Monteverdi, Claudio, *Il quarto libro de madrigali* (Venice, 1603)
—— *Madrigali guerrieri et amorosi . . . libro ottavo* (Venice, 1638)
Morel, Jacques, *1^r. Livre de pieces de violle* (Paris, [1709])
Pandolfi Mealli, Giovanni Antonio, *Sonate a violino solo* (Innsbruck, 1660)
Playford, John, *The Division Violin* (London, 2/1685)
Reincken, Johann Adam, *Hortus Musicus* (Hamburg, 1688)
Reusner, Esaias, *Delitiae testudinis* (Breslau, 1667); as *Erfreuliche Lauten-Lust* (Leipzig, 2/1697)
—— *Neue Lauten-Früchte* ([Berlin], 1676)
Schenck, Johann, *Scherzi musicali per la Viola da Gamba con Basso Continuo ad libitum* Op.6 (Amsterdam, [1698]); ed. H. Leichtentritt (Amsterdam: J. Müller, 1907)
—— *Le nymphe di Rheno* Op.8 (Amsterdam, [1702]); ed. K.H. Pauls, DEdM 44 (Kassel, 1956)
—— *L'Echo du Danube* Op.9 (Amsterdam, [1704]; Paris, 1742); ed. K.H. Pauls, DEdM 67 (Kassel, 1973)
Schmelzer, Johann Heinrich, *Sonatae unarum fidium, seu a violino solo* (Nuremberg, 1664); ed. E. Schenk, DTÖ 93 (Vienna, 1958)
Telemann, Georg Philipp, *Six Sonates à Violon seul, accompagné par le Claveßin* (Frankfurt am Main, 1715)
—— *Kleine Cammer-Music* (Frankfurt am Main, 1716)
—— *Six Trio* (Frankfurt am Main, 1718)
—— *Der getreue Musikmeister* (Hamburg, 1728)
—— *12 fantaisies à traversière sans basse* (Hamburg, 1732–3)
—— *Fantasie per il violino senza basso* [Hamburg, 1735]
Uccellini, Marco, *Sonate over Canzoni . . . Opera Quinta* (Venice, 1649)
—— *Compositioni armoniche sopra il violino . . . opera settima* (Venice, 1660)
Veracini, Francesco, *Sonate a Violino solo, e Basso . . . Opera Prima* (Dresden, 1721)
Vilsmaÿr, Johann Joseph, *Artificiosus Concentus pro Camera, distributus in sex Partes, seu Partias à Violino Solo con Baßo bellè imitante* (Salzburg, 1715); ed. Nobes 2000b
Vivaldi, Antonio, *Sonate a Violino e Basso per il Cembalo . . . Opera Seconda* (Amsterdam, [1712])
—— *VI Sonate . . . Opera Quinta* (Amsterdam, [1716])
Viviani, Giovanni Bonaventura, *Sinfonie . . . opera quarta* (Rome, 1678)
Walther, Johann Jakob, *Scherzi da Violino solo con il Basso Continuo* (Leipzig and Frankfurt, 1676, 2/1687)
—— *Hortulus Chelicus* (Mainz, 1688, 2/1694)
Westhoff, Johann Paul, *Sonate a Violino Solo con Basso Continuo* (Dresden, 1694)
—— [pieces for violin solo (Dresden, 1696)]; facsimile ed. W. Reich and M. Fechner, *Sechs Suiten für Violin Solo* (Leipzig: Edition Peters, 1974)

3. Modern editions

Bach, Johann Sebastian, *Sonates de Suites pour violon seul*, ed. J. Champeil (Paris: Heugel, 1959)
—— *Sonaten und Partiten für Violine allein*, ed. J. Joachim and A. Moser (Berlin: Bote & Bock, 1908)
—— *Lute Suite in C minor*, ed. H. Ferguson (London: Schott, 1950)
—— *Keyboard Music from the Andreas Bach Book and the Möller Manuscript*, ed. R. Hill (Cambridge MA: Harvard University Press, 1991)
—— *Six Suites for Solo Violoncello Transcribed for Viola*, ed. S. Rowland-Jones (London: Edition Peters, 1998)
Bononcini, Antonio, *Complete Sonatas for Violoncello and Basso Continuo*, ed. L.E. Lindgren (Madison WI: A-R Editions, 1996)
Couperin, François, *Oeuvres complètes de François Couperin. IV: Musique de chambre 3: Les Nations*, ed. A. Gastoué, rev. K. Gilbert and D. Moroney (Monaco: Éditions de l'Oiseau-lyre, 1987)
Dall'Abaco, Evaristo Felice, *Ausgewählte Werke. Erster Teil*, ed. A. Sandberger, DTB 1 (Leipzig: Breitkopf & Härtel, 1900)
—— ... *Zweiter Teil*, DTB 16 (1908)
—— ... *3. Teil*, ed. H. Schmid, DTB Neue Folge 1 (Wiesbaden: Breitkopf & Härtel, 1967)
Farina, Carlo, *Capriccio stravagante*, ed. N. Harnoncourt (Wilhelmshaven: Otto Heinrich Noetzel Verlag, 1970)
Gallot, Jacques, *Oeuvres des Gallot*, ed. M. Rollin (Paris: CNRS, 1987)
Geminiani, Francesco, *Sonate g-moll* [recte B-dur], ed. K. Gerhartz (Munich: Tischer & Jagenburg, [1911])
Goebel, Reinhard (ed.), *Dresden Sonatas* (Middleton WI: A-R Editions, 2006)
Kapsberger, Giovanni Girolamo, *Libro primo d'intavolatura di chitarone* (Venice, 1604), transliterated for keyboard by K. Gilbert (Bologna: Ut Orpheus Edizioni, 1998)
Lonati, Carlo Ambrogio, *The Violin Sonatas. Milan 1701*, ed. F. Giegling (Winterthur: Amadeus Verlag, 1981)
Montanari, Antonio, *The Three 'Dresden' Sonatas*, ed. M. Talbot (Launton: Edition HH, 2005)
Marais, Marin, *The Instrumental Works Volume I*, ed. J. Hsu (New York: Broude, 1980)
Pachelbel, Johann, *Organ Works*, ed. M. Seiffert (New York: Dover Publications, R/1994)
Pez, Johann Christoph, *Ausgewählte Werke*, ed. B.A. Wallner, DTB 1/35 (Augsburg: Dr. Benno Filser Verlag, 1928)
Quantz, Johann Joachim, *Solfeggi pour la flute traversiere avec l'enseignement Par Monsr. Quantz*, ed. W. Michel and H. Teske (Winterthur: Amadeus Verlag, 1978)
—— *Caprices, Fantasias and Beginner's Pieces for Flute Solo and with Basso Continuo*, ed. W. Michel and H. Teske (Winterthur: Amadeus Verlag, 1980)
Sweelinck, Jan Pieterszoon, *Opera Omnia Volume I, Fascicle I: Fantasias and Toccatas*, ed. G. Leonhardt (Amsterdam: Vereniging voor Nederlandse Muziekgeschedenis, 2/1974)
Walther, Johann Gottfried, *Gesammelte Werke für Orgel*, ed. M. Seiffert and H.J. Moser, DdT 1/26 and 27 (Wiesbaden: Breitkopf & Härtel, 2/1958)
Weckmann, Matthias, *Complete Free Organ and Keyboard Works*, ed. S. Rampe (Kassel: Bärenreiter, 1991)
Weiss, Silvius Leopold, *Lautenmusik des 17./18 Jahrhunderts: Ausgewählte Werke von Esaias Reusner and Silvius Leopold Weiss*, ed. H. Neemann, DEdM 12 (Frankfurt: Litolff, 1939)
—— *Complete Works for Lute Volume 3: The London Manuscript... Transcription Part I*, ed. D.A. Smith (Leipzig: C.F. Peters, 1985)
—— ... *Volume 4: The London Manuscript... Transcription Part II* (1990)
—— ... *Volume 5. The Dresden Manuscript. Facsimile of the Tablature. Part I* ed. T. Crawford, DEdM *Sonderreihe Band 11* (Kassel: Bärenreiter, 2002)

—— ... *Volume 6* ... *Part II* ... *Band 12* (2002)
Westhoff, Paul von, *Suite A-Dur*, ed. K. Gerhartz (Munich: Tischer & Jagenberg, [1925])

4. Literature before 1850

Adlung, Jakob, *Musica mechanica organoedi* (Berlin, 1768); facsimile intro. C. Mahrenholz (Kassel: Bärenreiter, 1961)
Altenburg, Johann Ernst, *Versuch einer Anleitung zur heroisch-musikalischen Trompeter- und Pauker-Kunst* (Halle, 1795); trans. E.H. Tarr, *Essay on an Introduction to the Heroic and Musical Trumpeters' and Kettledrummers' Art* (Nashville TN: The Brass Press, 1974)
Bach, Carl Philipp Emanuel, *Versuch über die wahre Art das Clavier zu spielen Zweyter Theil* (Berlin, 1762); trans. W.J. Mitchell, *Essay on the True Art of Playing Keyboard Instruments* (London: Cassel, 1947)
Bacilly, Bénigne de, *Remarques curieuses sur l'art de bien chanter* (Paris, 1668); trans. A.B. Caswell, *A Commentary upon the Art of Proper Singing* (Brooklyn NY: The Institute of Mediæval Music, 1968)
Baron, Ernst Gottlieb, *Historisch, theoretisch und praktische Untersuchungen des Instruments der Lauten* (Nuremberg, 1727); trans. D.A. Smith, *Study of the Lute* (San Francisco: Musica Antiqua, 1976)
Brossard, Sébastien de, *Dictionaire de Musique* (Amsterdam, 3/1705)
Burney, Charles, *The Present State of Music in Germany, The Netherlands, and United Provinces*, 2 vols (London, 1773)
Corrette, Michel, *Méthode pour apprendre aisément à joüer de la flute traversière* (Paris, c.1740); trans. C.R. Farrar, *Michel Corrette and Flute-Playing in the Eighteenth Century* (Brooklyn NY: The Institute of Mediæval Music, 1970)
—— *Méthode théorique et pratique pour apprendre en peu de temps le violoncelle dans sa perfection* (Paris, 1741); trans. in Graves 1971
Couperin, François, *L'Art de toucher le clavecin* (Paris, 2/1717)
Danoville, *L'Art de toucher le dessus et basse de violle* (Paris, 1687)
Forkel, Johann Nikolaus, *Über Johann Sebastian Bachs Leben, Kunst und Kunstgewerbe* (Leipzig, 1802); trans. in NBR
Freillon-Poncein, Jean Pierre, *La véritable manière d'apprendre à jouer en perfection du hautbois, de la flûte et du flageolet* (Paris, 1700); trans. C.P. Smith, *On Playing Oboe, Recorder, and Flageolet* (Bloomington IN: Indiana University Press, 1992)
Fux, Johann Joseph, *Gradus ad Parnassum* (Vienna, 1725), German trans. Mizler 1742
Geminiani, Francesco, *The Art of Playing on the Violin* (London, 1751)
Ganassi, Silvestro di, *Opera intitulata Fontegara* (Venice, 1535)
Hawkins, Sir John, *A General History of the Science and Practice of Music* (London, 1776; London: Novello, R/1853) facsimile intro. C. Cudworth (New York: Da Capo, 1963)
Heinichen, Johann David, *Der General-Bass in der Composition* (Dresden, 1728); partial trans. in Buelow 1986
Hiller, Johann Adam, *Lebensbeschreibungen berühmter Musikgelehrten und Tonkünstler neuerer Zeit. Erster Theil* (Leipzig, 1784)
Hotteterre, Jacques, *Principes de la flute traversiere* (Paris, 1707); trans. D. Lasocki, *Principles of the Flute, Recorder, and Oboe* (London: Barrie & Rockliff, 1978)
—— *L'Art de preluder sur la flute traversiere, sur la flute-à-bec, sur le hautbois* (Paris, 1719)
Kircher, Athanasius, *Musurgia Universalis* (Rome, 1650); partial German trans. in A. Hirsch, *Philosophischer Extract und Auszug, aus deß Welt-berühmten Teutschen Jesuitens Athanasi Kircheri von Fulda Musurgia Universali* (Schwäbisch Hall, 1662)
Kirnberger, Johann, *Die Kunst des reinen Satzes in der Musik* (Berlin, 1771, 1776, 1777, 1779); partial trans. in D. Beach and J. Thym, *The Art of Strict Musical Composition* (New Haven CT: Yale University Press, 1982)

Le Blanc, Hubert, *Defense de la basse de viole contre les entreprises du violon et les prétentions du violoncel* (Paris, 1740)
Marpurg, Friedrich Wilhelm, *Abhandlung von der Fuge* (Berlin, 1753, 1754)
Mattheson, Johann, *Das neu-eröffnete Orchestre* (Hamburg, 1713)
—— *Critica Musica* (Hamburg, 1722, 1725)
—— *Grosse General-Baß-Schule* (Hamburg, 1731)
—— *Kern melodischer Wissenschaft* (Hamburg, 1737)
—— *Der vollkommene Capellmeister* (Hamburg, 1739); trans. E.C. Harriss (Ann Arbor MI: UMI Research Press, 1981)
—— *Grundlage einer Ehrenpforte* (Hamburg, 1740)
Mizler, Lorenz, *Gradus ad Parnassum . . . von Johann Joseph Fux . . . aus dem Lateinischen . . . übersetzt* (Lepizig, 1742)
Montéclair, Michel Pignolet de, *Principes de musique* (Paris, 1736)
Mozart, Leopold, *Versuch einer gründlichen Violinschule* (Augsburg, 1756); trans. E. Knocker, *A Treatise on the Fundamental Principles of Violin Playing* (Oxford: Oxford University Press, 3/1985)
Muffat, Georg, *Florilegium primum* (Augsburg, 1695); ed. H. Rietsch, DTÖ 2 (Vienna, 1894)
—— *Florilegium secundum* (Passau, 1698); ed. H. Rietsch, DTÖ 4 (Vienna, 1895)
—— *Außerlesener . . . Instrumental-Music Erste Versamblung* (Passau, 1701); ed. E. Lutz, DTÖ 23 (Vienna, 1904); English translation of all Muffat's prefaces in Wilson 2001
Niedt, Friederich Erhardt, *Musicalische Handleitung zur Variation des General-Basses* (Hamburg, 2/1721); trans. Poulin and Taylor 1989
Playford, John, *An Introduction to the Skill of Musick . . . The Twelfth Edition. Corrected and Annotated by Mr. Henry Purcell* (London, 1694)
Quantz, Johann Joachim, *Versuch einer Anweisung die Flöte traversiere zu spielen* (Berlin, 1752); trans. E.R. Reilly, *On Playing the Flute* (London: Faber and Faber, 2/1985)
Rousseau, Jean, *Traité de la viole* (Paris, 1687); trans. N. Dolmetsch, *The Consort* xxxiv (1978) 302–11, xxxvi (1980) 365–70, xxxvii (1981) 402–11, xxxviii (1982) 463–66
Saint Lambert, M. de, *Les Principes du clavecin* (Paris, 1702); trans. R. Harriss-Warrick, *Principles of the Harpsichord by Monsieur de Saint Lambert* (Cambridge: Cambridge University Press, 1984)
Scheibe, Johann Adolph, 'Compendium Musices Theoretico-practicum' (c.1730); ed. in P. Benary, *Die deutsche Kompositionslehre des 18. Jahrhunderts* (Leipzig: Breitkopf & Härtel, 1961)
Simpson, Christopher, *The Division Violist* (London, 1659)
Tartini, Giuseppe, *A Letter from the late Signor Tartini to Performers on the Violin* (London, 1771)
Walther, Johann Gottfried, 'Praecepta der musicalischen Composition' (1708), ed. P. Benary (Leipzig: Breitkopf & Härtel, 1955)
—— *Musicalisches Lexicon* (Leipzig, 1732)
Weigel, Johann Christoph, *Musikalisches Theatrum* (Nuremberg, c.1722)

5. Literature after 1850

Abravaya, Ido, *On Bach's Rhythm and Tempo* (Kassel: Bärenreiter, 2006)
Allsop, Peter, *Arcangelo Corelli* (Oxford: Clarendon Press, 1999)
—— *Cavalier Giovanni Battista Buonamente* (Aldershot: Ashgate, 2005)
Altschuler, Eric Lewin, 'Were Bach's Toccata and Fugue BWV 565 and the Ciaccona from BWV 1004 lute pieces?', *The Musical Times* cxlvi/1893 (Winter 2005) 77–86
Apel, Willi, *Italian Violin Music of the Seventeenth Century*, ed. T. Binkley (Bloomington IN: Indiana University Press, 1990)

Argent, Mark, 'Decoding Bach 3: stringing along', *The Musical Times* cxli/1872 (Autumn 2000) 16–23

Aschmann, Rudolf, 'Das deutsche polyphone Violinspiel im 17. Jahrhundert: ein Beitrag zur Entwicklungsgeschichte des Violinspiels' (Dr diss., University of Zurich, 1962)

Babitz, Sol, *The Six Solos for Violin without Bass Accompaniment by Johann Sebastian Bach marked by Sol Babitz with the Taste and Technique described in the Sources & provided with a Preface on Baroque Performance Using a corrected Facsimile of the First Edition – Simrock 1802* (Los Angeles: Early Music Laboratory, 1972)

Badiarov, Dmitry, 'The violoncello, viola da spalla and viola pomposa in theory and practice', *The Galpin Society Journal* lx (4/2007) 121–45

Barnett, Gregory, 'The Violoncello da spalla: shouldering the cello in the Baroque Era', *Journal of the American Musical Instrument Society* xxiv (1998) 81–106

—— *Bolognese Instrumental Music 1660–1710* (Aldershot: Ashgate, 2008)

Bartel, Dietrich, *Musical-Rhetorical Figures in German Baroque Music* (Lincoln NE: University of Nebraska Press, 1997)

Bartels, Ulrich, 'Bearbeitungsproblematik und Echtheitszweifel. Überlegungen zur Sonate BWV 964 und zum Adagio BWV 968', *Vom Klang der Zeit . . . Klaus Hofmann zum 65. Geburtstag*, ed. U. Bartels and U. Wolf (Wiesbaden: Breitkopf & Härtel, 2004)

Beach, David W., *Aspects of Unity in J.S. Bach's Partitas and Suites: An Analytical Study* (Rochester NY: University of Rochester Press, 2005)

Beckmann, Gustav, *Das Violinspiel in Deutschland vor 1700* (Leipzig: N. Simrock, 1918); music supplement, 5 fascicles (1921)

—— 'Johann Pachelbel als Kammerkomponist', *Archiv für Musikwissenschaft* i/2 (1/1919) 267–74

Beisswenger, Kirsten, 'Zur Chronologie der Notenhandschriften Johann Gottfried Walthers', *Acht kleine Präludien und Studien über Bach. Georg von Dadelsen zum 70. Geburtstag*, ed. Collegium of the Johann Sebastian Bach Institute, Göttingen (Wiesbaden: Breitkopf & Härtel, 1992) 11–39

—— (ed.), *Johann Sebastian Bach . . . Six Suites for Violoncello Solo* (Wiesbaden: Breitkopf & Härtel, 2000)

Blum, David, *Casals and the Art of Interpretation* (London: Heinemann, 1977)

Borris, Siegfried, *Kirnbergers Leben und Werk und seine Bedeutung im Berliner Musikkreis um 1750* (Kassel: Bärenreiter, 1933)

Boyd, Malcolm, *Bach* (Oxford: Oxford University Press, 3/2000)

—— and John Butt (eds), *Oxford Composer Companions: J.S. Bach* (Oxford: Oxford University Press, 1999)

Boyden, David, *The History of Violin Playing from its Origins to 1761* (London: Oxford University Press, 1965)

Braubach, Jürgen, 'Die Sprache der Figuren. Zur Hermeneutik der Bachschen Lautenfuge am Beispiel der Fuga c-moll BWV 997', *Gitarre und Laute* viii/3 (5–6/1986) 51–6

Braun, Werner, 'Sans basse, senza accompagnamento, ohne Clavir. Formen kunstvoller Einstimmigkeit zwischen 1680 und 1780', *Archiv für Musikwissenschaft* xxxvi (1979) 254–78

Breig, Werner, 'Bach und Marchand in Dresden: eine überlieferungskritische Studie', *Bach-Jahrbuch* (1988) 7–18

Brewer, Charles E., *Solo Compositions for Violin and Viola da gamba with basso continuo from the Collection of Prince-Bishop Carl Liechtenstein-Castelcorn in Kroměříž* (Madison WI: A-R Editions, 1977)

Brooks, Brian Paul, 'The Emergence of the Violin as a Solo Instrument in Early Seventeenth-Century Germany' (Ph.D. diss., Cornell University, 2002)

—— 'Étienne Nau, Breslau 114 and the early 17th-century solo violin fantasia', *Early Music* xxxii/1 (2/2004) 49–72

Brown, Howard Mayer, *Embellishing Sixteenth-Century Music* (Oxford: Oxford University Press, 1976)
Buelow, George G., *Thorough-Bass Accompaniment according to Johann David Heinichen* (Lincoln NE: University of Nebraska Press, 2/1986)
Burguéte, André, 'Die Lautenkompositionen Johann Sebastian Bachs. Ein Beitrag zur kritischen Wertung aus spielpraktischer Sicht', *Bach-Jahrbuch* (1977) 26–52
—— 'Johann Sebastian Bachs Lautenwerke—Ende eines Mythos', *Gitarre & Laute* xvi/2 (3–4/1994) 66–72; '*Teil 2*', xvi/3 (7–8/1994) 50–3
Butt, John, *Bach Interpretation* (Cambridge: Cambridge University Press, 1990)
Bylsma, Anner, *Bach, the Fencing Master: Reading Aloud from the First Three Cello Suites* (Amsterdam: [author], 1998)
Castellani, Marcello, 'J.S. Bachs "Solo pour la flûte traversière": Köthen oder Leipzig?', *Tibia* xiv (1989) 567–73
Chafe, Eric, *The Church Music of Heinrich Biber* (Ann Arbor MI: UMI Press, 1987)
Cipriani, Paolo (ed.), *Johann Sebastian Bach: Opere per liuto* (Rovereto: E. Cipriani, 1977)
Coelho, Victor, 'Frescobaldi and the lute and chitarrone toccatas of "Il Tedesco della Tiorba"', *Frescobaldi Studies*, ed. A. Silbiger (Durham NC: Duke University Press, 1987) 137–56
Collins, Michael, '*Notes inégales*: a reexamination', *Journal of the American Musicological Society* xx/3 (Fall 1967) 481–5
Cowling, Elizabeth, *The Cello* (London: Batsford, 1975)
Crawford, Tim, 'New sources in the music of Count Losy', *Journal of the Lute Society of America* xv (1982) 52–83
—— *Sources manuscrites en tablature. Luth et théorbe (c.1500–c.1800). Catalogue descriptif.* Vol. III/2, ed. F.-P. Goy, P. Kiraly, C. Meyer (Baden Baden: Valentin Koerner, 1999)
—— 'S.L. Weiss's use of the lower bass courses', *Journal of the Lute Society of America* xxxiv (2002) 10–22
Curti, Martha, 'J.S. Bach's Chaconne in D minor: a study in coherence', *The Music Review* xxxvii/4 (11/1976) 249–65
Dadelsen, Georg von, 'Urtext und Spielpraxis. Einige Gedanken anhand des Allegro aus Bachs Violin-Solosonate a-Moll, BWV 1003', *Logos Musicae. Festschrift für Albert Palm*, ed. R. Görner (Wiesbaden: Franz Steiner, 1982) 19–23 [1982a]
—— 'Über den Anteil der Interpretation an der Dokumentation', *Quellenforschung in der Musikwissenschaft*, ed. G. Feder (Wolfenbüttel: Herzog August Bibliothek, 1982) 33–56 [1982b]
—— 'Bach der Violinist: Anmerkungen zu den Soli für Violine und für Violoncello', *Beiträge zur Bachforschung* 9/10 (1989) 70–6
—— 'Das Autograph: Entstehung und Überlieferung', in Seiffert 1991: 39–49
—— (ed.), *Joh. Seb. Bach. Suiten, Sonaten, Capriccios und Variationen* (Munich: Henle, 1975)
—— (ed.), *Faksimile-Reihe Bachscher Werke und Schriftstücke: Band 22 Sei Solo a Violino senza Basso accompagnato BWV 1001–1006* (Leipzig: Bach-Archiv, 1988)
Dammann, Rolf, *Der Musikbegriff im deutschen Barock* (Cologne: Arno Volk, 1967)
Davis, Nathan J., 'The Baroque Violoncello and the Unaccompanied Cello Suites of J.S. Bach, BWV 1007–1012' (Ph.D. diss., New York University, 1986)
Delang, Kerstin, 'Couperin–Pisendel–Bach. Überlegungen zur Echtheit und Datierung des Trios BWV 587 anhand des Quellenfundes in der Sächsischen Landesbibliothek– Staats- und Universitätsbibliothek, Dresden', *Bach-Jahrbuch* (2007) 197–202
Dirksen, Pieter, *The Keyboard Music of Jan Pieterszoon Sweelinck* (Utrecht: Koninklijke Vereniging voor Nederlandse Muziekgeschiedenis, 1997)
Dolmetsch, Arnold, *The Interpretation of the Music of the Seventeenth and Eighteenth Centuries* (London: Novello, 2/1946)

Dombois, Eugen M., 'The Allegro from J.S. Bach's Prelude, Fugue and Allegro in E flat major BWV 998', *The Lute Society Journal* xiv (1972) 25–8
—— 'The Fugue and Prelude from J.S. Bach's Prelude, Fugue and Allegro in E flat major BWV 998', *The Lute Society Journal* xv (1973) 37–47
Drescher, Thomas, '"Virtuosissima conversazione" Konstituenten des solistischen Violinspiels gegen Ende des 17. Jahrhunderts', *Basler Jahrbuch für historische Musikpraxis* xx (1996) 41–59
—— *Spielmännische Tradition und höfische Virtuosität* (Tutzing: Hans Schneider, 2004)
Dreyfus, Laurence, *Bach's Continuo Group* (Cambridge MA: Harvard University Press, 1987)
—— *Bach and the Patterns of Invention* (Cambridge MA: Harvard University Press, 1996)
—— (ed.), *Joh. Seb. Bach: Drei Sonaten für Viola da gamba . . . und Cembalo BWV 1027–1029* (London: Peters Edition, 1985)
Drüner, Ulrich, 'Violoncello piccolo und Viola pomposa bei Johann Sebastian Bach. Zu Fragen von Identität und Spielweise dieser Instrumente, *Bach-Jahrbuch* (1987) 85–112
Dürr, Alfred, *Studien über die frühen Kantaten J.S. Bachs* (Leipzig: Breitkopf & Härtel, 1951)
—— 'Tastenumfang und Chronologie in Bachs Klavierwerken', *Festschrift Georg von Dadelsen*, ed. T. Kohlhase and V. Schierliess (Neuhausen-Stuttgart: Hänssler, 1978) 73–88
—— *Die Johannes-Passion von Johann Sebastian Bach* (Kassel: Bärenreiter, 1988); trans. A. Clayton, *Johann Sebastian Bach, St John Passion* (New York: Oxford University Press, 2000)
—— 'Philologisches zum Problem Violoncello alto piccolo bei Bach', *Festschrift Wolfgang Rehm . . . 1989*, ed. D. Berke and H. Heckmann (Kassel: Bärenreiter, 1990) 45–50
—— *Die Kantaten von Johann Sebastian Bach* (Kassel: Bärenreiter, 6/1995); trans. R.D.P. Jones, *The Cantatas of J.S. Bach* (New York: Oxford University Press, 2005)
Efrati, Richard R., *Treatise on the Execution and Interpretation of the Sonatas and Partitas for Solo Violin and the Suites for Cello by Johann Sebastian Bach* (Zurich: Atlantis Verlag, 1979)
Eichberg, Hartwig, 'Unechtes unter Johann Sebastian Bachs Klavierwerken', *Bach-Jahrbuch* (1975) 7–49
Eisert, Christian, *Die Clavier-Toccaten BWV 910–916 von Johann Sebastian Bach* (Mainz: Schott, 1994)
Eller, Rudolf, 'Über Charakter und Geschichte der Dresdner Vivaldi-Manuskripte', *Vivaldiana* i (1969) 57–67
Eppstein, Hans, 'Chronologieprobleme in Johann Sebastian Bachs Suiten für Soloinstrument', *Bach-Jahrbuch* (1976) 35–57
Erickson, Raymond, 'Secret codes, dance and Bach's great "Ciaccona"', *Early Music America* viii/2 (Summer 2002) 34–43
Fanselau, Clamens, *Mehrstimmigkeit in J.S. Bachs Werken für Melodieinstrumente ohne Begleitungen* (Berlin: Studio, 2000)
Fechner, Manfred, *Studien zur Dresdner Überlieferung von Instrumentalkonzerten deutscher Komponisten des 18. Jahrhunderts* (Laaber: Laaber Verlag, 1999)
Ferreira, Manuel Pedro, 'The "French Style" and Corelli', *Studi Corelliani V* (Florence: Olschki, 1996) 379–88
Field, Elizabeth Imbert, 'Performing Solo Bach: An Examination of the Evolution of Performance Traditions of Bach's Unaccompanied Violin Sonatas from 1802 to the Present' (D.M.A. diss., Cornell University, 1999)
Fischer, Wilhelm, 'Zur Entwicklungsgeschichte des Wiener Klassischen Stils', *Studien zur Musikwissenschaft* iii (1915) 24–84
Flassig, Fred, *Die solistische Gambenmusik in Deutschland im 18. Jahrhundert* (Göttingen: Cuvillier Verlag, 1998)

Fontijn, Claire A., 'Quantz's *unegal*: implications for the performance of 18th-century music', *Early Music* xxiii/1 (2/1995) 55–62

Franklin, Don, 'Composing in time: Bach's temporal design for the Goldberg Variations', *Irish Musical Studies*, ed. A. Leahy and Y. Tomita (Dublin: Four Courts Press, 2004) 103–28

Fuchs, Josef Rainerius, 'Halbglissando und Imitation der Orgeltremulanten in Bachs Musik', *Die Musikforschung* xliii (1990) 247–52

Gilbert, Kenneth (ed.), *François Couperin: Pièces de clavecin Premier livre* (Paris: Heugel, 1972)

Glover, Jane, *Cavalli* (London: Batsford, 1978)

Goebel, Reinhard, 'Bachs geschichtlicher Ort', in Seiffert 1991:127–43

Golan, Lawrence, *Bach Three Sonatas & Three Partitas for Solo Violin, BWV 1001–1006*. Includes the Performance Practice Essay: Performing Bach (Pacific MO: Mel Bay Publications, 2006)

Graves, Charles Douglas, 'Theoretical and Practical Method for Cello by Michel Corrette: Translation, Commentary and Comparison with Seven other Eighteenth-Century Cello Methods' (Ph.D. diss., Michigan State University, 1971)

Grossman, Robert Allen, 'Der Intavolator als Interpret: Johann Sebastian Bachs Lautensuite g-moll, BWV 995, im Autograph und in zeitgenössischer Tabulatur', *Basler Jahrbuch für historische Musikpraxis* X (1986) 223–44

—— 'The Lute Suite in G minor BWV 995 by Johann Sebastian Bach: A Comparison of the Autograph Manuscript and the Lute Intabulation in Leipzig Sammlung Becker, Ms.III.11.3' (D.M. diss., Indiana University, 1987)

Grüss, Hans, 'Über Stricharten und Artikulation in Streichinstrumentenstimmen Johann Sebastian Bachs', *Bericht über die wissenschaftliche Konferenz zum V. Internationalen Bachfest der DDR . . . Leipzig 1985*, ed. W. Hoffmann and A. Schneiderheinze (Leipzig: VEB Deutscher Verlag für Musik, 1988) 331–40

Grützbach, Erwin A., *Zur Interpretation der sechs Suiten für Violoncello von Johann Sebastian Bach* (Eisenach: Karl Dieter Wagner, 3/1993)

Gustafson, Bruce and David Fuller, *A Catalogue of French Harpsichord Music 1699–1780* (Oxford: Clarendon Press, 1990)

Hefling, Stephen, *Rhythmic Alteration in 17th- and 18th-Century Music* (New York: Schirmer, 1993)

Henkel, Hubert, *Musikinstrumenten-Museum der Universität Leipzig. Katalog: Band 4 Clavichorde* (Leipzig: VEB Deutscher Verlag für Musik, 1981)

Henning, Uta and Rudolf Richter, 'The most beautiful among the claviers', *Early Music* x/4 (10/1982) 477–86

Hepokoski, James, *Sibelius: Symphony No.5* (Cambridge: Cambridge University Press, 1993)

Herz, Gerhard, *Essays on Bach* (Ann Arbor: UMI Research Press, 1985)

Hill, Robert, 'The Möller Manuscript and the Andreas Bach Book: Two Keyboard Anthologies from the Circle of the Young Johann Sebastian Bach' (Ph.D.diss., Harvard University, 1987)

Hilton, Wendy, *Dance and Music of Court and Theater* (Stuyvesant NY: Pendragon Press, 1997)

Hoffmann-Erbrecht, Lothar, 'Der Lautenist Sylvius Leopold Weiß und Johann Sebastian Bach', *Gitarre und Laute* ix/6 (11–12/1987) 19–23

Hofmann, Klaus, 'On the instrumentation of the E-major Suite BWV 1006a by Johann Sebastian Bach', *A Bach Tribute: Essays in Honor of William H. Scheide*, ed. P. Brainard and R. Robinson (Kassel: Bärenreiter, 1003) 143–54

Holman, Peter, *Four and Twenty Fiddlers: The Violin at the English Court 1540–1690* (Oxford: Clarendon Press, 1993)

Horn, Victoria, 'French influence in Bach's organ works', in Stauffer and May 1986: 256–73

Houle, George, *Meter in Music 1600–1800* (Bloomington IN: Indiana University Press, 1987)
Hsu, John, *A Handbook of French Baroque Viol Technique* (New York: Broude, 1981)
Hulshoff, G., *De Zes Suites voor Violoncello-Solo van Johann Sebastian Bach* (Arnhem: Van Loghum Staterus, 2/1962)
Husmann, Heinrich, 'Die Viola pomposa', *Bach-Jahrbuch* (1936) 90–100
Hutchings, Arthur, *The Baroque Concerto* (London: Faber and Faber, 3/1978)
Jarvis, Martin W.B., 'Did Johann Sebastian Bach write the Six Cello Suites?' (Ph.D. diss., Charles Darwin University, 2007)
Jones, Richard D.P., *The Creative Development of Johann Sebastian Bach. Volume I: 1695–1717* (New York: Oxford University Press, 2007)
Jones, Sterling Scott, *The Lira da braccio* (Bloomington IN: Indiana University Press, 1995)
Jung, Hans Rudolf, 'Johann Georg Pisendel (1687–1755): Leben und Werk: Ein Beitrag zur Geschichte der Violinmusik in der Bach-Zeit' (Dr diss., Friedrich-Schiller-Universität Jena, 1956)
Junghänel, Konrad, 'Bach und die zeitgenössische Lautenpraxis', *Johann Sebastian Bachs Spätwerk und dessen Umfeld. Bericht . . . Duisburg 1986*, ed. C. Wolff (Kassel: Bärenreiter, 1988) 95–101
Kahl, Willi, *Selbstbiographien deutscher Musiker des XVIII. Jahrhunderts* (Cologne: Staufen-Verlag, 1948)
Kassler, Michael (ed.), *The English Bach Awakening* (Aldershot: Ashgate, 2004)
Kast, Paul, *Die Bach-Handschriften der Berliner Staatsbibliothek* (Trossingen: Hohner-Verlag, 1958); expanded edition (Munich: Saur, 2003)
Kehr, Günter, 'Allgemeine Erläuterungen zu Bachs Sonaten und Partiten für die Violine allein', *Das Orchester* xxvii/10 (1979) 825–7
Keller, Hermann, *Die Klavierwerke Bachs* (Leipzig: Edition Peters, 4/1950)
Kennaway, George, 'Editing Bach's cello Suites', *The Strad* xci/1088 (12/1980) 561–3
Kinney, Gordon James, 'The Musical Literature for Unaccompanied Violoncello' (Ph.D. diss., Florida State University, 1962)
Klein, Hans-Günter, *Der Einfluß der Vivaldischen Konzertform im Instrumentalwerk Johann Sebastian Bachs* (Strasbourg: Heitz, 1970)
Klenz, William, *Giovanni Bononcini of Modena* (Durham NC: Duke University Press, 1962)
Knapp, Raymond, 'The Finale of Brahms's Fourth Symphony: the tale of a subject', *19th-Century Music* xiii/1 (Summer 1989) 3–17
Kobayashi, Yoshitake, 'Zur Chronologie der Spätwerke Johann Sebastian Bachs', *Bach-Jahrbuch* (1988) 7–72
—— 'Noch einmal zu J.S. Bachs "Solo pour la flûte traversière" BWV 1013', *Tibia*, (1991) 379–82
Kollpacher-Haas, Ingrid, 'Pierre-Gabriel Buffardin: Sein Leben und Werk', *Studien zur Musikwissenschaft* xxv (1962) 298–306 (*Festschrift Erich Schenk*)
König, Ernst, 'Die Hofkapelle des Fürsten Leopold zu Anhalt-Cöthen', *Bach-Jahrbuch* (1959) 160–7
Köpp, Kai, *Johann Georg Pisendel (1687–1755) und die Anfänge der neuzeitlichen Orchesterleitung* (Tutzing: Hans Schneider, 2005)
Kotsoni-Brown, Stavria, 'The Solo Cello Concertos of Antonio Vivaldi' (Ph.D. diss., University of Liverpool, 2000)
Krautwurst, Franz, 'Anmerkung zu den Augsburger Bach-Dokumenten', *Festschrift Martin Ruhnke zum 65. Geburtstag*, ed. K.-J. Sachs (Neuhausen-Stuttgart: Hänssler, 1986) 176–84
Kuijken, Barthold (ed.), *Johann Sebastian Bach, Solo for flute in A minor BWV 1013* (Wiesbaden: Breitkopf & Härtel, 1990)
Leahy, Anne, 'Bach's Prelude, Fugue and Allegro for Lute (BWV 998): a Trinitarian statement of faith?', *Journal of the Society for Musicology in Ireland* i (2005) 33–51

Leaver, Robin A., 'Überlegungen zur "Bildniβ-Sammlung" im Nachlaβ von C.P.E. Bach', *Bach-Jahrbuch* (2007) 105–38
Ledbetter, David, *Harpsichord and Lute Music in 17th-Century France* (London: Macmillan, 1987)
—— 'What the lute sources tell us about the performance of French harpsichord music', *Proceedings of the International Harpsichord Symposium Utrecht 1990*, ed. P. Dirksen (Utrecht: STIMU, 1992) 59–85
—— *Continuo Playing according to Handel* (Oxford: Oxford University Press, 3/1995)
—— 'On the manner of playing the Adagio: neglected features of a genre', *Early Music* xxix/1 (2/2001) 15–26
—— *Bach's Well-tempered Clavier: The 48 Preludes and Fugues* (New Haven CT: Yale University Press, 2002)
—— '*Les goûts réunis* and the music of J.S. Bach', *Basler Jahrbuch für historische Musikpraxis* xxviii (2004) 63–80
—— 'A question of genre: J.S. Bach and the "mixed style"', *Music and its Questions: Essays in Honor of Peter Williams*, ed. T. Donohue (Richmond VA: OHS Press, 2007) 205–24
Legl, Frank, 'Between Grottkau and Neuburg: new information on the biography of Silvius Leopold Weiss', *Journal of the Lute Society of America* xxxi (1998) 49–77
Leisinger, Ulrich (ed.), *Johann Sebastian Bach. Suites for Violoncello Solo BWV 1007–1012* (Vienna: Wiener Urtext Edition, 2000)
—— *Partita a-Moll für Flöte solo BWV 1013*, ed. H.-P. Schmitz, revised U. Leisinger (Kassel: Bärenreiter, 2001)
Lester, Joel, 'Problems in the *Neue Bach Ausgabe* of the E major Partita for violin alone', *Current Musicology* xviii (1972) 64–7
—— *Bach's Works for Solo Violin: Style, Structure, Performance* (New York: Oxford University Press, 1999)
—— 'Heightening levels of activity in J.S. Bach's parallel-section constructions', *Journal of the American Musicological Society* liv/1 (Spring 2001) 49–96
Lindley, Mark and Ibo Ortgies, 'Bach-style keyboard tuning', *Early Music* xxxiv/4 (11/2006) 613–23
Little, Meredith, and Natalie Jenne, *Dance and the Music of J.S. Bach* (Bloomington IN: Indiana University Press, 2/2001)
Lohmann, Ludger, *Studien zur Artikulations-Problemen bei den Tasteninstrumenten des 16.–18. Jahrhunderts* (Regensburg: Gustav Bosse, 2/1990)
Lundberg, Robert, 'The German Baroque lute, 1650 to 1750', *Journal of the Lute Society of America* xxxii (1999) 1–34
Lutterman, John Kenneth, 'Works in Progress: J.S. Bach's Suites for Solo Cello as Artifacts of Improvisatory Practices' (Ph.D. diss., University of California at Davis, 2006)
Luttmann, Stephen, 'The Music of Johann Schenck: some observations', *Journal of the Viola da Gamba Society of America* xviii (1981) 94–120
Mann, Alfred, *The Study of Fugue* (London: Faber and Faber, 1958)
Mansure, Victor Newell, 'The Allemandes of Johann Sebastian Bach: a Stylistic Survey' (D.M.A. diss., University of Oregon, 1992)
Markevitch, Dimitry, *The Solo Cello: A Bibliography of the Unaccompanied Violoncello Literature* (Berkeley CA: Fallen Leaf Press, 1989)
Marshall, Robert L., *The Compositional Process of J.S. Bach* (Princeton NJ: Princeton University Press, 1972)
—— *The Music of Johann Sebastian Bach* (New York: Schirmer, 1989)
Mather, Betty B., *Interpretation of French Music from 1675 to 1775* (New York: McGinnis and Marx, 1973)
—— and David Lasocki, *Free Ornamentation in Woodwind Music 1700–1775* (New York: McGinnis & Marx, 1976)

―― and Dean M. Karns, *Dance Rhythms of the French Baroque* (Bloomington IN: Indiana University Press, 1987)
―― and Elizabeth A. Sadilek, *Johann Sebastian Bach. Partita in A minor for Solo Flute BWV 1013 with Emphasis on the Allemande* (Nashua NH: Falls House Press, 2004)
McVeigh, Simon and Hehoash Hirschberg, *The Italian Concerto 1700–1760: Rhetorical Strategies and Style History* (Woodbridge: The Boydell Press, 2004)
Maul, Michael and Peter Wollny (eds), *Weimarer Orgeltabulatur. Die frühesten Notenhandschriften Johann Sebastian Bachs sowie Abschriften seines Schülers Johann Martin Schubart*, facsimiles and edition (Kassel: Bärenreiter, 2007)
Milliot, Sylvette and Jérôme de la Gorce, *Marin Marais* (Paris: Fayard, 1991)
Moens-Haenen, Greta, 'Zur Frage der Wellenlinien in der Musik Johann Sebastian Bachs', *Archiv für Musikwissenschaft* xli/3 (1984) 176–86
―― *Das Vibrato in der Musik des Barock* (Graz: Akademische Druck- und Verlagsanstalt, 1988)
Moser, Andreas, 'Zu Joh. Seb. Bachs Sonaten und Partiten für Violine allein', *Bach-Jahrbuch* (1920) 30–65
―― *Geschichte des Violinspiels* 2 vols, rev. H.-J. Nösselt (Tutzing: Hans Schneider, 1966, 1967)
Murata, Margaret (ed.), *Source Readings in Music History: The Baroque Era* (New York: W.W. Norton, 1998
Neumann, Frederick, 'External evidence for uneven notes', *The Musical Quarterly* lii/4 (10/1966) 448–64
―― 'Some performance problems of Bach's unaccompanied violin and cello works', *Eighteenth-Century Music in Theory and Practice*, ed. M.A. Parker (Stuyvesant NY: Pendragon Press, 1994) 19–48
Nobes, Pauline Heather, 'Neglected Sources of the Violin Repertory before *ca.* 1750' (Ph.D. diss., University of Exeter, 2000) [**2000a**]
―― (ed.), *The Unaccompanied Solo Violin Repertory before 1750: Klagenfurt Manuscript, Dances and Scordatura Suites*, facsimile with introduction (Middlesex: Rhapsody Ensemble Editions, 1999)
―― (ed.), *Six Vilsmaÿr Partitas*, introduction, facsimile and edition (Middlesex: Rhapsody Ensemble Editions, 2000) [**2000b**]
North, Nigel, Review of E. Cipriani and P. Cherici editions of Bach's lute works, *Music & Letters* lxiii (1982) 147–8
Öhm-Kühnle, Christoph, 'Zum Notentext der Suite e-Moll (BWV 996) – Eine textkritische Untersuchung der Abschrift von Heinrich Nikolaus Gerber', *Bach-Jahrbuch* (2006) 295–302
Oleskiewicz, Mary, 'The flute at Dresden: ramifications for eighteenth-century woodwind performance in Germany', *From Renaissance to Baroque*, ed. J. Wainwright and P. Holman (Aldershot: Ashgate, 2005) 145–65
Oppel, Reinhard, 'Zur Fugentechnik Bachs', *Bach-Jahrbuch* (1921) 9–48
Pirro, André, 'J.-S. Bach et la musique française', *Musica* vi/61 (10/1907) 149–50
Poulin, Pamela and Irmgard C. Taylor, *Friederich Erhardt Niedt: The Musical Guide* (Oxford: Oxford University Press, 1989)
Powell, Ardal, 'Vivaldi's flutes', *Early Music* xxxvi/1 (2/2008) 120–2
―― and David Lasocki, 'Bach and the flute: the players, the instruments, the music', *Early Music* xxiii/1 (2/1995) 9–29
Pratt, George, 'Bach's first cello Suite – a question in the Gigue', *The Strad* lxxxix/1065 (1/1979) 811–13
―― 'Editing of Bach's cello Suites: some unanswered questions', *The Strad* xci/1091 (3/1981) 813–14
Prinz, Ulrich, *Johann Sebastian Bachs Instrumentarium* (Kassel: Bärenreiter, 2005)

Rabey, Wladimir, 'Der Originaltext der Bachschen Soloviolinsonaten und -partiten (BWV 1001–1006) in seiner Bedeutung für den ausführenden Musiker', *Bach-Jahrbuch* (1963/64) 23–46

Rackwitz, Werner (ed.), *Georg Philipp Telemann: Singen ist das Fundament zur Musik in allen Dingen. Eine Dokumentsammlung* (Wilhelmshaven: Hinrichshofen, 1981)

Rampe, Siegbert and Dominik Sackmann (eds), *Bachs Orchestermusik* (Kassel: Bärenreiter, 2000)

Renwick, William, 'Praeludia et Fugen del Signor Johann Sebastian Bach?', *Bach Perspectives Volume Four*, ed. D. Schulenberg (Lincoln NE: Nebraska University Press, 1999) 137–58

—— *The Langloz Manuscript* (New York: Oxford University Press, 2001)

Robertson, Michael, '"Ex Vratislava ad Neöburgiam": a tale of three Fischers', *Early Music Performer* xv (5/2005) 45–57

Rostal, Max, 'Zur Interpretation der Violinsonaten J.S. Bachs', *Bach-Jahrbuch* (1973) 72–8

Rothfarb, Lee A. (ed. and trans.), *Ernst Kurth: Selected Writings* (Cambridge: Cambridge University Press, 1991)

Sackmann, Dominik, *Bach und Corelli* (Munich: Katzbichler, 1999)

—— '"Französischer Schaum und deutsches Grundelement" – Französisches in Bachs Musik', *Basler Jahrbuch für historische Musikpraxis* xxviii (2004) 81–93

Sadie, Stanley (ed.), *The New Grove Early Keyboard Instruments* (London: Macmillan, 1989)

Sardelli, Federico Maria, *Vivaldi's Music for Flute and Recorder* (Aldershot: Ashgate, 2007)

Saslav, Isodor, 'The *alla breve* "March": its evolution and meaning in Haydn's string quartets', *Haydn Studies*, ed. J.P. Larsen, H. Serwer, J. Webster (New York: Norton, 1981) 308–14

Schachter, Carl, 'The Gavotte en Rondeaux from J.S. Bach's Partita in E major for unaccompanied violin', *Israel Studies in Musicology* iv (1987) 7–26

—— 'The Prelude from Bach's Suite No.4 for Violoncello Solo', *Current Musicology* lvi (1994) 54–71

Scheck, Gustav, *Die Flöte und ihre Musik* (Mainz: Schott, 1975)

Schenker, Heinrich, 'The Largo of J.S. Bach's Sonata No.3 for unaccompanied violin', *The Music Forum* iv (1976) 141–59

Schmitz, Hans-Peter, *Querflöte und Querflötenspiel in Deutschland während des Barockzeitalters* (Kassel: Bärenreiter, 1958)

—— 'Marginalien zur Bachschen Flötenmusik', *Musica-Mens-Musici. Im Gedenken an Walther Vetter* (Leipzig: VEB Deutscher Verlag für Musik, 1969) 169–72

Schrammek, Winfried, 'Viola pomposa und Violoncello piccolo bei Johann Sebastian Bach', *Bericht über die wissenschaftliche Konferenz . . . Leipzig 1975*, ed. W. Felix, W. Hoffmann, A. Schneiderheinze (Leipzig: VEB Deutscher Verlag für Musik, 1977) 345–54

Schröder, Jaap, *Bach's Solo Violin Works: A Performer's Guide* (New Haven CT: Yale University Press, 2007)

—— et al., 'Jaap Schroeder discusses Bach's works for unaccompanied violin', *Journal of the Violin Society of America* iii/3 (Summer 1977) 7–32

Schröder, Karl-Ernst, 'Zur Interpretation der Präludien und Fantasien von Silvius Leopold Weiss', *Bach: Das Wohltemperierte Klavier I . . . Ulrich Siegele zum 70. Geburtstag*, ed. S. Rampe (Munich: Katzbichler, 2002) 181–218

Schubert, Klaus, 'Studien sur motivisch-thematischen Gestaltung und Dramaturgie in den Fugen der drei Sonaten für Violine solo von Johann Sebastian Bach' (Dr diss., Martin-Luther-Universität Halle-Wittenberg, 1985)

Schulenberg, David, *The Keyboard Music of J.S. Bach* (New York: Routledge, 2/2006)

Schulze, Hans-Joachim, 'Wer intavolierte Johann Sebastian Bachs Lautenkompositionen?', *Die Musikforschung* (1966) 32–9

—— '"Monsieur Schouster" – ein vergessener Zeitgenosse Johann Sebastian Bachs', *Bachiana et alia musicologica: Festschrift Alfred Dürr zum 65. Geburtstag*, ed. W. Rehm (Kassel: Bärenreiter, 1983) 243–50

—— *Studien zur Bach-Überlieferung im 18. Jahrhundert* (Leipzig: Edition Peters, 1984)
—— 'The French influence in Bach's instrumental music', *Early Music* xiii/2 (5/1985) 180–4
—— (ed.), *Johann Sebastian Bach: Drei Lautenkompositionen in zeitgenössischer Tabulatur (BWV 995, 997, 1000)* (Leipzig: Zentralantiquariat der Deutschen Demokratischen Republik, 1975)
Schwemer, Bettina and Douglas Woodfull-Harris (eds), *J.S. Bach. 6 Suites a Violoncello Solo senza Basso BWV 1007–1012* (Kassel: Bärenreiter, 2000)
Scott, Marion, 'The violin music of Handel and Bach', *Music & Letters* xvi/3 (7/1935) 188–99
Segerman, Ephraim, 'The name "tenor violin"', *The Galpin Society Journal* xlviii (3/1995) 181–7
Seiffert, Reinhard (ed.), *J.S. Bach Sei Solo: Sechs Sonaten und Partiten für Violine. Interpretation, Aufführungspraxis, Authentizität* (Munich: Edition Praxis und Hintergrund, 1991)
Siegele, Ulrich, *Kompositionsweise und Bearbeitungstechnik in der Instrumentalmusik Johann Sebastian Bachs* (Neuhausen-Stuttgart: Hänssler, 1975)
—— 'Bachs vermischter Geschmack', *Dortmunder Bachforschungen* ii (1999) 9–17
Siegmund-Schultze, Walther, 'Das konzertante Prinzip in Bachs Sonaten und Partiten für Violine solo BWV 1001–1006', *Bach-Studien* 6 (1981) 95–100
Silbiger, Alexander, 'Bach and the Chaconne', *Journal of Musicology* xvii/3 (Summer 1999) 358–85
Smit, Lambert, 'Towards a more consistent and more historical view of Bach's violoncello', *Chelys* xxxii (2004) 45–58
Smith, Douglas Alton, 'A biography of Silvius Leopold Weiss', *Journal of the Lute Society of America* xxxi (1998) 1–48
Smith, Mark M., 'The cello bow held viol-way: once common, but now almost forgotten', *Chelys* xxiv (1995) 47–61
—— 'Joh. Seb. Bachs Violoncello piccolo: Neue Aspekte-offene Fragen', *Bach-Jahrbuch* (1998) 63–81
Stauffer, George and Ernest May (eds), *J.S. Bach as Organist* (London: Batsford, 1986)
Stinson, Russell, 'J.P. Kellner's copies of Bach's Sonatas and Partitas', *Early Music* xi/4 (5/1985) 199–211
—— *The Bach Manuscripts of Johann Peter Kellner and his Circle* (Durham NC: Duke University Press, 1990)
Stowell, Robin, 'Bach's Violin Sonatas and Partitas', *The Musical Times* cxxviii/1731 (5/1987) 250–6
—— *The Early Violin and Viola: A Practical Guide* (Cambridge: Cambridge University Press, 2001)
Strunk, Oliver (ed.), *Source Readings in Music History: The Baroque Era* (New York: Norton, 1965)
Studeny, Bruno, *Beiträge zur Geschichte der Violinsonate im 18. Jahrhundert* (Munich: Wunderhorn-Verlag, 1911)
Tagliavini, Luigi Fernando, 'Bach's organ transcription of Vivaldi's "Grosso Mogul" Concerto', in Stauffer and May 1986: 240–55
Talbot, Michael, 'The concerto Allegro in the early eighteenth century', *Music & Letters* lii/2 (1971) 8–18, 159–72
Talle, Andrew, 'Nürnberg, Darmstadt, Köthen – Neuerkenntnisse zur Bach-Überlieferung in der ersten Hälfte des 18. Jahrhunderts', *Bach-Jahrbuch* (2003) 143–72
Tanenbaum, Faun S., 'The Sarabande of J.S. Bach's Suite No.2 for unaccompanied violoncello, BWV 1008: analysis and interpretation', *Theory and Practice* v/1 (1980) 40–56
Tarling, Judy, *Baroque String Playing* (St Albans: Corda Music, 2/2001)

Tatlow, Ruth, 'Collections, bars and numbers: analytical coincidence or Bach's design?', *Understanding Bach* ii (2007), 37–58
<www.bachnetwork.co.uk/ub2/tatlow.pdf>
Thoene, Helga, *Johann Sebastian Bach, Ciaccona–Tanz oder Tombeau?* (Oschersleben: Ziethen, 2002)
Timms, Colin, *Polymath of the Baroque: Agostino Steffani and his Music* (New York: Oxford University Press, 2003)
Tomita, Yo, 'Anna Magdalena as Bach's copyist', *Understanding Bach* ii (2007) 59–76
<www.bachnetwork.co.uk/ub2/tomita.pdf>
Urchueguía, Cristina (ed.), *Arcangelo Corelli. Historisch-kritische Gesamtausgabe der musikalischen Werke Band III. Sonate a Violino e Violone o Cembalo Opus V* (Laaber: Laaber Verlag, 2006)
Vanscheeuwijck, Marc (ed.), *Domenico Gabrielli: Ricercari per violoncello solo. . .*, facsimile with commentary (Bologna, Arnaldo Forni, 1998)
—— (ed.), *Giovanni Battista degli Antonii. Ricercate sopra il violoncello o clavicembalo e Ricercate per il violino*, facsimile with commentary (Bologna: Arnaldo Forni, 2007)
Vogl, Emil, 'The lute music of Johann Anton Losy', *Journal of the Lute Society of America* xiv (1981) 4–58
Vogt, Hans, *Johann Sebastian Bach's Chamber Music* (Portland OR: Amadeus Press, 1988)
Watkin, David, 'Corelli's Op.5 Sonatas: "Violino e violone *o* cembalo"?', *Early Music* xxiv/4 (11/1996) 645–63
Webber, Geoffrey, *North German Church Music in the Age of Buxtehude* (Oxford: Clarendon Press, 1996)
Wessel, Frederick T. 'The Affektenlehre in the Eighteenth Century' (Ph.D. diss., Indiana University, 1955)
Whitman, George, 'J.S. Bach: master of bowing technique', *The Strad* lxxix/946 (2/1969) 431–3
Wiemer, Wolfgang, 'Ein Bach Doppelfund: verschollene Gerber-Abschrift (BWV 914 und 994) und unbekannte Choralsammlung Christian Friedrich Penzels', *Bach-Jahrbuch* (1987) 29–73
Wiermann, Barbara (ed.), *Carl Philipp Emanuel Bach: Dokumente zu Leben und Wirken aus der zeitgenössischen Hamburgischen Presse (1767–1790)* (Hildesheim: Georg Olms, 2000)
Williams, Peter, 'A Chaconne by Georg Böhm: a note on German composers and French styles', *Early Music* xvii/1 (2/1989) 43–54
—— *The Chromatic Fourth during Four Centuries of Music* (Oxford: Clarendon Press, 1997)
—— *The Organ Music of J.S. Bach* (Cambridge: Cambridge University Press, 2/2003)
—— *J.S. Bach: A Life in Music* (Cambridge: Cambridge University Press, 2007)
Wilson, David K., *Georg Muffat on Performance Practice* (Bloomington IN: Indiana University Press, 2001)
Winternitz, Emanuel, *Musical Instruments and their Symbolism in Western Art* (New Haven CT: Yale University Press, 2/1979)
Wissick, Brent, 'The cello music of Antonio Bononcini: violone, violoncello da spalla, and the cello "schools" of Bologna and Rome, *Journal of Seventeenth-Century Music* xii/i (2006) <http://sscm-jscm.press.uiuc.edu/v12/no1/wissick.html>
Wolff, Christoph, 'Das Trio A-Dur BWV 1025: Eine Lautensonate von Silvius Leopold Weiß, bearbeitet und erweitert von Johann Sebastian Bach', *Bach-Jahrbuch* (1993) 47–67
—— *Johann Sebastian Bach, the Learned Musician* (Oxford: Oxford University Press, 2000)
—— 'Invention, composition and the improvement of nature: a propos Bach the teacher and practical philosopher', *The Keyboard in Baroque Europe*, ed. C. Hogwood (Cambridge: Cambridge University Press, 2003) 133–9
Zaslaw, Neal, 'Ornaments for Corelli's violin sonatas', *Early Music* xxiv/1 (2/1996) 95–115

Zingel, Hans Joachim, 'Bach auf der Harfe', *Schweizerische Musikzeitung* civ (9–10/1964) 286–8
Zohn, Steven, *Music for a Mixed Taste: Style, Genre, and Meaning in Telemann's Instrumental Works* (New York: Oxford University Press, 2008)

Select Discography

Bach, Johann Sebastian, *The Sonatas and Partitas for Violin Solo*, John Holloway (ECM, 2006) 476 3152
—— *Sonata in G minor BWV 1001, Partita in B minor BWV 1002*, Maya Homburger (Maya Recordings, 2003) MCD 0301
—— *Lute Music*, Jacob Lindberg (BIS, 1994) BISCD 587/8
—— *Bach Lute Works*, Andreas Martin (Harmonia Mundi Iberica, 2004) HMI 987051
—— *Bach on the Lute Volume Two*, Nigel North (Linn Records, 1994) CKD 029
—— *Les Voix humaines*, Jordi Savall (Alia Vox, 1998) AV9803
—— *Sonatas and Partitas BWV 1001–1006 lute versions*, Hopkinson Smith (Astrée, 2000) E 8678
Biber, Heinrich Ignaz Franz von, *8 Sonatae a violino solo (1681)*, Andrew Manze (Harmonia Mundi, 1994) HMU 907134–5
Demachy, *Pieces de Violle*, Jordi Savall (Astrée, 2000) ES 9946
Farina, Carlo, *Capriccio stravagante*, Skip Sempé (Harmonia Mundi, 1992) 05472 77190 2
Fischer, Johann Caspar Ferdinand, *German Consort Music, 1660–1710*, The Parley of Instruments, Peter Holman (Hyperion, 1983) CDA 66074
Lonati, Carlo Ambrogio, *Violin Sonatas*, Christoph Timpe (Capriccio, 2004) 67 075
Marini, Biagio, *Early Italian Violin Sonatas*, Convivium (Hyperion, 1998) CDA66985
—— *Curiose & Moderne Inventioni*, Romanesca (Harmonia Mundi, 1997) 907175
Muffat, Georg, *Armonico tributo*, Les Muffatti (Ramée, 2005) RAM 0502
Pez, Johann Christoph, *Ouvertures-Concerti*, Les Muffatti (Ramée, 2007) RAM 0705
Pisendel, Johann Georg, *Pisendel & Dresden*, Martina Graulich (Carus, 2003) 83.162
Reusner, Esaias, *European Lute Music Vol. 2*, Konrad Junghänel (Harmonia Mundi, 1992) RD77230
Schenck, Johann, *Wieland Kuijken Viola da Gamba Solo Recital* (Denon, 1993) CO-75659
Vilsmaÿr, Johann Joseph, *The Unaccompanied Violin: 18th-Century Portuguese and Austrian Music*, Pauline Nobes (Rhapsody Ensemble Edition, 1998) REE.01
Walther, Johann Jakob, *Scherzi da violino solo con il basso continuo*, Pavlo Beznosiuk (ET'CETERA, 2000) KTC 1224
—— *Hortulus Chelicus Mainz, 1688*, David Plantier (Zig Zag Territoires, 2006) ZZT 060902
Westhoff, Johann Paul, *Sonates pour Violon & Basse continue*, David Plantier (Zig Zag Territoires, 2004) ZZT 050201
—— *Suites for Solo Violin*, Pavlo Beznosiuk (ET'CETERA, 2000) KTC 1224
—— *Complete Suites for Solo Violin*, Kolja Lessing (Capriccio, 2004) 67 083

Index

References to music examples are in **bold**; references to Notes are *italic*.

Adlung, Jacob (1699–1762), 118, 240, 245
accent, 146
Agricola, Johann Friedrich (1720–74), 17, 57, 118, 252–4, 268
air de cour, 38
Albertini, Ignazio (*c*.1644–85), 19
Albicastro, Henricus (Heinrich Weissenberg)(*c*.1660–*c*.1730), 23, 63, 96, 101, *302*
Albinoni, Tomaso (1671–1751), 22, 63
Altnickol, Johann Christoph (1719–59), 119
Andreas Bach Buch, 3, *306*
Ansbach, 29
Antoni (Antonii), Giovanni Battista degli (1660–96), 36
Apollo, 15, 18
Arne, Thomas Augustine (1710–78), 88
Arnstadt, 8, 45, 268, *317*
arpeggiando, 25, 32, 121, *285*
Augsburg, 22, 29
August III, King of Poland, see Friedrich August II, Elector of Saxony

Bach, Anna Magdalena (1701–60), 3–5, 7, 8–9, 11, 16, 43, 136, 185, 194, 204, 209, 211, 214–15, 226–8, *299*, *308–10*; *Clavier-Büchlein* (1722), 73; *Clavier-Büchlein* (1725), 86, 184
Bach, Carl Philipp Emanuel (1714–88), 8–9, 14–15, 17, 22, 44, 54, 56, 60, 85, 99, 149, 252, 255, 260, 268, *301*
Bach, Johann Ambrosius (1645–95), 13
Bach, Johann Christoph (1642–1703), 21–2
Bach, Johann Christoph (1671–1721), 3, 13, 22, 63, *306*

Bach, Johann Nicolaus (1669–1753), 57, 245
Bach, Johann Sebastian (1685–1750),
VOCAL WORKS, cantatas, BWV 12: 95, *307*, BWV 21: 266, BWV 29: 13, 165, 167, **168–9**, 268, 272, *313*, BWV 56: *317*, BWV 68: 46, BWV 71: 37, BWV 78: 137, 141, BWV 94: 272, BWV 132: 37, BWV 140: 90, BWV 147: 116, BWV 163: 37, BWV 172: 37, BWV 173a: 60, BWV 184a: 60, BWV 198: 57, BWV 199: 37; Mass in B minor, 15; St Matthew Passion, 37, 57, 111, 116; St John Passion, 56, 252, 264, *306*
ORGAN WORKS, BWV 526: 121, BWV 529: 196, BWV 530: 121, BWV 532: 36, BWV 535a: *317*, BWV 539: 102, 104, 265, BWV 540: 244, BWV 542: 95, **96**, 149, 166, BWV 543: **82**, 218, BWV 545: 196, BWV 548: 155, BWV 572: 166, BWV 582: 137, 145, BWV 587: 63, BWV 588: 152, **153**, BWV 594: 95, **104**, 165, BWV 598: 176; *Orgel-Büchlein*, 16; Schübler chorales, BWV 645: 224; 'Eighteen' chorales, BWV 654: 212; *Clavier-Übung* III, 132, BWV 552: 212, BWV 682: 132; BWV 770: *317*
CLAVIER WORKS, Inventions and Sinfonias, viii, 10, 16–17, 73, 85–8, 90, 196, 248, *299*, *300*, *308*, *321*; English Suites, 110, 124, 154, 165, 248, 257, 272, BWV 806: 47, 199, 222, 249–50, BWV 807: 122, 124, BWV 808: 165, 184, BWV 809: 110, BWV 810: 199, BWV 811: 184, 234, 251; French Suites, viii, 10, 16, 73, 77, 80, 88, 108, 248, *307*, BWV 812: 77, 116, 130, 199, 222, 250, *310*, BWV 813: 78,

Bach, Johann Sebastian (1685–1750),
CLAVIER WORKS, Inventions and Sinfonias
(*cont.*), 114–15, 199, 226, BWV 814: 78,
114–15, BWV 815: 78, BWV 816: 55, 78,
171, *314*, BWV 817: 55, 78, 115, 193,
312; BWV 822: *319*; *Clavier-Übung* I, 3,
247, *310*, BWV 825: 133, BWV 826: 253,
317, BWV 827: 199, BWV 828: 231,
BWV 829: 242; *Clavier-Übung* II, 214,
300, *315*, BWV 831: 215, 219; *The Well-
tempered Clavier* I, 10–11, 16–17, 30, 63,
73, 87–8, 122, **130**, 138, 154, 176, 193,
244, 248, 264, 270–1; *The Well-tempered
Clavier* II, 30, 117, 254, 260–1, 264, *310*,
318; BWV 903: 30, 54, 95, 99; Toccatas,
BWV 914: 247, **248**, 249; BWV 918: 254;
BWV 964: 13, 118–19, 147, BWV 965:
98, BWV 968: 13, 119, 146–7, 153;
Sixteen Concertos, BWV 972: 127, BWV
974: 127, 145, BWV 981: 146; Goldberg
Variations, 88, 215, *332*
LUTE WORKS, BWV 995: 12, 57, 78, 206,
214–16, 220, **221**, 225, **226**, 238–40, **241**,
242, **243**–4, 246, 249–50, 253, 255, 261,
264–5, 267, *318*, BWV 996: 34, 57, 78,
92, 196, 234, 245–8, **249**, 250–1, 253,
BWV 997: 52, 57, 91, 108, 239, 252–9,
261–2, 276, *318*, BWV 998: 52, 57, 91,
93, 155, 252, 257, 259–63, *318*, BWV
999: 263–5, BWV 1000: 57, 100, 239,
265–7, *318*, BWV 1006a: 52–3, 57, 169,
171, 172, 174–5, 252, 267–9, 272, *316*,
318
CHAMBER WORKS, *Sei Solo* for violin, BWV
1001: 5, **6**–7, 22, 30, 32, 78, 83, 89, **93**,
94–8, **99**, 100–1, **102**, 103–7, **108**, 113,
120–4, 126–7, 134, 137, 155, 160, 170,
190, 221, 231, 263, 265, BWV 1002: 3, 5,
11, 17, 69, 72, 80, 108–12, **113–14**,
115–18, 120, 130, 134, 146, 164, 184,
193, 208, 218, 225, 271, BWV 1003: 22,
30, 92, **93**, 118–28, **129**, 131, 137–8, 147,
153, 155, 160, 199, 211, 227, 273, BWV
1004, 3, 5, 11, 48, 72, 78, 80, 89, 103,
129–30, **131**, 132, **133**, 134–5, **136**,
137–8, **139–40**, 141–5, 163–4, 167, 180,
186, 191–2, 208, 213, 234, 274, BWV
1005: 5, 13, 15, 53, 89, 92, **93**, 103, 119,
123, 126, 138, 145–6, **147–8**, 149, **150–2**,
153–63, **164**, 167, 196, 202, 257, BWV
1006: 3, 5, 11, 13, 53, 89, 128, 137,
164–5, **166**, 167–70, **171**, 172–5, 196–7,
211, 214, 227–8, 267–8, 270, 272, *318*; 6

Suites for cello, BWV 1007: 30, 54, 78,
83, 89, 176, **177**, 178, **179**, 180–1, **182**,
183–7, 194, 198, 200, 203, 206, 208, 228,
230, 249–50, 275, BWV 1008: 55, 78, 89,
107, 186, **187**, 188–9, **190–1**, 192–4, **195**,
198, 202, 216, 223, BWV 1009: 9, 53, 78,
117, 196, **197**, 198, **199**, 200, **201**, 202–4,
216, 233, BWV 1010: 53, 78, 89, 107,
134, 204, **205**, 206, **207**, 208, **209**,
210–11, **212**, 213, 215, 233, 236, 271,
BWV 1011: 8, 32, 49, 53, 75, 78, 86, 92,
93, 110, 165, 184, 213–16, **217**, 218–19,
220, 221, **222**, 223, **224**, 225–7, 231, 236,
250, 255, 265, 276, BWV 1012: 44–6, 54,
78, 116, 225, 227–8, **229**, 230–1, **232–3**,
234–7, 251, 258, 275; *Solo* for flute,
BWV 1013: 10, 59–60, 78, 270–2, **273**,
274–7; Six Sonatas for obbligato
harpsichord and violin, BWV 1015: 122,
BWV 1016: 95, BWV 1017: **210**; BWV
1025: 52, 57, 252, 254, 258, *317*; BWV
1026: 14, *311*, BWV 1028: 37, 259, BWV
1034: 60, 272, BWV 1035: 132
ENSEMBLE WORKS, BWV 1042: 171; Six
Brandenburg Concertos, 15–17, BWV
1046: 35, 95, 102, BWV 1049: 146–7,
154, BWV 1050: 36, 60, 104, 121, 133,
BWV 1051: 185; Overture-suites, 86,
259, BWV 1066: 14, 68, 73, **75**, **76**, 77,
113, 222, BWV 1067: 14, 276, BWV
1068: 127, 172, 215, BWV 1069: 215
SPECULATIVE WORKS, BWV 1076: 88;
Musical Offering, 15, 261, *312*; *The Art of
Fugue*, 17, 158
Bach, Wilhelm Friedemann (1710–84), 15,
44, 52, 72, 119; *Clavier-Büchlein*, 16–17,
86, 88
Badiarov, Dmitry, 46, *304*
Baltzar, Thomas (?1631–63), 38, *301–2*
bariolage, 25, 30, 55, 125, 144, 165–7,
177–8, 227–8, 230, 267–8, 320
Barnett, Gregory, *304*
Baron, Ernst Gottlieb (1696–1760), 51–2,
54, 56
bass viol, 1, 4, 22–3, 25, 37–43, 46, 50, 55,
58, 61–2, 96, 101, 111, 121, 133, 145,
183, 189, 192–4, 199, 204, 211, 214, 223,
225, 227, 231, 259, *303–4*, *312*
bass violin, *304*
Bebung, 169, *313*
Beethoven, Ludwig van (1770–1827), 32,
157
Beisswenger, Kirsten, 9

Benda, Franz (1709–86), 17, 44, 253, *303*
Berlin, 8, 17, 35, 48, 56, 59, 268, *304*
Berlioz, Hector (1803–69), 19
Biber, Heinrich Ignaz Franz von (1644–1704), 16, 19–20, 23–6, 28, 31, 63, 105, 142, 145, 166, 213, 247, **281**–4, *301*–*3*
Bitti, Martin(ell)o (1655/6–1703), 29
Blavet, Michel (1700–68), 59
Bleyer, Nicolaus (1591–1658), 22
Blochwitz, Johann Martin (*fl.* 1720–30), 59, *319*
Bogenclavier, 268
Böhm, Georg (1661–1733), 141, **142**
Bononcini, Antonio Maria (1677–1726), 42, *304*
Bononcini, Giovanni (1670–1747), 35, 42
Bononcini, Giovanni Maria (1642–78), 20
Bordoni, Faustina (1697–1781), 39, *303*
Boyden, David, 103
Brahms, Johannes (1833–97), 135, 144
Breslau (Wroc_aw), 48, 50, 52
Bruckner, Anton (1824–96), 261
Bruhns, Nicolaus (1655–97), 23, *301*
Buffardin, Pierre-Gabriel (*c.*1690–1768), 59–60, 80, 270, *306*
Buonamente, Giovanni Battista (*c.*1600–42), 19
Burguéte, André, 265, 268, *317*–*8*
Burney, Charles (1726–1814), 88
Butt, John, 115, 162
Buxtehude, Dietrich (*c.*1637–1707), 26, 141, 145, 196, 246, 248

campanella (see also bariolage), 20, 49, 55, 227, 244, 254, *305*, 320
Campra, André (1660–1744), 62, 63, 68, 72, 165, **170**
canon, 36, 88, 161, *312*
caprice (also capriccio), 17–18, 33, 41, 53, 54, 253
Carl, Landgrave of Hessen-Kassel (1677–1730), 40
Carlsbad (Karlovy Vary), 4
Casals, Pablo (1876–1973), 180, 216
Castelli, Francesco (?–1631), 18
Castello, Dario (*fl.* first half of 17th century), 24, 47, 64
Cartier, Jean-Baptiste (1765–1841), 15
Cavalli, Francesco (1602–76), 186
Champeil, Jean André, 103
Chafe, Eric, *302*
chorale melodies, 'An Wasserflüssen Babylon', 149, 151, **152**; 'Komm heiliger Geist, Herre Gott', 149, **152**; 'Wohl mir, dass ich Jesum habe', 116–17
Christiane Eberhardine, Electress of Saxony (1671–1727), 27
Cipriani, Ernesto, *305*
clavichord, 12, 14, 96, 118–19, 259–60, 267–8
col legno, 19, 38
Cologne, 45
Colombi, Giuseppe (1635–94), 20
contredanse, 271, 276
Corelli, Arcangelo (1653–1713), 2, 13, 20, 22–3, 26–7, 31–5, 42, 45, 52, 55, 58, 62–5, 68, 78–9, 96–7, 100, 113, 117, 148, 161, 171, 185, 231, 250, *301*, *304*, *307*, *318*; Op.2: 64, **65**, 67, **68**, 75, 78–9; Op.3: 128, 166; Op.4: 65, **66**–**7**; Op.5: 19–20, 26, 30, 32, 58, **70**, 96, **97**, 100, 109, 113, 128, **161**, 166, **198**, 208, 231, graces, 30, 96, **97**, 231, *308*; Op.6: 63–4, 67–8, **69**, **71**
Corrette, Michel (1707–95), 271, *319*
Cöthen, 5, 14, 17, 35, 42, 45, 51, 56, 59–60, 73, 149, 265, 270
coulé de tierce, 75, **77**, 111, 115, 131–2, 134, 161, 172, 181, 183, 189, 193, 203, 219, 221, 225, 232, 275, *307*, 320
Couperin François (1668–1733), 2, 10, 27, 39, 58, 63, 68, 70–2, 77–9, 111, 130, 181, 221–2, 250, *306*–*7*; First Book: 47, 70, 85, 111; Second Book: 58; *L'Art de toucher le clavecin*: 70; Third Book: **74**, 111, *297*; *Concerts Royaux*: 75, **76**, 77, 106, 250
Cuzzoni, Francesca (1696–1778), 39, *303*

da braccio, 35
Dadelsen, Georg von, 5, 173, *310*
da gamba, 35, 43, 46
D'Agincourt, François (1684–1758), *316*
Dall'Abaco, Evaristo Felice (1675–1742), 111
D'Anglebert, Jean Henry (1629 or before–91), *305*
Danzig, 21
Darmstadt, 59
da spalla, 35, 37, 43–6
David, Ferdinand (1810–1873), 138
Demachy (*fl.* second half of 17th century), 38, **192**, 193, 211, 225
Dieupart, (Charles) François (?after 1667–*c.*1740), 41

divisions, 21, 38, 43, 67–9, 72, 78, 80, **81**, 82, 92, 105, 109, 112, 115–7, 125, 132–3, 135, 141, 157, 167, 171, 173, 183–4, 190–91, 193–5, 203, 208, 217–18, 222–3, 225, 236, 250–1, 257–8, 271, *300*, *315*, 320
Dolmetsch, Arnold, 116, 173, 235, *310*
Dörffel, Alfred, 100, 118, 121, 136, 214, *309*
double stops (see also multiple stops), 18, 22–4, 26, 38, 41, 101, 105, 138, 148, 152, 159, 173, 194, 216, 225, *301*
Dresden, 15, 18–19, 22–3, 27, 29, 32–3, 37, 44, 52, 59, 64, 80, 113, 184, 240, 252, 268, 270, *305–6*
Drüner, Ulrich, 45
Dudelsack, 203
Dufaut, François (before 1604–before 1672), 48, 50
Düsseldorf, 41, 56
dynamics, 38, 57, 119, 230, 254, 273, 276; echo, 38, 68, 125, 128, 131, 136, 174–5, 211, 213, 227–8, 254, 263, 276

Eberlin, Daniel (1647–1715), 22
Efrati, Richard, 207
Eisenach, 21–2, 42
enjambement, 70, 75, 77, 130, 222, 225, 320
Eppstein, Hans, 10
Erfurt, 22, 240
Ernst August of Sachsen-Weimar, Duke (1688–1748), 57, 245, *304*
Ernst Ludwig of Hessen-Darmstadt, Landgrave (1667–1738), 42
Evelyn, John (1620–1706), 29
Eylenstein, Gregor Christoph (1682–1749), 37

Falckenhagen Adam (1697–1754), 53, 57, 239, 244, 316
Fanselau, Clemens, 22
Farina, Carlo (*c*.1604–39), 18–19, 21
Ferguson, Howard, 259, *317*
figurae, 135, 206, *314*, *316*, 321
first practice (see also *stile antico*), 322
Fischer, Johann (1646–?1716/17), 22
Fischer, Johann Caspar Ferdinand (1656–1746), 30, 53, 141, 164, *311*
Florence, 27, 29
Forkel, Johann Nicolaus (1749–1818), 12, 14–15, 21, 36, 44, 53, 257, 270, *310*
Forqueray, Antoine (1672–1745), 38–9, 42
Frankfurt am Main, 29, 34
Frankfurt an der Oder, 60
Freillon-Poncein, Jean-Pierre (*fl.* 1700–08), 58

Frescobaldi, Girolamo (1583–1643), 13, 49, 80, 129, 138, 247
Freytag, Johann Heinrich (?–1720), 59–60, *306*
Friedrich II, King of Prussia (1712–86), 268, 275
Friedrich-August II, Prince-Elector of Saxony (Augustus III, King of Poland)(1696–1763), 29, 112
Friedrich Wilhelm, Elector of Brandenburg (1620–88), 48
Froberger, Johann Jacob (1616–67), 13, 48, 54, 154, *302*
Furchheim, Johann Wilhelm (*c*.1635/40–82), 19, 22, *301*

Gabrielli, Domenico (1659–90), **36–7**, 176, 223
Gaultier, Denis (1597/1603–1672), 48–51, 54
Gaultier, Ennemond (1575–1651), 49, 51, *305*
Gallot family, 51, 55
Geminiani, Francesco (1687–1762), 29, 31–4, 96, 101, 122, **289–91**, *302–3*
Gerber, Ernst Ludwig (1746–1819), 42, 44
Gerber, Heinrich Nicolaus (1702–75), 44, 73, 245, 247–9
Gerhartz, Karl, 31–2, *302*
Gleichmann, Johann Georg (1685–1770), 268, *318*
glissando, 19, 121, 227
Goldberg, Johann Gottlieb (1727–56), 254
golden section (see also proportions), 144, 154, *312*, 321
Gottsched, Johann Christoph (1700–66), 253
Gottsched, Luise (?–1762), 52, 253
gout, *313*
Graun, Johann Gottlieb (1702/3–71), 15, 44
Graupner, Christoph (1683–1760), 110–11, 133, 258
Grützbach, Erwin, 206
guitar, 39, 49

Hamburg, 9, 13, 148–9, 252
Handel, George, Frideric (1685–1759), 13, 23, 53–6, 65, 82, 85–6, 88–9, 91, 106, 143, 234, *300*, *303*; *Rinaldo*: 234; harpsichord Suites: 109, *316*; 'Zadok the priest': 89; *Israel in Egypt*: *317*; Op.6: 143; *Messiah*: *309*
harp, 268, *319*
harpsichord, 2, 14, 39, 47–8, 51–2, 58, 60,

70, 79–80, 109–11, 127–8, 210, 214, 219, 227, 252, 259–60, 267–8, *305, 309, 317*
Haussmann, Elias Gottlieb (1695–1774), 88, 161
Hausswald, Günther, 5, 10, 100
Haydn, Joseph (1732–1809), 54, 135, 157, *304–5*
Hertel, Johann Christian (1697–1754), 42
Hesse, Ernst Christian (1676–1762), 42
hexachord, 11, 321–2
Hildebrandt, Zacharias (1688–1757), 56–7
Hiller, Johann Adam (1728–1804), 42, 44
Hochbrucker, Simon (1699–*c*.1750), 268
Höffler, Konrad (1647–in or before 1705), 40
Hoffmann, Johann Christian (1683–1750), 44, 46, 56, 240, *305*
Hofmann, Klaus, 267
Hohlfeld, Gottfried (1711–70), 268, *318*
horn, 35, 57, 185, 237
Hotteterre, Jacques (1674–1763), 58, 68, *306–7, 319*
Hutchings, Arthur, 213

Ilmenau, 268
improvisation, 30–3, 38, 56, 80, 82, 87–8, 119, 149, 151–2, 176, 246–7, 249, 260–1, 264, *300–1, 317*
inégalité (inequality), see *notes inégales*
inganno, 256, 321
Innsbruck, 19

Jena, 57, 245–6
Joachim, Joseph (1831–1907), 103, *299*
Johann Ernst of Sachsen-Weimar, Duke (1664–1707), 13
Johann Ernst of Sachsen-Weimar, Prince (1696–1715), 34
Johann Wilhelm II, Elector Palatine (1658–1716), 41

Kapsberger, Johann Hieronymus (1580–1651), 247, 265, *318*
Kassel, 40
Kayser, Bernhard Christian (1705–58), *319*
Kehr, Günter, 115
Keller, Hermann, 119, 261
Kellner, David (*c*.1670–1748), *316*
Kellner, Johann Peter (1705–72), 3–5, 8–11, 43, 45, 60, 102–3, 144, 154, 199, 203, 209, 211, 213, 228, 231, 235–6, 263–4, *299, 309, 311–12, 314*
Kelz, Matthias (*c*.1635–95), 22, *301*
Kerll, Johann Caspar (1627–93), 13

key schemes, 11, 32, 131, 163, 166, 179, 190, 261
Kinsky, Georg, 45
Kirnberger, Johann Philipp (1721–83), 8, 12, 15, 78–9, 116, 216, 225, 235, 253, *300*; *Die Kunst des reinen Satzes in der Musik*: 12
Kittel, Johann Christian (1732–1809), *300*
Klagenfurt manuscript (A-Klagenfurt, Landesmuseum für Kärnten Inv. Nr. M73), 24, *302*
Knüpfer, Sebastian (1633–76), 48
Kohaut, Karl (1726–84), *318*
Köhler, Johann Friedrich (1756–1820), 44
Kräuter, Philipp David (1690–1741), 13
Krebs, Johann Ludwig (1713–80), 57, 261
Krebs, Johann Tobias (1690–1762), 245–6
Krieger, Johann (1651–1735), *300*
Kroměříž (Kremsier), 25
Kropfgans, Johann (1708–*c*.71), 50, 52–3, 57, 252
Kuhnau, Johann (1660–1722), 3, 51, 247
Kühnel, August (1645–*c*.1700), 40–1, 56, 101, *304*
Kühnel, Johann Michael (1670–1728), 56, *304*
Kuijken, Barthold, *306*
Kuijken, Sigiswald, 46

La Barre, Michel de (*c*.1675–1745), 58
Langloz manuscript (*D-B* Mus.ms.Bach P 296), **153**
Lautenwerk, 2, 4, 34, 57, 78, 239, 245–6, 253, 255, 260, 265, 268, *306*
Le Blanc, Hubert (?–?1729), 39
Leclair, Jean-Marie (1697–1764), 34
Legrenzi, Giovanni (1626–90), 22
Leipzig, 3–4, 10, 12, 14, 29, 42, 44, 48, 50, 52, 56–7, 59–60, 64, 123, 151, 154, 176, 238–40, 247, 253, 268, 270, *300*
Leisinger, Ulrich, 9, *319*
Leopold I, Holy Roman Emperor (1640–1705), 32
Leopold of Anhalt-Cöthen, Prince (1694–1728), 4, 17, 35, 40, 149
Le Roux, Gaspard (?–1707), *307*
Lesage de Richée, Philipp Franz (*fl. c*.1695), 50–1, 53, 55
Lester, Joel, 83, 98, 100, 104, 151
Levasseur, Jean-Henri (1764–1823), 9
Liechtenstein-Castelcorn, Carl, Prince-Bishop of Olmütz (1624–95), 21, 25
Linike, Christian Bernhard (1673–1751), 35, 56, *304*

lira da braccio, 18
lirone, 18
Locatelli, Pietro (1695–1764), *303*
Lonati, Carlo Ambrogio
  (*c.*1645–*c.*1710/15), 31–2, *303, 309*
London, 15, 29, 52, *300*
Losy von Losinthal, Jan Antonín
  (*c.*1650–1721), 51–3, 55, *305*
Louis XIV, King of France (1638–1715), 27
Lübeck, 23, 38
Lully, Jean-Baptiste (1632–87), 42, 49–51,
  62–3, 65, 79, 85–6, 137–8, 141–4, 164–5,
  194, 214, 216, 235
Lüneburg, 22, 141, *312*
lute-harpsichord, see Lautenwerk
Luther, Martin (1483–1546), 15
Lyra viol, 38, 225, *301*

Mainz, 23, 25
Marais, Marin (1656–1728), 38–40, 42–3,
  58, 62, 65, 96, 121, 133, **189**, 190–1, 225,
  303
Marcello, Alessandro (1669–1750), 127,
  145–6
Marcello, Benedetto (1686–1739), 146, 248
Marchand, Louis (1669–1732), 29, 64
Maria Casimira, Queen of Poland
  (1641–1716), 52
Marini, Biagio (1594–1663), 18–20, *301*
Marpurg, Friedrich Wilhelm (1718–95),
  91, 160, 216, 268, 321
Marsyas, 16
Matteis, Nicola, the younger (?late
  1670s–1737), 29–32, 34, **286–8**
Mattheson, Johann (1691–1764), 43–4, 59,
  93, 110, 122–3, 148–9, **150–1**, 152–3,
  156, 160, 170, 255, *310*
Maximilian III Joseph, Elector of Bavaria
  (1727–77), *304*
Mendelssohn, Felix (1809–47), 32
Mercure galant, 27
Mesangeau, René (?late 16th
  century–1638), 47, 54, 64
messanza, 163, 167, 321
Modena, 36
Möller manuscript, 3, 63, 141, 314
Montanari, Antonio (1676–1737), 29, 33–4
Montéclair, Michel Pignolet de
  (1667–1737), 146, *311*
Monteverdi, Claudio (1567–1643), 24, 49,
  62, 88, 135, 152, 322
Morel, Jacques (*fl. c.*1700–49), 133
Moser, Andreas, 31, 148

Mouton, Charles (1617–pre1699), 50, 54,
  305
Mozart, Leopold (1719–87), 105, 199, 207
Mozart, Wolfgang Amadeus (1756–91),
  304, 320
Muffat, Georg (1653–1704), 28, 63–4, 68,
  116, 137, 145, 169, **170**, 193, 235, *316*
Mühlhausen, 57
Multiple stops (see also double stops),
  18–20, 23, 31, 36–7, 158
Murschhauser, Franz Xaver Anton
  (1663–1738), 30
musette, 170–1, 173–4, 237

Naples, 2, 29, *321*
Nau, Étienne (*c.*1600–47), *300*
Neuburg an der Donau, 18
Niedt, Friedrich Erhard (1674–1708),
  246–7, 249, 264
Nobes, Pauline, 28
Norblin, Louis (1781–1854), 9, 187
North, Nigel, *318*
notes inégales (*inégalité*, inequality), 41, 48,
  58, 65, 68–70, 78–80, 87, 105, 111, 116,
  132–3, 135, 141, 170, 174, 183, 191–4,
  210, 216, 218, 223, 235, *307, 309, 314*
Nuremberg, 25, *300*

ondeggiando, 25, 122, **285**, 321
organ, 14, 16, 23, 26, 56, 63, 83, **84**, 87, 95,
  96, 101–3, **104**, 137, 145, 148–9, 152,
  153, 165–7, 176–8, 218, 221, 224, 245–7,
  252, 265–6, 268, *300, 312, 317*
overture, 10, 41, 53, 58, 85–6, 110, 119–20,
  146, 165, 214–5, 218–20, 246, 248–9
overture-suite, 109, 111, 165, 214, 259

Pachelbel, Johann (1653–1706), 13, 22, 26,
  151, **153**, *301*
Pandolfi Mealli, Giovanni Antonio (*fl.*
  1660–69), 19
Paris, 2, 9, 27, 36, 40, 42, 58, 63, 268, *307*
partia, 3–4
partita, 3, 40–1, 72, 129, 138
Pasquini, Bernardo (1637–1710), 64
passepied, 28, 107, 216, 263, *315*
perfidia, 165
Petrini (after 1710–50), 268
Pez, Johann Christoph (1664–1716), 63,
  111, *306*
Pinel, Germain (early 1600s–1661), 51
Pisendel, Johann Georg (15, 17, 19, 29,
  31–4, 44, 63–4, 80, 108–9, 113, 120, 270,
  292–6, *300–3, 306*

pizzicato, 19, 26, 38, 211, *315*
Poelchau, Georg (1773–1836), 5, *311*
Potsdam, 132
Praetorius, Michael (1571–1621), 268, 271
Prague, 51
Prinner, Johann Jakob (1624–94), 16
proportions (see also golden section), 124, 144, 155, 203, *300, 310*, 321
Purcell, Henry (1659–95), 23, 26, 85, 137, *300, 314, 321*

Quantz, Johann Joachim (1697–1773), 23, 33–4, 59, 63, 78, 80, 104–5, 110, 116, 162, 173, 193, 220, 222, 235, 271–2, 275, *303, 306–7, 309, 319*

Ragazzi, Antonio (?1680–1750), 29, **31**, 34
Raphael Sanzio (1483–1520), 18
Rameau, Jean-Philippe (1683–1764), *311*
Rebel, Jean Féry (1666–1747), 19
recorder, 59, 147
Reichardt, Johann Friedrich (1752–1814), 17, 52, 260
Reincken, Johann Adam (1643–1722), 49, 97–8, 149, 151, 160, *312*
Renwick, William, 152
Reusner, Esaias, the younger (1636–79), 48–51, 193, *305, 316*
Rheinsberg, 268
rhetoric, 87, 255, 321
ribattuta, 199
ritornello, 81–4, 87, 91, 101, 115, 124, 127, 135, 154–5, 165, 174, 181, 191, 195, 200, 210, 212, 214, 216, 228, 250, 254, 256–7, 272, *307*
Rome, 2, 13, 19, 22, 29, 33, 52, 58, 63–4, *306*
Rost, codex, 22
Rousseau, Jean (1644–99), 38
Ruppin, 268

St Petersburg, 5
Salomon, Johann Peter (1745–1815), 15, *300*
Salzburg, 25, 28, 64
sans chanterelle, 46, 49, 51, 55
Scarlatti, Alessandro (1660–1725), 52
Scarlatti, Domenico (1685–1757), 52
Schachter, Carl, *313–4*
Scheibe, Johann Adolph (1708–76), 85–6, 255
Schenck, Johann (1660–after 1710), 41–2, 96, 101, 133, 145, 223, 231, *304*
Schenker, Heinrich, 162, *312, 314*

Schering, Arnold, 97
Schmelzer, Johann Heinrich (*c.*1620/23–1680), 16, 19–21, 25, *302*
Schnittelbach, Nathanael (1633–1667), 22–3
Schönborn family, 25, 28, 37
Schouster, see Schuster
Schrammek, Winfried, 45
Schröter, Johann Georg (1683–*c.*1749), 268
Schulenberg, David, 264
Schumann, Robert (1810–56), 102
Schuster, Jacob (?1685–1751), 238–9
Schütz, Heinrich (1585–1672), 18
Schwanberg, Georg Heinrich Ludwig (1696–1744), **frontispiece**, 3–5, 8, 10
Schweitzer, Albert, 148, *308*
scordatura, 8, 10, 18, 20–2, 24–5, 27–8, 31, 46, 48, 213–4, 225, 239, *315–6*, 322
second practice (see also *stile moderno*), 24, 46, 232, 322
Simpson, Christopher (*c.*1602–6–1669), 38, 80
Smith, Hopkinson, *318*
Smith, Mark M., 45–6
Sobiesky, Prince Alexander (1677–1714), 52
Sophie-Charlotte, Queen of Prussia (1668–1705), 35
sources, *A-Wn* Musiksammlung Mus.Hs.5007: 9; *D-B* Mus.ms.40644 see Möller manuscript, Mus.ms.Bach P 218: 119, 253, P 267: 5, 311, P 268: **frontispiece**, 4–5, 7, 211, P 269: 4–5, 185, 194, P 289: 9, 213, 222, P 296: **153**, P 650: 252, 317, P 801: 245, 251, *307*, P 804: 5, 8, 154, 199, 263–4, *314*, P 967: 4–5, **6**, 8, 11, *309*, P 968: 270; *D-LEm* III.8.4 see Andreas Bach Buch; *F-Pn* Rés.Vm7 673 see Rost codex; see Chapter Five for lute/Lautenwerk sources
Spiess, Joseph (?–1730), 17
Spitta, Philipp (1841–94), 105, 108, 119, 138, 144, 146, 148, 221
Steffani, Agostino (1654–1728), 63
Steglich, Rudolf, 119
stile antico (see also first practice), 26, 42, 148, 154, 165, *312*, 322
stile moderno (see also second practice), 154
Stinson, Russell, 5, 8, 103
Stölzel, Gottfried Heinrich (1690–1749), 51, **86**
Straube, Rudolf (1717–*c.*1780), 57
Strungk, Nicolaus Adam (1640–1700), 19, 22–3

style brisé, 48–9, 51, 55, 102, 116, 126, 159–60, 193, 223, 225, 235, 267, 269
style: concertante, 32, 67–8, **69**, **71**, **73**, 83, 86, 128, 157, 174, 211; dance, 41, **65**, **68**, **72**, **73**, 77, 87, 109, 169, 171, 174, *308*; French, 38–40, 42, 47–51, 55, 58, 63–4, 70, 75, 108, 130, 141, 169–71, 181, 191, 193, 218, 221, 235, 250, *307*; galant, 34, 53, 87, 110, 132, 193, 208–9, 218, 261–3, *321*; Italian, 2, 18, 33, 58, 63, 132, 169–70, 214, *307*; Lombardic, 34, 79; mixed, vii, 2, 4, 41–2, 49–53, 57–9, 62–4, 70, 72, 79–80, 109, 111, 115, 132, 165, 174, 185, 191, 194, 210, 214, 219, 221–2, 250; sonata, 41–2, 47, 53, 55, 58–9, **66–7**, **70**, 72, 77, 80, 109, 111, 117, 142, 160, 171, 173–4, **182**, 194, 200, 203, 223, 225, 228, 236, 251, 275, *308*
Stylus phantasticus, 20, 41, 247
suite, 3–4, 10, 17, 22, 27–8, 37–8, 41, 47–8, 50, 53, 55, 63, 66, 69, 72, 80–2, 108–9, 129, 164–5, 173, 199, 214, 221, 227, 235, 251, 259, *305*, *307*
sul ponticello, 19
Sweelinck, Jan Pieterszoon (1562–1621), 151–2, 153, 160

tablature, 56, 213, 239, **241**, 242–3, **244–5**, 260, *309*
Tartini, Giuseppe (1692–1770), 113
Tatlow, Ruth, *300*
Telemann, Georg Philipp (1681–1767), 23, 29, 34, 59, 63, 85, 96, 111, 134, 146, 165, 223, 274, *300*, *306*, *308*, *312–13*; *Six Sonates*: 3, 34–5, 110, 113, 208, 227; *Six Trio*: 59; *Kleine Cammer-Music*: 59; *Der getreue Musikmeister*, 33, 44; Fantasias for flute: 223–4, 255, **276**; Fantasias for violin: 30, 115
theorbo, 38, 40, 48, 52, 57, 176, 211, 247, 265, 267, *305*, *316*
tierce coulée, *307*
tirer et rabattre, 49
Torelli, Giuseppe (1658–1709), 29, 63, 165
Traeg, Johann (1747–1805), 9
tremolo (see also vibrato, bow), 18, 24, 38
trumpet, 19, 36, 96, 167, **168–9**, 196, 203, 228, *313*

Uccellini, Marco (1610–80), 20, 24, 26

Vega 'Bach' bow, 56, *308*
Venice, 2, 29, 63

Veracini, Francesco Maria (1690–1768), 111, **112**, 113, 134, 143
vibrato (see also *Bebung*), 58, 119, 121, 183, 194, 227, 321; bow vibrato (see also tremolo), 19, 121–2, 227
Vienna, 19, 21, 25, 29, 31–2, 268, *301*
Violdigambenwerk, see *Bogenclavier*, 15
Vilsmaÿr, Johann Joseph (1663–1722), 28–9
viola, 8, 14, 37, 43–6, 68, 85, *304*
viola da gamba, see bass viol
viola da spalla, 43, 45–6
viola pomposa, 43, 44–6
violino in tromba, 19
violino piccolo, 102
violoncello piccolo, 10, 43–5, 271
Vivaldi, Antonio (1678–1741), 29, 31, 33–5, 37, 63, 83, **84**, 95, **103**, 110, 127, 134, 142, 164–5, 172, 211, 213, 256, 268, *303*, *306*
Viviani, Giovanni Bonaventura (1638–after 1692), 19
Voltaire, François Marie Arouet de (1694–1778), 275
Volumier (Woulmyer), Jean Baptiste (*c*.1670–1728), 64, *302*

Wagner, Richard (1813–83), 146, 167
Walther, Johann Gottfried (1684–1748), 22, 28–9, 38, 43, 162, 171, 245, *301*, *312–13*, *316*
Walther, Johann Jakob (*c*.1650–1717), 19, 21, 23–8, 63, 105, 121–2, 145, **285**
Watkin, David, 198
Wecker, Christoph Gottlieb (1706–74), 60
Weckmann, Matthias (*c*.1616–74), **247**
Weigel, Johann Christoph (1661–1726), *300*
Weimar, 5, 10, 13–14, 27–9, 37, 43, 56–7, 63, 73, 97, 110, 239, 245, 265, *304*, *316*
Weiss, Silvius Leopold (1687–1750), 50–3, **54**, 55–7, **82**, 110, 209, 234, 240, 247, 251–2, 258, 260–1, 277, *305*, *316*, *318*
Weissenfels, 40, 239
Westhoff, Johann Paul (1656–1705), 19, 24, 26–9, 41, 152, **153**, 154, *302*
Weyrauch, Johann Christian (1694–1771), 57, 239, 252–4, 259, 265, *305*
Wiemer, Wolfgang, 245
Wild, Friedrich Gottlieb (1700–1762), 60
Wittenberg, 27
Würdig, Johann Gottlieb (1681–1728), 60
Würzburg, 37

Zelenka, Jan Dismas (1679–1745), 80